ALTRUISTIC EMOTION, COGNITION, AND BEHAVIOR

CHILD PSYCHOLOGY

A series of books edited by **David S. Palermo**

ALTRUISTIC EMOTION, COGNITION, AND BEHAVIOR

Nancy Eisenberg
Arizona State University

LAWRENCE ERLBAUM ASSOCIATES, PUBLISHERS
1986   Hillsdale, New Jersey   London

Lawrence Erlbaum Associates, Inc., Publishers
365 Broadway
Hillsdale, New Jersey 07642

Library of Congress Cataloging in Publication Data

Eisenberg, Nancy.
  Altruistic emotion, cognition, and behavior.

  Bibliography: p.
  Includes indexes.
  1. Altruism. 2. Emotions. 3. Cognition. 4. Values.
I. Title.
BF637.H4E37   1986   150   85-1586
ISBN 0-89859-624-6

Printed in the United States of America

10 9 8 7 6 5 4 3 2 1

Contents

Preface and Acknowledgments

This book is an effort to integrate thinking and research concerning the role of emotion and cognition in altruistic behavior. I have not undertaken this task alone; in addition to the coauthors of several chapters, many people have contributed to this effort.

Several researchers have had a powerful influence on my thinking about altruism and moral reasoning over the past decade. These psychologists, all of whom have shaped the field through their work, include Martin Hoffman, Lawrence Kohlberg, Jane Piliavin, Shalom Schwartz, and Ervin Staub. I have borrowed heavily from their work. Furthermore, many persons have contributed more directly. Among those who have provided critical feedback on drafts of chapters are C. Daniel Batson, Anne Colby, Robert Cialdini, Darwyn Linder, Ervin Staub, and Ross Thompson. Moreover, I have benefited from discussions with Paul Mussen, Sally Powers, and Carolyn Zahn-Waxler concerning issues relevant to this book.

In addition to those persons previously mentioned, I would like to thank both Sally Carney for the many hours she spent preparing the manuscript and the students who contributed to the research from our laboratory. I would also like to acknowledge with appreciation funds from the National Institute of Mental Health, The Foundation for Child Development, the German Academic Exchange Service, and Arizona State University that supported some of the research presented in several chapters. Moreover, completion of the book was greatly facilitated by an award from the Arizona State University Honors Program which provided release time from teaching. Finally, I would like to thank my husband, Jerry Harris, for both his editorial comments and patience throughout this project.

He had great natural kindliness, but it was a kindliness of instinct, which betokened no interest in the recipient: he would come to the rescue if you were in a fix, but if there was no getting you out of it would not bother you further. . . . Perhaps he was an intensely logical man. It could not be denied that he led a good life (if at least you did not confine goodness to conformity with your own sensual inclinations), for he was charitable and kindly, and he devoted his energies to the alleviation of pain, but if motive counts for righteousness, then he deserves no praise; for he was influenced in his actions neither by love, pity, nor charity. (p. 15)

Somerset Maugham, in
The Narrow Corner

1 Introduction

The history of the human race is replete with examples of human cruelty, aggression, and selfishness. Indeed, instances of atrocites and injustice can be found in accounts of nearly all cultures and societies, ancient or modern. Given the abundance of negative behavior among people, it would seem that the capacity for evil and destructiveness is a part of human nature. Yet humans are also capable of a wide variety of good, kind, and caring behaviors. Examples of such behavior, like instances of cruelty and aggression, are readily evident in everyday life as well as in historical or religious accounts.

The broad range of human potentialities for good and evil has inspired philosophical debates for thousands of years, as well as numerous psychological inquiries in recent decades. Few individuals deny that humans have the capacity for great selfishness and evil; indeed, philosophers such as Hobbs (1642/1973) and psychologists such as Freud (1925, 1930) and Lorenz (1966) have suggested that humans are egoistic and aggressive by nature. There is more disagreement, however, concerning humans' capacities for altruism, self-sacrifice, and unselfishly motivated behavior. Indeed, some philosophers have claimed that self-sacrifice is psychologically impossible for humans, and would be ethically inappropriate if possible (e.g., Hobbs).

Some of the disagreement regarding the existance of truly altruistic behavior is based on discrepancies in definitions of altruism. Altruistic behavior is often defined as voluntary behavior that is intended to benefit another and is not motivated by the expectation of external reward (Eisenberg, 1982; Staub, 1978). When defined in this manner, most modern philosophers and psychologists seem to agree that altruism does exist (e.g., Blum, 1980; Hoffman, 1981; Nagel, 1970; Rushton, 1980; Staub, 1978). However, although some psychologists view acts

1

of assistance that are internally rewarded as altruistic (e.g., acts motivated by guilt, the desire to maintain a positive self-image or sympathy; Mussen & Eisenberg-Berg, 1977; Staub, 1978), others believe such acts are basically hedonistic in nature (cf. Batson, 1984; Cialdini, Darby, & Vincent, 1973; Cialdini, Kenrick, & Baumann, 1982). Moreover, there is a lack of concensus concerning the proximal determinants of altruism, that is, the factors that produce an act of altruism in a specific situation. Both cognitive processes and affective responses frequently have been cited as potential motivators of altruism, but there is considerable disagreement concerning the relative contributions of each to the development and maintenance of altruistic behavior.

The purpose of this book is to consider the role of both prosocial emotions and cognitions in altruistic action. Altruism will be defined as described previously and, consequently, will include behaviors motivated by sympathy, guilt, and other self-evaluative reactions associated with internalized values. Altruism is considered to be but one subtype of prosocial behavior, that is, voluntary behavior intended to benefit another (regardless of motive). Although altruistic prosocial behaviors generally are perceived as being moral, prosocial acts can be motivated by nonmoral (e.g., the desire for social approval) or even immoral (e.g., the desire to manipulate another for one's own benefit) motives.

As was already suggested, the bases for altruism can be varied. Some altruistic acts seem to be based primarily (but not entirely) on emotional factors (e.g., sympathetically motivated behavior), whereas others are somewhat more cognitive in motivation (e.g., based upon conscious, cognitive values or norms, perhaps accompanied by self-evaluative emotions). This is not to say that any motive is solely cognitive or affective. Before considering this issue in further detail, let us turn briefly to the more general issue of the cognitive-affective interface.

COGNITION AND EMOTION

Determining the nature of the interrelations between cognition and emotion has been a thorny problem for psychologists. The issue that probably has generated the most attention is the "chicken and egg" dilemma; for years, writers have considered and debated the question of which comes first, cognition or affect. However, although numerous models of the affect-cognition link have been proposed, the issue is far from resolved.

A number of theorists and researchers have considered affect to be primarily a consequence of cognition (Mandler, 1975, 1980; Royce & Diamond, 1980; Schachter & Singer, 1962). They generally have regarded emotion as a product of the cognitive interpretation of events or arousal. This interpretation can be of any component of emotion, including the elicitors, expression, and experience of emotion (Lewis, Sullivan, & Michalson, 1984).

With regard to elicitors, researchers have suggested two types of theories: discrepancy and appraisal theories. According to appraisal theories, emotion is the result of an individual's appraisal of a situation (e.g., Averill, 1980; Lazarus, 1968; Lazarus, Averill, & Optin, 1970). If the appraisal of a situation is positive or benign, the individual's affective response will be positive; negative appraisals lead to negative affect. In contrast, in discrepancy theories, emotions are believed to be the consequence of discrepancies or incongruities between external events and the individual's cognitive representations (e.g., Berlyne, 1960; Kagan, 1978). Stimuli that are too novel or discrepant are viewed as evoking unpleasant affect, whereas an optimal degree of novelty evokes interest or other positive reactions.

A number of writers have been concerned with the relation of cognition to the expression rather than elicitation of emotion. In general, these investigators have suggested that facial and other emotional expressions are, at least in part, a consequence of learning. As part of the socialization process, children learn which expressions are appropriate at which times (Saarni, 1979, 1982), and which expressions are desirable or reinforced (Lewis & Michalson, 1983).

Still other writers have suggested that our experience of emotion is shaped by cognition. For example, James (1884, 1890) and Tomkins (1963) proposed that emotion is a response to the perception of physiological bodily changes such as trembling or facial expressions. One is fearful because he or she perceives the self to be trembling. Other researchers have asserted that the individual's cognitive interpretation of general arousal (Schacter & Singer, 1962; cf. Reisenzein, 1983) or other aspects of one's own functioning (thoughts, behaviors; Mandler, 1975, 1980) result in the experience of emotion.

Not all writers have focused on the causal effects of cognition. Others have proposed that affect preceeds and structures cognition. Darwin (1872/1965) concluded that emotions were biologically based, and that cognitively-based processes do relatively little to modify their expression. Similarly, for Freud (1933/ 1968), emotion was primary. In Freud's theory, the development of the *id* (containing irrational drives and instincts) is prior to the development of cognitive processes (the *ego*). Moreover, Freud believed that the *ego* functions in service of the *id*, and that irrational processes frequently disrupt cognitive functioning. Numerous other writers have proposed that affect is primary and central to human functioning, and can lead to behavior without much contribution from cognitive processing (Izard, 1977, 1984; Tomkins, 1981; Zajonc, 1980). Nonetheless, most investigators or theorists who have emphasized the independence or primacy of affect have acknowledged the role of cognition in affective responding (e.g., Freud, 1926; Izard, 1977; Tompkins, 1981; Zajonc & Markus, 1984).

In recent years, numerous psychologists have attempted to go beyond the issue of emotional versus cognitive primacy to propose more integrative approaches for conceptualizing the complex interactions between emotion and cognition (e.g., Cowan, 1982; Lewis et al., 1984; Plutchik, 1977). These conceptulizations vary somewhat. For example, Cowan adapted Piaget's (1981) perspective that emotions and cognitive are not totally separable; cognitive schemas are always accompanied by affect, and affect always has some cognitive organization. Moreover, he suggested that primarily affective schemas can lead to cognitive activities or vice versa. Lewis et al. also noted a complex interplay between emotions and cognition; they labeled the intercycling of the two the "cognitive emotional fugue." In their view, emotion and cognition are interwoven, in that one leads to the other in a continuing cycle. For example, emotion may sometimes precede cognition, which in turn leads to new emotions and cognitions.

The issue of the relation between affect and emotion is far from resolved. Clearly, the association is complex and probably is not unidirectional. Moreover, interrelations probably vary depending upon how one defines "cognition" and "affect" (cf. Izard, 1984). Consequently, there is unlikely to be a simple formula that can depict the relative inputs of cognition and affect for all aspects of human functioning.

Emotion and Cognition in Altruism

The notion of a complex interplay of emotion and cognition undoubtedly applies to altruistic responding. Individuals' cognitive evaluations of and expectations in a potential helping situation must affect their emotional reactions to a potential recipient of aid and the recipient's plight. For example, the attributions that a potential benefactor makes with regard to the origins of another's need will influence the likelihood that the potential benefactor will empathize with or devalue a needy other. Similarly, an individual's cognitive constructions of the nature of morality affect emotional responding in a given situation by influencing one's interpretation of that situation, and, consequently, anticipated self-evaluative responses for different behavioral choices. Furthermore, emotional reactions such as empathy and guilt may induce a more intensive cognitive appraisal of a situation or cognitive restructuring of the specific issue at hand (e.g., reinterpretation of the degree of the other's need).

At a more basic level, even the emotions associated with altruistic behavior are often based, at least in part, on cognitions, whereas moral cognitions associated with altruism have emotional concomittants. On the one hand, sympathy, which is believed by many to promote altruistic responding (see Chapter 3), is an emotional reaction apparently based on certain cognitive skills such as perspective taking (Hoffman, 1984a). Similarly, self-evaluative responses such as guilt and self-reward seem to derive from the comparison of one's behavior (or anticipated behavior) with behavior in accordance with internalized values and norms; these values and norms involve cognitive representations and often a complex cognitive network. On the other hand, cognitive consideration of values, norms, and other nonmoral factors is sometimes accompanied by emotional responding (e.g., the anticipated self-evaluative responses already discussed).

Moreover, cognitive attributional processes concerning a needy other or even one's own behavior often elicit emotional responding (see Chapters 5 and 6).

In summary, the contributions of emotion and cognition to altruism are multifaced, complex, and interrelated. One cannot really consider one without the other. Those aspects of cognition and emotion that are most directly related to altruistic motives and functioning will be the foci of interest in this book.

PURPOSE AND STRUCTURE OF THE BOOK

There is a vast body of research and theorizing concerning the development and maintenance of prosocial (including altruistic) behavior. At least a dozen volumes concerning altruism have been published (e.g., Latane & Darley, 1970; Mussen & Eisenberg-Berg, 1977; Rushton, 1980; Staub, 1978, 1979), as well as hundreds of articles in psychological journals. However, although these various published works are similar in their focus on altruism and other prosocial behaviors, they differ considerably in their level of analysis of the phenomenon.

In specific, writers and researchers have attempted to explain altruistic responding by reference to biological factors (e.g., Trivers, 1971; Wilson, 1975), cultural factors (e.g., Whiting & Whiting, 1975), variations in socialization within the family or school (e.g., Hoffman, 1970a, b), situational factors (e.g., Latane & Darley, 1970), the media (cf. Rushton, 1980), and aspects of intrapsychic functioning (e.g., Batson & Coke, 1981; Hoffman, 1975, 1976). All of these levels of analysis have something to contribute to an understanding of altruism. However, it is often useful to probe a single level of analysis in depth.

In this book, we focus primarily on intrapsychic factors involved in prosocial responding, especially emotions and cognitions believed to play a major role in altruistic behavior. Thus, we consider in some detail sympathy and emotions related to self-evaluative responses, both of which have been viewed as potential motivational bases for altruism (Chapters 3 and 10). Moreover, cognitions concerning individuals' conceptions of altruism and their evaluations of the degree to which specific acts are altruistic are examined (Chapters 4 and 5), as are altruistic values (which have a cognitive basis) and cognitive processes that are basic to moral decision making (Chapters 6 through 10). Each of these issues is examined in some detail, and relevant research and theory in developmental, social, and other areas of psychology are presented. As a developmentalist, I will consider issues related to development in some depth; however, the developmental literature is considered within the context of the larger body of research.

Although the primary focus of the book is upon a specific set of intrapsychic factors relevant to altruism, in the final chapters of the book these intrapsychic factors are discussed in relation to a variety of other relevant factors including socialization and situational influences on altruism. In specific, models including factors influencing both level of prosocial moral reasoning (Chapter 9) and pro-social behavior (Chapter 10) are presented. In this manner, the research and conceptualizing related to cognitive and emotional contributors to altruism are tied back into the larger body of work concerning moral development.

Because individuals' internal states, including motives, generally are not readily accessible, it frequently is impossible to distinguish altruistic from non-altruistic prosocial acts. Consequently, the research reviewed is not confined to that concerning solely altruistic prosocial behavior. Moreover, given that chil-dren's altruistic responding may develop from less moral modes of prosocial behavior, it is difficult to isolate the examination of altruism from the study of other forms of prosocial behavior. Nonetheless, as much as is possible, we attempt to differentiate altruism from other types of prosocial responding. Indeed, the theory and data concerning altruistic emotions and cognitions are examined with an eye to differentiating altruistic from nonaltruistic prosocial responding.

In summary, the purpose of this book is to examine psychological research and theory concerning those cognitions and emotions most relevant to altruism. However, the issue of the role of emotion and cognition in morality is neither new nor the sole domain of psychologists. Thus, before considering the relevant psychological research related to altruism, it is worthwhile to review the per-spectives of philosophers as well as psychologists concerning cognitive versus affective influences on morality. It is to these perspectives that we now turn.

2 Philosophical and Theoretical Roots

The sources of morality, including the role of cognition and affect in altruism, have been debated for centuries. As long ago as the golden age of Greece, Socrates argued that moral wisdom is the essence of morality. Moral wisdom, he claimed, leads to truly virtuous behavior.

More recently, philosophers who have disagreed with the doctrine of psychological and ethical egoism have sought to explain the existence of virtuous behaviors, including altruism. Among philosophers, the label "psychological egoism" customarily is used to identify any theory that implies that no human action is genuinely unselfish or truly altruistic. *Ethical egoism* refers to the argument or belief that it is unreasonable and unjustifiable for people to behave in a manner contrary to their own interests, even if they are able to do so (Brandt, 1959; Milo, 1973). Thomas Hobbs (1642/1973) was one of the most vocal advocates of the doctrine of self-love and egoism, a doctrine which was quite popular in some educated circles.

PHILOSOPHICAL ARGUMENTS

Cognitive Perspectives

Immanuel Kant (1788/1949, 1797/1964) was one of the best-known philosophers to refute the doctrine of ethical egoism. He argued that if an action is one's duty, that is reason enough to do it, independent of one's own interest. Consequently, Kant believed altruism to be the reasonable and ethical course of action in some situations. Moreover, according to Kant, duty stems from universal, impartial principles, principles that are rational and have nothing to do with emotions. Kant (1788/1949) described how duty influences behavior:

> It is a very beautiful thing to do good to men from love to them and from sympathetic good will, or to be just from love of order; but this is not yet the true moral maxim of our conduct which is suitable to our position amongst rational beings as *men* when we pretend with fanciful pride to set ourselves above the thought of duty, like volunteers, and, as if we were independent on the command, to want to do of our own good pleasure what we think we need no command to do. We stand under a *discipline* of reason, and in all our maxims must not forget our subjection to it, nor withdraw anything therefrom . . . duty and obligation are the only names that we must give to our relation to the moral law [p. 168].

Indeed, Kant (1788/1949, 1797/1964) thought that affect, including sympathetic reactions towards others, could not engender moral behavior because feelings are transitory, changeable, and are out of our conscious control. In other words, because we do not control our emotions, we are not responsible for our feelings. Consequently, feelings have nothing to do with morality, because morality must involve will and self-control. Moreover, because a person's affective responses to others differ depending on who the person is and on the circumstances, emotions were not viewed by Kant as having the universality or constancy that is required for morality. In brief, Kant viewed morality, including altruism, as a highly rational enterprise totally detached from humans' affective functioning.

Numerous philosophers and psychologists have followed the lead of Socrates and Kant by emphasizing the centrality of cognition or rationality in morality. For example, Henry Sidgwick (1874/1962) advocated the view that benevolence is a rational duty. Nagel (1970), a modern philosopher, has differeniated between "pure" rational altruism and behavior motivated by sympathy, love, or other emotions:

> The altruism which in my view underlies ethics is not to be confused with generalized affection for the human race. It is not a feeling. . . . Without question people may be motivated by benevolence, sympathy, love, redirected self-interest, and various other influences, on some of the occasions on which they pursue the interests of others, but that there is also something else, a motivation available when none of those are, and also operative when they are present, which has genuinely the status of a rational requirement on human conduct. There is in other words such a thing as pure altruism (though it may never occurs in isolation from all other motives). It is the direct influence of one person's interest on the actions of another, simply because in itself the interest of the former provides the latter with a reason to act. If any further internal factor can be said to interact with the external circumstances in such a case, it will be not a desire or an inclination but the structure represented by such a system of reasons [pp. 3, 80].

Clearly, according to Nagel, the involvement of affect in the helping process taints its purity.

Lawrence Kohlberg, who has developed a psychological model of moral development based on cognitive-developmental theory (this theory will be discussed in Chapters 7 and 9), was clearly influenced by the writings of philosophers such as Kant. Kohlberg delineated a sequence of stages of moral reasoning that he views as the basis of moral development (Kohlberg, 1969, 1971, 1976, 1981). These stages are described as being invariant in sequence, universal to all persons, and as having a hierarchical structure (i.e., each stage is more advanced than the previous). Moreover, each stage is purportedly a mode of thinking or problem solving that is qualitatively distinct from previous stages. Advancement through the stages is a function of cognitive development as well as of life experiences that stimulate the growth of social cognition. Although Kohlberg does not claim that his stages are strictly cognitive, they are viewed as mediated by changes in reasoning.

> What is being asserted, then, is not that moral judgment stages are cognitive but that the existence of moral stages implies that moral development has a basic structural component. While motives and affects are involved in moral development, the development of these motives and affects is largely mediated by changes in thought patterns . . . Moral judgment stages or sequences are to be described in cognitive structural terms even in regard to "affective" aspects of moral judgment, like guilt, empathy, etc. [1969, p. 390].

> It is evident that moral judgments often involve strong emotional components, but this in no way reduces the cognitive component of moral judgment, though it may imply a somewhat different functioning of the cognitive component than is implied in more neutral areas. An astronomer's calculation that a comet will hit the earth will be accompanied by strong emotion, but this does not make his calculation less cognitive than the calculation of a comet's orbit which had no earthly consequences. Just as the quantitative strength of the emotional component is irrelevant to the theoretical importance of cognitive structure for understanding the development of scientific judgment, so the quantitative role of affect is relatively irrelevant for understanding the structure and development of moral judgment [1971, p. 189].

Other modern social scientists and educators have taken a position even stronger than Kohlberg's (1969, 1971) with regard to the contribution of cognition to moral functioning. For example, Bailey (1980) argued "that morality is largely to do with reason and little to do with feelings or affections"[p. 114]. His argument that duty and rationality rather than emotions are the bases of morality is quite reminiscent of Kant's (1788/1949) thesis. Indeed, with the exception of stylistic differences, much of Bailey's analysis, including the following, is clearly adopted from Kant:

If I go by my feelings as they actually exist I have strong sympathetic feelings towards some people, weaker feelings for others, indifference to yet others and positive feelings of hostility and lack of accord towards some few . . . We cannot base a morality on the existence of these various and multitudinous shades of feeling . . . the real test is how I react to those least in harmony with me, those I positively dislike. Towards such as these I can only exercise a morality that is based on some rational and cognitive awareness of the worthiness for respect of all mankind. . . . Reason and principle tell me my duty in a way that feeling can never do [p. 120].

Thus, Kant's emphasis on cognition is still evident in modern thinking about morality.

Affective Perspectives

Although some influential philosophers and psychologists have minimized or denied affect a sizable role in morality, many theorists have been unwilling to conclude that emotion cannot be a legitimate part of the moral process. For example, David Hume (1777/1966) argued that sympathy and empathy (called benevolence, sympathy, or humanity) play a major role in morality:

it follows, that everything, which contributes to the happiness of society, recommends itself directly to our approbation and good-will. Here is a principle, which accounts, in great part, for the origin of morality: And what need we seek for abstruse and remote systems, when there occurs one so obvious and natural? . . . Have we any difficulty to comprehend the force of humanity and benevolence? Or to conceive, that the very aspect of happiness, joy, prosperity, gives pleasure; that of pain, suffering, sorrow, communicates uneasiness? . . . The signs of sorrow and mourning, though arbitrary, affect us with melancholy; but the natural symptoms, tears and cries and groans, never fail to infuse compassion and uneasiness. And if the effects of misery touch us in so lively a manner; we can be supposed altogether insensible or indifferent towards its causes; when a malicious or treacherous character and behaviour are presented to us? [pp. 219–220].

Like Hume, Arthur Schopenhauer (1841/1965), in his critique of Kant's (1788/1949) work, argued that compassion is one of the fundamental incentives of human action, and that moral behaviors are often based upon one person's sympathizing with another:

There are generally only *three fundamental incentives* of human actions, and all possible motives operate solely through their stimulation:

  a) Egoism: this desires one's own weal (is boundless).
  b) Malice: this desires another's woe (goes to the limits of extreme cruelty).
  c) Compassion: this desires another's weal (goes to the length of nobleness and magnanimity).

Every human action must be attributable to one of these incentives, although two can also act in combination [p.145].

Some more recent philosophers have suggested that sympathy, although being a morally valued motive, is inferior to the rational motive of duty (Ross, 1930), or is a moral motive because the same types of actions are engendered by sympathy and duty (meaning conscientiousness; Mercer, 1972). Still others, such as Iris Murdoch (1971), have suggested that philosophers have over emphasized the role of cognitive self-awareness in morality: "Instances of the facts, as I shall boldly call them, which interest me and which seem to have been forgotten or 'theorized away' are the fact that an unexamined life can be virtuous and the fact that love is a central concept in morals [pp. 1–2]."

Bernard Williams (1973) challenged Kant's (1788/1949) assertions regarding the role of emotions by pointing out that moral principles, like emotions, are not merely rational. In Williams' view, principles are part of the individual's inner self:

The idea that people decide to adopt their moral principles seems to me a myth, a psychological shadow thrown by a logical distinction; and if someone did claim to have done this, I think one would be justified in doubting either the truth of what he said or the reality of those moral principles. We see a man's genuine convictions as coming from somewhere deeper in him than that; and, by what is only an apparent paradox, what we see as coming from outside him. So it is with the emotions [p. 227].

Moreover, Williams (1973) pointed out that acts resulting from feelings of benevolence may sometimes have more positive consequences for the recipient than acts based on cold rational principle.

Is it certain that one who receives good treatment from another more appreciates it, thinks the better of the giver, if he knows it to be the result of the application of principle, rather than the product of an emotional response? He may have needed, not the benefits of universal law, but some human gesture. It may be said that this is obviously true enough in many cases, but it has nothing to do with morality; it just shows that people place other sorts of value on human conduct besides moral value. Well, this may be said, and Kant indeed said it, but it leads to an uncomfortable dilemma. Either the recipient *ought* to prefer the ministrations of the moral man to the human gesture, which seems a mildly insane requirement; or, alternatively, if it be admitted that it is perfectly proper and rational of the recipient to have the preference he has, the value of moral men becomes an open question, and we can reasonably entertain the proposal that we should not seek to produce moral men, or very many of them, but rather than those, whatever their inconsistencies, who make the human gesture [p. 227].

The modern philosopher who has probably taken the strongest and most eloquent stance concerning the role of affect in morality, particularly altruism, is Lawrence Blum (1980). Just as most other theorists who assert that affect is a legitimate source of moral action, Blum has not denied that cognition is a contributor to morality and moral behavior. Rather, he suggested that altruism may be prompted by either moral cognitions or altruistic emotions such as sympathy, concern, or compassion. According to Blum, "the crucial distinction is between concern for one's own good and concern for the good of others, rather than between emotional (or interested considerations) and rational considerations" [p. 124]. Blum pointed out that rational processes do not always produce moral action; as we all know, cognitive "reasons" can be twisted or distorted in such a way that they can be used to justify immoral behavior. Blum asserted that the sense of duty (which was seen by Kant [1788/1949] as rational) is no more immune to the distorting, rationalizing, self-deceiving, and weakening effects of personal feelings than are sympathy, compassion and concern for others' welfare.

Blum (1980) defined altruism as "a regard for the good of another person for his own sake, or conduct motivated by such a regard [pp. 9–10]." Based upon his definition, he asserted that altruistic behavior often is motivated by altruistic emotions such as compassion or sympathy. Indeed, according to Blum, emotions such as sympathy are sometimes more likely than rationality to lead to altruistic behavior because "sympathy and compassion themselves impel, or can impel, the necessary reflection when the situation presents elements of complexity, when it is not evident how best to carry out one's beneficent intent [p. 110]." In other words, individuals may be induced to take the other's perspective when they sympathize, and consequently may be better able to assist another or may even be more likely to assist. Moreover, Blum argued that the quality of helping induced by sympathy may often be superior to helping based upon cold rationality rather than concern.

One of Kant's (1788/1949) primary reasons for asserting that emotions have little or no moral value is that emotional responses are not universal; our emotional responses vary as a function of the other person and the situation. Blum (1980) denied that a morally good action must be universal. To Blum, a sympathetic act of assistance is a direct response deriving from regard for the good of another, and therefore is of moral value even if the act is not motivated by some principle that is universal or applicable to all situations. Blum's view is that universality may be a valid criterion for moral principles but not moral behavior: "It may be that universality is a valid requirement for acceptable moral principles. I have been concerned, however, with a different issue, namely whether universalizability is a valid requirement for moral (i.e., morally good) action. It is only the latter role for universalizability which I have denied [p. 116]." In brief, Blum believes that Kant's criteria for moral action are incorrect and that, contrary to Kant's perspective, some emotions can and do engender moral action.

A number of modern psychologists clearly would agree with Blum's (1980) argument that emotions such as empathy and compassion can be motivating factors in truly moral behavior, especially altruism (e.g., Aronfreed, 1970; Batson & Coke, 1981; Hoffman, 1975, 1976, 1982a; Mussen & Eisenberg-Berg, 1977; Staub, 1978, 1979). Indeed, for most psychologists whether emotionally induced positive behaviors are moral is not the question, but rather to what degree are behaviors such as altruism a consequence of emotional reactions, and in what situations might the causal relation between empathy (or sympathy) and prosocial behavior be strongest (e.g., Eisenberg, 1983c; Underwood & Moore, 1982). In essence, for psychologists, questions concerning the role of emotion in morality tend to be of an empirical nature and concern how and when moral behavior is elicited by emotion, whereas for philosophers the issue is one of defining pure or real morality.

THE ROLE OF EMOTION AND COGNITION IN DEVELOPMENTAL THEORIES OF MORALITY

The precepts of the major developmental theories are clearly reflected in the varying perspectives of psychologists regarding the contributions of emotion and cognition to moral development, including altruism. Moreover, although prosocial emotions and cognitions are not explicitly mentioned by many theorists, theorists' views related to affect and cognition in general can provide insights into the ways in which prosocial affects and cognitions are likely to be conceptualized. Consequently, it is useful to review relevant aspects of the major theories in the history of developmental psychology (psychoanalytic, social learning, and cognitive developmental) as well as components of other theories relevant to the study of prosocial behavior (biological theories, action theories).

Psychoanalytic Theory

Although Sigmund Freud and other traditional psychoanalytic theorists have had relatively little to say about altruism, they have theorized extensively regarding moral development in general (Freud, 1930, 1955, 1968; Hall & Lindzey, 1954). Indeed, Freud advanced one of the first fully developed theories of moral development. In this theory, as in psychoanalytic theory in general, both cognition and affect are considered, but the role of affect is primary.

According to traditional psychoanalytic theory, there are three major structures or systems that form an individual's personality. The most primitive of these is the id. The id is present from birth and is a composite of innate instinctual desires, including instincts related to self-preservation and, most notably, sexual desires and aggression. The function of the id is to gratify the individual's instinctual desires and thereby maintain a tensionless state in the organism. Thus, the id is composed almost entirely of affective impulses.

In contrast, the ego, which purportedly develops after birth, is the rational, cognitive part of the personality. In it are the organism's perceptual and cognitive processes. The function of the ego is to mediate between the demands of the external (primarily social) world and the desires of the id by devising the best ways to obtain gratification given the society's rules and sanctions regarding instinctual gratification. Thus, according to psychoanalytic theory, the primary purpose of the rational part of the individual is to obtain the most gratification possible at the least cost.

The third system of personality, the superego, is the most relevant to an understanding of moral development, including prosocial development. It is the internalized arbiter of moral conduct, the representation of moral rules and the ideal self as well as the enforcer of standards (the conscience). Freud (1959, 1968) believed that the superego develops as a byproduct of the process of identifying with one's same-sex parent at approximately 4–6 years of age.

The process of identification and superego development is believed to differ for boys and girls. The young boy, in the natural process of development, purportedly desires erotic bodily contact with his mother because it is pleasurable. The boy's father is seen as a rival for the mother's attention. Thus, the boy feels hostile and jealous toward his father. Moreover, the boy, due to the frustrations of parental discipline and intervention as well as those from the difficulties of everyday life, develops additional resentment of the father. As a consequence, the boy fears retaliation from his father. Because he assumes that females' penises have been cut off, the boy fears that the father's retaliation will take the form of castration. To relieve the anxiety that results from his fear of paternal revenge, the boy represses his resentment toward his father as well as any conscious desire for his mother. As part of this process, the boy identifies with his father, that is, adopts the values, beliefs, and behaviors of the father. In doing so, the boy can vicariously possess his mother, and also ensures his own safety because the father is relatively unlikely to injure someone similar to himself.

Freud's (1959, 1968) explanation of the process of identification is less clear for girls than for boys. According to his theory, the young girl notices that males have penises whereas she and her mother do not. Consequently, she envies boys for their penises, devalues her mother because she has none, and resents her mother for not giving her a penis (or for allowing her to be castrated). She denounces her love for her mother, and turns her affections toward her father because he has the valued appendage. The girl subconsciously believes that through her father she can possess a penis, both literally by taking it inside of her and symbolically by having his child. However, the girl fears both the resentment of her mother and losing the nurturance previously provided by the mother. Thus, she experiences intense anxiety. To deal with this anxiety, she, like the boy, represses her desire for the opposite-sex parent and her hostility for the same-sex parent, and identifies with her mother. As a result of the identificatory process, the girl adopts her mother's values, attitudes, and behaviors. More precisely, the child adopts the motives, attitudes, values, and behavior that she perceives to be characteristic of her mother, whether or not her perceptions are accurate. Failure to identify with the mother results in faulty or incomplete moral development.

The superego, the major consequence of identification, purportedly is composed of two subsystems: the conscience and the ego ideal. The ego ideal contains the moral standards or ideals that the individual aspires to obtain; the conscience serves to evaluate or regulate the individual's behaviors. When internalized moral standards or ideals are violated, the conscience punishes the individual with guilt feelings. These guilt feelings are the feelings of resentment and hostility formerly directed toward the same-sex parent that were turned inward as a result of identification. When the person fulfills the ideals of the superego, the conscience rewards the self with feelings of pride.

Many emotions are involved in Freud's (1925, 1959, 1968) traditional theory of superego or moral development. Hostility, erotic feelings, anxiety, jealousy, fear, guilt, and pride all play a role. Although the endproduct, the superego, contains representations of values and the ideal self, it is controlled by guilt.

According to the traditional psychoanalytic perspective, the role of cognition in moral development is minor. Even seemingly cognitive aspects of morality, such as principles of justice, are attributed to irrational, selfish desires. For example, Freud (1955) asserted that: "social justice means that we deny ourselves many things so that others may have to do without them as well, or what is the same, they may not be able to ask for them. This demand for equality is the root of social conscience and the sense of duty [p. 121]." In the view of Freud and his followers, guilt, envy, and self-destructive tendencies are the major forces underlying altruism and a sense of justice (Fenichel, 1945; A. Freud, 1937; Glover, 1968).

Indeed, according to Anna Freud (1937) and Flugel (1961), seemingly altruistic behaviors are often defense mechanisms used by the ego to deal with the superego. For example, a person may act in an apparently altruistic manner to conceal and keep in check avaricious tendencies. This type of defense mechanism—the development of a trait exactly opposite of the original trait—is called reaction formation (A. Freud, 1937). Similarly, the defense mechanism termed "altruistic surrender" (A. Freud) purportedly can produce prosocial behavior. This is when an individual vicariously satisfies his or her own needs and desires by taking pleasure in the successes of others. Although the latter defense mechanism is seen as being healthy in some circumstances (and pathological in others; cf.

Flugel), the fact that psychoanalysts view such empathic responses as defense mechanisms suggests that they believe the roots of altruism to be primarily irrational.

Not all psychoanalytically inclined theorists attribute as large a role in development to irrational processes as did Freud. A splinter group of psychoanalysts have placed much more emphasis on the contributions of cognition to development. These psychoanalysts, called ego psychologists, have argued that the blind internalization of parental values cannot adequately account for the principled moral reasoning of some adults. They also have rejected the idea that the formation of moral values is virtually completed by age 5 or 6. According to their perspective and that of many modern psychoanalysts, moral development is an ongoing process occurring throughout adolescence and on into adulthood (e.g., Breger, 1973; Solnit, 1972). Advances in intellectual development as well as changing perceptions of the self are important contributions to the individual's evolving moral code (Breger, 1973). For example, Flugel (1961) proposed that as part of normal ego development, the individual's moral orientation and attitudes change in a positive direction: from fear to security; from moral inhibition to spontaneous kindness and consideration; from egocentricity to sociality; from aggression to tolerance and love; and from heteronomy (the use of external standards and authorities for making moral decisions) to autonomy. Others (e.g., Settlage, 1972) have suggested that the superego is "re-externalized" in adolescence. Thus, in adolescence the moral values of the superego are accessible to conscious appraisal and are re-evaluated and sometimes tested out. As a result of this reappraisal and testing, some values will be reincorporated in the superego whereas others are discarded. This reappraisal is viewed as the consequence of an adolescent being exposed to the conflicting values and uncertainties of adult society—an experience that shakes the adolescent's faith in his or her values— and is assumed to be a more cognitive enterprise than the original identificatory process.

Much research and theorizing on moral development has been spurred by traditional psychoanalytic conceptions of the superego and the identificatory process. In this work, affective processes such as guilt as well as socialization practices related to the internalization of parental standards have been emphasized. For example, the concept of identification (albeit modified) was central in much research on altruism in the 1960s and early 1970s (e.g., Mussen, Rutherford, Harris, & Keasey, 1970; Rutherford & Mussen, 1968). Thus, the theory has had a sizable, although often indirect, impact on the study of altruism and other moral behaviors. However, because much of the theory is unverifiable— and the limited empirical research has, in general, not supported testable aspects of the theory—psychoanalytic theory (especially the traditional version) is not a major contributor to current research and theory on moral development. Moreover, because of psychoanalytic theorists' emphasis on the pathological and egoistic aspects of human nature, there is little in the theory concerning the development of humanistic, positive values and behaviors that are not the byproducts of egoism and other similar traits.

Social Learning Theory

In psychoanalytic theory, the individual is viewed as being irrational, egoistic, and driven to moral behavior only by emotions such as fear, anxiety, and guilt. In traditional learning theory or behaviorism, the forerunner of modern social learning theory, the organism is also conceptualized in nonrational terms. However, according to this perspective, people are not affectively driven, just nonrational. Moreover, the child is not viewed as being highly egoistic, merely as a passive being that must be molded by society if he or she is to adopt the appropriate moral values and behaviors. Thus, in the traditional learning-theory perspective, the individual's affective and cognitive functioning play a relatively minor role in development; the tools for socialization, including moral socialization, lie in the hands of societal agents who control and regulate the child's behavior.

The fact that affect and cognition play a minor role in the traditional learning-theory account of development is directly attributable to the views of the most prominent figures in behaviorism. John Watson (1922, 1928), the orginator of 20th century behaviorism, asserted that internal phenomena which could not be observed or measured, including emotional reactions and cognition, had no role in a theory of behavior. He considered overt, observable behavior and the external forces that shape it to be the proper units of study. Similarly, B. F. Skinner (1971) attributed moral behaviors, as well as other types of behaviors, to environmental contingencies, not to values, feelings, or other internal constructs. With reference to morality, Skinner stated:

> This is an area in which it is easy to lose sight of the contingencies. A person drives a car well because of the contingencies of reinforcement which have shaped and which maintain his behavior. The behavior is traditionally explained by saying that he possesses the knowledge or skill needed to drive a car, but the knowledge and skill must then be traced to contingencies that might have been used to explain the behavior in the first place. We do not say that a person does what he "ought to do" in driving a car because of any inner sense of what is right. We are likely to appeal to some such inner virtue, however, to explain why a person behaves well with respect to his fellow men, but he does so not because his fellow men have endowed him with a sense of responsibility of obligation or with loyalty or respect for others but because they have arranged effective social contingencies. The behaviors classified as good or bad and right or wrong are not due to goodness or badness, or a good or bad character, or a knowledge of right and wrong; they are due to contingencies involving a great variety of reinforcers, including the generalized reinforcers of "Good!" "Bad!" "Right!" and "Wrong!" [107–108].

Some classical learning theorists have even attempted to explain moral principles such as a sense of justice exclusively in terms of reinforcement. Thus, Skinner (1971) concluded that: "The issue of fairness is often simply a matter of good husbandry. The question is whether reinforcements are being used wisely [p. 106]." Others have described the development of conscience as the product of classical conditioning rather than operant conditioning, as, in the words of Eysenck (1960), a "conditioned anxiety response to certain types of situations and actions [p. 13]" formed by pairing certain stimuli (such as the desire to transgress) with punishments or other aversive stimuli.

Modern social learning theory is not a unified theory; there are many versions. Nonetheless, there are some basic similarities among the various versions. For example, most social learning theorists would agree that prosocial behaviors as well as other behaviors are the product of learning. According to Rushton (1982), a strong proponent of social learning theory: "From the social learning point of view, the degree to which a person engages in prosocial behavior, as well as the frequency and patterning of that behavior, is largely the result of the person's previous learning history . . . . Thus, if we wish to understand how children develop prosocial consideration for others, it is necessary first to understand the 'laws of learning' [p. 86]."

Different renditions of modern social learning theory vary in the degree to which the roles of cognition and affect are emphasized in accounts of moral development. In general, affect, especially prosocial affect, is relatively neglected in explanations of the development and maintenance of prosocial and other moral behaviors. The most obvious exceptions to this pattern are the accounts of morality based on respondent or classical conditioning. For example, anxiety and fear play a major role in Eysenck's (1960) explanation of the development of conscience. Indeed, conscience is defined as a conditioned negative emotional response that is experienced when one anticipates wrongdoing. Similarly, conditioned empathic responsiveness is the key element in Aronfreed's (1970) model for the development of altruism in childhood. In Aronfreed's view, prosocial actions are motivated by empathy that results from the repeated pairing of the child's feelings of pleasure with someone else's expression of positive affect.

Affect has been assigned a lesser but sometimes visible role in other recent social learning theory accounts of moral behavior. For example, positive and negative self-evaluative reactions, which are probably affective as well as cognitive in nature, are viewed by Bandura (1978) as an important component in his model of the self-regulation of behavior. According to Bandura, "much human behavior is regulated through self-evaluative consequences in the form of self-satisfaction, self-pride, self-dissatisfaction and self-criticism [p. 350]." Similarly, Mischel and Mischel (1976) stated that affective reactions to expected behavioral outcomes are an important determinant of moral behavior:

Even when different people share similar expectancies [regarding consequences for behavior], they may choose different patterns of behavior because of differences in the *subjective values* of the outcomes that they expect . . . . The subjective (perceived) value for the individual of particular classes of events (his stimulus preferences and aversions) is an important determinant of behavioral choices. *Subjective value* refers to stimuli that have acquired the power to induce positive or negative emotional states in the person and to function as incentives or reinforcers for his behavior [p. 91].

Thus, for both Bandura and the Mischels, affect is important in the evaluation of the consequences of behaviors, be the consequences self-evaluative or related to personal likes and dislikes. However, they have seldom discussed potentially prosocial emotions such as empathy.

Although emotion is assigned some importance in accounts of morality by many modern social learning theorists, often cognition is designated a more important role. Indeed, one of the most dramatic changes in social learning theory in recent years is the increasing importance of cognitive processes in the theory. In fact, some versions of social learning theory are now labeled as "cognitive social learning theory" (Mischel & Mischel, 1976).

Perhaps the primemover in modifying some learning theory to include cognitive processing is Bandura (1977, 1978). In his view:

If human behavior could be fully explained in terms of antecedents, inducements and response consequences, there would be no need to postulate any additional regulatory mechanisms. However, most external influences affect behavior through intermediary cognitive processes. Cognitive factors partly determine which external events will be observed, how they will be perceived, whether they leave any lasting effects, what valence and efficacy they have, and how the information they convey will be organized for future use. By manipulating symbolically the information that is derived from experience, one can comprehend events and generate new knowledge about them [1977, p. 160].

In social learning theory, people play an active role in creating information-generating experiences as well as in processing and transforming informative stimuli that happen to impinge upon them. This involves reciprocal transactions between thought, behavior, and environmental events. [1978, p. 356].

Observational learning is viewed by social learning theorists as a powerful means for establishing behavior (Bandura, 1977, 1978), including prosocial behavior (e.g., Rushton, 1980). Exposure to prosocial models is believed to facilitate learning as well as the performance of prosocial behaviors, at least in some circumstances. Moreover, many of the processes underlying observational learning are primarily cognitive. According to Bandura (1977), observational learning is governed by four component processes: attentional processes; retention processes; motor reproduction processes; and motivational processes. The retention processes include symbolic coding of observed stimuli, as well as cognitive organization of the information and symbolic rehearsal. Thus, the critical mechanism of modeling is conceptualized as being at least partially grounded in cognitive processing capacities.

In many versions of social learning theory, cognition is also assigned a role in a variety of other processes related to moral judgments and behaviors. For example, modern social learning theorists frequently view morality as a decision-making process. According to Rosenthal and Zimmerman (1978), the individual must process information concerning the situation at hand and then integrate this information with other factors including ethical rules or principles that are in themselves cognitively constructed:

> Social learning theory treats moral judgments as multidimensional social decisions. Many diverse criteria are utilized when an individual's responsibility for improper conduct is being determined. These criteria include such factors as the personal characteristics of the wrongdoers, the nature of the acts, the long-range as well as the immediate consequences of the acts, the setting in which the acts occurred, the precipitating conditions, the remorse of transgressors, the number and type of people who are victimized, and many other factors . . . . By means of diverse social experiences, we learn which of these considerations are relevant in a given situation. The rules are learned from social encounters by means of modeling, tuition, or evaluative feedback . . . . Thus, social learning theory treats moral decision-making as a highly intricate process, whose many inter-relating factors must be considered and weighed in each situation for their relevance to be determined [p. 151].

Cognition is not only a part of moral decision-making and the construction of principles in social learning theory, but also is involved in the self-evaluation that follows behavior (Bandura, 1978), and in self-regulatory processes (Mischel & Mischel, 1976). Moreover, according to one recent theoretical model for prosocial behavior, cognitions concerning values and beliefs are central to prosocial action and may even facilitate the elicitation of prosocial affects such as empathy (Staub, 1978). According to Staub:

> Most personal goals are likely to have an associated network of cognitions. It is of these cognitions, in a sense, that the goal consists. A person who regards helping others as a personal goal might evaluate other people positively and might think of others' welfare as something desirable and good, of others' distress as bad. Consequently, that person would want to help another in distress [p. 46].

> Individual differences in beliefs, values, and related norms may determine whether people will react empathically. For example, a value orientation that emphasizes concern with other people's welfare may lead to interpretations of others' distress and needs that arouse empathic emotional reactions. The distinction that has been traditionally maintained between empathy and values is probably unjustified—at least it has been too strongly drawn [p. 45].

Thus, in Staub's view, cognitions are an inherent part of the individual's moral orientation, including his or her personal goals and value hierarchy. Moreover, cognitions related to others' welfare can activate empathic responding and, consequently, prosocial behavior. However, Staub also has asserted that people's actions can result primarily from emotional rather than cognitive processes.

To summarize, modern social learning theorists differ considerably in the degree to which they include cognitive and affective factors, especially those explicitly related to prosocial cognitions and emotions, in models of moral behavior. In some theories, empathy or self-evaluative prosocial emotions such as guilt are viewed as a potential motivating factors for prosocial behavior; in other theories, prosocial emotion is assigned no more than a minor role. Moreover, in some theories but not others, a variety of emotions including anxiety, guilt, and fear are involved in both the evaluation of potential behavioral outcomes and in the processes related to value and goal formation. Similarly, although cognitions are relatively unimportant in some social learning models, cognitions concerning prosocial goals and values (or egoistic goals and values) are viewed as vital constructs in other social learning accounts of prosocial and other moral behaviors. These cognitions generally are viewed as the product of learning and experience and are believed to be one cognitive contribution, along with cognitive self-regulatory, learning, and decision-making skills, to moral decision-making and behavior. Comprehensive theories such as Staub's (1978, 1979, 1984), in which cognitive and affective factors are being integrated, are currently in the process of synthesis, and will undoubtedly contribute more to our understanding of prosocial action in the future.

Cognitive-Developmental Theory

Cognitive-developmental theory, sometimes called structuralism, is the most cognitively oriented of the major developmental theories. That is, cognitive-developmental theorists assign a more central role to cognition (and changes in the structure or organization of cognitions) in their descriptions and explanations of various phenomena than do theorists with a psychoanalytic or social learning orientation.

In cognitive-developmental theory, people are viewed as being active in their own development, not driven by instinctive impulses or molded by environmental factors. Individuals structure their environment by actively intepreting their surroundings. Knowledge is not merely a copy of reality or experience; it is actively constructed through the individual's interactions with people, tasks, and events in the environment, as well as through the individual's reflection on interactions. Thus, environmental factors contribute to development and behavior, but are themselves filtered through the individual's cognitive apparatus. According to Piaget (1970), the foremost cognitive theorist:

In order to know objects, the subject must act upon them, and therefore transform them; he must displace, connect, combine, take apart and reassemble them . . . knowledge is constantly linked with actions or operations, that is, with transformations . . . . Knowledge, then, at its origin neither arises from objects nor from the subject, but from interactions . . . between the subject and those objects [p. 704].

In cognitive-developmental theory, development is characterized as a sequence of qualitative changes from simpler to more complex and differentiated forms of organization. Theorists and researchers frequently have attempted to portray the sequence of changes by delineating stages or levels of reasoning about specific issues or phenomena. Examples of such stages are Piaget's (1970) stages of cognitive development, Kohlberg's (1969, 1976, 1978) stages of moral reasoning, and Turiel's stages of conceptions concerning social conventions (1983).

Kohlberg (1973) outlined several essential characteristics of Piaget's cognitive-developmental stages:

1. Stages imply distinct or qualitative differences in structures (modes of thinking) which still serve the same basic function (e.g., intelligence) at various points in development.
2. These different structures form an invariant sequence, order of succession in individual development. While cultural factors may speed up, slow down, or stop development, they do not change its sequence.
3. Each of these different and sequential modes of thought forms a "structured whole." A given stage-response on a task does not just represent a specific response determined by knowledge and familiarity with that task or tasks similar to it; rather, it represents an underlying thought-organization.
4. Stages are hierarchical integrations. Accordingly, higher stages displace (or, rather, reintegrate) the structures found at lower stages [p. 498].

Thus, development is viewed as proceeding through a universal, invariant sequence of stages, each of which is more advanced than the previous stage and integrates in it less mature forms of thought. Development consists of changes in the structure of rational processes used to conceptualize actions and the world in which they are embedded.

Piaget (1932/1965) conducted the first empirical research on stages of moral development. In this work, he examined age-related changes in children's evaluations of actors' morality and conceptions of justice. However, although he presented "stages" of development for moral conceptions, in this early work he did not attempt to apply all the criteria of developmental stages to his levels of moral judgment. For instance, Piaget suggested that in some cultures the sequence of development might be partially reversed due to cultural beliefs and pressures. Indeed, Piaget apparently became disenchanted with his early work on moral judgment because of its focus on content (thinking about specific topics) rather than structure.

Kohlberg (1969, 1971, 1976, 1981) expanded on and modified Piaget's (1932/ 1965) early work on moral judgment. His goal was to construct true cognitive-developmental stages of reasoning, that is, stages with the characteristics listed previously. The result was a six-stage sequence (although the validity of the sixth stage has been questioned; Gibbs, 1977; Kohlberg, 1978). These stages are believed by Kohlberg to reflect changes in the structure of reasoning used to resolve all types of moral conflicts. More recently, however, researchers have asserted that the structure of reasoning differs depending on the domain of knowledge (moral, societal, and psychological; Turiel, 1983), or the type of social interaction (e.g., friendship, authority, relations, prosocial interactions) being considered (Damon, 1977; Eisenberg, 1982).

With regard to prosocial behavior, the cognitive-developmental perspective has served to highlight the issue of conscious cognitive motivations or reasons underlying prosocial actions (e.g., Bar-Tal, 1982; Eisenberg, 1982; Krebs, 1982). Clearly, prosocial behaviors can be performed for a variety of reasons, ranging from the selfish to the highly altruistic and morally principled. Indeed, behaviors that result in a benefit for another are labeled as altruistic or nonaltruistic based on the motives or reasons attributed to the actor. Thus, the reasoning behind the behavior, not the behavior itself, determines its meaning. Inquiry into age-related changes in such reasoning has been stimulated by cognitive-developmental theory.

In contrast to that of cognition, the role of affect in cognitive-developmental theory is relatively minor. Kohlberg (1969, 1971) has asserted that in the moral realm emotion is structured by cognition. In his view, emotion may accompany moral judgments, but is irrelevant to the structure of moral judgments (Kohlberg, 1971). Although not all modern cognitive developmentalists assign as little importance to affect as does Kohlberg, few emphasize emotion in their accounts of development.

Interestingly, the most prominent cognitive developmentalist, Piaget, attempted to formulate a model that encompassed both cognitive and emotional components of development. Piaget's (1981) position was that cognitive and emotional development follow two parallel, complementary courses. Cognition is viewed as providing the structure for development; emotion supplies the fuel or energetic component. Piaget forcefully argued that affect and cognition are inseparable, that there is no thought without emotion and no emotion that occurs without cognition. Moreover, in Piaget's view, the one is irreducible to the other.

Piaget (1981) outlined stages of affective development that parallel his stages of cognitive development (cf. Cowan, 1982; Hesse & Cicchetti, 1982). According to this model, during the sensorimotor stage (from birth to approximately 2 years), intraindividual feelings are present or are acquired. Hereditary structures are present at birth; other feelings, including affects regulating intentional behavior, are then acquired. During the preoperation stage of development (approximately 2–7 years of age), elementary interpersonal feelings and the beginnings of moral feelings, such as respect and obedience, emerge. The stage of concrete operations (approximately 7–11 years) is characterized by the appearance of autonomous moral feelings and "will" (the ability to coordinate conflicting values and conflicting wills so that an initially weaker impulse can become the stronger). According to Piaget, *"the will is simply the affective analogue of intellectual decentration*1[p. 65]." Finally, during the formal operational stage (11–12 years onward), indealistic goals and feelings for collective ideals emerge. In brief, Piaget not only relegated a role to affect in his theory of development, but also delineated stages in the development of affect, including moral affects. Unfortunately, except to a limited degree in a few papers, Piaget did not integrate any of his ideas concerning affect in his theory and research on cognitive or moral development.

It is possible that emotion will play a larger role in cognitive-developmental theory in the future. A few individuals with a primarily cognitive-developmental perspective have recently attempted to expand on Piaget's model of affective development (e.g., Cowan, 1982). Some philosophers and social scientists concerned with moral education (e.g., Crittenden, 1979; Pahel, 1979; Peters, 1979) have also emphasized the role of affect in the cognitive-developmental model of moral development. Moreover, as selected aspects of cognitive-developmental theory are integrated in mini-theories or research related to social behaviors such as prosocial behavior (e.g., Bar-Tal, 1982) and emotion (Hesse & Cicchetti, 1982), cognitive-developmental conceptions may be modified or expanded to better account for the influence of emotion in development.

Biological Theories

Psychoanalytic, social learning, and cognitive-developmental theories frequently are accorded the status of "grand" theories, because they are relevant to explanations for a broad range of developmental phenomena. Biological or sociobiological approaches have a more limited place in developmental theory in that these approaches are used to account for a more limited number of phenomena. However, the popularity of theories involving a genetic component has increased substantially over the last decade or two (although earlier in the century biological theories were much more influential than today), and some writers have integrated biological mechanisms into theories of altruism. For this reason, the role of emotion and cognition in biological theories concerning social behavior will be discussed briefly.

Numerous writers have considered the possibility that altruism has survival value for the human species and perhaps the individual, and therefore may have been favored by natural selection (e.g., Holmes, 1945; Wilson, 1975). However, explaining the evolution of altruism has been difficult because altruism is a paradox for Darwinian theory of evolution. Given that altruists frequently may risk their own safety and well-being when they assist others, one would expect altruists to have less reproductive success than would more selfish persons.

Consequently, evolutionary pressures should serve to eliminate altruism from the species. Yet altruism still exists.

Several processes have been proposed to explain the paradox of altruism including group selection (Wynn-Edwards, 1962), kin selection (Hamilton, 1964, 1971, 1972; Wilson, 1975), and reciprocal altruism (Trivers, 1971). According to the group-selection theory, altruism is advantageous to the group; groups with altruistic members are more likely to survive, even if specific altruists do not. In contrast, the central idea in kin-selection theory is that through self-sacrificing actions, the altruist increases the probability that close relatives, who share the altruist's genes, will survive and reproduce. Consequently, the gene for altruism will often be passed on to the next generation through an altruistic actor's relatives. Finally, in the theory of reciprocal altruism, it is argued that the altruist him or herself frequently benefits from an act of altruism and therefore is more likely to survive and reproduce. Although altruistic acts are dangerous and provide no immediate benefit for the altruist, the beneficiary of an altruistic act may reciprocate in the future when the altruist is sorely in need of assistance.

The merits and inadequacies of the various explanations for the evolution of altruism are not especially relevant to this chapter, and, consequently, will not be discussed here (for relevant discussions, see Campbell, 1975; Hoffman, 1981; Ridley & Dawkins, 1981; Rushton, Russell, & Wells, 1984; Staub, 1978; Wilson, 1975, 1978). What is important is the significance of prosocial cognitions and affects in biological explanations of altruism. Not surprisingly, the constructs of affect and cognition are seldom mentioned in these theories; the emphasis is on the unit of biological transmission, the gene, and its survival in the gene pool. Nonetheless, a few individuals have integrated aspects of cognitive and affective functioning in evolutionary explanations of altruism (e.g., Hoffman, 1981; Trivers, 1971). For example, Hoffman argued that empathic capacities are the mediator of altruistic action, and that it is empathy, not the altruistic action itself, that has been the object of natural selection (cf. Matthews, Batson, Horn, & Rosenman, 1981). In Hoffman's view, empathy (vicarious affective responding that is appropriate to someone else's situation rather than one's own) is a universal human response based upon physiological structures (e.g., the limbic system). Furthermore, Hoffman integrated cognitive capacities into his model by delineating the multiple roles of cognition in empathy (Hoffman, 1981, 1982a), as well as in selecting whom to assist. Hoffman suggested that the fact that people empathize more with similar than dissimilar others is based upon cognitive processing, and is consistent with the theory of kin selection (because similar individuals are more likely than dissimilar persons to share genes with the empathizer). Thus, in Hoffman's view, empathy, a primarily affective capacity that becomes increasingly integrated with cognitions with age, is the key element in the evolution of altruism in humans.

MacLean (1982), like Hoffman (1981), has suggested that the capacity for empathy is the basis of much prosocial behavior, and has evolved in the human species. In his view, the evolutionary forerunner of empathy (as well as conscience) is the capacity for mammals to provide nurturant mothering of their offspring. MacLean noted that the capacity for parental behavior and family affiliation in mammals appears to derive from the limbic system. Moreover, he has suggested that the development of the prefrontal neocortex has led to further enhancement of parental behavior and has provided humans with the capacity for foresight, which is hypothesized to underlie our striving for the welfare of our progeny as well as others.

Hoffman's (1981) and MacLean's (1982) propositions regarding the role of empathy in the evolution of altruism are relatively unique; few writers have elaborated on the role of emotion and cognition in biological theories of altruism. Of course, cognitive decision-making processes could be an element in popular biological theories; for example, potential altruists would be more likely to assist kin if they developed cognitive classificatory mechanisms by which they could differentiate kin from nonkin (kin-selection theory). Moreover, in reciprocal-altruism theory, the altruist would survive longer if he or she were prudent in picking whom and when to assist. Nonetheless, as currently conceived, most biological theories have contributed relatively little to an understanding of prosocial cognitions and emotions.

Action Theory

The primary focus of cognitive-developmental theory is on cognition. In contrast, social learning theorists tend to emphasize overt, observable behavior, although some have made considerable progress in integating cognition into their models. This emphasis of the major theories on one or another component of action, rather than on all aspects of functioning, has limited the usefulness of these theories.

The limited explanatory power of the traditional theories in developmental and other areas of psychology apparently served as an impetus to the emergence of a "new" theoretical orientation, action theory. This approach has rapidly been gaining acceptance in Europe, especially in the German-speaking countries. Action theory was first introduced and discussed by general psychologists (e.g., von Cranach, Kalbermatten, Indermuhle, & Gugler, 1982) and industrial psychologists (e.g., Hacker, 1978; Volpert, 1974), but recently has been used in relation to developmental issues and phenomena (Chapman & Skinner, in press; Eckensberger, 1979; Eckensberger & Reinshagen, 1980; Eckensberger & Silbereisen, 1980a, b; Mischel, 1983; Silbereisen, in press; Skinner & Chapman, 1983), applied developmental and counseling research (Baumgardt, Kueting, & Silbereisen, 1981; Brandstadter, 1981, 1983), and the study of crosscultural development (Eckensberger, 1979).

The action theoretical approach is quite complex, and, in reality, is a number of related theories that are still evolving at a rapid pace. Although action theory is new in that it has only recently been labeled as such and outlined in detail (e.g., Eckensberger & Silbereisen, 1980a,b; von Cranach & Harre, 1982; von Cranach et al., 1982), it has a diverse historial and philosophical basis. Action theorists have borrowed many ideas from "naive" theories of behavior, especially Laucken's (1973) and Heider's (1958) tenets about how people in everyday life develop elaborate networks of thinking about action and their causes. From sociology, for example, symbolic interactionism (Mead, 1934), psychologists have borrowed the notion that manifest behavior is governed by cognitions which themselves derive from society (e.g., Goffman, 1963, 1969). Further intellectual input has come from industrial psychology (e.g., Hacker, 1978; Volpert, 1974), from work on systems theory and problem solving (Miller, Galanter, & Pribram, 1960), and from Marxist theory (cf. Volpert, 1974; von Cranach et al., 1982).

Among the major propositions of an action theoretical orientation is the assertion that human beings are self-reflective and that some behaviors, those called actions, are guided by mental representations. Concepts such as goals, intentions, values, self-monitoring during action, and self-regulation by feedback cycles are fundamental aspects of the theory. Furthermore, society and its rules, norms, and conventions are essential elements of action theoretic formulations. According to an action orientation, because the individual always acts in the environment, culture influences behavior via the specific circumstances surrounding an action (Lantermann, 1980; von Cranach et al., 1982). Moreover, the individual's cognitions and actions are governed by society's rules, norms, and conventions (von Cranach et al., 1982), and individuals, in turn, shape their culture by means of the consequences of their actions (Eckensberger, 1979).

Mario von Cranach and his colleagues (1982), some of the better known action theorists, introduced the term "action" in the following manner:

> Our key concept is that of "action" (*Handeln*). By that we mean a type of behaviour that is (in part, at least) conscious, directed towards a goal, planned and intentional (or willed) . . . . The word "conscious" is intended to express the fact the subjective experiences, accessible to the doer himself and relating to the action are associated with the objection performance of the action; the action is represented in a cognitive manner . . . we do not expect all parts of action will be conscious . . . . We will assume that the cognitive representation of actions, takes the form of goals and plans. [pp. 16–17].

Action is viewed as serving, according to von Cranach et al., "to maintain the actor's self by the adaptation to the demands of his environment [p. 76]."

Action theory is primarily a cognitive theory. According to von Cranach et al. (1982), action is cognitively organized behavior. Indeed, they stated that, "our theory is drawn up essentially as a cognition theory [p. 80]." Conscious cognitions are viewed as controlling and regulating action. They do so via symbolic coding that forms an information processing system; a system for determining which tasks are superior and superordinate to other systems of functioning. Actions are organized hierarchically into the levels of goal determination, strategies to accomplish the goal, and operations (the level at which action steps are organized in minute detail through self-regulation). Attentional processes are an important component of the theory; cognitions related to actions become conscious through attentional processes when the organization of action requires it.

Although action theorists deal primarily with the role of cognition in action, they include emotion in their theoretical framework. As von Cranach et al. (1982) stated:

Motives and emotions determine the goals and sub-goals of concrete actions and affect the subconscious self-regulation . . . . They influence, chiefly, the choice of goal in all levels and also the decision between competing goals and so decision-behaviour and conflict-behaviour; they influence the resolve to perform and finally, with other factors, they structure behaviour on the lower organization levels [p. 80].

Clearly, prosocial affects such as empathy could play a role in goal selection and resolution of goal conflict. However, because emotions and motivations are not readily accessible to empirical measurement, von Cranach et al. (1982) and many other action theorists have chosen to focus on the cognitive and behavioral components of action.

Values, including moral values, are an important component of action theory models of behavior. Values are defined by von Cranach et al. (1982) as "an enduring, non-specific cognition the content of which is esteemed and to be striven for. A negative value is a long-term, non-specific cognition the content of which is rejected to be avoided. A value object is a positively evaluated and a negative value object is a negatively evaluated, animate or inanimate object in the environment [p. 91]." Values and value goals (as well as negative values and objects) influence the choice of action goals, and thereby are a means of influencing behavior. Values are primarily cognitive in their nature; however, emotions as well as values are viewed as influencing the individual's choice of goals, and thereby, behavior.

At this time, action theory is primarily a conceptual theory, a system of concepts and definitions. von Cranach et al. (1982) labeled action theory as a "framework theory," because they assume the theory can be used to integrate a number of empirically-based theories. They also noted that action theory is primarily a description theory because at this time it is easier to use the concepts in the theory to describe empirical findings than to make predictions.

Because of its emphasis on values, goals, behavior, and emotion as well as cognition, the action theory perspective may provide a useful framework for future models of moral development. Indeed, some theorists have already been formulating models for aspects of moral functioning based upon action theory conceptualizations. For example, Eckensberger and Reinshagen (1980) have reconceptualized Kohlberg's (1969, 1971) stages of moral judgment in an action theory framework. In doing so, they have analyzed the relation between content and structure of Kohlberg's stages in terms of goals, means to goals, and consequences. Based on their analysis, Eckensberger and Reinshagen propose a somewhat different model of moral judgment, one in which Kohlberg's higher stages (4, 4½, and 5) are viewed as a horizontal decalage, that is, as subtle extensions of Stage 1, 2, and 3 reasoning respectively and not as new stages.

Eckensberger and Reinshagen's (1980) work is an example of the provocative models that can emerge from an action theoretic perspective. However, they focused primarily on a limited aspect of action theoretic concepts. The study of prosocial development would undoubtedly benefit from action theoretic ideas related not only to values, value conflict, and goal setting, but also to the links between values and goals and actual behavior.

CONCLUSION

Philosophers and psychologists have differed substantially in the degree to which they have incorporated cognition and emotion in their theories and models concerning human functioning. In general, those who have emphasized one element have either belittled or neglected the role of the other in human behavior. Consequently, writers who have attributed prosocial behavior to both cognitive and affective variables generally have found it necessary to go beyond the scope of any single theoretical perspective (e.g., Hoffman, 1976, 1982a; Staub, 1978, 1979, 1982). Cognitive developmental tenets have been borrowed or adapted to explain the development of conscious cognitions underlying helping actions (e.g., Bar-Tal, 1982; Eisenberg, 1982; Hoffman, 1975; Krebs, 1982), whereas social learning principles have been the basis for research and theorizing concerning the socialization and learning of altruism (e.g., Gelfand & Hartmann, 1982; Hoffman, 1970b, 1977; Rushton, 1980, 1982; Staub, 1979). Integrative approaches obviously are necessary to adequately explain prosocial development and are the goal of many current theorists.

3 Prosocial Emotion: Methods and Current Research

Caring, sympathetic concern, and vicarious responding to another's emotion are frequently considered prosocial or altruistic responses (Hoffman, 1975, 1982a; Mussen & Eisenberg-Berg, 1977; Zahn-Waxler & Radke-Yarrow, 1982), and have been cited by philosophers and psychologists as the basis of much moral behavior (Barnett, 1984; Blum, 1980; Feshbach, 1982; Hoffman, 1981; Hume, 1777/1966; Rushton, 1980; Staub, 1978). Such reactions are, by definition, based at least in part on affective responding. Moreover, self-evaluative emotions— for example, guilt or pride—are also considered by some theorists to play a role in the development and maintenance of prosocial behavior (Hoffman, 1982a; Staub, 1978, 1979). Theory and research concerning these various forms of "altruistic" emotions will now be examined.

EMPATHY AND SYMPATHY

Definition of Empathy

Over the years, empathy has been defined in several different ways. In the past, researchers often described empathy as social insight (Dymond, 1949), or as the cognitive ability to comprehend the affective (and sometimes cognitive) status of another (Borke, 1971, 1973; Deutsch & Madle, 1975; Hogan, 1969). However, more recently, the ability to understand another's cognitive state has been labeled by developmentalists as "cognitive role taking," whereas the ability to discern and interpret another's affective responses has been called "affective role taking" (Ford, 1979; Shantz, 1975; Underwood & Moore, 1982).

In recent work, empathy has been defined in two different but related ways. Some writers have viewed empathy as the vicarious feeling of another's emotional state, e.g., as the vicarious matching of emotional responses (Feshbach & Roe, 1968; Stotland, 1969). Hoffman (1982a) describes this response as: "a vicarious affective response that is more appropriate to someone else's situation than to one's own [p. 281]." On the other hand, Batson and Coke (1981) have defined empathy as concern or compassion for another's welfare, for example, as "an emotional response elicited by and congruent with the perceived welfare of another [p. 169]." In some operationalizations of empathy, elements of both emotional matching and sympathy are included (e.g., Bryant, 1982; Davis, 1983a; Mehrabian & Epstein, 1972), that is, empathy is considered a vicarious response that is not inconsistent with the perceived welfare of another, and often involves sympathetic concern.

It is my view that there are at least three types of emotional reactions that frequently have been labeled as "empathy," and that these three reactions should be differentiated. In some instances, the individual merely reflects the emotion of the other. In this situation, the individual feels the same emotion as the other, and is neither highly self-concerned nor other-directed in orientation. I would suggest that this type of emotional orientation be labeled as "empathy" or "emotional contagion," and that pure empathic responding occurs most frequently among very young children.

In other situations, the individual responds to another's emotion with an emotion that is not identical to the other's emotion, but is congruent with the other's emotional state and his or her welfare. An example of this reaction would be when an individual feels concern for another who is distressed or sad. This type of reaction frequently has been labeled as "sympathy" (e.g., Wispe, 1984) or "sympathetic distress" (Hoffman, 1984b). This type of emotional responding should be especially likely to motivate altruistic behavior.

The third type of reaction that often has been mislabeled as empathy is a negative, self-oriented concern in reaction to another's emotional state. For example, an individual may feel worried or anxious rather than sympathetic in response to another's distress. As for sympathy, there is not necessarily an exact match between the emotion of the observer and the other. However, unlike sympathy, the response is self-oriented rather than other-oriented. Batson (Batson & Coke, 1981) has labeled such a self-oriented reaction as "personal distress."

Empathy (as defined above) is a relatively noncognitive response, one that might occur in very young children who do not clearly differentiate between one's own distress and that of another. Moreover, children and adults may initially respond to emotion-eliciting events involving others with an empathic response which, via cognitive processing, becomes either personal distress (if the focus is on the self) or sympathy (if the focus is upon another). For persons aged 1–2 years or older who can differentiate between their own and others' distresses (Radke-Yarrow, Zahn-Waxler, & Chapman, 1983), it is likely that initial vicarious emotion will be appraised or interpreted by the empathizer (cf. Giblin, 1981). This is not to say that empathizing necessarily occurs prior to sympathizing or personal distress; an individual's cognitive assessment in a situation could lead directly to feelings of personal distress or sympathy.

Because empathy, sympathy, and personal distress are very different reactions, most likely with different antecedents and consequences, differentiation of these reactions when possible would undoubtedly result in both increased conceptual clarity and more comprehensible empirical findings. In this book, I will use the terms "empathy," "sympathy," and "personal distress" as defined above when possible. However, many theorists and researchers have not distinguished among these terms; thus, when reviewing their research and conceptualizations, it often is impossible to determine whether they were referring to or assessing empathy, sympathy, or personal distress. Moreover, in some situations it is difficult to distinguish among the three types of responses. Consequently, I will often use the word "empathy" to refer to undifferentiated emotional responsiveness that could be sympathy, empathy, or personal distress.

Altruism and Empathy/Sympathy: Conceptual Models

Over the years, the relation between altruism and empathy/sympathy has been conceptualized in a variety of ways. Some conceptualizations include developmental components; others do not.

Aronfreed (1968, 1970) and Hoffman (1975, 1976, 1982a) are two psychologists who have proposed developmental accounts of the relation between empathy and altruism. According to Aronfreed's social learning account, empathy is acquired by a conditioning process, that is, by the repeated pairing of the child's own feelings of pleasure or distress (elicited by external stimuli) with corresponding emotions in others. As a result of this process, cues of others' emotions acquire the capacity to elicit corresponding emotions in the child. Moreover, the child learns that behaviors that make others happy or relieve another's distress are pleasurable for the child as well. Thus, with time, the child learns that helping behaviors are self-reinforcing.

Hoffman (1975, 1976, 1982a) has proposed the most detailed account of the development of an association between empathy and altruism. According to his model, in the first year of life, before the child has acquired person permanence (the understanding that people are permanent objects separate from the self that exist over time), others' distress cues elicit global distress responses, that is, "a fusion of unpleasant feelings and of stimuli that come from the infant's own body, from the dimly perceived 'other,' and from the situation [1982a, p. 287]." However, because the child does not yet clearly differentiate between self and other, it is often unclear to the child who is experiencing the distress.[1] In terms

---

[1] It should be noted, however, that some developmental psychologists studying infants believe that the self and other are differentiated from early in life (e.g. Campos, personal communication, April, 1985).

of our definitions, Hoffman appears to be saying that the infant experiences empathy, not sympathy.

According to Hoffman, as the child acquires person permanence near the end of the first year of life, the child gradually learns to differentiate between another's and one's own distress. However, because young children cannot clearly differentiate between their own internal states and those of others, they often confuse the two. Consequently, children's helping behaviors are "egocentric," that is, children attempt to alleviate the other's distress with actions that are likely to diminish their own distress. Hoffman (1976) suggested that these early helping behaviors are "quasihedonistic" in motive, that is, that young children assist a suffering person to alleviate their own distress.

As children develop the ability to role take (the capacity to understand others' affective and cognitive states), Hoffman (1975, 1976, 1982a) assumes that they increasingly differentiate between their own and others' perspectives and feelings. In my view, this ability to differentiate clearly between one's own and others' emotional states is necessary for the beginning of sympathetic responding. Hoffman further suggested that, as a consequence of advances in role-taking skills, the 2–3-year-old child's helping behaviors are more appropriate and responsive to others' needs and feelings than are those of younger children. This is because children learn with age to seek out information about others that is relevant to an understanding of the other's distress, information that can be used to formulate effective helping strategies.

According to Hoffman (1975, 1976, 1982a), there is further change in the relation between empathy/sympathy and altruism as the child develops the understanding that the self and others are individuals with different and separate histories and identities, and that people have feelings beyond the immediate situation. Although children continue to be aroused by others' immediate distresses, their arousal may be intensified by the knowledge that the other's distress is not transitory but chronic. The child may imagine another's repeated experiences of distress, even if there are no cues of distress in the immediate situation. Thus, at Hoffman's highest level of empathic involvement, a variety of types of information—including expressive cues from the needy other, immediate situational cues, and knowledge of the other's life condition—can elicit empathic responding.

Hoffman's (1975, 1976, 1982a) theory is unique because he has outlined developmental changes in the contributions of emotion (personal distress/empathy/sympathy) and cognition to prosocial behavior. Most writers who have discussed the relation of empathy to altruism, especially social psychologists, have focused on the capacities of adults or older children, and thereby have neglected to account for the influence of the dramatic changes in cognitive development in childhood.

One of the more elaborate social psychological accounts of the relation between empathy and altruism is that of Piliavin, Dovidio, Gaertner, and Clark (1981, 1982). They have proposed a model of the process by which bystanders come to intervene in emergencies, crises, and other situations in which the need for assistance is immediate. Emotional arousal, as well as the cognitive calculation of costs and rewards in a particular situation, is central to the model.

In the Piliavin et al. model (1981, 1982), arousal that results from observing an emergency is aversive, and the bystander consequently is motivated to reduce it. To accomplish this goal, the bystander will select the response to the emergency that will most quickly and effectively reduce the arousal while, at the same time, incurring as few net costs (costs minus rewards) as possible. The costs for not assisting that are included in the cost/reward analysis may include both emotional costs (an awareness that observing the other's continued suffering will result in one's own personal distress) and self-probation, as well as other personal costs. However, Piliavin et al. also noted that in some circumstances and for some people with specific personality characteristics, emergency helping may be very irrational and impulsive, that is, it may be almost a reflexive response, not a response based on a cost/reward analysis. Piliavin et al. suggested that such reflexive helping is probably related to especially high levels of arousal in the helping situation.

In their model, Piliavin et al. (1981) attempted to differentiate between personal distress and sympathy: "To the extent that arousal is interpreted as alarm and concern rather than disgust and upset and the salience of empathic costs for not helping exceed personal cost considerations, the motive for helping has a sympathetic rather than selfish tone" (pp. 239–240). [These empathic costs] "involve internalizing the need or suffering of the victim and produce a continued and perhaps increased level of unpleasant arousal (p. 236)." It is unclear whether sympathetic reactions are believed to lead to helping due to the actor's desire to reduce his or her own aousal. This is because Piliavin et al. (1982) seem to view sympathy as leading to a lack of differentiation between one's own needs and those of others, sometimes resulting in the needs of others being "incorporated into the bystander's best interest [p. 286]."

Batson, Coke, and their colleagues (Batson, 1984; Batson & Coke, 1981; Batson, Duncan, Ackerman, Buckley, & Birch, 1981; Batson, O'Quin, Fultz, Vanderplus, & Isen, 1983; Coke, Batson, & McDavis, 1978; Fultz, 1982; Toi & Batson, 1982). have proposed a model of empathetically induced prosocial behavior that is similar in some aspects to that of Piliavin et al. (1981, 1982). In their view, taking the perspective of a person in need tends to increase one's empathic emotional response, which, in turn, increases the potential helper's desire to see the other's need reduced (Baton, 1984; Coke et al., 1978). However, two types of emotional arousal may occur in helping contexts: empathy (an other-oriented concerned response) that may result in only altruistically motivated helping (helping motivated by the desire to increase the needy other's welfare), and personal distress (self-oriented emotions such as anxiety, alarm, or worry), which tends to facilitate egoistic helping (helping motivated by the desire to reduce the aversive personal distress created by arousal). Batson's definition of empathy is what I have labeled sympathy.

Batson (1984) has proposed a model for differentiating between altruistically (sympathetically) motivated helping and egoistically (personal distress) motivated helping. In his view, because the altruist's goal is to reduce the other's distress, the costs for not helping are high, whereas there is little gain for the potential helper in escaping (leaving before helping). In contrast, if the goal for helping is primarily egoistic (the reduction of aversive personal arousal), this goal can be more easily achieved by escaping than helping, if escape is possible and easy. Thus, the cost/reward analysis in a helping situation varies, as does the pattern of helping behavior, depending whether the potential helper's arousal is primarily altruistic or egoistic.

Both Piliavin et al. (1981, 1982) and Batson and Coke (1981) have described models in which the potential helper is assumed to be capable of cost-benefit analyses and decision-making based on these analyses. Moreover, such decision-making presupposes that the potential helper has some intuitive understanding of the basis of his or her arousal. Thus, social psychological models of the empathy/altruism association may be of somewhat limited usefulness for explaining the young child's prosocial actions. As was noted by Hoffman (1976, 1982a) and observed by Radke-Yarrow and Zahn-Waxler (Radke-Yarrow & Zahn-Waxler, 1984; Zahn-Waxler & Radke-Yarrow, 1982), very young children often have difficulty even pinpointing the source of their distress, much less analyzing factors that might increase or alleviate their arousal. Thus, their helping behaviors may tend to be less cognitively controlled than those of adults in noncrisis situations (adults' reactions may also be reflexive in crises; Piliavin et al., 1981). However, cognitive abilities such as the capabilities to assess and weigh the costs and benefits of various actions clearly improve in the early years of life as the child becomes better able to consider various factors simultaneously (Piaget, 1970). Developmental advances in these cognitive skills as well as in role taking and moral judgment undoubtedly affect that nature of the relation between empathic responsiveness and prosocial behavior, and need to be considered in future models of prosocial action.

ASSESSING EMPATHY/SYMPATHY

In studies concerning the association of empathy/sympathy with prosocial behavior, researchers have used a variety of techniques to measure empathy. Because the results of this research are a function, to some degree, of the methodology employed, it is useful to analyze procedures for assessing empathy and sympathy prior to examining the results of the research.

In the vast majority of studies concerning the proposed empathy-altruism link, one of six measures of empathy has been used: (1) individuals' reports (verbal or nonverbal pointing responses) of emotional response or mood, usually directed to the experimenter, after hearing stories or viewing pictures containing information about a hypothetical other's affective state (e.g., Brehm, Powell, & Coke, 1984, Eisenberg-Berg & Lennon, 1980; Fay, 1971; Feshbach, 1982; Iannotti, 1975, 1977, 1978, 1981, 1985; Lennon, Eisenberg, & Carroll, 1983b; Sawin, Underwood, Weaver, & Mostyn, 1981; Staub & Feinberg, 1980); (2) self-report (usually via pencil and paper measures) of emotional responsiveness in simulated distress situations, for example, after viewing someone in need or distress (e.g., Batson et al., 1983; Coke et al., 1978, Experiment 2; Toi & Batson, 1982; Wispe, Kiecott, & Long, 1977; Zahn-Waxler, Friedman, & Cummings, 1983); (3) observers' ratings of individuals' facial, gestural, and/or vocal (tone of voice) reactions to another's (usually a hypothetical other's) emotional state or predicament (Leiman, 1978; Lennon et al., 1983b; Sawin et al., 1981; Zahn-Waxler et al., 1983; Zahn-Waxler, Iannotti, & Chapman, 1982); (4) self-report scales specially designed to measure empathy and/or sympathy including items such as "I tend to get emotionally involved with a friend's problems" and "Seeing people cry upsets me" (e.g., Barnett, Howard, King, & Dino, 1980; Davis, 1983a, b; Eisenberg, Pasternack, & Lennon, 1984; Eisenberg-Berg & Mussen, 1978; Kalliopuska, 1980; Mehrabian & Epstein, 1972; Stotland, Mathews, Sherman, Hansson, & Richardson, 1978); (5) physiological responsiveness to another's distress (Byeff, 1970, reported in Piliavin et al., 1981; Gaertner & Dovidio, 1977; Gaertner, Dovidio, & Johnson, 1979; Krebs, 1975; Piliavin, Piliavin, & Trudell, 1974, reported in Piliavin et al., 1981; Sawin, 1979; Wilson & Cantor, 1985); and (6) other-report (e.g., peers' or teachers') of individuals' empathy/sympathy (e.g., Barnett, Howard, Melton, & Dino, 1982; Sawin et al., 1981). Moreover, in some research concerning altruism, investigators have not directly measured empathy but have assumed that certain manipulations induce an empathic set (e.g., Aderman & Berkowitz, 1970; Batson et al., 1981; Coke et al., 1978, Experiment 1.).

Various measures of empathy differ somewhat from one another with regard to definition of empathy. With some measures (e.g., most in grouping 1), empathy has been operationalized as the vicarious matching of one's own emotional response to that of another; with others, empathy has been defined, at least in part, as sympathy or concern for others (most studies in groupings 2, 4, and 6). Of course when empathy is operationalized as physiological or facial/gestural/vocal responses to another's emotional (usually negative) state (measures 3 and 5), it is difficult to determine whether an emotional reaction reflects empathy (vicarious experiencing of the same emotion as another), sympathy, or some other emotional response such as personal distress. Similarly, when empathy has been operationalized as an individual's self report of a global negative state (e.g., sadness), it is impossible to determine whether the negative response reflects emotional matching (empathy), sympathy, or personal distress.

The various measures of empathy also can be differentiated into those assessing the trait of empathy or sympathy (measures 4 and 6), and those for which emotional responding in a specific circumstance (assessment of an emotional state) is assessed (measures 1, 2, 3, and 5). In studies involving the trait of empathy, empathy generally has not been experimentally manipulated. In contrast, in studies concerning state empathy, researchers usually have either attempted to directly manipulate subjects' empathic responding or have manipulated the experimental situation so that the likelihood of subjects experiencing empathic responding is enhanced (e.g., Batson et al., 1981; Coke et al., 1978; Krebs, 1975).

Researchers have tended to use different indices of empathy/sympathy with different age groups. Techniques involving subjects' reports to the experimenter of emotional responsiveness in reaction to a hypothetical character's situation have been used primarily with children. In contrast, self-report via pencil and paper measures of empathy in a staged or videotaped situation has been used more frequently with adults. Physiological measures have been used mostly with adults, whereas facial/gestural indices have been used solely with children. Lastly, researchers have used tests or scales to assess the trait of empathy/sympathy primarily with adults, but also with children school-aged and older. The fact that researchers have tended to assess children's and adults' empathy with different measures is important because, as will soon be discussed, the results of research concerning the association between empathy and prosocial behavior differ depending on the age of the subjects in a particular study.

Each measure of empathy/sympathy would appear to have its own advantages and disadvantages. Picture/story measures of empathy, those for which children are told stories (or see pictures) about others in emotion-evoking situations and then are asked how they feel, are perhaps the most problematic. Typically children are told very short stories (often composed of three sentences) about a sad, happy, angry, or fearful other (e.g., a child who has lost his or her dog), and then is asked: "How do you feel?"; "Tell me how you feel?"; "How did that story make you feel?" (Feshbach & Roe, 1968; Roe, 1982); or "After hearing this story, how do you feel?" (Eisenberg-Berg & Lennon, 1980). In the original research of this type, that conducted with the Feshbach and Roe Affective Situations Test for Empathy (commonly referred to as the FASTE), only children's verbal responses were scored; in some more recent research, nonverbal indices of the child's affective response (children have been asked to point to pictures of faces to indicate how they feel) have also been obtained (e.g., Eisenberg-Berg & Lennon, 1980; Iannotti, 1975, 1978, 1985). Responses typically are coded such that children receive a high score on empathy if their self-reported emotion matches the emotion that is supposed to be conveyed by the story (e.g.,

"I feel sad" for a sad story) and a low score if the valence of their reported emotion differs from that of the story protagonist. However, some researchers who have used picture/story techniques have scored more than one type of emotional response; for example, they have assessed both the match between the child's and story protagonist's affect and report of sympathetic feelings (Staub & Feinberg, 1980).

Picture/story measures have been criticized on both methodological and conceptual bases. With regard to methodology, there are several potential problems. First, it is not at all clear that the short hypothetical scenarios that are the basis of these measures are intense enough to elicit empathy/sympathy (Eisenberg-Berg & Lennon, 1980; Sawin et al., 1981), or that a child's emotions can be so easily manipulated that they can shift rapidly from story to story (Hoffman, 1982b). Second, although intensity of a vicarious response may be an important index of emotional responding (Feshbach, 1982), intensity of empathic/sympathetic affect has seldom been measured. Third, it is likely that the use of verbal responses and the presence of demand characteristics (the child is repeatedly asked how he or she feels) makes the measure vulnerable to the effects of social desirability (Eisenberg & Lennon, 1983; Hoffman, 1982b). Fourth, for some stories, more than one type of affect could be elicited, yet only one is scored as empathic. For example, in one story intended to elicit anger, a child is playing with a friend, the friend breaks a window, and the principal blames the first child. It is reasonable to assume the hypothetical character might feel fear as well as anger, yet only anger is considered the correct response (Hoffman, 1982b).

Fifth, it appears that children's responses vary depending on sex of the child and sex of the experimenter. Boys appear to be more reluctant to report negative emotions such as fear and more willing to report happiness than are girls (Brody, 1983). Moreover, children score higher on story/picture measures of empathy if interviewed by same-sexed rather than opposite-sexed adults (Lennon, Eisenberg, & Carroll, 1983a). Indeed, the correlation between sex of the experimenter and the degree of a gender difference in empathic responding is quite high (.80; Eisenberg & Lennon, 1983). Although it is not entirely clear why children score higher on empathy if interviewed by same-sexed investigators, it is likely that children are more highly motivated to seek approval from same-sexed than opposite-sexed experimenters (and thus, to provide "correct" answers). Alternatively, children may be more likely to attend to, or are less fearful or, same-sexed adults. Whatever the reason, the fact that children's empathy scores vary as a function of sex of experimenter is a problem, especially because most investigators have not systematically varied sex of experimenter.

A conceptual issue related to the validity of story/picture indices of empathy concerns the unidimensionality of empathy/sympathy. Researchers usually assess empathy by measuring vicarious responding to a variety of emotions (e.g., anger, sadness, fear, happiness), and then obtain an overall empathy score by combining children's responses across different affects. The assumption behind this procedure is that people who empathize with someone experiencing one emotion are likely to empathize with others experiencing different emotions. However, this may not be the case; in fact, empathizing with another's sadness or distress has been more closely associated with helping behaviors than has empathizing with positive affects, especially for boys (Feshbach, 1982; Sawin et al., 1981). It is possible that different types of people tend to empathize/sympathize with different emotions, perhaps because of the differential costs and rewards for empathizing with positive versus negative emotions. Some individuals may actively block experiencing another's negative emotions due to the consequent discomfort, and may try to empathize with others' positive states in an attempt to elevate their own mood. Alternatively, the emotions that children empathize with could easily be a function of prior experiences; people may be more likely to vicariously respond to another's affect if they themselves have been in a similar situation or have experienced similar emotions. Clearly, it is premature to assume that empathy is unidimensional and that empathizing with one emotion is similar to and associated with empathizing with another emotion.

Another conceptual issue related to the use of story/picture measures with children concerns the fact that such assessment instruments require that children be both aware of their feelings and able to label them correctly. It is quite possible that younger children cannot always verbalize what they are feeling; indeed, young children have difficulty even labeling emotions such as anger and fear (e.g., Borke, 1971, 1973; Eisenberg-Berg & Lennon, 1980). Moreover, because children younger than 8 or 9 years of age do not understand that a person can feel two feelings simultaneously (Harris, 1983; Harter, 1982), it is unlikely that young children are capable of reporting the full range of feelings that they may experience in a single situation.

Some of the potential limitations of picture/story measures of empathy probably also apply to other self-report measures of empathy. For example, it may be difficult for some people, especially children, to label either exactly how they feel in a specific situation (in experimental studies) or how they generally respond in sympathy-evoking circumstances (as is required on questionnaires concerning empathy/sympathy). Moreover, the self-report of emotional responsiveness in simulated distress situations or via questionnaires may be contaminated by individuals' desire to respond in a socially acceptable manner. Indeed, in many studies involving these types of measures, there are probably demand characteristics that influence subjects' responses. The fact that there are significant sex differences favoring females in individuals' self report of empathy but not for nonverbal and physiological measures of empathy is consistent with the idea that social stereotypes and sex-role expectations influence report of empathy (Eisenberg & Lennon, 1983). In our culture, emotionality and nurturance are part of the stereotypic feminine role (e.g., Best, Williams, Cloud, Davis, Robertson, Edwards, Giles, & Fowles, 1977; Block, 1973, 1981; Williams, Bennett,

& Best, 1975). Consequently, the sex difference in self report of empathy is probably due to females being more willing than males to present themselves as empathic.

Nonverbal measures of empathy, such as indices of physiological responding and facial or gestural reactivity, are less likely to be contaminated by social desirability effects than are self-report measures because they generally are less obtrusive. Nonetheless, there are potential difficulties with these measures. It is possible that the tendency for children to nonverbally express emotions in a clearly identifiable fashion increases with age (Giblin, Bezaire, & Agronow, 1982; Lennon et al., 1983b; Morency & Krauss, 1982), as does the ability (and understanding of the ability) to purposefully monitor facial expressions (Saarni, 1979, 1982; Shennum & Bugenthal, 1982). Thus, young children's facial expressions may be difficult to read, whereas older persons' nonverbal responses may not be indicative of their actual feelings.

The difficulties with physiological measures of empathy are primarily methodological (cf. Lang, 1971; Sroufe & Waters, 1977; Thompson & Frodi, 1984). It is difficult to interpret physiological indices, in part because different people have different baseline responses and reaction rates. Moreover, particular physiological responses may indicate a variety of emotional reactions, and various physiological indices do not always interrelate in the expected manner (cf. Duffy, 1972; Mandler, Mandler, Kremen, & Skoliton, 1961). Empathic responding also may be reflected in some physiological reactions but not others, and cognitive processes as well as mere body movement and speech influence physiological responses.

An additional problem with nonverbal indices of empathy is that empathic responses may not always be expressed simultaneously via all channels of expression (e.g., facially and physiologically), and different people may tend to express emotion in different ways. Buck and his colleagues have found that children (Buck, 1977) and adults (Buck, Miller, & Caul, 1974; Buck, Savin, Miller, & Caul, 1972) who communicate emotion in a specific situation via facial expressions tend to exhibit relatively few physiological reactions in the same situation (see also Notarius & Levenson, 1979). Although not all researchers have obtained a negative relation between an individual's physiological responding and the accuracy of their facial communication (Zuckerman, Klorman, Larrance, & Spiegal, 1981), it appears that for a specific person, one mode of emotional response may frequently predominate over and perhaps inhibit alternative channels of response. Consequently, any single nonverbal measure of empathy may or may not accurately reflect empathic reactivity.

To summarize, there are potential pitfalls for all indices of empathy/sympathy currently in use. Consequently, in interpreting research concerning the relation of empathy/sympathy to altruism, one must always be aware of possible methodological limitations. Indeed, because of the methodological concerns, it is best to base conclusions regarding empathy on a broad base of research involving several different indices of empathy.

THE RELATION BETWEEN EMPATHY AND PROSOCIAL BEHAVIOR: EMPIRICAL FINDINGS

Despite the fact that many philosophers and psychologists have assumed that empathy/sympathy is an important mediator of altruism and other prosocial behaviors (e.g., Archer, 1984; Batson & Coke, 1981; Blum, 1980; Hoffman, 1981, 1982a; Hume, 1777/1966; Staub, 1978), the empirical support for this assumption is mixed. In some studies a positive relation between the two has been noted; in many others, it has not (cf. Eisenberg, 1983c; Underwood & Moore, 1982). Indeed, Underwood and Moore computed a meta-analysis for a number of relevant studies, and found no significant relation between empathy and prosocial responding. However, it is important to note that most of the studies included in this analysis were conducted with children.

Many researchers have assessed children's empathy with picture/story instruments such as the Feshbach and Roe Affective Situations Test (FASTE). Although empathy as assessed with such measures has occasionally been positively related to prosocial behavior (e.g., Marcus, Telleen, & Roke, 1979, but their measure of cooperation was primarily an index of sociability; S. M. Miller, 1977, for girls; Sawin et al., 1981, for some affects), generally the relation has been negative, inconsistent, or nonsignificant (Eisenberg-Berg & Lennon, 1980; Fay 1971; Iannotti, 1977, 1978, 1981, 1985; Sawin, et al., 1981). However, when researchers have used instruments other than picture/story measures to assess empathy, preschoolers' and elementary school children's empathizing has been positively related to prosocial behavior (Brehm et al., 1984; Leiman, 1978; Lennon et al., 1983b; Peraino & Sawin, 1981; Zahn-Waxler et al., 1982).

As was noted by Underwood and Moore (1982), the strength of the association between empathy and prosocial behavior seems to increase with age. When empathy has been operationalized as responses to empathy questionnaires and as other-report of empathy (which often reflect sympathy as well as empathy), empathy generally has been positively related to adolescents' prosocial behavior (Barnett, Howard, King, & Dino, 1981; Barnett et al., 1982; Eisenberg-Berg & Mussen, 1978, for boys only), although not all investigators have obtained this association (Peraino, 1977). For example, adolescents' self report of empathy on questionanires has been associated with boys' volunteering of time to assist with a boring task (Eisenberg-Berg & Mussen, 1978) and males' and females' making of booklets for retarded and crippled children (Barnett et al., 1981). Similarly, empathy frequently has been associated with prosocial behavior in correlational research involving questionnaire or scale measures of empathy/

sympathy with adults (Barnett et al., 1981; Batson et al., 1983; Davis, 1983a, b; Marks, Penner, & Stone, 1982; Mehrabian & Epstein, 1972; Ornum, Foley, Burns, DeWolfe, & Kennedy, 1981) as well as in laboratory studies in which level of empathy or sympathy was manipulated (Archer, Diaz-Loving, Gollwitzer, Davis, & Foushee, 1981; Batson et al., 1981; Coke, et al., 1978; Krebs, 1975; Toi & Batson, 1982).

Indeed, the research findings for adults are relatively consistent. Physiological arousal that is presumed to reflect empathy or sympathy—for example, measures of heart rate or galvanic skin responses—have been associated with speed of assisting in emergencies (e.g., Gaertner & Dovidio, 1977; Gaertner et al., 1979; Sterling & Gaertner, 1984) and with willingness to sacrifice earnings to assist another who was receiving electric shock (Krebs, 1975). Moreover, when empathy/sympathy has been induced by leading subjects to believe they are similar to another (e.g., Batson et al., 1981) or by directing subjects to imagine how the needy other feels (Toi & Batson, 1982), subjects who were induced to empathize assisted the person with whom they empathized more than did individuals not induced to empathize, particularly when it was easy to escape the negative consequences of not assisting (i.e., when subjects did not have to observe the other in distress any longer or would not have future contacts with the needy other). Moreover, when adults' interpretation of their arousal has been manipulated by the use of misattribution procedures (i.e., a person is led to mistakenly attribute his or her arousal to another source, e.g., a placebo), individuals who were not induced to attribute their arousal when viewing a distressed or needy other to nonempathic factors were more likely to assist the needy other than were individuals who were induced to attribute their arousal to other factors (Coke et al., 1978; Harris & Huang, 1973). Similarly, when adults were induced by false physiological feedback to believe that they were aroused in response to hearing a broadcast appeal for help from a needy other, they were more likely to perceive themselves as empathic and to assist the needy other than were subjects who were not told that they were aroused (Coke et al., 1978), especially if the subjects were those high in self report of the disposition of empathy/sympathy and if there were demand characteristics in the experimental setting (i.e., the subjects were asked to evaluate their emotional state before helping and if helping behavior was public; Archer et al., 1981). Finally, prosocial behavior has been associated with adults' self report of trait empathy/sympathy (via questionnaires, Liebhart, 1972; Mehrabian & Epstein, 1972) and self-report of state sympathy or arousal when observing another in distress (Batson et al., 1983; Gaertner & Dovidio, 1977; Marks et al., 1982).

In the past, one could have argued convincingly that the empirical association between adults' empathy and prosocial action was the consequence of the aversive affects of empathizing, i.e., personal distress (Hoffman, 1982a; Piliavin et al., 1981; cf. Batson, 1984). If responding to another's emotional state results in a negative vicarious state for an individual, he or she may assist the other out of the desire to reduce personal distress, not because of concern for the other person. However, according to the results of recent research conducted by Batson and his colleagues (Batson et al., 1981; Batson, O'Quin, Fultz, Vanderplus, & Isen, 1983; Coke, 1980; Coke et al., 1978; Fultz, 1982; Toi & Batson, 1982) and Davis (1983b), personal distress and sympathy seem to be two qualitatively distinct motives for helping. Although feelings of personal distress and sympathetic arousal may be somewhat correlated (e.g.,Archer et al., 1981; Batson, 1984; Davis, 1983b; Toi & Batson, 1982), they are not always highly associated (Batson et al., 1983), they factor analyze into distinct factors (Batson, 1984), and they are related to different patterns of helping behavior. Sympathetic arousal appears to be more likely than personal distress to lead to helping (Coke et al., 1978; Davis, 1983a), especially in situations in which aroused individuals are not forced to deal extensively with the arousal-producing stimulus (e.g., Batson et al., 1981; Batson et al., 1983; Toi & Batson, 1982). In brief, it appears that feelings of personal distress, unlike sympathetic arousal, mediate helping only when helping is either necessary or the easiest way to relieve one's own uncomfortable affective state. In contrast, sympathetically motivated helping is less likely to vary as a function of egoistic concerns, although even individuals who generally are sympathetic may become self-concerned if the cost of helping is too high (Batson, O'Quin, Fultz, Vanderplus, & Isen, 1983).

Given the relatively consistent relation between empathy/sympathy and prosocial action in adulthood, it is important to analyze carefully the contradictory findings concerning this relation in childhood. The inconsistency in research findings seems to be a function, in part, of the method of assessing empathy/ sympathy. Although empathy, when assessed with picture/story indices (e.g., Eisenberg-Berg & Lennon, 1980; Fay, 1971; Iannotti, 1977, 1978, 1981, 1985) and questionnaires (Eisenberg, Pasternack, & Lennon, 1984) has not been reliably associated with children's positive behaviors, nonverbal measures of empathy have been more consistently positively correlated with helping or sharing behaviors (e.g., Leiman, 1978; Lennon et al., 1983b; Peraino & Sawin, 1981; but not Zahn-Waxler et al., 1983).

For example, in a study involving preschoolers, Lennon et al. (1983b) found that a composite measure of anonymous prosocial behavior was positively related to children's nonverbal distress, as coded from their facial expressions and gestural reactions (turning of head, covering face with hands) when viewing videotapes of injured children. For boys, but not girls, level of nonverbal empathy was especially related to assisting the victims with whom the children had empathized. Similarly, Peraino and Sawin (1981) presented first-grade girls with three different distress sequences, and provided the girls with opportunities to alleviate the distress of the children depicted in the tapes. They found that nonverbal measures of empathy (facial expressions, behavioral gestures, reaction time, and looking away) were related to helping and sharing with (but not comforting of) both the individuals with whom they were just empathizing and persons in need in other situations. Moreover, Radke-Yarrow and Zahn-Waxler (1984; Zahn-Waxler & Radke-Yarrow, 1982) have found that even among 2-year-olds, seemingly sympathetic reactions to real-life distresses (primarily as reported by mothers) are often associated with subsequent attempts to help or comfort the needy other. The relation between nonverbal measures of empathy and prosocial behavior would probably be even more consistent if one could differentiate personal distress from empathy/sympathy when observing facial expressions.

There are at least two other bodies of research that can be viewed as providing evidence, albeit indirect, of an sympathy–altruism link in childhood. In the research related to children's moral judgments about prosocial moral conflicts (see Chapters 7 and 8 for more details), researchers have consistently noted that children often justify helping actions in hypothetical situations with reasons related to empathy and role taking (e.g., Eisenberg, Boehnke, Schuhler, & Silbereisen, 1985; Eisenberg, Lennon, & Roth, 1983; Eisenberg-Berg, 1979a; Eisenberg-Berg & Neal, 1981). Moreover, even preschoolers frequently justify their own real-life helping behaviors with rationales suggesting that they acted prosocially because of an awareness of another's need (e.g., statements such as "he's hurt" or "she needs help"; Eisenberg, Pasternack, Cameron, & Tryon, 1984; Eisenberg-Berg & Neal, 1979). The other body of empirical research that is supportive of the sympathy–altruism link in childhood is embedded in the socialization literature. Although the research is not entirely consistent (e.g., Feshbach, 1975; Mussen et al., 1970), socializers' use of disciplinary techniques that are likely to focus the child's attention on another's affective state or plight (use of reasoning) tend to be associated with level or degree of prosocial responding (e.g., Bar-Tal, Nadler, & Blechman, 1980; Dlugokinski & Firestone, 1974; Eisenberg, Pasternack, & Lennon, 1984; Hoffman, 1975; Karylowski, 1982a; Zahn-Waxler, Radke-Yarrow, & King, 1979, cf. Hoffman, 1970b, 1977, and Radke-Yarrow et al., 1983). For example, moral preachings in which adults point out the affective consequences of a child's helping or sharing for another (e.g., "our giving will make those children happy") have been positively associated with children's subsequent prosocial behaviors (Burleson & Fennelly, 1981; Dressel & Midlarsky, 1978; Eisenberg-Berg & Geisheker, 1979; Midlarsky & Bryan, 1972; Perry, Bussey, & Freiberg, 1981; Sims, 1978). Indeed, such empathy-inducing appeals have been found to be effective when appeals that were power-assertive (involved threats of disapproval; Perry et al., 1981), normative (referred to norms relating to altruism; Eisenberg-Berg & Geisheker, 1979), or self-oriented (referred to hedonistic reasons for assisting; Burleson & Fennelly, 1981) in content were ineffective. Thus, it appears that there is some association between the use of empathy-inducing socialization practices and prosocial responding among children.

In short, it seems that sympathetic responsiveness is sometimes associated with prosocial behavior even in childhood, and that the strength of the empirical association between empathy/sympathy and prosocial behavior is a function of both age of the sympathizer and method for assessing empathy. As has been noted by Hoffman (1975, 1976) and Zahn-Waxler and Radke-Yarrow (1982; Radke-Yarrow & Zahn-Waxler, 1984), very young children often may empathize, but empathizing may not be associated with helping because the child does not know how to assist appropriately, or does not realize that assistance is appropriate. With age, children most likely learn how to assist, and that assisting can produce positive consequences for both the needy other and the self (e.g., relief from personal distress or production of positive vicarious affect). Moreover, with age, children's emotional reactions are more likely to involve sympathetic concern (Hoffman, 1976, 1982a), and it appears that sympathetic concern is somewhat more likely to be associated with prosocial behavior than is mere vicarious responding (e.g., in fantasy) to another's state (Davis, 1983a). Consequently, the link between empathizing and prosocial behavior should be strengthened with age-related learning and the development of the capacity for nonegocentric sympathetic responding. Indeed, the fact that many researchers have operationalized empathy in childhood as mere vicarious responding and not as sympathetic concern may explain, in part, the low association between many measures of children's empathy (e.g., picture/story measures) and their prosocial behavior.

THE RELATION BETWEEN EMPATHY AND PROSOCIAL BEHAVIOR: CONCEPTUAL ISSUES

Implicitly or explicitly, most writers who have proposed that empathy/sympathy mediates prosocial behavior have limited the domain of prosocial behaviors with which they were concerned to altruistic behaviors (e.g., Hoffman, 1982a; Underwood & Moore, 1982). In other words, most theorists and researchers have asserted that empathy (particularly sympathy) mediates behavior that is voluntary and intentional, and benefits another without conscious concern for one's own self-interest. The implication is that empathy or sympathy would not be expected to mediate the performance of prosocial behaviors that are involuntary, unintentional, and/or motivated in some way by self-concern, external pressures, or the desire for social approval. Of course, personal distress could be expected to mediate nonaltruistic prosocial behavior.

Nature of Altruism

If sympathetic responding is, in reality, a major motivator for altruistic behavior, one would expect a strong positive association between empathic/sympathetic responding and the occurrence of altruistic behavior. The empirical association between the two should be somewhat attenuated, however, if (1) altruism is often motivated by factors other than sympathy, or (2) the "altruistic" behaviors studied by researchers frequently are really less than altruistic in motivation.

Both of these conditions seem to be true. With regard to the first issue, numerous writers have suggested that altruism can be motivated by a variety of factors besides empathy or sympathy including abstract moral principles (Bar-Tal, 1982; Bar-Tal & Raviv, 1982; Eisenberg, 1982; Staub, 1982) and guilt (Hoffman, 1982a). Research is consistent with this suggestion: Adolescents and adults frequently justify their prosocial behaviors with references to abstract values (e.g., Fellner & Marshall, 1981; Petrovich, 1982). Moreover, in studies concerning moral reasoning about prosocial moral dilemmas, adolescents sometimes discuss the role of abstract principles (and guilt or positive affect related to living up to these principles) in decisions regarding prosocial actions (Eisenberg-Berg, 1979a). Thus, because altruistic behaviors are sometimes motivated by factors other than sympathy, one should not expect an association between sympathy and altruistic behavior in all situations for all people.

Even if altruistic behaviors were always motivated by sympathetic concerns, the behaviors that have been deemed to be altruistic in most studies are not necessarily truly altruistic in motivation. Typically, researchers assess altruism (or prosocial behavior) by providing subjects with opportunities to share or assist others, or by observing naturally occuring helping, sharing, or comforting behaviors. In most cases, there is no way to ascertain whether the individual's positive behavior is altruistically motivated or is a consequence of any of a number of nonaltruistic considerations (e.g., fear of punishment, hedonistic concerns, need for approval). If the behavior is not altruistically motivated, there is no theoretical reason to expect it to be associated with sympathetic responding.

State Versus Trait Assessments of Empathy

Another factor that may influence the degree of empirical association between empathy/sympathy and altruism is the type of emotional response that is assessed. Most researchers or theorists believe that altruism in a specific situation is related to both empathic arousal (usually sympathy) in that situation (*state empathy*) (e.g., Aronfreed, 1970; Batson, Coke, & Pych, 1983; Coke et al., 1978; Hoffman, 1982a; Piliavin et al., 1981; Staub, 1978) and/or to the general disposition to be empathic (*trait empathy*). Presumably this is because one with such a disposition is more likely to react empathically/sympathetically (and, thus, to help) in any given situation (e.g., Eisenberg-Berg & Mussen, 1978; Feshbach, 1982; Hoffman, 1982a; Mehrabian & Epstein, 1972). However, if there is an association between empathic responding and altruism, one would expect the relation to be stronger and more consistent for state than trait empathy. This is because, in any given situation involving the potential for altruism, there may or may not be cues that are likely to elicit empathy, and the cues may or may not evoke empathy in any specific person who is high on the *trait* of empathy.

In short, for reasons either within the individual or specific to the situation, an individual's normal or typical level of empathic responding may be irrelevant to the likelihood of altruism in that situation.

Although limited in quantity, there are empirical data consistent with the suggestion that trait empathy may be related to prosocial behavior in some circumstances but not others, depending on the characteristics of the specific situation. For example, Earle, Diaz-Loving, and Archer (1982) found that dispositional sympathy was positively related to adults' helping, but only in a situation that was not particularly sympathy-inducing (a situation in which help was requested via a written appeal). In the situation in which sympathy was likely to be induced in most people (a "live" appeal for help), prosocial values, but not the "trait" of sympathy, were related to helping. Although it is possible that the results of this study were due to factors in the experimental situation other than the degree to which it was sympathy-inducing (e.g., the degree to which a live versus written appeal could evoke feelings of guilt or need for approval), Earle et al.'s findings are consistent with the view that dispositional or trait empathy may mediate individual differences in helping in some situations but not others.

Other researchers have also obtained findings suggesting that the expression of trait empathy varies as a function of the empathy-evoking cues in a specific situation. For example, Barnett et al. (1982) found that sixth graders high on dispositional sympathy helped needy others more than did less sympathetic children, but only in a situation in which the children had been affectively primed, that is, had been induced to think about sad events that had happened to another child. When the children were asked to discuss either negative events that had happened to themselves or affectively neutral events, there were no differences in the subsequent helping of children high and low in dispositional sympathy.

There is also limited evidence to support the assertion that the relation between state empathy and altruism is somewhat stronger than the association between trait empathy and altruism. Peraino and Sawin (1981) examined the association of first grade girls' empathy (operationalized as facial responsiveness to viewing another's distress on videotape, reaction time to response, self-report of affect, gestural reactions to anothers' distresses) to their sharing, helping, or comforting of others in three different distress situations. They found that empathic responsiveness in a given situation was more closely related to prosocial behavior directed toward the needy other in the same situation (state empathy: for 8 of 18 possible correlations) than to empathic responsiveness in other situations (trait empathy: 6 of 32 correlations).

If state empathy is more related to altruism than is trait empathy, some of the inconsistencies in the empirical findings concerning empathy/sympathy and prosocial behavior could be due to differences in type of empathy (trait or state) assessed. Much (but certainly not all) of the research conducted with adults has involved measures of state empathy (e.g., Archer et al., 1981; Batson et al.,

1981, 1983; Coke et al., 1978; Krebs, 1975; Toi & Batson, 1982). In contrast, in most of the research conducted with children, measures of the trait of empathy have been correlated with prosocial responding (cf. Underwood & Moore, 1982). Thus, if altruism is more likely to be a consequence of state than trait empathy, one would expect to find a more consistent positive relation between empathy and prosocial behavior in the adult research literature.

Similarly, the distinction between state and trait empathy could account for some of the discrepancies in the empirical research concerning the relation between empathy and altruism during childhood. In nearly all of the studies in which empathy has been positively related to prosocial behavior, empathy was operationalized as state empathy (Brehm et al., 1984; Leiman, 1978; Lennon et al., 1983b; Peraino & Sawin, 1981). In contrast, in most of the research in which empathy has been unrelated or negatively related to prosocial behavior, empathy has been operationalized as a trait (e.g., Eisenberg, Pasternack, & Lennon, 1984; Eisenberg-Berg & Lennon, 1980; Fay, 1971; Iannotti, 1978, 1981, 1985; Sawin et al., 1981).

In brief, it is important to distinguish between trait and state empathy (and/or sympathy) when examining the association between empathy and prosocial behavior. Conceptually, one would expect state empathy to be more closely related to altruism than is trait empathy. Researchers who have examined the relation between trait empathy and altruism have not directly tested the theoretical proposition that altruism is mediated by empathy arousal for the potential recipient of aid in the given situation. Rather, research concerning the relation between trait empathy and prosocial behavior can be viewed as an indirect test of the empathic arousal/altruism link.

Personal Distress, Sympathy, and Their Association To Altruism

In addition to all of the factors discussed above, there is yet another reason why empathy and altruism may sometimes be unrelated or negatively associated in the empirical research. As was discussed previously, with most measures of empathy it is impossible to differentiate personal distress from empathy. This is because most indices involve no more than self report of a general negative state, or measurement of a general negative physiological or facial/gestural reaction. Thus, the empirical association between indices of empathy and prosocial behavior has probably been attentuated in the research due to the fact that arousal from personal distress often has been labeled as sympathy. In such situations, arousal that mistakenly has been called sympathy may frequently be negatively, not positively, associated with prosocial behavior. For example, Stotland et al. (1978) found that highly empathic nurses were more likely than less empathic nurses to avoid contact with patients. Indeed, if potential helpers experiencing personal distress can escape the aversive situation without paying too high a cost, they will tend to do so (Batson & Coke, 1981; Batson, O'Quin, Fultz, Vanderplus, & Isen, 1983). In contrast, people who experience concern for the needy other rather than personal distress will tend to assist, even if escape from the situation is possible (unless the cost of helping is very high; Batson et al., 1983). Thus, as researchers develop methods of distinguishing among personal distress, sympathy, and empathy, the empirical support for the association between empathy and altruism should be stronger than it is at the present time.

Summary

The empirical findings concerning the relation between empathy and prosocial behavior (an inconsistent relation in childhood, a positive association in adulthood) apparently are influenced by several factors. First, it is likely that empathy actually becomes a more effective mediator of prosocial action with age, especially as vicarious emotional responding involves a greater degree of sympathetic concern. Second, the inconsistent findings for children seem to be due, in part, to the facts that (1) much of the research has involved measures of trait rather than state empathy, and (2) the validity of some of the measures of empathy used with children is questionnable. Moreover, in many studies, the relation between empathy and helping may have been attenuated by the use of measures of "altruism" that were motivated by nonaltruistic considerations, and by indices of empathy that cannot be used to differentiate among personal distress, empathy, and sympathy. In summary, although empathy or sympathy would not be expected to mediate all types of prosocial behaviors, it is likely that the degree to which empathy is a mediator of altruism has been underestimated in the empirical research.

PRIDE, GUILT, AND OTHER POTENTIALLY PROSOCIAL AFFECTS

Empathic/sympathetic responding is not the only type of emotional reaction that mediates or is associated with altruistic action. In a helping situation, potential helpers are often aware of relevant prosocial values and norms, as well as the consistency of one's own behaviors with these values or norms. Emotional reactions frequently accompany the self-evaluation process; pride and feelings of self-satisfaction may be associated with prosocial action once the individual is aware of norms related to helping or has internalized values concerning altruism, whereas guilt, self-punishment, or other negative affects are associated with behavior at odds with relevant norms or values. Moreover, individuals may anticipate that they will experience positive or negative self-evaluative affective reactions depending upon the consistency of their behavior with altruistic norms or values.

Self-evaluative emotions differ from empathic (and sympathetic) emotion in important ways. Empathy is a vicarious response; in contrast, guilt, pride, and other self-evaluative emotions are reactions evoked by evaluation of one's own behavior in a situation, not the other's state. Moreover, self-evaluative emotions would appear to be more cognitively based than are many empathic reactions, the former being based on an evaluative (cognitive) process. Finally, it is likely that mere cognitions concerning impending self-evaluative emotion (i.e., anticipation of feelings of guilt or pride) serve to guide behavior more frequently than does anticipation of empathic and sympathetic reactions.

Theory

The roles of self-evaluative and value-related affects in prosocial action have been discussed and studied much less frequently than has empathy. Nonetheless, numerous writers have at least implied that such affects exist in their discussion and models of prosocial action.

Staub (1978, 1982, 1984) as well as Hoffman (1970a) noted two types of value orientations, one characterized by concern for the welfare of others and the other by concern for doing what is right, that is, upholding one's duty and adherence to norms and rules. Moreover, Staub (1978, 1984) has suggested that based upon these internalized norms and values, a person develops "personal norms," that is, "a person's expectation that he will engage in certain kinds of behavior, presumably derived from personal values and beliefs [p. 43]." Adherence to personal norms is viewed as being motivated by self-reactions, including positive or negative self-evaluation, self-reward, and guilt.

Schwartz and Howard's (1981, 1982, 1984) concept of "personal norms" is somewhat akin to that of Staub's (1978, 1982, 1984) in that it also involves anticipatory self-satisfaction or dissatisfaction. However, Schwartz's and Staub's definitions of personal norms also differ somewhat. Like Staub, Schwartz and Howard view personal norms as behavioral expectations generated from one's own internalized values. However, unlike Staub's concept of personal norms, Schwartz and Howard's personal norms are defined as being situationally specific, that is, they refer to one specific action. These expectations are experienced as feelings of moral obligation, and are backed by self-administered sanctions and rewards. Thus, Schwartz and Howard's conception of personal norms, like Staub's, includes both a cognitive component (value-based expectations) and an emotional component (feelings of obligation and anticipatory rewards and sanctions), but is less general than Staub's conception. Both components are viewed as affecting the probability that an individual will engage in a specific prosocial action.

Numerous other writers have also noted the role of self-evaluative affective responses, especially anticipatory self-evaluative reactions, in altruism. For example, Piliavin et al. (1981, 1982) cited self-censure and its reverse as among the various types of costs and rewards that people consider when deciding whether to help. Moreover, Hoffman (1976, 1982a) outlined in some detail the role of guilt in prosocial development. His (1982a) definition of guilt included cognitive, affective, and motivational elements, with the affective component being a "painful feeling of dis-esteem for the self [p. 298]."

Hoffman (1982a) proposed that guilt stemming from an awareness of another's distress and from some vague feelings of responsibility for this distress develops in the first couple of years of life, whereas guilt based on a clear awareness of the impact of one's own behavior on another develops a bit later. In Hoffman's view, guilt based on the awareness that one's act, or contemplated behavior, is discrepant from internalized norms develops considerably later. Moreover, "existential guilt," or guilt based on the awareness of differences in the well-being between oneself and others, is also viewed as being an important determinant of some adults' altruistic behavior.

Hoffman (1982a) views empathetic distress as a prerequisite for the development of guilt, although guilt and empathy may often be independent at a subsequent point in development. He believes that guilt (especially guilt over omission or inaction), as well as empathy, may be the "quintessential prosocial motives, since they may transform another's pain into one's own discomfort and make one feel partly responsible for the other's plight whether or not one has actually done anything to cause it" [p. 304].

In brief, numerous writers have included moral affects other than empathy in models of altruistic motivation, particularly emotions related to self-evaluation. These self-evaluative emotions are assumed to be the consequence of comparing one's own behavior or contemplated behavior with internalized values or norms. Moreover, the self-evaluative process is viewed as influencing both (1) the consistency of one's behavior (or contemplated behavior) with the content of the altruistic norm itself (i.e., with values related to the importance of assisting another), and (2) the degree to which one has, or plans to, behave in a manner consistent with rules and norms, regardless of their content. In other words, self-evaluation can concern either adherence to the content of norms, rules, and values related to helping, or adherence to the more general issue of upholding of one's duty to conform with internalized norms and values.

Empirical Data

Unfortunately, there is relatively little research directly concerning norm- and value-related prosocial affects. This is because researchers concerned with concepts such as personal norms and prosocial affect often have failed to differentiate between cognitive and affective components in their operationalizations of individuals' internalized value orientations, or have assessed primarily the role of cognition in norm- or value-induced prosocial behavior.

Values and Self-Evaluative Emotions.   As was discussed previously, both Schwartz and Howard (1981, 1982, 1984) Staub (1978, 1982, 1984) have emphasized the role of self-evaluative affective reactions in altruistic behavior originating from altruistic norms and values. Moreover, these researchers have empirically examined the role of such values and norms in altruism (e.g., Schwartz, 1973, 1978; Schwartz & Fleishman, 1978). However, Staub and his students generally have assessed individuals' prosocial orientations, that is, the degree to which they hold values consistent with prosocial behavior, not the role that emotion plays in the individual's adherence to internalized values (Feinberg, 1978; Grodman, 1979; Staub, 1974). For example, Staub typically has studied variables such as the degree to which individuals hold Machiavellian values, ascribe responsibility for action to themselves, or hold norms related to social responsibility. Similarly, Schwartz generally has measured individuals' tendencies to ascribe responsibility to the self and the degree to which individuals report that they feel a moral obligation to perform specific helping behaviors (personal norms). Thus, he has not directly and specifically examined self-evaluative emotions.

For example, typical items on Schwartz's ascription of responsibility scale (used by Staub, 1974; Schwartz, 1968b, 1973; Schwartz & Clausen, 1970) are "Being very upset or preoccupied does not excuse a person for doing anything he would ordinarily avoid" or "If a person is nasty to me, I feel very little responsibility to treat him well" (Schwartz, 1968b). Although it is true that people who ascribe responsibility to the self should be more likely to have experienced self-evaluative reactions in response to the acceptance or avoidance of prosocial responsibilities, such reactions are not directly assessed. Similarly, items such as "If a stranger to you needed a bone marrow transplant and you were a suitable donor, would you feel a moral obligation to donate bone marrow?" are typical of those on Schwartz's (1973) index of personal norms. These items seem to tap subjects' endorsement of specific prosocial actions deriving from prosocial values, but not the degree to which performance (or nonperformance) of specific acts is accompanied by self-evaluative reactions.

Other researchers have obtained evidence that more directly demonstrates the role of self-evaluative affects in prosocial behavior. For example, Fellner and Marshall (1981) found that persons who donated kidneys frequently reported positive self-evaluative reactions. Similarly, Eisenberg-Berg (1979a) and Karylowski (1982a, b) found that adolescents who were interviewed regarding hypothetical moral dilemmas occasionally reported that self-evaluative affects (e.g., pride and guilt) would be important determinants of choosing an altruistic versus egoistic course of action. Such reports were virtually absent before high school age (Eisenberg-Berg, 1979a), but were salient in the reasoning of a small minority of high school students. In specific, these older students said that they would feel guilt or other negative emotions if they did not live up to their self-image or values, and positive affect if they did. Similarly, Petrovich (1982) found that a few retarded adolescents, but not younger children, defined "good acts" (including prosocial behaviors as well as other "good" behaviors) based upon self-evaluative reactions.

Interestingly, Thompson and Hoffman (1980) found that some elementary school children reported that they would feel guilty for violating justice principles (e.g., such as the importance of mutual trust or personal rights) if they transgressed against another child or failed to assist a needy peer (responses to hypothetical transgression and helping situations were combined to form a composite score). References to the use of internal principles concerning right and wrong in explanations of guilt feelings increased with age of the child from first to fifth grade. Differences in the findings of Thompson and Hoffman and Eisenberg-Berg (1979a) with regard to the age at which children expressed guilt feelings were probably due to differences in both stringency of coding guilt responses and in the type of hypothetical offenses being considered. Thompson and Hoffman also found that children who were induced to empathize with a hypothetical victim were more likely than those not induced to empathize to report feelings of guilt, as well as concern, for the victim.

It is important to note that children may experience a rudimentary form of guilt before they are able to verbalize feelings of guilt. Indeed, Zahn-Waxler, Radke-Yarrow, and King (1983) noted signs of conscience or guilt in the second year of life. Some children not only attempted to make reparation for distresses they had caused others, but also exhibited guilt-like or apologetic reactions. Children who exhibited guilt-like reactions were those most likely to see themselves as responsible for stresses they had not caused, and were more altruistic than other children when they were bystanders to (rather than perpetrators of) another's distress. Whether the guilt reactions observed by Zahn-Waxler et al. represented true guilt (i.e., guilt based upon the supposition that one has committed an act that is morally wrong) or an emotional reaction based on empathy, fear of punishment, or some other factor is unclear. Regardless, it is likely that the reactions described by Zahn-Waxler et al. constitute a rudimentary form of guilt.

Guilt versus Mood Induction. In research with adults, investigators have found that people who accidently harm another person frequently provide subsequent help to the victim (e.g., Freedman, 1970; Freedman, Wallington, & Bless, 1967; McMillen, 1971; Wallace & Sadalla, 1966). Some researchers have suggested that such helping is either an attempt to restore one's self-esteem (Filter & Gross, 1975; McMillen, 1971; McMillen, Jackson, & Austin, 1974) or a consequent of guilt feelings (e.g., Freedman, 1970) due, perhaps, to the fact that transgressions evoke memories of social norms (Harvey & Enzle, 1981). Findings of a relation between transgression and helping are consistent with the view that altruism is frequently motivated by self-evaluative affects. However, it is also possible that people assist after committing transgressions in an attempt to restore equity (because feelings of inequity are uncomfortable; Walster, Berscheid, & Walster, 1970), or because helping simply serves a hedonistic function (Cialdini, Baumann, & Kenrick, 1981; Cialdini, Darby, & Vincent, 1973; Cialdini & Kenrick, 1976; Cialdini, Kenrick, & Baumann, 1982).

Cialdini and his colleagues (1973, 1981, 1982) have argued that people who have injured others and who therefore might feel guilt or other negative self-evaluative emotions subsequently assist others not because of internalized values, but merely to lift their own spirits. In Cialdini's view, the sight of someone being harmed makes one feel bad (regardless of whether the observer was responsible for the harm), and prosocial behavior is one means among many that people use to make themselves feel better. Thus, the personal feelings of distress caused by a transgression can be reduced by engaging in prosocial behavior, as well as by any other rewarding (positive) event (e.g., eating an ice-cream cone). Cialdini and his colleagues assume that prosocial acts are rewarding for adults and older children because, through the socialization process, such acts have acquired the properties of a secondary reinforcer. In other words, because altruism is frequently rewarded in childhood (with approval and other types of rewards), helping behaviors gradually become rewarding in themselves to older children and can be used as a method of self-reinforcement.

As support for their position, Cialdini et al. (1981, 1982) point to the facts that (1) transgressors assist nonvictims as well as victims after a transgression (Carlsmith & Gross, 1969; Darlington & Macker, 1966; Rawlings, 1968); (2) observers as well as transgressors assist another who has been injured in some manner (Konecni, 1972; Rawlings, 1968; Regan, 1971); and (3) transgressors are less likely to assist a victim after receipt of rewarding or positive events than if there were no such intervening event (Cialdini et al., 1973; McMillen & Austin, 1971). Moreover, researchers have found that helping by adults is more likely after exposure to a variety of negative events (besides a transgression) including being embarrassed (Apsler, 1975), being injured oneself (Greenglass, 1969), receiving deviant feedback about oneself (Filter & Gross, 1975) or being forced to advocate a counterattitudinal position (Kidd & Berkowitz, 1976). Indeed, even exposure to a positive event before viewing or committing a transgression seems to reduce subsequent helping of a person who was not the victim of the transgression (Cunningham, Steinberg, & Grev, 1980). Furthermore, consistent with the model, exposure to a negative event does not produce more helping if the act of helping is so costly that it would probably result in negative affect rather than positive affect (Weyant, 1978). Finally, the relation between negative affect and helping apparently increases with age in childhood, as would be expected if prosocial acts become self-reinforcing as a result of the socialization process (Cialdini & Kenrick, 1976; Kenrick, Baumann, & Cialdini, 1979).

What Cialdini and his colleagues (1973, 1981, 1982) have attempted to do is to provide a parsimonious explanation for a wide variety of research findings. In general, they view altruism as a hedonistically motivated act. In their view, what researchers have labeled as "guilt" is just one of many negative affects that a person may wish to relieve by engaging in prosocial behavior. This perspective is similar to that of writers who have suggested that people frequently help in an effort to reduce their own personal distress (Batson & Coke, 1981; Piliavan et al., 1981, 1982), although Cialdini has suggested that any of a variety of concrete reinforcers will provide relief whereas Batson and Coke and Piliavin et al. have referred more specifically to relief provided by the reduction of one's own emotional arousal or tension. Moreover, Cialdini's theory is reminiscent of Sears' (1957) and Whiting and Child's (1953) assertions that self-critical responses become secondary reinforcers during childhood due to the fact that parental evaluative responses have been associated with positive stimulus characteristics of the parents, for example, their nurturance. According to this perspective, by imitating parental evaluative reponses, children can provide themselves with a reinforcing, pleasurable experience.

If Cialdini and his colleagues (1973, 1981, 1982) are correct, one might conclude that feelings of guilt, although associated with prosocial behavior, are not really moral because they lead to a hedonism or self-focus rather than to an other-orientation or value-focus. However, it has not been demonstrated that the subjects in the research who assisted after harming another actually felt guilt. In studies, of this sort, subjects generally accidently injured another by actions such as dropping files or beaking a camera. In is quite possible that these people, who had not intentionally injured another, felt embarrassment, frustration, empathy for the victim, anxiety over the potential cost to the self of the accident, or any number of negative emotions other than guilt. Certainly, there is no reason that persons who have accidently damaged an object should feel that they violated internalized values or norms.

In brief, it is not at all clear that genuine guilt—that is, a negative self-evaluative reaction based on the self-perception of violation of internalized standards or norms—is associated with helping merely because guilty persons want to feel better. Moreover, not all subjects behaved in the same manner in the studies on transgression and altruism. For those who felt genuine guilt, subsequent helping behavior may have been motivated by the desire to act in a manner consistent with internalized norms and values, not by the need to change their mood. Such persons may have been those for which exposure to a positive event did not reduce subsequent helping. Indeed, if the subjects had really experienced guilt, only an expiatory response, not receipt of a positive experience should have lessened their negative affect.

Methodological Issues

A major difficulty in studying guilt and related emotions is the lack of an adequate methodology for use in research. Self-evaluative emotions, like empathy, are internal responses with possible external correlates such as specific facial expressions. Thus, self-evaluative responses are not necessarily observable. Moreover, there are probably large individual differences as well as developmental differences in the tendency to experience self-evaluative, value-based affects. It is likely that young children are incapable of true guilt, although they do sometimes exhibit behaviors that may represent a rudimentary form of guilt (Hoffman, 1982a; Zahn-Waxler, Radke-Yarrow, & King, 1983). Moreover, adults would be expected to experience true guilt only if they have developed an internalized moral orientation with regard to values concerning others or rule-upholding. Consequently, it may be difficult for researchers to create experimental situations in which most people will experience guilt or other self-evaluative responses.

Even when people have been experimentally induced to behave in ways that are relatively likely to violate moral standards—for example, are induced to lie (McMillen, 1971; McMillen et al., 1974)—some subjects may have viewed their behavior as being inconsequential or as being unrelated to moral values. Moreover, in studies with children, subjects may verbalize self-critical comments (sometimes believed to be indices of guilt), accept responsibility for a transgression, or report that a hypothetical child would confess to wrongdoing (e.g., Aronfreed, Cutick, & Fagen, 1963; Luria, Goldwasser, & Goldwasser, 1963; Sears, Rau, & Alpert, 1965) merely to present a socially acceptable image, to lessen their own anxiety, or to deter punishment (Aronfreed, 1968; Hoffman, 1970a, b).

At this time, I am aware of no physiological index that can be used to distinguish guilt from other negative reactions. Consequently, it is premature to assess guilt with physiological measures, although the development of reliable physiological indices of guilt would be extremely beneficial to the study of moral development. Thus, self-report indices or semi-projective measures (Thompson & Hoffman, 1980) may be the best way to assess guilt and other self-evaluative reactions. However, such measures are susceptible, of course, to intentional and unconscious distortions or misrepresentations. Moreover, young children may be unable to verbalize self-evaluative moral affects even if they feel them.

Perhaps researchers could use facial expressions as an index of guilt, especially for reasearch with very young children (who have not yet learned to mask their expressions). As yet, this approach apparently has not been tried. Such innovative techniques may be necessary if our understanding of self-evaluative moral affects is to be broadened.

CONCLUSIONS

Although the research is spotty and inconclusive, there is empirical support for the theoretical assumption that altruism frequently is engendered by empathy or sympathy and self-evaluative emotions related to internalized norms and values. The relation between these emotional responses and prosocial behavior seems to be more consistent with age, partially due to the fact that guilt reactions and empathic responses (especially those involving sympathetic concern) develop or change in quality with age as a function of cognitive development and socialization influences. In the case of guilt and similar self-evaluative affects, one could not expect an association with altruism until at least middle childhood when children begin to internalize relevant values and norms. For empathy, responding seems to change with age from a primarily reflexive, vicarious response (empathy) to one which often involves an orientation toward the needy other and his or her situation (sympathy), a change that would be expected to be associated with a stronger association between vicarious arousal and altruism. The development of prosocial tendencies is undoubtedly influenced by prosocial emotions; consequently, the development of these emotions must be central in any comprehensive model of altruism.

4 Attributions About Others and Their Prosocial Actions

Altruistic acts, by definition, involve some degree of conscious cognitive processing. Such acts are intentional and voluntary, and thus must be proceeded by some cognitive consideration of the behavior to be performed. Moreover, altruistic actions are defined as being enacted for internal reasons that are likely to be at least partially cognitive and conscious. Thus, to understand the nature of altruistic behavior, one must examine individuals' conceptions of altruism, and the cognitive processes associated with the decision to act in an altruistic or nonaltruistic manner.

As has been pointed out by action theorists, cognition plays a multifaceted, complex role in most human behaviors. Cognitive inputs to action influence the selection of values, goals, and specific behaviors, as well as the coordination and execution of behaviors. Consequently, to discuss all the ways in which cognition is involved in altruism would require a detailed model, one in which all facets of human action from value formation, to decision making, to self-regulation and the execution of concrete behaviors are delineated. Such a model is well beyond the scope of this book and is a goal to which psychologists can, at present, only strive to achieve. Consequently, in this book only the cognitive processes most relevant and unique to prosocial and altruistic functioning will be considered in any detail.

There are four types of cognitions that seem especially important to an understanding of altruism. Three are general classes of inferential or attributional processes; the fourth is an aspect of cognition involved in the decision-making process. The three types of inferential/attributional processes are (1) individuals' attributions about the kindness of others' prosocial behaviors (or the kindness of a prosocial actor himself or herself), (2) actors' self-attributions or self report concerning the virtue of their own prosocial behaviors or motives, and (3) inferential processes or inferences about other persons that may influence the likelihood of an individual perceiving another's need and/or directing prosocial action toward the other person. Examples of the latter category include the processes of making inferences about either others' internal states (e.g., role taking) or the causes (e.g., internal or external) of another's situation.

The component of the moral decision-making process that will be examined is moral judgment, that is, the individual's judgments about why one should or should not behave in a given manner in a situation in which there is a moral conflict (i.e., a conflict among various values and/or needs or desires). In my opinion, as in the view of some others (Berndt, 1981; Staub, 1982), people's values and goals are reflected in their moral judgments. Whereas attributions and inferences generally concern behaviors or states that have occurred in the past (and also may be existing in the present), moral judgments most often are elicited when making decisions concerning future actions or abstract, hypothetical possibilities.

There are numerous other conceptual and methodological distinctions that can be made with regard to moral judgments, attributions, and inferences. Many of these will become evident in this and subsequent chapters as we consider research and theory concerning these cognitive processes.

VERBAL REPORT OF COGNITIVE PROCESSES

To study individuals' attributions, inferences, and moral judgments, investigators usually elicit either directly or indirectly people's verbal reports of their own mental processes. For example, in research of this type, people are often asked questions such as "Why do you think that?" or "Why did you do that?" Whether people have direct access to their own internal mental processes has been a matter of considerable debate. Indeed, ever since the Wurzburg investigations that relied heavily on introspective processes, writers have intermittently discussed the validity of introspective procedures (e.g., Watson, 1928).

The issue of access to mental processes was recently reintroduced by Bem (1972) and Nisbett and Wilson (1977). In his behavioristic "self-perception theory," Bem proposed that individuals have relatively little access to their own internal states. Cognitions concerning these states are really just self-attributions based on observation of one's own behavior. In Bem's words:

> Individuals come to "know" their own attitudes, emotions, and other internal states partially by inferring them from observations of their own overt behavior and/or the circumstances in which this behavior occurs. Thus, to the extent that internal

cues are weak, ambiguous, or uninterpretable, the individual is functionally in the same position as an outside observer, an observer who must necessarily rely upon those same external cues to infer the individual's inner states [p. 2].

According to Bem (1972), children learn to describe themselves as a result of interactions with others who label the child's internal states (based on external cues) when they occur. Thus, both internal and external cues may be used to infer one's own states, with external cues predominating when internal cues are "weak, ambiguous, or uninterpretable [p. 5]."

It is important to note that Bem does not deny that internal stimuli can, at times, be used to interpret one's own behavior or internal states. Indeed, he delineated those situations in which external rather than internal cues predominate in interpretation or understanding of one's own behavior or state (when internal cues are weak, ambiguous, or uninterpretable). In Bem's view, one of the important distinctions between self-perception and interpersonal perception is that the self has access, albeit limited, to internal stimuli:

All of us have approximately 3–4 ft of potential stimuli inside of us which are unavailable to others but which are available to us for self-attributions. The thrust of Skinnerian analysis of self-attributions is not that we can make no discriminations among internal stimuli, but only that we are far more severely limited than we suppose in this regard because the verbal community is limited in how extensively it can train us to make such discriminations [pp. 40–41].

Nisbett and Wilson's (1977) position regarding the accessibility of internal states and our knowledge of these states is more radical that that of Bem (1972). Their arguments can be summarized as follows:

1. People are unaware of critical stimuli that influence a response.
2. People often are unaware of an inferential process that has occurred.
3. People often are unaware of their own responses to stimuli.
4. When attempting to explain the effects of a stimulus, people often do not access their memories of the cognitive processes used in connection with the stimulus; rather they may base their explanations on a priori theories about the causal relation between stimulus and response.
5. Even when subjective reports concerning higher mental processes are correct, the veracity of such reports is due to the correct use of a priori causal theories.

In brief, Nisbett and Wilson (1977) asserted that we have virtually no access to our own internal process, including those processes related to decision making, motivational states, and evaluative actions: "The evidence reviewed is then consistent with the most pessimistic view concerning people's ability to report accurately about their cognitive processes . . . . The relevant research indicates that such reports, as well as predictions, may have little value except for whatever utility they may have in the study of verbal explanations per se [p. 247]."

After making such a sweeping denounciation of verbal report, Nisbett and Wilson (1977) introduced an idea that limited the breadth of their conclusions, stating that they apply only to cognitive processes and not to cognitive content:

> The individual knows a host of personal historical facts; he knows the focus of his attention at any given point in time; he knows what his current sensations are and has what almost all psychologists and philosophers would assert to be "knowledge" at least quantitatively superior to that of observers concerning his emotions, evaluations, and plans . . . The only mystery is why people are so poor at telling the difference between private facts that can be known with near certainty and mental processes to which there may be no access at all [p. 255].

Unfortunately, Nisbett and Wilson did not clearly define content and process. Apparently, content can include awareness of emotions, evaluations, and plans, although not awareness of how these internal contents are elicited, change, and influence behaviors.

Nisbett and Wilson's (1977) conclusions have been criticized on several accounts. First, as was noted above, the differentiation between content and process is unclear (von Cranach, Kalbermatten, Indermuhle, & Gugler, 1982; Smith & Miller, 1978; White, 1980). Thus, it is difficult to know whether many internal phenomena such as intentions, values, and goals are contents or processes. Second, as was noted by von Cranach et al. (1982), Nisbett and Wilson based many of their conclusions on the fact that subjects in experiments were unaware of subtle experimental manipulations that influenced behavior. Given that the experimenters often were attempting to deceive the subjects, it is somewhat unreasonable to expect subjects to see through these manipulations. Moreover, because subjects were asked to report on a behavior that was a product, in part, of the experimenter's manipulations in a situation controlled by the experimenter, the process about which the individual was to report had not gone on entirely within the person (Shotter, 1981). Third, the methods of data analysis used to disclose *individual* cognitions were often inappropriate because they tested differences among groups (von Cranach et al., 1982). Fourth, Nisbett and Wilson's arguments are presented in a nonfalsifiable form; if subjects can correctly identify mental processes, their success is automatically attributed to a priori causal theories rather than to introspective awareness. Fifth, Nisbett and Wilson's theory of self-perception does not explain why self-perceptions that do not serve to justify one's own behavior occur. For example, they do not account for simple conscious decision making or problem solving (von Cranach et al., 1982).

Another important problem with Nisbett and Wilson's (1977) argument is that they did not differentiate between reasons and causes. According to Locke and Pennington (1982), *causes* are what explain human behavior (and other events) if one observes the behavior "from the outside, looking for empirical regularities, and preferably constant conjunctions between particular behaviors and various features of the environment, the agent's history and so on [p. 212]." *Reasons* are those aspects of people's situation, themselves, their action or its consequences that people cite when explaining their own behavior. According to Locke and Pennington, reasons are a type of cause, and are important determinants (along with other causes) of behavior. Reasons are viewed as motivating behavior because they make behavior seem sensible and appropriate to the actor.

Although people may sometimes be unaware of external causes of behavior, they frequently are fully aware of the reasons for their actions. Reasons may be arbitrary or even based on false information; nonetheless, people are often neither ignorant nor mistaken about what their reasons are (Locke & Pennington, 1982). Thus, if reasons are considered as one cause of human behavior, people may have excellent access to some mental processes underlying behavior.

Another important distinction that Nisbett and Wilson (1977) failed to consider is between behaviors that are intentional and those that are nonintentional (Morris, 1981). In general, the inaccurate reports discussed by Nisbett and Wilson concerned nonintentional behavior (e.g., liking of an object), not intentional behavior. It is quite possible that subjective self reports of intentional behavior are more likely to be accurate than self reports of nonintentional acts. Indeed, it is likely that Nisbett and Wilson would consider intentions as being in the category of cognitive content rather than cognitive process.

In conclusion, it appears that Nisbett and Wilson's (1977) assertions regarding the inaccessibility of our internal processes may be overstated, and are also somewhat vague and ambiguous with regard to specific processes that are unavailable. People do seem to be aware of some aspects of their internal processing, including many of their reasons for actions and intentions. As was suggested by Smith and Miller (1978), a more productive approach to the issue might be to determine when (not whether) people are able to report accurately on their mental processes. Smith and Miller noted that self reports are likely to be more accurate if the tasks or actions are novel and interesting, rather than so routine, overlearned, or boring that they can be performed in a mindless fashion. Moreover, accuracy of self reports may be relatively high if the behavior in question is intentional. Thus, one would expect people to have some understanding of the causes (including reasons) for judgments or prosocial behaviors that follow internal conflict or a difficult decision-making process, and perhaps less awareness of the causes of trivial judgments or attributions and insignificant, automatically performed prosocial acts.

COGNITIONS CONCERNING THE KINDNESS OF
ACTORS OR ACTIONS

In research concerning people's inferences or attributions about others' or their own behaviors, individuals generally are requested to explain their own motives for prior behaviors, or to make attributions about others' actions. If people have some access to their mental processes, their reports of their own reasons should be at least partially accurate, given that the individual is not motivated to hide his or her real reasons. Moreover, their understanding of the criteria they use to evaluate others and others' actions should be at least partially correct. In contrast, if people really have no access to internal processes, people's reports of reasons for their own actions and of the criteria used to make attributions about others could be little more than self-attributions based upon the individual's a priori theories concerning behavior and situational cues that can be used to interpret actions.

In the remainder of this chapter and Chapter 5, individuals' cognitions and conceptions about the goodness or kindness of both others' (this chapter) and their own (Chapter 5) positive behaviors will be discussed. In the case of cognitions about others' behaviors, we are in essence examining the issue of people's *attributions* about the kindness of others' behaviors. Because one does not have direct access to others' internal functioning, the cognitions that a person has concerning the motives underlying another's behavior may or may not be valid, and are at best inferences. In the case of cognitions regarding the kindness of one's own actions, it is less clear if the individual is making an attribution (i.e., does not have direct access to his or her own internal motives) or is providing veridical reports concerning his or her internal states (e.g., motives, reasoning). As has been suggested previously, it is likely that factors such as saliency of the action determine, in part, the accessibility of relevant cognitions (von Cranach et al., 1982).

ATTRIBUTIONS ABOUT OTHERS' POSITIVE
BEHAVIORS

To understand the nature of altruistic behavior, it is important to know the criteria people use to evaluate kindness or altruism. Psychologists generally define altruistic acts as voluntary, intentional behaviors that benefit another and are not motivated by external factors such as rewards and punishments. By studying people's attributions regarding others' positive actions, it is possible to determine whether laypersons evaluate the merit of positive behaviors in a manner consistent with psychologists' conceptions. Moreover, by examining developmental change in children's attributions of kindness, one can delineate changes with age in children's conceptions of altruism.

In general, the research on people's attributions regarding the intentionality of others' positive behaviors has been modeled after the work of Piaget (1965). In contrast, research concerning other criteria for evaluation of altruism (e.g., evaluation of the motives underlying an action) generally has been designed to test assumptions from, and has been modeled after, work related to attribution theory (e.g., Heider, 1958; Kelley, 1967, 1972). For the most part, the results of the research on attributions about others' prosocial actions or dispositions has been consistent with the larger body of research on attributions about others and their behaviors.

The Criteria of Intentionality

In general, an actor's intentionality is considered an important factor in the evaluation of moral and social actions (e.g., Heider, 1958; Piaget, 1965). This is certainly true for evaluations of positive behaviors; adults do not view behaviors that unintentionally result in positive consequences as especially meritorious or kind (Baldwin & Baldwin, 1970; Baldwin, Baldwin, Castillo-Vales, & Seegmiller, 1971; Breznitz & Kugelmass, 1968). Similarly, prosocial acts performed under pressure are not viewed as particularly kind (Breznitz & Kugelmass, 1968).

The use and relative importance of the criterion of intentionality for judging prosocial acts apparently varies as a function of age. Researchers have examined these age-related changes by adapting the story procedures used by Piaget (1965) to study children's understanding of the role of motives and intentions in morality. Piaget frequently elicited children's attributions (and the reasons for their attributions) by presenting children with two or more scenarios involving moral (or immoral) actors, asking the children which story protagonist was "naughtier" or which story solution was fairest, and then eliciting the children's justifications for their decisions. Perhaps the best known of Piaget's stories is the following:

A. A little boy who is called John is in his room. He is called to dinner. He goes into the dining room. But behind the door there was a chair, and on the chair there was a tray with fifteen cups on it. John couldn't have known that there was all this behind the door. He goes in, the door knocks against the tray, bang go the fifteen cups and they all get broken!

B. Once there was a little boy whose name was Henry. One day when his mother was out he tried to get some jam out of the cupboard. He climbed up on to a chair and stretched out his arm. But the jam was too high up and he couldn't reach it and have any. But while he was trying to get it he knocked over a cup. The cup fell down and broke. [p. 122].

Piaget (1965) discussed his findings in relation to what he labeled as the shift from objective to subjective morality, believed to occur at approximately age 6–7 years. In Piaget's vernacular, objective morality denotes a focus on the external features of action, such as its consequences, when determining the morality of an action. In contrast, a subjective orientation is characterized by the child's focusing on internal, subjective processes, including motives and intentionality, when evaluating actors and their behaviors. Piaget's intention was not to clearly distinguish between the use of intentionality versus motives as criteria for judging morality; indeed, these two concepts were often used somewhat interchangeably by Piaget. As a consequence, in his research paradigm, Piaget sometimes did not clearly control for either the valence of a story protagonist's motives or the intentionality of the protagonist's behavior. Moreover, he also tended to confound the dimensions of consequences and motives in his stories. For example, in the story pair presented above, the positively motivated act resulted in large consequences whereas the ill-motivated act resulted in smaller consequences (see Grueneich, 1982; Karniol, 1978; and Keasey, 1978, for further discussion of these issues).

Only a few experimenters have explicitly examined children's understanding of the role of intentionality in evaluating the morality of behaviors or actors (e.g., Berndt & Berndt, 1975; King, 1971; Peterson & Keasey, cited in Keasey, 1978; Walden, 1982; cf. Shantz, 1983), especially positive behaviors. In one of the few relevant studies, Peterson and Keasey (cited in Keasey, 1978) presented three groups of preschoolers (mean ages = 3:8, 4:4, and 4:11 years/months) with three stories, all of which ended with the protagonist producing identical positive consequences. However, in one story, the outcome was an accident, whereas in the remaining two the outcome resulted from either a good or bad motive. The children were asked to evaluate the story protagonists, and to provide reasons for their evaluations. Peterson and Keasey found that their preschool children did not use intentionality in any systematic way to evaluate behaviors that resulted in positive outcomes. Their ratings of the accidental stories were randomly distributed. Moreover, only one of 36 children in the study gave a reason for his or her evaluation of the accident that came close to identifying its unintentional nature.

The results of the remaining relevant studies are consistent with Peterson and Keasey's (cited in Keasey, 1978) findings. Berndt and Berndt (1975) studied children's evaluations of motive and intentionality in four types of situations (altruism, instrumental aggression, displaced aggression, and accidental). They found that even 5-year-old children made inferences based on intentionality, and that this result was marginally significant for the altruism story (see Keasey, 1978, p. 243 for a reanalysis of the data). However, Berndt and Berndt noted that differences in intentionality did not affect the evaluative ratings of preschoolers. In general, improvement in the children's ability to use intentionality as a criterion for evaluations increased substantially during the elementary school years.

Baldwin and Baldwin (1970; Baldwin et al., 1971), in a study of children's evaluations of the kindness of various actors, found that the use of intentionality as a criterion for judging kindness increased significantly from age 5 to 7 (they did not include younger children in their research). Because the Baldwins' procedures will be discussed in detail in the next section, they will not be outlined here. Nonetheless, the Baldwins' data are consistent with other research in indicating that the use of intentionality as a criterion for judging others increases dramatically from the preschool to elementary school years.

Identification of Positive Versus Negative Motives and Causal Schema

Interestingly, children seem to be able to use motives to differentiate between various behaviors that result in positive consequences before they can distinguish between intentional and accidental positive behaviors. For example, Peterson and Keasey (cited in Keasey, 1978) found that the same 3- and 4-year-olds who could not differentiate intentional and accidental positive behaviors did evaluate positively motivated story characters more highly than negatively motivated story protagonists (the consequences of all story characters' behaviors were positive). In other research, investigators have found that 3-year-old (Nelson, 1980) and 4- to 6-year-old children can differentiate between positively and negatively motivated acts that have positive consequences (and sometimes might be considered prosocial; e.g., Costanzo, Coie, Grumet, & Farnell, 1973; Feldman, Klosson, Parsons, Rholes, & Ruble, 1976; Keasey, 1978), although, in one study, children could not consistently differentiate antisocial from prosocial motives until age 5 (Lyons-Ruth, 1978). However, even though children can use motives to evaluate positive behaviors, for young children (e.g., kindergartners) but not older children, the consequences (positive or negative) of a behavior are more important than the actor's motives when evaluating behaviors (Surber, 1982). Moreover, Nelson found that preschool children tend to distort their recall of motives when the valences of outcomes (consequences) and motives are inconsistent. In other words, if the outcome of a behavior is positive and the protagonist's motive is negative, young children might report that the protagonist's motives were less negative than might be expected.

Although young children demonstrate some capacity to differentiate between negatively and positively motivated acts that have positive consequences, their attributions regarding the kindness of acts that result in benefits for others are still quite different from those of adults. In specific, when judging the kindness of actors or their behaviors, young children differ in some ways from adults in their use of covariation principles and causal schemes.

According to Kelley's (1967, 1972) model of attributional processes (the covariation principle), adults are likely to attribute the cause of a behavior to the person (internal causes) rather than the situation if the person acts consistently toward a specific target (high consistency), if the agent (actor) responds in the same way to many different targets (low distinctiveness), and if other actors respond differently toward the specified target (low consensus). Thus, according to Kelley's theory, people should judge a person who assists a specified recipient consistently, who assists many different people, and who assists people that others do not help as more kind than persons who do not assist a target consistently, who do not assist many different people, and/or who assist only persons that others have also assisted.

According to the limited research, it appears that adults generally do use consistency, distinctiveness, and consensus information to make judgments about the kindness of an act (DiVitto & McArthur, 1978; Leahy, 1979). Moreover, even elementary school children apparently use these criteria, at least to some degree, to define the concept of kindness. For example, Leahy found that first and fifth graders, as well as adults, rewarded hypothetical story protagonists relatively more than other story protagonists if they were consistent in their positive behavior and if they helped more than one person. However, children apparently cannot use consensus information to evaluate an actor's kindness until mid- to late elementary school age (DiVitto & McArthur, 1978). The data on consensus information are consistent with the findings that (1) children frequently do not use consensus information in their evaluations until approximately age 7–8 (Dix & Herzberger, 1983) (although the age for the emergence of the use of consensus information is not entirely clear; see Sedlak & Kurtz, 1981), and (2) adults acquire consensus information to a lesser degree, and utilize it less, than distinctiveness or consistency information (Major, 1980; McArthur, 1972, 1976). The delayed and less frequent use of consensus information may be due, in part, to the fact that actors who behave in a manner similar to others are not perceptually salient. Consequently, people may find it more difficult to attribute the cause of a behavior to the actor (rather than the situation) if consensus rather than consistency or distinctiveness information is available (Dix & Herzberger, 1983).

Researchers interested in the development of cognitions about altruism have studied complex causal schema such as the multiple-sufficient schema and graded-effects schema (Kelley, 1967, 1972; Kun, Murray, & Sredl, 1980) more frequently than covariation principles. According to one aspect of the multiple-sufficient schema, the discounting principle (called inverse compensation in the graded-effects model; cf. Kun et al., 1980; Sedlak & Kurtz, 1981), a given cause (e.g., the assumption that an act was motivated by kindness) is minimized when another plausible facilitory cause (e.g., a formal obligation or duress) is present. In contrast, according to the augmentation principle (or direct compensation in the graded-effects model), the presence of an inhibiting cause (e.g., the previous refusal to help by the potential recipient of aid or threats of physical harm to the potential benefactor if he or she helps) leads to the inference that the facilitory cause (e.g., kindness of the actor) is greater. Although the graded-effects schema and not the multiple-sufficient schema is probably the model used by children and many adults (Sedlak & Kurtz, 1981) and, consequently the terms "inverse compensation" and "direct compensation" are more accurate and appropriate than the terms discounting and augmentation, the latter terms will be used henceforth. This is because these terms have commonly been used in the literature as names for the processes that will be discussed.

Clara and Alfred Baldwin were among the first researchers to adopt Piaget's (1965) methods to study the attributional strategies used by people to evaluate the kindness of people and their actions (Baldwin & Baldwin, 1970; Baldwin et al., 1971; Baldwin, Baldwin, Hilton, & Lambert, 1969). In their research, the Baldwins (1970) defined kindness as "a motivation that is sometimes inferred from the fact that one person benefits another, provided the circumstances are appropriate [p. 30]." Some of the circumstances that they hypothesized would influence an observer's evaluation of the kindness of an actor (besides intentionality of the actor) were whether (1) the benefactor had a choice; (2) the benefactor was acting in obedience to a request or command from authority; (3) the benefactor was acting in his or her own self-interest (for example, helping in an attempt to bribe another or to promote trade); and (4) the benefactor was acting in accordance with a social obligation. The social obligations discussed by the Baldwins were the obligation to (1) benefit an invited guest; (2) return a favor; (3) equalize the total benefits in a situation; and (4) help someone who is in serious trouble. The Baldwins hypothesized that an actor who benefits another will be viewed as less kind by an observer if the behavior is not by choice or is not intentional, or if the act benefits the actor himself or herself or fulfills a social obligation.

The Baldwins (1970) tested their hypotheses in a series of studies with a picture-story technique reminiscent of Piaget's (1965). In one study, people in kindergarten, second, fourth, sixth, and eighth grade and in college were presented with 10 story pairs. In each pair of stories, the actual benefit of the protagonist's behavior for another was the same, but some feature of the scenario was varied to provide a contrast which, according to the Baldwins' hypotheses, should make the behavior in one story seem kinder than the behavior in the other. For example, to test the role of obedience in attributions regarding kindness, in one story the protagonist's behavior was requested by his mother (the child gave some of his toys to his baby brother after his mother requested him to do so) whereas, in the other story, the sharing was spontaneous (the child shared without being asked to do so). The children and adults were presented with the story pairs, asked to select the story in which the child was kinder, and then were requested to explain their decision.

In general, the Baldwins (1970) found that subjects tended to make attributions in a manner consistent with their predictions and with the discounting principle. Adults judged actors as kinder if their behavior was voluntary, involved self-sacrifice, did not benefit the actor, and did not fulfill a social obligation. Moreover, there were developmental changes in the children's attributions. For second graders, only attributions regarding the kindness of an actor who assisted to promote a trade were similar to those of adults. By fourth grade, children did not differ from adults in their attributions regarding the role of choice, obedience to authority, self-sacrifice, or obligation to a guest. Eighth-grade children were similar to adults in most attributions regarding kindness, including attributions concerning the role of returning a favor. Only the evaluation of one social obligation (equalization of benefits) showed further development from eighth grade to adulthood.

In a more recent study, Leahy (1979) examined developmental changes in children's use of the augmentation as well as discounting principles. Using a picture-story technique very similar to that of the Baldwins (1970), he found that first-grade children, but not fifth graders or adults, viewed actors as kinder if the actors received a reward (versus was not rewarded) for assisting. Thus, the youngest children did not use the discounting principle; rather they demonstrated use of what has been labeled as either the additive principle (Karniol & Ross, 1976) or as augmentation error (Sedlak & Kurtz, 1981). In contrast, in accordance with the discounting principle, fifth graders and adults believed an actor less kind if the assistance resulted in either a reward or avoidance of punishment. Moreover, consistent with either the augmentation or discounting principles, fifth graders and adults also judged actors who assisted in spite of the threat of harm as more kind than actors who assisted when doing so resulted in the avoidance of physical harm. Similarly, adults, unlike first or fifth graders, believed an individual to be kind if help was offered when there was a reciprocity-related reason not to assist, for example, when the potential recipient had not shared with the potential benefactor on a previous occasion. Unfortunately, Leahy did not actually test the augmentation principle separately from the discounting principle because he did not compare helping at a cost to the actor with helping at no cost (the same general limitation applies to the Suls, Witenberg, & Gutkin, 1981 study).

In brief, Leahy (1979) noted an increase with age in the use of the discounting principle, and obtained data consistent with (but not necessarily indicative of) a similar developmental pattern with regard to use of the augmentation principle. Young children did not evidence usage of either of these principles; rather, Leahy found that first graders assumed that actors' motives were positively related to the outcome of their behavior.

Several other researchers who have examined children's attributions regarding prosocial behaviors have obtained similar data. Other investigators have noted that young children use the additive principle (or demonstrate augmentation error) and, thus, view rewarded or self-beneficial behavior as more meritorious than unrewarded behaviors when evaluating both prosocial behaviors (Butzin, 1979; Cohen, Gelfand, & Hartmann, 1981; DiVitto & McArthur, 1978; Jensen & Hughston, 1973) and other types of social behaviors (e.g., Costanzo, Grumet,

& Brehm, 1974; Karniol & Ross, 1976). In general, children's use of the additive principle has been found to decrease significantly during the elementary school years (Cohen et al., 1981; DiVitto & McArthur, 1978).

Similarly, a number of investigators have noted an increase in the use of the discounting or augmentation principles with regard to both prosocial behavior (Benson, Hartmann, & Gelfand, 1981; Butzin, 1979; Cohen et al., 1981; Peterson, 1980; Peterson & Gelfand, 1984; Shure, 1968; Suls, Witenberg, & Gutkin, 1981) and other behaviors (Costanzo et al., 1974; Karniol & Ross, 1976, 1979). True, some kindergarteners seem to be able to use the discounting principle to some degree (Berndt, 1977). However, summarizing across studies, it appears that older children or adults, in comparison with younger children, are more likely to attribute an actor's helpfulness to external rather than internal causes (i.e., to a helpful disposition) if the benefactor's helpfulness was materially rewarded (Cohen et al., 1981; Jensen & Hughston, 1973; Leahy, 1979; Peterson & Gelfand, 1984); if there were positive reciprocity-based reasons for assisting (Baldwin et al., 1971; Baldwin & Baldwin, 1970; Peterson, 1980; Peterson, Hartmann, & Gelfand, 1977); or if the act of assistance was not voluntary, was performed under duress, was an act of obedience, or was in accordance with social obligations (Baldwin et al., 1971; Baldwin & Baldwin, 1970; Kritt & Baldwin, 1980; Leahy, 1979; Peterson & Gelfand, 1984). Younger children (e.g., first and fourth graders), as well as adults, seem most likely to discount the kindness of helping performed to avoid physical punishment or criticism; children but not older individuals apparently view praised helping as intrinsically motivated (Peterson & Gelfand, 1984). Moreover, adults, but not children, view empathically motivated or prosocial behavior without any apparent (explained) motive as more internal than praised helping or sharing, which in turn is viewed as more internal than prosocial behavior motivated by tangible rewards, reciprocity considerations, and compliance with norms of helping (Peterson & Gelfand, 1984).

Use of the discounting principle in attributions concerning prosocial behavior seems to increase rapidly during the elementary school years, changes little after age 12–13 with regard to situations involving material reward (Cohen et al., 1981; Peterson & Gelfand, 1984), and continues to increase into adulthood, especially for situations related to the equalization of benefits (adults discount helping when such an obligation exists; Baldwin & Baldwin, 1970) and reciprocity-related helping (adults are more likely than children to discount helping involving returning a favor, Leahy, 1979; Peterson & Gelfand, 1984; Suls et al., 1981). Similarly, use of the augmentation principle when judging the kindness of an actor apparently increases during the elementary school years and into adulthood. For example, researchers have found that adults view those who help despite previous refusals by the potential recipient to assist the benefactor as kinder than those who are merely returning a favor (Suls et al., 1981).

Although children's use of the discounting principle is not reliable before age 7 to 9, younger children (for example, kindergarteners) will discount an actor's internal motivation when they are helped to attend to or understand the inducement value of certain variables (Benson et al., 1981; Karniol & Ross, 1979; Peterson & Gelfand, 1984). Ways of enhancing children's understanding of the inducement value of various factors seem to include increasing the salience of an actor's ulterior motives, either by explicitly pointing out possible manipulative motives or external pressures (Benson et al., 1981; Karniol & Ross, 1979; Peterson & Gelfand, 1984) or by depicting the course of events visually (with films) as well as with auditory input (Shultz & Butkowsky, 1977).

Specific Motives for Positive Behaviors

In the research discussed above, only two aspects of attributions about others' positive behaviors were assessed: (1) children's identification of positive versus negative motivations; and (2) individual's application of covariation principles and causal schema to the attribution process. In none of the studies reviewed did investigators elicit and report individuals' attributions regarding the specific motives that engendered positive acts. In other words, in most of the studies on attributions about others, subjects merely rated or ranked others on dimensions such as goodness or kindness; they did not indicate whether the actor's positive behavior was due to factors such as the desire for rewards, need for social approval, an empathic reaction, or internalized values.

There are relatively few studies in which the investigators have both elicited observers' attributions regarding others' motives for positive acts and reported the data in terms of the specific motives elicited (rather than combining all motives into a single index of dispositional versus trait attributions or positive versus negative motives). In research of this type, the investigators were sometimes attempting to assess level of moral judgment and not people's attributions about others (e.g., O'Connor, Cuevas, & Dollinger, 1981). Moreover, the coding of attributed motives generally has been modeled after Kohlberg's system (1971, 1976) for scoring moral judgment, rather than after coding systems devised to assess attributions. However, these studies have differed from those on moral judgment in that subjects have not resolved a moral dilemma (e.g., have not decided whether or not someone should assist in a particular situation) or justified their decision; rather, they have been presented with the description of a positive act already performed by another and asked to explain the actor's behavior. Thus, although research of this sort concerns content similar to research on prosocial moral judgment (i.e., specific motives for helping), subjects in these studies merely have attributed motives to another rather than resolved a moral conflict. Although it is quite possible that the motives individuals attribute to others frequently reflect the concerns that would predominate if they resolved the moral dilemma themselves, it is possible that people attribute motives to others that would be relatively unimportant in their own decision making.

Two studies concerning attributions about others' specific motives for positive behaviors were located (Schlenker, Hallam, & McCown [1983] and Stephan [1975] discussed only composite indices of motives). O'Connor et al. (1981) presented third, fifth, and seventh graders with hypothetical vignettes in which the story protagonist assisted another and then asked children to pick from a list of six reasons the one best explaining "why the child helped [p. 270]." Conceptual/normative motives (e.g., "Dick thinks it is good to make another person's work lighter when possible," or "Dick thinks it is wrong if you don't help someone who needs it") were chosen by the majority of subjects; empathic reasons and reasons related to reciprocity were chosen by approximately 10% of children. Egocentric (emphasis on rewards for the helper), authority-oriented (emphasis on obeying authorities and avoiding punishment), and relationship (concerns with social approval) motives were infrequently selected. When motives were stated in positive tems (e.g., "Dick felt sorry for Scott") rather than negative terms (e.g., "Dick didn't like feeling sorry for Scott"), there was an increase with age in level of attribution (with egocentric, authority, and relationship motives being relatively low, and empathy, reciprocity, and conceptual/normative being somewhat higher). All categories decreased in use with age except conceptual/normative, which increased in frequency of use (although it is unclear if these changes were significant).

In a study with kindergarteners, second, fourth, and sixth graders, Battistich, Watson, and Solomon (1983) used a procedure similar to that of O'Connor et al. (1981). Children were presented with vignettes concerning parent-child, older sibling-younger sibling, and peer helping and were asked why the helper assisted. Battistich et al. found that pragmatic considerations and benefits to the helper were the most frequently mentioned motives at all grade levels. Mention of these two motives declined somewhat with age (nonsignificantly), whereas mention of other types of motives (self concern and desire for superiority, joint benefit/reciprocity, role obligation/expression of a caring relationship, and helping as a value or principle) increased significantly with age. The increase in reference to abstract values or norms with age is consistent with O'Connor et al.'s (1981) findings, although the increase in reciprocity and egocentric (self-concern/superiority) motives is not.

The differences in O'Connor et al.'s (1981) and Battistich et al.'s (1983) findings are probably due to several factors. First, the vignettes differed considerably; in the latter study, the vignettes frequently involved family members, not peers. Second, the coding categories for motives differed somewhat. Finally, and probably of most importance, the two studies differed considerably in mode of eliciting the children's attributions. O'Connor et al. asked children to pick among predetermined motives; Battistich et al. elicited the children's own inferences. Given that children are able to recognize and seem to prefer higher-level concerns or motives before they can spontaneously generate these motives (Rest, 1973, 1979), it is not surprising that the children in O'Connor et al.'s study cited higher-level motives (more normative and conceptual motives and fewer pragmatic and self-oriented, egocentric motives) than did the children in the Battistich et al. study. As will be discussed in Chapters 5 and 7, the motives spontaneously offered by the children in the Battistich et al. study are quite similar in type and developmental pattern (with the exception of the increase in self-concerned reasons) to responses in studies of both children's attributions about their own prosocial behaviors (Eisenberg et al., 1984; Eisenberg-Berg & Neal, 1979) and children's moral judgments about prosocial moral dilemmas (e.g., Eisenberg, Lennon, & Roth, 1983; Eisenberg-Berg, 1979a; Eisenberg-Berg & Hand, 1979). In contrast, the motives cited by the children in O'Connor et al.'s study were more sophisticated than those obtained in most studies on prosocial moral judgment or motives for one's own assisting.

THE RELATION OF ATTRIBUTIONS ABOUT OTHERS' PROSOCIAL BEHAVIORS TO PERSONAL BEHAVIOR

It is reasonable to assume that the way in which people conceptualize and evaluate kindness (as reflected in their attributions) should relate, at least to some degree, to the quantity or quality of their own prosocial behaviors. Based upon the limited research, this appears to be true, at least if level of conceptualization of attributions is operationalized in terms of use of covariation principles and causal schema. For example, Dlugokinski and Firestone (1973, 1974) found that fifth and eighth graders' attributions (as assessed with the technique developed by Baldwin et al., 1969) were positively related to both nominations by peer for considerateness and donations to charity (especially for eighth graders). Similarly, Seegmiller and Suter (1977) found that level of children's attributions was positively related to cooperative behavior, although attributions were unrelated to an index of helping.

With regard to the specific motives attributed to others, the findings are quite mixed. Battistich et al. (1983) noted few significant relations between a low-cost helping behavior and the motives that kindergarteners and second, fourth, and sixth graders attributed to hypothetical helpers. O'Connor and Cuevas (1982) did obtain an association between level of motive attributed to others and teachers' ratings of prosocial, empathic behavior, but only for seventh graders and not for third or fifth graders (although consistency of attributions was positively related to behavior for fifth graders). Moreover, in a study involving 4–11 year olds, Zahn-Waxler et al. (1982) found that children who attributed prosocial intentions to story protagonists who had either hurt another or had viewed someone who was feeling badly were more likely to assist a crying infant (but less likely to assist an adult who had injured herself) than were other children.

Attributions of guilt were positively related to helping of adults but negatively related to assisting an infant. Of course, one would not expect an especially strong relation between level of attributions about others' and one's own behavior; just because an individual is relatively sophisticated in the ability to deduce others' motives (a cognitive capacity) does not mean that they themselves will be motivated to act in a manner that people (including themselves) will judge to be kind.

CONCLUSION

Children's attributions concerning positive behaviors change dramatically with age. The use of intentionality as a criterion for judgment increases rapidly from the preschool to school years. Moreover, although even preschoolers can distinguish between good and bad motives, they differ from adults in their use of covariation and causal schema when making attributions about the kindness of others. Young children, like adults, judge actors who assist many people and help consistently (covariation schema) as kinder than actors who are less consistently helpful. However, according to the limited data, they do not use consensus information (information concerning whether other persons also helped) until somewhat later. Moreover, in early elementary school, children frequently use the additive principle rather than the discounting principle when evaluating the kindness of others' behaviors. By mid-elementary school, however, children often discount the kindness of acts that may have been motivated by external consequences or pressures, and the use of discounting strategies when making inferences regarding positive acts increases into adulthood. In addition, although the existing data concerning this issue are scarce and somewhat unclear, it appears that older children, but not young children, view acts of assistance as more kind if they are performed despite potential costs to the self (the augmentation principle). Use of the augmentation principle in cases involving negative reciprocity (helping someone who refused to assist the potential helper in the past) apparently increases in frequency into adulthood. In brief, young children do not define kindness in the same way as do adults; however, with age, children's definitions of kindness and altruism more closely approximate those of adults.

It is important to note that the available research on the topic is not only limited in quantity but subject to a variety of criticisms. As was pointed out by Fiedler (1982), researchers who have sought to demonstrate the existence of general cognitive schemata that are used to explain causal relations often have done little more than show that specific stimulus/reaction relations elicit certain specific explanations. Moreover, much of the research can be criticized for its lack of ecological or phenomenological validity. For example, in the attribution research in general, investigators often unjustifiably assume that their operationalizations of particular causes in a situation are perceived in the same ways by subjects as by themselves (Weiner, 1983). Researchers also assume that the process of eliciting attributions (e.g., asking subjects about their attributions) does not significantly alter the attributional process; this may not be a valid assumption (Enzle & Schopflocker, 1978).

Furthermore, in most research, the task used to elicit causal schemata does not have a structure similar to that in a naturally occurring causal problem (Fiedler, 1982; McArthur & Baron, 1983). When presented with brief hypothetical story analogues, the subject often is not forced to engage in the process of choosing which environmental information in an experience to encode and to then use in making relevant judgments; the selection of relevant information has already been completed by the experimenter and has been labeled semantically. For example, in many studies, the individual need not decide if a particular positive behavior is intentional or not; he or she is told if the act was accidental. Nonetheless, in reality the process of encoding relevant information is basic to the attribution process. Fiedler has suggested that one can improve future research by: (1) prestructuring stimulus materials so that there is some degree of uncertainty regarding the best interpretation of the empirical raw events; (2) including in the stimulus materials some cues pointing to plausible causes, apart from the description of an effect to be examined; (3) avoiding linguistic artifacts, that is, verbal concepts that are semantically independent and therefore may predetermine the individual's reasoning; and (4) including cues to more possible causes than turn out to be relevant so that the complexity of real-life stimulus situations is replicated.

In brief, it is clear that the procedures used to assess individuals' attributions about others' as well as their own prosocial behaviors are relatively simplistic and that the attributions elicited with the use of these materials are not entirely analogous to naturally occurring attributional processes. Whether children's attributions are more or less advanced (with regard to the use of causal schemes) in the real world is unclear. Although the stimuli to be encoded and utilized in making attributions are much more complex in reality than in the lab, children may rely on certain information in the environment when making attributions that generally is not available in experimental settings. Although it is quite possible that the pattern of developmental change noted in the research would also be obtained if children's attributions about real-life behaviors were examined, it would not be surprising if the ages at which specific capacities have been found to exist would differ somewhat from what has been noted previously.

Of what relevance is information regarding children's attributions about others' prosocial actions to an understanding of the performance of prosocial (including altruistic) behavior? Such information is useful in at least three ways. First, observers' conceptions of kindness will affect how they react to an individual's positive behaviors, and consequently, the type of feedback an actor is likely to receive for different positive behaviors. For example, a helping behavior that results in an expectable concrete reward would probably be evaluated highly by young children, but not by adults; thus, children but not adults would be likely to react relatively positively to such a helping behavior (be they observers or the recipients of aid; see Eisenberg, 1983b). In accordance with the notion that even children's reactions to others are influenced by the motives they attribute to others, Graziano, Brody, and Bernstein (1980) found that third and sixth graders rewarded peers more for their prior performances if these performances were hindered by the peer's altruistic motives than if they were hindered by aggressive motives. Second, the manner in which individuals define or characterize kind behaviors is likely to influence the manner in which, and conditions under which, they behave in a prosocial manner. For example, an adult who desires to act in an altruistic manner and who does not want to behave in a manner that appears (to oneself or others) to be self-serving would probably prefer to assist in situations in which they will not be rewarded; this would not be expected for children who use the additive principle in evaluating the kindness or actions or actors. Finally, the manner in which individuals define kindness will influence the self-attributions or self-evaluations that follow the performance of positive behaviors. For example, older children or adults who expect a reward for assisting another would not be likely to perceive themselves as kind as a result of performing the positive act. In contrast, young children may view themselves as especially kind if they are rewarded for helping. Because such self-attributions appear to affect the likelihood of subsequent prosocial action for children approximately age 8 and older (see Chapter 5), individuals' definitions of altruism and kindness have implications for their own prosocial functions. We will now turn to the issue of self-attributions and the perception of one's own motives.

5 The Development of Self-Perceptions

Nancy Eisenberg, Jeannette Pasternack, Teresa Lundy

As was discussed in Chapter 4, there appear to be developmental changes in the manner in which people construe others' positive behaviors. Thus, it should not be surprising that self report of motives and self-evaluations for positive acts also seems to change somewhat systemically with age. The form of these changes as well as the significance of self-perceptions related to positive behaviors are considered in this chapter.

THE NATURE OF SELF-ATTRIBUTION

Despite Nisbett and Wilson's (1977) assertion that individuals' explanations for their own behaviors generally are little more than self-attributions (see Chapter 4), it is likely that there are important differences between attributions about others and explanations or attributions about one's own behavior. Bem (1972) outlined four significant differences between interpersonal attributions and self-perceptions. The first is that an actor has access to some internal stimuli that observers can not detect. For example, an actor knows if he or she is trying hard at a task. Second, people have knowledge of their own past behavior, knowledge that can influence attributions. Others lack such historical information. Third, Bem suggested that in some (but not all) situations, "motivational effects may enter as the self seeks to protect his esteem or defend against threat [p. 41]." Finally, Bem referred to Jones and Nisbett's (1971) suggestion that an actor's attention is focused outward toward situational cues whereas, for an observer, the actor's behavior is a figural stimulus against the ground of the situation. Thus, according to Jones and Nisbett, an actor should attribute personal behavior to situational requirements, whereas an observer should be more likely to attribute the actor's behavior to stable personal dispositions.

Although Bem (1972) acknowledged that self-perceptions differ in some ways from perceptions of others, he asserted that in many instances self-perceptions are really self-attributions. Others have disagreed. For example, von Cranach et al. (1982) have argued that people have considerable direct access to their internal states via a finely structured system of categories that has been perfected by society for the classification of inner experiences as social representations. Moreover, von Cranach et al. suggested that we learn to classify our inner experiences by constant wrestling with our own problems. In their view, the differences between interpersonal attributions and self-perceptions are considerably larger than was suggested by Bem.

Biases in Report of Self-perceptions

Despite the lack of agreement regarding the degree to which self-perceptions and interpersonal attributions differ, it is clear that differences do exist. Numerous researchers have obtained findings that are at least partially supportive of Jones and Nisbett's (1971) assertion that people are inclined to view their own behaviors as being situationally determined, whereas they attribute others' behaviors to dispositional qualities (e.g., Cunningham, Starr, & Kanouse, 1979; Monson & Snyder, 1977; Nisbett, Caputo, Legant, & Marecek, 1973; Smith, 1984; cf. Van der Pligt, 1981). Indeed, even school-aged children exhibit the actor-observer difference in their perceptions (Abromovitch & Freedman, 1981). Based solely on the actor-observer bias described by Jones and Nisbett (1971), one would expect persons who act prosocially to attribute their own behavior to external, situational causes (e.g., the other's need, concrete rewards for assisting), whereas observers would be more likely to attribute the actor's helpfulness to internal causes (e.g., altruistic motivations).

The situation is not as simple as that, however. If the actor/observer difference were to hold true in the cause of prosocial acts, actors would be more likely to attribute their own helping behaviors to external, nonmoral factors such as desire for concrete rewards or approval than to internal positive motivations. Such belittlement of one's own motives and actions is contrary to the bulk of the social psychological evidence. Indeed, people tend to report judgments and perceptions that are based in their favor, that is, they take credit for positive behaviors and attribute negative behaviors to external factors (e.g., Arkin, Gleason, & Johnsten, 1976; cf. Snyder, Stephan, & Rosenfield, 1978).

The reasons for the self-bias in perceptions of contingencies are unclear and have been a topic of considerable debate. Miller and Ross (1975) and others (Miller, 1978; Nisbett & Ross, 1980) have suggested that the self-enhancing attributions found in the literature might not, as many have proposed, be a function of self-enhancing motives. Rather, they proposed that the bias in favor of the self might be due to perceptual or other cognitive processing biases. For example, Miller and Ross (1975) suggested that self-serving biases regarding perceptions of personal success and failure might be due to the tendencies of people: (1) to expect their own behavior to produce successes; (2) to detect a closer covariation between their behavior and its outcome in the case of increasing success rather than constant failure; and (3) to erroneously formulate their judgments of contingency between response (e.g., their behavior) and outcome in terms of the occurrence of the desired outcome (i.e., success) rather than in terms of any actual degree of contingency.

In their discussion of self-serving biases, Miller and Ross (1975) were concerned with biases in attributions concerning the causality of one's own successes and failures. However, similar egocentric biases have also been noted with regard to people's attributions concerning their own versus others' contributions to a group outcome. For example, people's own contributions to a group product are recalled more often than are others' contributions, and individuals often accept more responsibility for a group product than others attribute to them (Ross & Sicoly, 1979). As for the egocentric biases in attributions of causality, it has been suggested by some researchers that this actor/observer egocentric bias frequently could be due to nonmotivational explanations such as: (1) selective encoding and storage of self-generated versus other-generated responses: (2) differential retrieval from memory of information related to one's own versus others' contributions; or (3) differences in the information available to the self versus others concerning an actor's contributions or behavior (Ross & Sicoly, 1979).

In contrast to Miller and Ross (1975; Miller, 1978), some investigators have argued that attributional biases that enhance one's own causality, contribution or responsibility often serve an ego-inflating or defensive purpose, that is, may be accounted for by "motivational" rather than "cognitive" factors. For example, the self-serving biases noted in the research have been attributed to the need to enhance or preserve one's own self-esteem (cf. Snyder et al., 1978), the need to maintain or gain a positive public self-image (Bradley, 1978; Weary, 1979, 1980), or the need to maintain or enhance the value of success and to avert the aversive experience of failure (Boski, 1983). By taking credit for positive outcomes and by denying responsibility for negative outcomes, people may be able to bolster their self-esteem, their affect, and in some situations, their public image. In fact, there is now a substantial body of research consistent with the proposition that self-enhancing biases in the attribution process often are a function of motivational factors (e.g., Cunningham et al., 1979; Miller, 1976; Schlenker et al., 1983; Sicoly & Ross, 1977). Although selective retrieval (e.g., Ross & Sicoly, 1979) as well as other nonmotivational factors may also contribute to the appearance of self-enhancing attributions, in some instances ego-enhancing motivational factors appear to be the most plausible explanation for these biases (Bradley, 1978; Schlenker et al., 1983; Sicoly & Ross, 1977).

It is also true, however, that the data on the origins of self-serving biases are far from conclusive. As was pointed out by Tetlock and Levi (1982), cognitive and motivational explanations have not been adequately differentiated; one can always devise a cognitive explanation to explain egoistic biases because "in order to arouse a need or motivational state in perceivers . . . researchers must experimentally vary the information available to perceivers [p. 74]." Tetlock and Levi were probably correct in their suggestion that the dichotomy between cognitive and motivational explanations will become increasingly blurred as the two theoretical perspectives are refined. Thus, perhaps the best way to approach the cognitive/motivational issue would be to attempt to delineate the degree to which affective reactions—especially those that have an ego-enhancing, maintaining, or defensive function—interact with cognitive operations in creating or preserving attributional biases.

To summarize, there is evidence to suggest that attributional processes (especially those of adults) about oneself versus others are systematically influenced by two factors: self-enhancing biases (regardless of the origin of these biases) and the actor/observer bias in perspective (the tendency for actors to focus on situational contributions to their behavior and for observers to focus on dispositional factors). In the case of prosocial behaviors, the predictions concerning the differences in actors' and observers' attributions generated from these two types of biases are partially inconsistent. For example, based on the actor/observer bias, one would predict that people would be more likely to attribute others' positive behaviors to an internal, altruistic disposition than they would their own positive acts. In contrast, based on the research concerning self-serving biases, one would expect people to be more likely to attribute their own than others' positive behaviors to ego-enhancing, internal, positive dispositions.

In the remainder of this chapter, the nature and development of individuals' perceptions of their own positive behaviors will be examined. However, before focusing on people's self-perceptions per se, we will examine the nature of both actor/observer differences and self-serving biases in the prosocial realm.

Variation in Attributions Concerning the Self versus Others

Based on the literature concerning both the actor/observer difference and self-serving biases, one would expect people to differentially attribute intentionality and responsibility to their own versus others' positive behaviors. Although this is probably the case, there is virtually no empirical research directly relevant to the issue. Those investigators who have examined differences in actors' and observers' attributions of intentionality and responsibility (rather than motives) have tended to focus on nonmoral acts (e.g., Ross & Sicoly, 1979; Weary, 1980). Moreover, several investigators who have focused on attributions of responsibility or intentionality in situations involving moral behaviors have compared individuals' attributions for their own versus another's hypothetical behaviors (rather than attributions from two sets of individuals, actors and observers; Fincham & Jaspars, 1979; Keasey, 1977; Nummedal & Bass, 1976) or individuals' attributions about others versus those they would attribute to others (Saltzstein & Weiner, 1982). Although these researchers have found a tendency for children (1) to more frequently justify their own than others' behaviors (including well-intentioned behaviors) with references to intentions (Keasey, 1977) and (2) to assume that they would use intentionality as a criterion for judgment more than would adults (Saltzstein & Weiner, 1982), it is unclear whether actors and observers differ in their judgments regarding the intentionality of behaviors that are either positively intentioned or have positive outcomes.

The empirical findings with regard to attributions or judgments about *motives* for positive acts, albeit limited in quantity, are considerably clearer. The tendency of individuals to attribute their own behaviors to situational factors and others' behaviors to dispositional causes does not seem to hold in the case of prosocial behaviors. Rather, it appears that people view their own positive behaviors as more internal and morally motivated than do observers. In fact, this pattern appears to hold for positively valanced behaviors in general. For example, Eisen (1979) found that actors reported their own positive behaviors (including emotions, beliefs, actions, and accomplishments) to be less distinctive and more consistent with their past behavior than did observers, whereas the reverse was true for a variety of negative behaviors. These same adults were more likely to attribute positive behaviors to their own internal dispositions than were observers, whereas the opposite pattern of results was found for negative behaviors. Moreover, in another study, Eisen (1979) found that actors made more internal attributions for positive than negative behaviors, and somewhat (nonsignificantly) more internal attributions for positive responses than did observers.

In regard to prosocial behaviors, Stephan (1975) found that actors and observers did not differ significantly in the degree to which they attributed adults' assistance (helping to look for a "lost" contact) to situational versus dispositional factors. Rather, he reported that adult actors tended to give more positive reasons for their behaviors than did observers (Stephan did not, however, report the appropriate test of simple effects to support the latter finding). In another study with adults, Schlenker et al. (1983) found that actors were more likely than observers to attribute their helping (sharing of a token so that a confederate might engage in an interesting activity) to positive motives, and less likely to attribute their behavior to nonpositive motives. Positive motives included wanting to help another person, the desire to do the right thing, and references to the other's need, whereas neutral and negative motives included the desire to gain or maintain social approval, helping merely because it was expected, or assisting simply because there was no reason not to assist. The actors' self-enhancing attributions were somewhat stronger when the consequences of helping were large rather than small, and occurred when report of motives was both public (known to others) and private.

There is virtually no research concerning differences in the perceptions of children who enact versus observe prosocial behaviors. Gelfand and Hartmann (1982), however, have noted an interesting pattern across two studies that they have conducted. In one experiment, second-and third-grade children received either no consequences, social (praise or reproof) or material (two-penny reward or fine) consequences, or combined social and material consequences for donating and failing to donate (Smith, Gelfand, Hartmann, & Partlow, 1979). The children in this study discounted the kindness of their own behaviors, i.e., attributed their behavior to external (fines or rewards) rather than internal (desire to help or concern about another) motives, when they had received material consequences. However, they attributed their generosity to internal causes when they had received social consequences or no consequences. Most interestingly, when the consequences were both social and material, the children's attributions were more internal than when their behaviors were followed by solely material consequences. In contrast, in another experiment, elementary-school children (especially sixth graders) attributed *others'* helping to extrinsic factors (material rewards or punishment) when the hypothetical other had received either solely material or combined social and material consequences (Cohen et al., 1981). Thus, children appear to be somewhat more likely to discount the intrinsic motivation of others (in comparison to oneself) when the consequences for helping or not helping are both material and social.

Gelfand and Hartmann (1982) suggested that the difference in children's attributions about the self versus others is due to motivational factors, i.e., self-serving biases. In their view, self-image maintenance and self-esteem are better served by attributing one's own (but not another's) prosocial actions to internal motivations rather than to extrinsic, self-oriented motives. However, it is also possible that the pattern noted by Gelfand and Hartmann is due, at least in part, to differences in the age of subjects in the Cohen et al. (1981) and Smith et al. (1979) studies. The children in the Smith et al. study (the group that did not discount their own helpfulness in the social-plus-material consequences) were in second and third grade. In contrast, in the Cohen et al. experiment, the children who significantly discounted others' prosocial actions in the social-plus-material condition were sixth graders. The third graders in this research—i.e., the children similar in age to Smith et al.'s subjects—did not discount others' helping in the social-plus-material-consequence condition significantly more than helping in either the social- or material-consequence only conditions (although the mean score for the social-plus-material-consequence condition was closer to that in the material- than social-consequence condition). In brief, although the findings discussed by Gelfand and Hartmann may indeed indicate a self-serving bias in children's attributions regarding their own and others' prosocial behaviors, it is not entirely clear whether the pattern of findings is due to real differences in attributions for self versus others or to a difference in age of subjects across studies.

In summary, although the research is limited and only suggestive, it appears that people (perhaps adults more than children) are somewhat more likely to attribute their own than others' prosocial behaviors to positive, flattering motives (e.g., an altruistic disposition or sympathetic concern). It is likely that there is a motivational reason for this bias, i.e., that self-serving biases of this type serve to enhance individuals' self-esteem and self-image (see Gelfand & Hartmann, 1982, and Schlenker et al., 1983, for discussions of the issue of motivational versus perceptual/cognitive explanations). Given this pattern of findings, one cannot assume that people's attributions about others' prosocial behaviors are always accurate indices of how people make judgments about their own helpful behaviors.

THE DEVELOPMENT OF ATTRIBUTIONS ABOUT PERSONAL PROSOCIAL BEHAVIORS

Most researchers who have investigated individuals' attributions about others' positive or prosocial actions have been attempting to examine one of two issues: peoples' use of intentionality as a criterion for evaluating the morality of actors or their behaviors (an issue stemming from Piaget's [1965] work) or the use and development of the causal schemata and principles outlined in attribution theory (Heider, 1958; Kelley, 1972). In contrast, researchers who have examined individuals' self-attributions with regard to prosocial actions have generally been concerned with the development of prosocial behavior per se, in specific, with the development of altruistic motives and the cognitive processes underlying prosocial actions at various ages or in various situations. Due to the differing goals and interests of researchers concerned with interpersonal versus intrapersonal attributions for positive behaviors, the resulting bodies of research differ considerably in typical design, procedures, and measures.

In the majority of the studies on interpersonal attributions, subjects (both adults and children) have been presented with hypothetical helping situations and then have been requested to make attributions about the helper in the scenario. In many instances, these attributions have been in the form of ratings of "goodness" or "kindness," or have consisted of choosing the kinder of two story protagonists, or the one who most liked helping. Only infrequently have subjects in studies on interpersonal attribution of prosocial intent been asked to attribute specific motives to others (e.g., Battistich et al., 1983; O'Connor et al., 1981; Schenkler et al., 1983; Stephan, 1975). Moreover, in only two of these studies was the prosocial other a real-life person, and in these investigations, the experimenters did not report the attributed motives in any detail (different types of positive or negative motives were combined to compute composite indices, and subjects picked motives from an a priori list; Schenkler et al., 1983; Stephan, 1975).

In contrast, in studies concerning self-attributions or expressed motives, researchers typically have induced experimental subjects to behave in a prosocial manner, and then have questioned the subjects regarding their reasons or motives for their behavior. Frequently the subjects have been given the opportunity to help in a variety of situations in a given sequence (e.g., Bar-Tal, Korenfeld, & Raviv, in press; Bar-Tal, Raviv, & Leiser, 1980; Raviv, Bar-Tal, & Lewis-Levin, 1980) or have been assigned to various experimental conditions differing in important situational variables such as the type of consequence for helping or not helping (Bar-Tal & Nissam, 1984; Guttman, Bar-Tal, & Leiser, 1979; Smith et al., 1979) or level of prior reward from the intended recipient (Dreman, 1976). Moreover, in contrast to the studies on interpersonal attributions, self-expressed motives (i.e., self-perceptions) almost always have been self-generated rather than selected from a list of alternatives.

In much of the research on individuals' perceptions of reasons for their own prosocial behavior, the subjects have been children. In many of their studies (e.g., Bar-Tal et al., 1980, in press; Dreman, 1976; Dreman & Greenbaum, 1973; Raviv et al., 1980; Smith et al., 1979; Ugurel-Semin, 1952), the prosocial act was suggested or otherwise instigated by an adult; in others, prosocial behavior was self-initiated or peer-initiated (Eisenberg, Pasternack, Cameron, & Tryon, 1984; Eisenberg-Berg & Neal, 1979). As is discussed in some detail later, the results of the various studies are no doubt a function, in part, of the parameters of the experimental design in the typical study on intrapersonal perception of prosocial motives. But first, the research concerning self-attributions and expressed motives for prosocial behaviors will be reviewed.

The Use of Causal Schemas for Prosocial Self-attributions

Although self-attributional processes similar to discounting have been examined with regard to a number of behaviors—for example, the undermining of intrinsic interest (e.g., Deci, 1975; Kassin & Lepper, in press; Lepper, Greene, & Nisbett, 1973)—there is a paucity of research related to people's use of the covariation principles or causal schema when discussing motives for their own prosocial actions. There is evidence, however, that children in mid-elementary school discount the kindness of their own prosocial behaviors if they have received concrete rewards for assisting (Smith et al., 1979). Moreover, as has been found with regard to their attributions about others, children do not discount the kindness of their own behaviors when the consequences of those behaviors are merely social (social approval or disapproval; Smith et al., 1979). However, as was discussed previously, children may be more likely to discount others' prosocial motives than their own when a prosocial action results in both material and social consequences (Gelfand & Hartmann, 1982). Additional empirical data concerning this issue are clearly needed.

Developmental Changes in Reasoning

Laboratory Studies.   In some of the research concerning children's reasoning about their own prosocial behaviors, all subjects have been provided with a single, identical opportunity to assist another and then have been interviewed regarding their subsequent behavior. An example of this type of study is that of Ugurel-Semin (1952). In this study, Turkish children aged 4–16 were asked to divide an uneven number of nuts between themselves and a peer, and then were questioned regarding their sharing (or nonsharing) behaviors. Ugurel-Semin found that the children's reasons for their sharing could be coded into the following categories: egocentrism (e.g., confusion of self with other, selfish attitude, fixation on numerical perspective, mean age = 7 years, 3 months); sociocentrism (obedience to moral and religious rules and customs, mean age = 9 years, 2 months); awareness of social reaction (e.g., shame, mean age = 9 years, 3 months); superficial reciprocity (emphasis on equality, mean age = 9 years, 5 months); deeper and enlarged reciprocity and cooperation (mutual interest, maintaining good relations with friends, mean age = 10 years, 5 months); altruism (sympathy, sacrifice, moral joy, mean age = 10 years, 5 months); and justice (e.g., justice demands equal sharing, mean age = 10 years, 10 months). Ugurel-Semin found that the youngest children reasoned in an egocentric manner, that is, they exhibited a purely selfish orientation or confused the self with others, or the material with the moral. Children about 9 years of age reasoned primarily in terms of obedience to stereotypic, socially accepted rules and norms (concerning when and with whom one shares) and shame for violation of these rules. In contrast to the younger children, the children at about 10–11 years of age or older emphasized the importance of maintaining positive interpersonal relationships, empathic reasons for sharing, and internalized values regarding altruism and just behavior.

Other researchers have found that young children's self-reported motives for their own prosocial behaviors may be less egocentric than Ugurel-Semin's (1952) data would indicate. In a pilot study involving 12 preschool children, using a procedure similar to that of Ugurel-Semin, Damon (1971) found that children's reasoning regarding why they shared with a peer was frequently empathic (indicated concern about the consequences of behavior for others), as well as pragmatic and self-oriented (concerned either the reciprocal consequences of sharing for the friendship or for oneself). Similarly, when Dreman and Greenbaum (1973) asked kindergarten-aged Israeli children to share candies with classmates who could either reciprocate the sharing or could not reciprocate, they found that children justified previous sharing with a classmate with the following expressed motives (in order of importance from most to least): (1) norm-directed (labeled "social responsibility," i.e., the child feels obligated to share with a dependent other because of the prevailing social norms); (2) empathic ("altruism," i.e., the child desires to make the recipient happy; no interpersonal profit or loss is supposedly involved); and (3) interpersonally oriented ("ingroup," i.e., the child wants to perpetuate existing friendships or repay friends for past services). Thus, the children frequently attributed their sharing to altruistic (empathic) or norm-related motives. Indeed, reciprocity-oriented considerations (the desire to repay immediate services rendered or the desire for future gain) were seldom mentioned as reasons for sharing, even though the study was designed so that one of the experimental manipulations involved potential reciprocity considerations (i.e., the recipient was told who gave him or her the candy).

Perhaps the largest body of research related to self-attributions about one's own prosocial behaviors is that of Bar-Tal and his colleagues in Israel. In a few of their studies, they have used designs similar to those of Dreman and Greenbaum (1973) or Smith et al. (1979), that is, subjects were assigned to various conditions differing on important dimensions such as the availability of rewards for helping, were given the opportunity to assist another, and then were interviewed regarding their reasons for assisting (Bar-Tal & Nissim, 1984; Guttman et al., 1979). However, in most of their research, Bar-Tal and his colleagues have used a paradigm that is relatively unique. This experimental design has involved presenting children with a series of opportunities to assist another, proceeding from the least explicit (with regard to pressure and/or the offer of concrete rewards) to the most explicit. If and when children do assist, they are questioned regarding their motives for doing so. For example, in one study (Bar-Tal et al., 1980), children played a game with a peer, won candy as a prize, and then were provided with a series of opportunities to share the candy with the peer (the sequence of opportunities ended when the child did indeed share). The various conditions in which the children could share (in order of occurrence) were as follows: (1) altruistic condition (the child was left alone for 3 minutes with the loser); (2) normative condition (the child could share after the experimenter explicitly and at length referred to the norm of sharing); (3) internal initiative and concrete reward (the experimenter told the child that he or she would get a reward for sharing); (4) compliance (the experimenter told the winner to share with the loser and moved aside for a couple of minutes); and (5) compliance and concrete-defined reinforcement (the experimenter told the winner to share and promised a big prize for sharing). After children shared in any of the above conditions, they were interviewed regarding their reasons for sharing.

In Bar-Tal's studies, the children's expressed motives have been coded into various categories that are identical or similar to those used by Bar-Tal et al. (1980) and Raviv et al., (1980): (1) concrete reward (prosocial behavior occurred because of the promised reward); (2) compliance (prosocial behavior occurred because the experimenter told the child to do so); (3) internal initiate with concrete reward (prosocial behavior occurred because the child believed that a concrete reward would be received for performing the act); (4) normative (prosocial behavior occurred because of a normative belief prescribing sharing with other children; conformity with this norm brings social approval, e.g., "It's nice to share)"; (5) generalized reciprocity (prosocial behavior occurred because of a belief in a generalized social rule that people who act prosocially will receive aid when they are in need); (6) personal willingness without expectation of an internal reward but with expressions of self-satisfaction, e.g., "I like to share to give others satisfaction"; (7) personal willingness to act prosocially without any reward, e.g., "Candy should be shared to make the other children happy."

In general, Bar-Tal and his colleagues have found that with age children are more likely to exhibit "higher-quality" helping behavior, that is, they are more likely to assist without being told to do so or before being offered concrete rewards (Bar-Tal et al., 1980; Raviv et al., 1980). Moreover, children's self-reported reasons for assisting tend to become more sophisticated with age (Bar-Tal et al., 1980; Guttman et al., 1979). In specific, Bar-Tal and his colleagues have found that normative reasoning (stereotypic references to norms and concern for the social approval that accompanies compliance to the norm) is used frequently by kindergarteners, school-aged children, and young adolescents to justify their actions (Bar-Tal & Nissim, 1984; Bar-Tal et al., 1980; Guttman et al., 1979). Younger children, especially kindergarteners, also frequently explain their actions with references to concrete rewards when such rewards are offered (Guttman et al., 1979). Young children report altruistic, internal, or clearly empathic motives relatively infrequently (Bar-Tal et al., 1980), but references to these motives increase with age (Bar-Tal & Nissim, 1984; Bar-Tal et al., 1980; Guttman et al., 1979).

Bar-Tal and his colleagues (Bar-Tal, 1982) view the types of motives listed previously as comprising a developmental sequence. However, although there does seem to be development in the predicted direction with age, it is unclear whether report of these motives actually progresses through the exact sequence delineated by Bar-Tal, or if the relation between motives and age is due to age changes in the use of only a few of the motivational categories. This problem in interpretation is due to the fact that Bar-Tal and his colleagues frequently have combined adjacent stages in statistical analyses (due to the infrequent use of some categories) or have not coded all categories of reasoning. In addition, they frequently have used chi-square or similar analyses to examine the association between level of reasoning and age; thus, dramatic developmental change in the use of one or two categories could account for the overall relation between age and level of motive. Moreover, because different children in some of the studies (e.g., Bar-Tal et al., 1980; Raviv et al., 1980) frequently were reasoning about very different situations (recall that the children in some studies were questioned regarding their motives only after they assisted and not all children helped in the same situation), developmental changes in the children's self-reported motives may have been due to differences in the circumstances in which they shared. Indeed, level of motive was related to type of situation in which the children first shared as well as with age, and older children helped more often in higher-level situations. Furthermore, in another study, expressed motives for assisting were obtained from only the relatively small proportion of subjects who both agreed to assist and showed up to help at a different time (Bar-Tal & Nissim, 1984). In this study, fewer eleventh graders came to help than did seventh or ninth graders; thus, age differences in reasoning could have been due to the fact that only the most altruistic eleventh graders were interviewed whereas a more diverse group of younger persons was interviewed. (It should be noted that some of the difficulties in interpreting Bar-Tal and his colleagues data are due to the fact that they were not primarily concerned with specific age changes in expressed motives.)

Studies in Naturalistic Settings. In all the research on expressed motives already discussed, the prosocial behaviors in questions were elicited in contrived circumstances by an adult experimenter. In such circumstances, the individuals' choices of action often were relatively constrained, and the children's references to adult-sanctioned norms (and associated social approval) were probably enhanced. Indeed, in most of the conditions in these studies, sharing or helping was requested (directly or indirectly) or demanded by adults. Moreover, in Bar-Tal's and his colleagues' research, children were offered rewards by adults for assisting, a procedure that undoubtedly increased the likelihood of reward-related expressed motives. Thus, it is likely that the range and frequency of self-reported motives in these studies, was, in part, a consequence of salient features of the sharing situation, including the presence of adults and rewards.

Using a different method, Eisenberg (Eisenberg, Pasternack, Cameron, & Tryon, 1984; Eisenberg-Berg & Neal, 1979) has examined children's reasoning about their own naturally-occurring prosocial behaviors rather than experimentally-elicited behaviors. In this research, preschoolers have been casually interviewed by familiar adults in the classroom whenever the adults saw them perform a prosocial act. Under these circumstances, the children most frequently explained their prior peer-oriented prosocial behavior by referring to the needs of others ("He wanted it," "She doesn't have any") or to pragmatic concerns ("It was dirty"). References to rewards, punishment, approval, or norms were relatively infrequent, although hedonistic concerns and references to liking of the recipient were verbalized approximately 5–15% of the time.

Using a methodology similar to that of Eisenberg, Hertz-Lazarowitz (1983) obtained somewhat similar data with Israeli school-aged children. She interviewed children in grades 1–2, 3–4, and 5–6 who had assisted a peer in the classroom. At all ages, children were likely to cite pragmatic or hedonistic motives for assisting; for the children in grades 1–2 and 3–4, needs-oriented reasons were also very common. A few children also expressed approval-oriented motives, or verbalized stereotypic, global conceptions of "nice" behavior. Surprisingly, the oldest children's expressed motives were the most hedonistic. However, only a total of 30 children were interviewed (approximately 10 at each grade), so the findings were based on the responses of relatively few children.

The procedure of questioning children about their motives for naturally occurring prosocial behaviors has been used to examine adult-initiated and adult-directed as well as peer-initiated and peer-directed behaviors. Eisenberg, Pasternack, and Lundy (1985) asked children their reasons both for complying with adults' requests for assistance and for spontaneously helping or sharing with adults in the preschool classroom. As for peer-related prosocial acts, children frequently justified both their own spontaneous and requested prosocial behaviors with pragmatic reasoning (25% and 39% of the cases, respectively). Similarly, needs-oriented (primitive-empathetic) justifications, which preschoolers often use to explain peer-oriented or peer-initiated prosocial acts, were also frequently used to justify adult-related behaviors, but only when the behavior was spontaneous (32%) rather than requested (2%). Moreover, hedonistic reasoning, which is seldom used by preschoolers to explain their peer-related behaviors (Eisenberg et al., 1984; Eisenberg-Berg & Neal, 1979), was frequently verbalized in relation to adult-oriented prosocial acts (31% for spontaneous prosocial acts; 44% of requested behaviors). This apparently was because the teachers and teachers' aides often asked the children to help them with exciting or desirable tasks (such as getting snacks or making cookies), and children often spontaneously offered to assist with "fun" or interesting activities (e.g., feeding the gerbil).

Interview Studies.   In three studies in which interview techniques were used, some of the same self-expressed motives as those discussed by Ugurel-Semin (1952), Damon (1971), Bar-Tal (Bar-Tal et al., 1980), and Dreman (1976; Dreman & Greenbaum, 1973) were noted. Petrovich (1982) asked mentally handicapped children aged 9, 11, 13, 15, and 17 years from Yugoslavia to name "the best thing" they had ever done, and to indicate why it was the best. Approximately 50% of the children named "helping others" as their best act. "Consideration of others" as well as rewards were the most frequently named reasons for the subjects judging their "good" acts (including helping as well as several other behaviors) as good. References to the reason "consideration of others" increased significantly with age. Less frequently mentioned reasons included reciprocity, acceptance of general norms, and self-respect for doing right.

In another study in which people were questioned about a general category of behavior rather than a specific, recent prosocial act, Furby (1978) asked American and Israeli children and adults (American sample only) why they themselves share, and why they think people in general should share tangible possessions. Responses to these two different questions were not reported separately, so it is not possible to separate the subjects' intrapersonal and interpersonal attributions. Nonetheless, developmental trends in the reasons given were noted. For the American sample of 5–6 year-olds, the most frequently mentioned considerations regarding sharing were: (1) whether the recipient was liked or nice; (2) if the recipient was a family member; (3) the belief that sharing is good or nice; and (4) potential for damage to the shared object. Seven- to 8-year-olds mentioned the same types of reasons, although references to the niceness of sharing (the norm of sharing) were more frequent, as were references to negative reciprocity ("If someone does not share with me, I do not share with her"). Ten- and 11-year-olds tended to mention more reasons than did younger children, but used most of the same types of reasons. However, the relative importance of considerations was somewhat different; negative reciprocity and evaluation of the other person were the most frequently mentioned dimensions, closely followed by the belief that sharing is a good thing to do. Also frequently mentioned at this age was concern for the other's welfare. Most of the dimensions mentioned by the fifth graders were also mentioned frequently by 16–17-year-old students, although the other's honesty and responsibility and the manner in which the shared object would be used were also frequently discussed by the adolescents. Finally, the same reasons mentioned by 16–17-year-olds were relevant for the 40–50-year-olds. However, the adults, but not the younger subjects, also stated that sharing made them feel good—they received internal affective rewards (empathic or otherwise) when they shared.

Furby (1978) noted several crosscultural differences in reported motives for sharing. Israeli 5–6-year-olds, especially those on the kibbutz, were less likely than American children of comparable age to refer to the norm of sharing. For both the older group of Israeli children and Americans (aged 10–11), concern for others was of major importance. Yet the 10–11-year-old Americans still mentioned the norm of sharing more than the Israelis did, whereas the Israelis were especially likely to say that sharing depends on the particular object, that one should share to create harmonious social interactions, and that one should share with those whom one likes.

In one last set of studies (Silbereisen, Boehnke, & Reykowski, 1984) related to self report of motives for assisting, Polish and German (West Berlin) children and adolescents (grades 6, 9, 10, and 12) responded to a number of vignettes describing a situation in which they themselves assisted another (e.g., tidied up the kitchen for one's mother). After each vignette, the following five possible types of motives for assisting were presented: (1) hedonism (involving pleasure or protection from physical pain); (2) self-interest; (3) conformity; (4) task orientation (e.g., "If you don't clean up the kitchen right away, it's much more work to do it later"); and (5) other-interest (concern for or orientation to another's needs). Participants rated each of the five motives after each vignette on a scale indicating the degree to which "I would probably think that way." Although the results were very complex, in general the endorsement of all types of motives except intrinsic (other-oriented or task-oriented helping) declined with age. However, self report of motives was highly influenced by the type of school subjects attended (in both countries, there is a highly structured tracking system). More educated students were more likely to prefer intrinsic (other-oriented or task-oriented) motives. In both countries, other-oriented motives were endorsed most often, followed by task-oriented, conformistic, hedonistic, and self-interested motives (in that order). In brief, other-oriented and task-oriented motives were reported most often, and were the only motives that well-educated and older subjects were as willing to accept as were less educated and younger subjects.

Summary. There are both consistencies and inconsistencies in the research related to children's self report of motives for their own prosocial behaviors. The inconsistencies are undoubtedly due, in part, to the variability in samples (the children in the studies reviewed above were from five different cultures), and to the fact that the situations in which the children assisted varied dramatically across studies. In some of the studies, there were adults present immediately before or when the children assisted; in others, there were no adults involved in the helping situation. Furthermore, in some of the research (especially that of Bar-Tal and his colleagues; Bar-Tal et al., 1980; Raviv et al., 1980), most of the children did not share or help until they were directed to do so or were offered a concrete reward for assisting. Consequently, in many instances, the children's behavior was a response to a command and may not have been planned or voluntary. In contrast, in other research, the children were not explicitly directed to share, and were not offered concrete rewards for assisting another; thus, the children's potential motives were probably less constrained.

Despite the inconsistencies in the research paradigms and data, one can draw some tentative conclusions regarding children's self report of motives for their own prosocial actions. In general, preschoolers' and elementary-school children's reasoning seems to be predominately pragmatic, empathic, self-oriented, or reward-oriented (including being oriented to direct reciprocity concerns and to the desirability of assisting someone important to the child) (Bar-Tal et al., 1980; Dreman, 1976; Dreman & Greenbaum, 1973; Eisenberg et al., 1984; Eisenberg-Berg & Neal, 1979; Furby, 1978; Guttman et al., 1979; Smith et al., 1979; Ugurel-Semin, 1952). Normative motives seem to be expressed by young children primarily when an adult either is present during the prosocial act or instigates it. It is likely that the presence of an adult increases the probability that a child will focus on normative standards and social sanctions that are part of adult society. Moreover, references to rewards seem to occur primarily when children are explicitly offered rewards for assisting (although hedonistic reasoning was frequently used to explain attempts to assist adults with interesting activities in one study with preschoolers). In none of the studies have children frequently reported that their prosocial behavior was motivated by fear of punishment or blind obedience to authorities' dictates, even if an adult told the child to share or help.

From age 4 into the elementary-school years, report of reward-oriented expressed motives appears to decrease (Bar-Tal et al., 1980; Guttman et al., 1979; Ugurel-Semin, 1952). Simultaneous with the decrease in reference to these types of expressed motives, self report of other-oriented, altruistic reasons (reasons indicating a willingness to share without the expectation of external rewards, and which often reflects self-reflective role taking, empathic responding, or an emphasis on equality and justice) increases in frequency of use (Bar-Tal & Nissim, 1984; Bar-Tal et al., 1980; Furby, 1978; Ugurel-Semin, 1952). Self report of normative, stereotypic concerns (e.g., about "nice" behavior) and approval-oriented motives apparently becomes more common with age in the elementary-school years (although it is not clear if these changes are significant; Raviv et al., 1980; Ugurel-Semin, 1952) and may decrease somewhat during high school (Bar-Tal & Nissim, 1984; Furby, 1978). Thus, in general, it appears that the cognitions associated with children's prosocial actions become more internal and less related to external gain with development.

Expressed Motives Concerning Adult versus Peer Interactions

In much of the research concerning self-reported motives in prosocial situations, children's prosocial behaviors were either instigated or requested by adults. Consequently, even if the recipient of the behavior were a peer, the children may have perceived themselves as helping, or complying with, an adult. Thus, it is important to ask whether report of motives in this type of circumstance really differs from expressed motives in situations that involve only other children.

The answer is yes. It appears that children both define adult-oriented and peer-oriented kindness differently, and report somewhat different motives for adult-instigated versus peer-instigated prosocial acts.

Youniss (1980) examined the issue of qualitative differences between child-child and adult-child interactions in a series of studies concerning children's conceptions of adult- versus peer-directed acts of kindness or "unkindness." To elicit children's thoughts concerning this issue, Youniss asked children to generate stories of adult-child or child-child interactions in which one person did something kind (or unkind) to another, or to judge stories with regard to the kindness of actors' behaviors. He found that children, especially those in early elementary school, generally viewed adult-directed and peer-directed kindness very differently. For the young children (approximately 6–8 years of age), kindness towards adults consisted of being obedient, or being good or polite, whereas unkindness was the reverse. Older children (approximately 12–14 years of age) defined adult-directed kindness not only as obedience and "being good," but also as doing one's chores and, occasionally, as showing concern for an adult in need. Unkindness for the older children consisted of misbehaving, talking back, and occasionally, not helping an adult. In contrast, peer-directed kindness was described as involving giving and sharing, playing together, giving physical assistance (especially for 9–14-year-olds), and occasionally (for children 9 years and older) understanding or teaching. Unkindness toward peers consisted of not sharing, aggression, or, for older children, not sympathizing or social exclusion. In brief, Youniss found that children, especially younger children, differentiated peer from adult interactions primarily with regard to the issues of equality and unilateral constraint, with adult-directed acts of kindness being characterized by obedience and compliance, and peer-directed interactions involving more equalitarian and prosocial elements. Moreover, based upon additional studies in which Youniss asked children to describe what the recipient of an unkind act would do, he found that child-child interactions often were characterized by reciprocity in responding, whereas adult-child interactions frequently involved the concept of punishment.

Based on Youniss' (1980) findings, it would seem that children's peer-directed acts of "kindness" often are prosocial in that they are helpful or involve sharing, and consequently, frequently should be motivated by (or attributed to) concern for the other or reciprocity considerations. In contrast, adult-directed acts of kindness, which often involve (in children's eyes) obedience with adults' demands or expectations, should more often be motivated by (or attributed to) blind obedience to authorities, or concern over the possibility of punishment for not behaving in the proper manner. Research conducted by myself and my students is consistent with these assumptions (Eisenberg, Lundy, Shell, & Roth, 1985). In two different studies, we elicited from preschool children their expressed motives for naturally occurring compliant (including prosocial) behaviors. Compliant behaviors were defined as behaviors occurring in response to a request or mild command from another. Frequently these behaviors could be viewed as prosocial, i.e., as being behaviors such as helping or sharing that directly benefit another (e.g., the requested prosocial behaviors in Eisenberg, Cameron, Tryon, & Dodez, 1981; or Strayer, Wareing, & Rushton, 1979). At other times, the compliant behaviors had no prosocial consequences and appeared to have been primarily acts of obedience, to an authority, a dominant other, or a nonprosocial norm or rule implicitly or explicitly referenced by the requester. Because "kindness" was defined by Youniss' subjects as involving prosocial behaviors as well as acts of obedience, politeness, and "doing good," examination of children's compliant behaviors seemed to be a reasonable approach for exploring differences in adult-directed and peer-directed positive behaviors.

In both studies (Eisenberg et al., 1985), children were observed for a number of weeks (8–18) in their classrooms by adults with whom the children were familiar (the adults were present on a regular basis). The adult circulated around the room in a systematic manner, and whenever he or she noted a compliant behavior (the child complying with a request or mild command), the adult questioned the child with regard to the child's motives (e.g., said "Hey Johnny, can you tell me why you gave the hat to Cindy when she asked for it?").

The children's expressed motives were coded into the following categories: (1) authority/punishment orientation (references to demands and/or punishment); (2) hedonistic orientation (references to expected gain for the self); (3) direct reciprocity (references to benefits or costs directly deriving from reciprocity [or lack of it] from the one with whom the child complied); (4) pragmatic orientation (references to practical, nonmoral reasons); (5) needs-oriented reasoning (references to another's psychological or physical needs as a justification for behavior, e.g., "He wanted some clay"); (6) affectional-relationship orientation (references to the relationship between him/herself and either the requester or the recipient of aid); (7) approval and interpersonal orientation (references to social approval and/or the desire to enhance interpersonal interactions); and (8) stereotyped good/bad orientation (stereotyped reasons such as "It's nice to help"). Moreover, each incident was also coded to indicate if the behavior requested of the child was prosocial (an act that directly benefited another, usually, but not always, the requester) or resulted in compliance with a command or regulation that did not directly benefit a specific person (nonprosocial behavior). For example, if a teacher asked or told the child to share clay with another child, or if a child shared clay with a peer who requested clay, the compliant act would be scored as prosocial. However, if a child was asked or told to clean up a table that was soiled, the act was scored as nonprosocial.

In general, the children's justifications for adult-instigated and peer-instigated compliant behaviors differed in a manner consistent with Youniss' (1980) prior findings. Children used more authority and punishment reasoning to explain compliance with adults' than peers' prosocial and nonprosocial requests/commands. Moreover, they justified peer-instigated compliance more often than adult-initiated compliance with references to others' needs or one's relationship with or liking for another person (the latter for prosocial requests only). The patterns of findings were very similar in both experiments, although the results were stronger in the study involving the larger sample.

One reason that children may frequently attribute both their prosocial and nonprosocial adult-oriented compliant actions to authority- and punishment-related motives may be that they do not clearly differentiate between adults' requests and commands. Adults, unlike peers, generally are in positions of authority and frequently may punish children for lack of compliance; thus, it is possible that children often interpret adults' requests as commands. Consequently, children frequently may believe that they are complying with adults' requests (even prosocial requests) for external reasons such as the avoidance of punishment or merely to obey authorities.

In a third study (Eisenberg, Pasternack, & Lundy, 1984), we explored this possibility, that is, we examined whether preschool children make different attributions about their compliance with adults' requests versus commands for prosocial behavior. Each child, on two different occasions, was requested to help and directed to help by two different, familiar experimenters. If the child complied with the request, he or she was approached by a different experimenter who briefly interviewed the child to ascertain the reasons for helping.

According to the results, the children did not report different motives for their compliance with adults' requests and commands. The fact that approximately the same number of children eventually complied in the command and request condition also suggests that the children did not distinguish between the adults' requests and commands. Based on these findings, it would seem that one reason for the elevated amount of authority and punishment justifications associated with adult-directed prosocial behaviors is that children frequently interpreted adults' requests as commands, and consequently, often complied in order to escape the negative consequences frequently associated with defiance of a command.

Based upon the limited available data, there is reason to believe that children's expressed motives for adult- versus peer-instigated prosocial behaviors differ in important ways. Given the large discrepancy in the ways that children generally conceptualize adult-directed and peer-directed kind and unkind behaviors (Youniss, 1980), it is unlikely that the children's expressed motives for their compliant behaviors were always merely self-attributions formulated post hoc to performance of the behavior in question. Rather, it would seem that, at least in some situations, children's conscious motives for adult- and child-instigated behaviors differ considerably. Thus, it is likely that some of the differences previously noted in the research concerning expressed motives were due to the different nature of the prosocial interactions (e.g., adult- versus child-instigated) being examined.

THE ROLE OF EXPRESSED MOTIVES IN PROSOCIAL BEHAVIOR

Thus far we have discussed developmental changes in individuals' self-perceptions of their own motives for prosocial behavior, not the role of expressed motives in behavior. However, it obviously is important to determine whether people's self-perceptions of their own motives are related to the frequency or quality of prosocial behaviors.

Provision of Attributions

Based on recent research, there is reason to believe that the attributions individuals make regarding their own motives for prosocial actions affect the likelihood of subsequent prosocial action. In specific, researchers have found that when adults tell children that the children's prior positive behaviors were due to internal causes (e.g., kindness), children are more likely to behave in a prosocial manner on subsequent opportunities to assist (Grusec, Kuczynski, Rushton, & Simutis, 1978; Grusec & Redler, 1980; Holte, Jamruszka, Gustafson, Beaman, & Camp, 1984). For example, Grusec and her colleagues have found that elementary-school children generally are more likely to response to subsequent appeals for assistance if they have been told that an initial act of donating (in response to an adult's cues or prompts) was due to internal motives (the fact that they are helpful people and like to help others) than if donating was attributed to compliance with an adult's expectations (Grusec et al., 1978) or if no attribution was made by an adult (Grusec & Redler, 1980). Adults' provision to children of internal attributions also has been shown to enhance other behaviors such as cooperation (Jensen & Moore, 1977), self-control (Toner, Moore, & Emmons, 1980), resistance to temptation (Dienstbier, 1978), tidiness (Miller, Brickman, & Bolen, 1975), and performance on tests of mathematics (Miller et al., 1975).

According to the limited available research, the effectiveness of socializers' altruistic attributions seems to increase with age during the elementary-school years (Grusec & Redler, 1980). It is likely that this is due to the fact that children's ability to think in terms of enduring personality characteristics, which produce consistency in behavior, increases with age (Eisenberg & Cialdini, 1984). Unless children understand the concept of stability in personality, i.e., the idea of dispositional traits, they should not be motivated to behave in ways consistent with their own or others' conceptions of the child's personality. In other words, if younger children do not view themselves in terms of enduring personality traits, they should be less inclined than older children or adults both to believe in intraindividual consistency and to attempt to maintain a consistent self-perception or public image. Although even 5-year-olds have some conception of personality traits (Heller & Berndt, 1981), it is clear that both the use of the concept of personality (Barenboim, 1981; Peevers & Secord, 1973; Snodgrass, 1976) and the ability to perceive personality consistency across time and situations increases substantially from age 5 to approximately 8–9 years of age (Dix & Grusec,1983; Rholes, 1982; Rholes & Ruble, 1984; Rotenberg, 1982). Consequently, it should not be surprising that Grusec and Redler (1980) found that 8-year-olds' prosocial behaviors, but not those of 5-year-olds, were affected by adults' provision of altruistic attributions.

The Relation between Expressed Motives and Behavior

Grusec and her colleagues (Grusec et al., 1978; Grusec & Redler, 1980) studied the role of the provision of adult-formulated attributions in children's prosocial behaviors, not the role of children's own expressed motives in subsequent prosocial development. In fact, relatively few investigators have examined the degree of association between individuals' self-reported motives and their actual pro-social responding. Nonetheless, this is an important issue because of the implications of the findings for an understanding of the role of cognition in prosocial behavior. If there is no association between self-reported motives and behavior, the logical assumption is either that people have little access to their motives or that in many situations prosocial behaviors are performed rather automatically (e.g., as part of a social script; Karniol, 1982; Langer, Blank, & Chanowitz, 1978). In contrast, if there is an association between reported motives and behavior, it would appear either that much prosocial behavior is consciously motivated and that these motives are accessible, or that people have very accurate a priori hypotheses regarding human behavior (Nisbett & Wilson, 1977).

The results of studies in which the association between expressed motives and prosocial behavior was examined are listed in Table 5.1. As can be seen from this table, there does seem to be some association between expressed motives and prosocial responding, especially when the expressed motives were obtained for the same situation in which prosocial behavior was assessed. In general, higher level (more internal) motives have been associated with assisting under more "altruistic" conditions (helping without the promise of rewards or without an adult telling the child to help; Bar-Tel et al., 1980, 1982; Raviv et al., 1980), and with greater quantity of helping or sharing (Dreman & Green-baum, 1973; Smith et al., 1979). However, when the relation between expressed motives for prosocial behavior across a sample of situations has been related to quantity of assisting across a broad sample of helping situations, the association between expressed motives and quantity of prosocial behavior has been much weaker (Eisenberg, Pasternack, Cameron, & Tryon, 1984).

Based on this pattern of data, it would seem that there is some consistency between expressed motives and prosocial behavior in a given situation. This could be because individuals' characteristic motives determine, in part, the range and type of situations in which people assist others, or because an individual's expressed motives are formulated based on the person's post hoc analysis of the situation and the possible determinants of one's own prior behavior. Although it is impossible at this time to adequately evaluate the merits of these two alternative explanations, there are some data related to this issue. At least for adults, the individual's post hoc analysis of the consequences of a prosocial action seems to determine, to some degree, the report of motives. Schlenker et al. (1983) found that individuals who were given differential feedback regarding the consequences of their helping behavior *after* the behavior was completed differed somewhat in their expressed motives. Individuals who were told that the consequences of their helping were relatively high (and positive) attributed more internal *and* external motives to themselves than did those told that the consequences of their helping were low. (Unfortunately, due to the fact that the specific comparisons between attributions for persons in the high versus low consequence conditions were not reported separately from those for an observer,

TABLE 5–1.

The Relation Between Prosocial Behavior and Expressed Motives

Study	Subjects	Measure of Prosocial Behavior	Measure of Reasoning	Relationship	Direction and Comments
Bar-Tal et al., 1980	Israeli K and grades 2 and 4	Sharing candy won in a game with a peer	Categories outlined on p. 86–87	Between expressed motive and amount sharing	+
Bar-Tal et al., (in press)	Israeli M & F grade 5	Donation of money to March of Dimes; children proceeded through a series of conditions varying in normative cues, promise of rewards, and/or adult demand for sharing	Level of expressed motive: (high to low); altruism, generalized reciprocity, normative, internal initiative with concrete reward, compliance	Between level of expressed motive and condition in which shared / Between expressed motive and amount shared	+ / +
Bar-Tal & Nissim, 1984	Israeli M & F grades 7, 9, 11	Volunteering time to help repair books for older person; conditions varied in availability and type of reward for helping	Level of expressed motive: (high to low); altruism, generalized reciprocity, normative, internal initiative with concrete reward, compliance	Between level of expressed motive and and helping in the various conditions / Between level of expressed motive and quantity of helping	0 / 0
Dreman, 1976	Israeli grades 1, 4, 7	Sharing candy received for doing a drawing; subjects' anonymity and likelihood of reciprocity varied across conditions	Expressed motive for sharing, categories outlined on p. 86	Between amount of candy and justification level	0—Complex interaction with situation; subjects gave more reciprocity reasons in reciprocity conditions
Dreman & Greenbaum, 1973	Israeli K	Sharing an odd number of candies; anonymity and likelihood of reciprocity (if donor would be known) varied across conditions	Expressed motive for sharing after opportunity to share; categories on p. 86	Between expressed motives and number of candies shared	+

			Expressed motives: author-ity/punishment oriented, hedonistic, pragmatic, needs-oriented, affectional relationship, approval/ interpersonally oriented, stereotypic	Spontaneous sharing with motives (especially if there were no cues of neediness)	+—Between shar-ing and both pragmatic and affectional rela-tionship motives
Eisenberg, Pasternack, Cameron, & Tryon, 1984	Preschoolers	Naturalistic observations of spontaneous sharing, requested sharing, sponta-neous helping, asked for helping		Spontaneous helping	0
				Requested sharing	0
				Requested helpings	0
Raviv et al., 1980	Israeli grade 4, 6, 8	Donation of prize money to crippled children; children proceeded through a series of conditions, varying in amount of normative cues, promise of concrete reward, and/or adult com-mand for sharing	Level of expressed motive (high to low): altruism, generalized reicprocity, normative, internal initia-tive with concrete reward, compliance	Between level of expressed motive and which condi-tion the children donated in	+
Smith et al., 1979	M & F 7–8 and 8–9 years	Giving pennies to help another child win a game; conditions varied in terms of type of consequences for sharing or not sharing (social, material, social & material	Self-expressed motives rated on degree of intrinsic ver-sus extrinsic motivation	Between internality of attribution and amount of donating	+
Wright, 1942a	Grade 3	Opportunities to share an attractive toy with friend or stranger	Expressed motives for pre-ferring friend or stranger after sharing	Between sharing with stranger (associated with higher sharing) and expressed motive given	+—Fewer self-oriented reasons were given for sharing with a stranger

it is impossible to know if this difference was statistically significant.) Thus, people attributed greater amounts of all types of motives to themselves if they believed that the consequences of their behavior were sizable. Given that the feedback was supplied subsequent to a performance of the behavior, subjects apparently formulated their expressed motives (at least to some degree) post hoc to the behavior.

Although post hoc evaluations of one's own behavior may have some effect on people's expressed motives, it also appears that their role is limited. Smith et al. (1979) provided children with social, material, or both types of rewards for donating, or with material, social, or both types of punishments for not donating. They found that children were more likely to attribute their donating behavior to external circumstances if they received material consequences (reward or punishment) than if they received either social or social and material consequences. However, although there was not a significant relation between type of consequence received and quantity of subsequent donating, there was a positive relation between amount of subsequent donating and internality of children's attributions within each condition (i.e., when the effects of contingencies for donating or not donating were controlled). Thus, individual differences in expressed motives were related to quantity of donating, whereas the environmental contingencies that might influence post hoc evaluations were not.

When might expressed motives be little more than self-attributions based on post hoc self-evaluations (as described by Bem, 1972) and when do they actually reflect people's a priori motives for assisting? One type of situation in which expressed motives are probably formulated post hoc is when people perform low-cost, prosocial acts in an automatic fashion. Several investigators have argued that such prosocial behaviors are not uncommon: We have social scripts in our memories prescribing the expected or normal course of action in common situations, and we frequently act in accordance with these scripts without much conscious deliberation (Abelson, 1981; Karniol, 1982; Langer et al., 1978). Especially in situations in which helping is not costly, does not have a strong positive effect on the recipient, and does not create cognitive conflict for the potential benefactor, there often may be no reason for the benefactor to consider cognitively whether to assist, and why one should do so. Moreover, one might expect that the probability of an individual's prosocial behavior being performed automatically would be especially high if the behavior in question is both low cost and requested by another. In such situations, people appear to react to the cue for helping (the request) without considering their reasons (Langer et al., 1978; Weyant, 1978). This line of reasoning is supported by Eisenberg, Pasternack, Cameron, and Tryon's (1984) finding that children's expressed motives for the performance of low-cost, requested prosocial acts were unrelated to the quantity of requested prosocial acts. Rather, the proportion of times that the child complied with requests to assist was related to a nonassertive social style, that is, to low frequencies of peer-oriented social interaction, requests for assistance from peers, attempts to take objects from peers, and attempts to defend objects in one's own possession. In contrast, frequencies of prosocial behaviors that were spontaneously emitted were moderately related to expressed motives as well as number of social interactions.

In brief, there is evidence to suggest that the greatest determinant of whether people comply with low-cost requests to assist (but not with spontaneously emitted behaviors) is their characteristic styles of responding to people, not a priori motives for assisting. In contrast, in situations in which the cost of a prosocial action is moderate or high, or the behavior is performed after mental deliberation, it is likely that there is a moderate causal relation between motives and prosocial behaviors. This conclusion is reminiscent of Smith and Miller's (1978) assertion that people have more access to cognitive processes when the tasks performed are not so routine or overlearned that they can be performed in a mindless manner. In summary, there appears to be a moderate relation between self-reported motives and prosocial responding in some situations. The role of self-reported motives in altruism will be addressed further in Chapter 10.

6

Role Taking, Attributions About the Origins of Another's Dependency, and Problem-Solving

Inferences about one's own and others' positive acts (examined in Chapters 4 and 5) are not, of course, the only aspects of social cognition that are relevant to the study of prosocial action. There are other inferential processes that occur prior rather than subsequent to the performance (or lack of performance) of prosocial behaviors that have been viewed as being particularly important to the development of prosocial behavior. Moreover, interpersonal problem-solving skills, a set of cognitive abilities that involve inferential processes as well as other social-cognitive abilities, are probably important in the formulation and execution of prosocial actions. The role of these capacities in prosocial development will now be considered.

ROLE TAKING

One of the inferential processes that has received the most attention in theories or models of prosocial behavior is role taking or perspective-taking (Batson, 1984; Hoffman, 1975, 1976; Krebs & Russell, 1981; Staub, 1979). Generally, role-taking has been subdivided into at least three types: (1) perceptual perspective-taking (the ability to understand the literal visual perspective of another); (2) cognitive perspective-taking (the ability to predict and understand another's thoughts, motives, intentions, and behaviors); and (3) affective perspective-taking (the ability to infer another's feelings and emotional reactions) (Ford, 1979; Shantz, 1975; Underwood & Moore, 1982). These three types of perspective-taking appear to be somewhat, but not highly, interrelated (Ford, 1979; Shantz, 1975; Staub, 1979).

Conceptually, it is reasonable to assume that cognitive and affective perspective-taking play a role in the development and elicitation of prosocial behavior. Young children (or adults) with limited role-taking abilities should be less likely than persons with more sophisticated perspective-taking capacities to infer that another is needy or distressed. Consequently, they should be relatively unlikely to empathize with and assist another. If an individual is unaware of another's feelings or wants, why should he or she assist the other person?

Perspective-taking may also facilitate sympathizing (and, consequently, prosocial behavior) even when another's need is obvious. Moreover, the knowledge obtained via perspective-taking may elicit a feeling of social responsibility based on internalized norms and values or may produce a state of cognitive discomfort akin to a sense of lack of closure or cognitive inconsistency (Krebs & Russell, 1981). One way to dissipate the discomfort associated with the recognition that another needs assistance is to provide that assistance.

Perspective-taking abilities have been especially prominent in developmental models of altruism. This is because some types of prosocial behaviors have been found to increase in frequency with age (Moore & Eisenberg, 1984; Mussen & Eisenberg-Berg, 1977; Radke-Yarrow et al., 1983; Rushton, 1980), and explanations for this age-related change are needed. Because perspective-taking capacities improve dramatically from 2–3 years of age into adolescence (e.g., Kurdek, 1977; Selman, 1971, 1980; cf. Shantz, 1983) and involve an understanding of others' thoughts and feelings, it is not surprising that these capacities have been viewed as a prime candidate for explaining the age-related increases in prosocial behavior.

Despite the attractiveness of the concept of role taking for models of prosocial development, the empirical relation between the two has not been highly consistent. For children, perspective-taking has been found to be positively related (Buckley, Siegal, & Ness, 1979; Elder, 1983; Hudson, Forman, & Brion-Meisels, 1982; Krebs & Sturrup, 1982; Olenjnik, 1975; Rubin & Schneider, 1973), unrelated (Eisenberg-Berg & Lennon, 1980; Emler & Rushton, 1974; Rushton & Wiener, 1975; Zahn-Waxler, Radke-Yarrow, & Brady-Smith, 1977), inconsistently related (Barrett & Yarrow, 1977; Green, 1975; Iannotti, 1975, 1978) and even negatively related (LeMare & Krebs, 1983) to prosocial behavior (see Krebs & Russell, 1981; Kurdek, 1978; Underwood & Moore, 1982 for detailed reviews). For adults, inducing a perspective-taking set by telling subjects to "imagine how another feels" has been associated with helping (Aderman & Berkowitz, 1970; Toi & Batson, 1982), as well as with physiological reactions believed to reflect empathy (Stotland, 1969); however, the research for adults is limited and the patterns of results generally have been complicated.

Based on this body of empirical research, Krebs and Russell (1981) concluded that the findings concerning the relation between perspective-taking and prosocial behavior are "woefully inconclusive [p. 137]." Others, after reviewing basically the same data, have come to a very different conclusion. In fact, Underwood and Moore (1982) computed a meta-analysis and obtained a highly sufficient relation between prosocial behavior and perspective-taking (perceptual and cognitive/affective). This relation was still significant when the effects of age were controlled.

The association between perspective-taking and prosocial behavior, albeit significant, is not large. This is probably due to a variety of conceptual as well as methodological factors. First, there is no reason to assume that role taking should always be related to prosocial behavior. A relation should hold only if the particular prosocial act requires or would be facilitated by the understanding of another's perspective. In many instances this is not the case. Performance of a particular prosocial behavior may be relatively automatic because of either its low cost (e.g., Langer et al., 1978; Karniol, 1982) or its compelling, crisis-like quality (Piliavin et al., 1981). Alternatively, the act may be one that is likely to be motivated by a variety of factors other than knowledge of another's internal status (e.g., approval if an adult or authority is present).

Moreover, frequently it is not necessary that people engage in perspective-taking in order to obtain information about another's state; in many cases, we need only to access information about people or situations (e.g., the fact that people have often said that a particular person is depressed) from our memories or to project our own feelings onto others. Higgins (1981), in an excellent paper on the concept of role taking, emphasized the latter point by redefining role taking in a more precise manner than has usually been the case. In this definition, he clearly stated that an inferential process is necessary for role taking: "Judgments involve role taking when there is an inference about a target's viewpoint (or response) under circumstances where the judge's own viewpoint is salient and different from the target's [p. 133]." If one accepts this definition of role taking (or either one of its component parts), then many prosocial acts do not involve or require role taking.

Another issue is the common expectation that all types of role taking should relate to prosocial behavior. Conceptually, one would expect cognitive, perceptual, and affective role taking to relate to different types of prosocial actions (Staub, 1978). Logically, affective perspective-taking should facilitate prosocial behaviors involving others' expressions of affect; perceptual perspective-taking might be most related to impersonal types of prosocial behaviors (because what is assessed is impersonal); and cognitive perspective-taking should relate most closely to prosocial acts in situations in which information regarding others' covert cognitions (e.g., intentions, motives) is relevant (Krebs & Russell, 1981). Although it is not clear that these relations hold (cf. Krebs & Russell, 1981), inconsistencies in the research could be due to failure to consider the type of perspective-taking required in a particular situation.

Another possible reason for the relatively weak relation between role taking and prosocial behavior is methodological. Many instruments used to assess perspective-taking may not adequately measure it. For some of these tasks, role taking (defined as an inferential process) is not necessary and/or sufficient for success (Higgins, 1981). For example, with some measures of affective role-taking (e.g., Borke, 1971; cf. Chandler & Greenspan, 1972), an emotional response may be directly elicited by the test stimulus (e.g., a hypothetical story in which a protagonist is in an upsetting situation), and this emotional response could then be projected onto the protagonist. For other role-taking tasks (e.g., the one in which children are asked to select appropriate gifts for their parents and peers; Shatz, 1978; Zahn-Waxler et al., 1977), the respondents may access "social category knowledge," that is, stored information regarding others' preferences, rather than engage in perspective-taking (Higgins & Parsons, 1983; Higgins, Feldman, & Ruble, 1980).

Developmental issues must also be considered when examining the relation between role taking and prosocial behavior. According to some research (e.g., Flavell, Botkin, Fry, Wright, & Jarvis, 1968; Selman, 1980; cf. Shantz, 1983), level or stage of role taking changes with age, and the various stages are qualitatively different. If this is true, selection of the instrument with which to assess role taking is critical. Even if the changes with age are more quantitative than qualitative, it would be important that the instrument used to assess perspective-taking not be so simple that one obtains a ceiling effect, and not be so difficult that there is insufficient variation in the resultant data. Clearly, given the wide variation in difficulty of the various measures of role taking, the choice of an instrument will have a profound effect on the findings. In many cases, failure to find an association between role taking and another variable (including prosocial behavior) could be due to use of an inappropriate or insensitive measure.

Even if the popular indices of role-taking were flawless, there would be another problem in the design of most research concerning the relation between it and prosocial behavior. In general (as is true for many studies concerning the relation between empathy and prosocial behavior; see Chapter 3), researchers have measured role taking in a laboratory setting, often with instruments involving hypothetical others, and have assessed prosocial behavior in a different situation. It is quite likely that the type of role taking assessed in the laboratory setting is frequently unnecessary or inappropriate to the helping situation in question. As was pointed out by Krebs and Russell (1981), researchers have seldom assessed whether subjects have taken the perspective of a potential recipient of aid.

The most direct test of the association between role taking and prosocial behavior probably would be to assess role taking in the helping situation. Perhaps the next best test would be to determine the relation between individuals' scores on an aggregate index of role taking (based on a battery of measures) and their helpfulness across a variety of situations (an aggregate measure of prosocial behavior). In general, the sum of a set of multiple measurements of a characteristic or behavior is a more stable and unbiased estimator than is any single measurement from the set (Epstein, 1979; Rushton, Brainerd, & Pressley, 1983). By combining across measures, the error associated with particular instruments may average out; moreover, the generality of the measure is enhanced.

Unfortunately, aggregated measures have seldom been utilized when examining the relation between perspective-taking and prosocial behavior. In one of the only studies of this type, Elder (1983) administered four measures of role taking and five laboratory measures of prosocial behavior to first graders. He also obtained three observational measures of prosocial behavior, as well as teachers' ratings of prosocial responding. Correlations between individual measures of role taking and prosocial behavior were low; however, the relation between the aggregated measures of role taking and prosocial behavior was much higher (.44; .52 after correcting for attenuation).

One last conceptual issue is of relevance. There is no reason to assume that perspective-taking invariably leads to altruistic cognitions or behaviors. True, it should result in a better understanding of the other and his or her situation. However, this understanding can be used for manipulative or Machavellian purposes. Role taking is merely an information-gathering process, one that is not intrinsically altruistic. Whether an individual uses the acquired information to assist, manipulate, or harm probably depends on the actor's values and own needs.

In summary, there does seem to be a positive empirical relation between level of role taking skills and quantity of prosocial behavior, albeit not strong or consistent. Undoubtedly, the empirical relation would be stronger if the measures of perspective-taking and prosocial behavior were always valid and reliable, if aggregation procedures were used, if role taking and prosocial behavior were assessed in the same situation, and if age and content-appropriate measures had been chosen in all studies. Moreover, although infrequently investigated, it is likely that level of perspective-taking is related to quality of assistance. For example, sensitivity of verbal, comfort-intended communications, a prosocial skill that increases dramatically with age in the school years (Burleson, 1982), has been related to perspective-taking as well as to other social-cognitive skills (e.g., construct differentiation; Burleson, 1984).

In many cases, there is no reason to believe that a particular act of assistance should be motivated by knowledge of another's perspective or feelings. Indeed, in many instances prosocial behaviors are undoubtedly the result of selfish or self-concerned rather than altruistic motives, or are automatically performed. Thus, it would appear that the most appropriate issue for future investigation would be the delineation of the circumstances in which perspective-taking is most likely to influence prosocial behavior.

ATTRIBUTIONS ABOUT THE ORIGINS
OF ANOTHER'S DEPENDENCY

In Chapter 4, people's inferences or attributions about the kindness of others' behaviors were discussed, as was the relation of these attributions to subsequent prosocial actions. Another type of attribution about others that appears to affect the probability of subsequent prosocial responding is attributions about the cause or basis of the potential recipient's dependency.

In general, the greater a person's need (or subjectively perceived need), the more both children (e.g., Fouts, 1972; Zinser & Lydiatt, 1976; Zinser, Perry, & Edgar, 1975) and adults (e.g., Bickman & Kamzan, 1973; Wagner & Wheeler, 1969; Weyant, 1978) assist. Nonetheless, people do not assist all needy persons equally; the reason for the other's need is a critical variable mediating helpfulness.

In early investigations with adults, researchers found that adults were more likely to assist a person whose need was due to another person's mistake or decision, rather than persons whose needs were due to an internal cause (e.g., taking it easy and not working hard, Berkowitz, 1969; refusal to complete a task, Ickes, Kidd, & Berkowitz, 1976; poor planning, Horowitz, 1968). Similarly, people were more likely to assist a potential recipient who could not complete a task without external assistance (who was totally dependent on another for helping) than those who merely chose to ask for assistance rather than to do the task themselves (Schopler & Matthews, 1965). These findings were initially interpreted as indicating that individuals are more likely to assist another if the other's need is based on external (environmental) rather than internal causes.

Ickes and Kidd (1976) challenged this internal/external locus of control interpretation. They suggested that the critical dimension is intentionality or controllability of the potential recipient's dependency. According to this view, when one's dependency is due to factors beyond one's own control, be they internal (e.g., lack of ability) or external (e.g., environmental constraints), the person is more likely to be viewed as deserving of assistance than if the person intentionally behaved in a manner that created the need (e.g., were lazy or careless).

The results of recent research are consistent with the view that the dimension of controllability of a potential recipient's need is a more critical variable influencing the likelihood of receiving assistance than is locus of control (e.g., Meyer & Mulherin, 1980). For example, Barnes, Ickes, and Kidd (1979) found that college students were more likely to lend others their class notes if the other's need for the notes was described as due to lack of ability rather than lack of effort (both internal causes). Furthermore, Bryan and Davenport (reported in Ickes and Kidd, 1976) reported that newspaper readers donated more at Christmas to people whose need was uncontrollable (e.g., child-abuse victims) than to people's whose dependency could be attributed to their own moral or psychological deficiencies.

Researchers have seldom examined the relation between children's attributions of causality for another's neediness and their helping behaviors. Nonetheless, there is research which is consistent with the view that children do make attributions about the reason for another's need, and that these attributions are related to their subsequent prosocial behavior. For example, Barnett (1975) found that fourth- and fifth-grade boys were more likely to share tokens (prizes) with peers who had none due to uncontrollable factors (the peer had not had an opportunity to win any tokens) than with peers who could be viewed as responsible for their needy state (they had no tokens because they lost in a competitive game). The boys also judged it fairer for the losers in the competition to not receive any tokens. In another study with fourth and fifth graders, Braband and Lerner (1975) obtained a similar pattern of findings but the results were not statistically significant. However, the children were significantly more likely to assist a peer if that peer was not responsible for the needy state *and* if the potential benefactor was not deserving of the free playtime that would be forfeited if assistance was offered. Finally, Miller and Smith (1977) found that fifth-grade children donated more money to peers who had no money due to factors beyond their control (the experimenter ran out of funds) than to children who had carelessly lost their own money (a controllable cause). However, this finding was significant only when the children had been either properly paid or underpaid for previous work; when they had been overpaid, they donated equally to children whose needy state was due to controllable versus uncontrollable factors.

It appears that the connection between attributions about the cause of another's dependency and an actor's prosocial behavior is, for the most part, not direct. Apparently, the effect of attributions regarding controllability and behavior is largely mediated by the actor's affective response to the personal attributions he or she makes. In two different research projects, Meyer and Mulherin (1980) and Weiner (1980) examined the effects of three different dimensions of causality (stability of the cause over time, internal versus external locus of the cause, and controllability of the cause) and their affective consequences on adults' reports of the likelihood that they would assist a needy other. Meyer and Mulherin asked people to rate the probability that they would assist hypothetical others in each of eight situations in which causality varied along three dimensions: stability, locus, and control (a 2 x 2 x 2 experimental design). The subjects also rated their affective reactions to each of the situations on 25 affect scales. Meyer and Mulherin found that, although the effect was moderated to some extent by stability and locus of causality, subjects were much more willing to help when the need for aid was due to uncontrollable rather than controllable causes (e.g., when the need for money was due to health reasons or to a disability obtained on the job, rather than to dislike of work or unwillingness to seek work out of town). Moreover, controllability was highly related to the subjects' reported emotional responses; in general, subjects reported more empathy and concern and less anger when the dependent other's need was due to uncontrollable rather than controllable causes. Furthermore, according to a path analysis, attributions concerning controllability had both a direct and indirect (through affect scores) effect on reported helping. However, the indirect effect was considerably larger than the direct effect. In brief, Meyer and Mulherin found that the effect of attributions of controllability on reported willingness to help was largely an indirect result of their influence on subjects' emotional reactions to the request.

In a series of studies, Weiner (1980) obtained findings very similar to those of Meyer and Mulherin (1980). In his first study, Weiner systematically manipulated the locus, stability, and controllability of a hypothetical person's dependency, and elicited adults' judgments of the likelihood that they would assist the dependent other (i.e., that they would lend class notes). Helping was influenced by both locus and controllability of the cause, and by the interaction of these two factors. Ratings of helping were lowest when the cause of need was both internal to the needy other and controllable (e.g., lack of effort).

In subsequent studies, Weiner (1980) examined the role of affect in the attribution-helping process. In general, adults were asked to report their affective reactions to, as well as the likelihood that they would assist, a person who was needy due to either illness (an uncontrollable cause) or being drunk (a controllable cause). Alternatively, subjects were provided with information about the attributions or affective reactions that they themselves purportedly had in a hypothetical situation involving either a drunk or ill dependent other, and were then asked to rate the probability that they would assist. Overall, Weiner found that ascription of causality to internal, controllable factors (e.g., drunkeness) maximized negative affective reactions (e.g., disgust and anger) and led to avoidance (low levels of helping). Ascription of causality to uncontrollable factors was associated with positive affective reactions such as pity and sympathy, and with reported willing to help. Although perceptions of the other's personal control were in themselves related to willingness to help, affective reactions accounted for a much larger percent of the variance in reported helping. In short, Weiner concluded that attributions of causality affected helping behavior primarily (but not solely) by guiding emotional reactions, and that these reactions "provide the motor and direction for behavior [p. 186]."

One limiation of the research described previously should be noted. In all of these studies, the individual who needed help for controllable (or internal; Berkowitz, 1969; Horowitz, 1968; Schopler & Matthews, 1965) reasons could have been viewed as having a character flaw, whereas this was not true for the people who did not have control over their dependency or need. For example, the needy individual in these studies was depicted as a drunk (Weiner, 1980), as being lazy (e.g., someone who did not work or worked only when in the mood; Barnes et al., 1979; Berkowitz, 1969; Meyer & Mulherin, 1980), as being a dependent, perhaps inadequate person (Horowitz, 1968; Schopler & Matthews, 1965), or as possibly being disagreeable (the needy other refused to participate in a study; Ickes et al., 1976). Thus, it is not surprising that subjects were less willing to assist these unattractive people than people without explicit or implicit character flaws. Perhaps attributions concerning controllability of the potential recipient's needs would not be related to help rendered if the person who was needy due to controllable factors was also attractive. For example, people might be equally willing to lend classnotes to individuals who missed class due to either illness (an uncontrollable cause) or to the decision to take care of a sick friend (a controllable cause). It is quite possible that attributions concerning the controllability of another's neediness are related to subsequent helping only if the needy other's controllable choices or behaviors are likely to put him or her in a negative light.

It is interesting to note that if individuals are unable to assist a needy or distressed other, they are likely to derogate (e.g., attribute negative characteristics to) the other, even if the needy person is not responsible for his or her own fate (e.g., Lerner & Simmons, 1966; cf. Lerner & Miller, 1978). Indeed, people are even more likely to derogate an unfortunate other who did not cause or choose his or her own fate than one who deliberately chose to be in negative circumstances (Lerner & Miller, 1978). Lerner has claimed that derogation occurs in these circumstances because people believe in a "just world," that is, in the idea that there is a relation between what people do and what happens to them. It is not clear, however, that derogation of others who are victims of misfortunes due to no fault of their own prevents subsequent helping of the victim by the derogator when an opportunity to assist arises. Indeed, in two studies in which people could assist needy others after having evaluated (and often derogated) the other, subsequent helping was not suppressed (Kenrick, Reich, & Cialdini, 1976; Lerner & Matthews, 1967). Although researchers have suggested a variety of reasons for the finding that derogation has not been related to depressed helping (e.g., sadistic motives for assisting, trivial measures of helping behavior; Lerner & Miller, 1978), at the present time there is no reason to assume that derogation of those who suffer uncontrollable, undeserved misfortunes consistently inhibits subsequent helping of the unfortunates. Of course, this does not mean that derogation of others based upon prejudice, stereotyping, or personal animosity, rather than belief in a just world, is unrelated to assistance provided to derogated individuals. In fact, there are myraid historical examples of instances when derogation or dehumanization of a group of people (e.g., Blacks, Jews, "the enemy") has served to justify aggression directed against the group (cf. Bandura, 1973).

INTERPERSONAL PROBLEM-SOLVING SKILLS

There is another aspect of social cognition that most likely is an important factor in the execution of prosocial behavior, and has been cited as such by researchers (e.g., Shure, 1982; Solomon, Watson, Battistich, Solomon, & Schaps, 1981). This skill (actually group of skills) has frequently been labeled as interpersonal problem-solving skills. These capacities are not, in themselves, merely inferential processes, although it is likely that people with better inferential (i.e., perspective-taking) capacities have more finely honed problem-solving skills (Marsh, Serafica, & Barenboim, 1980; Shure, 1982; Spivack & Shure, 1974). Indeed, Silbereisen (1985) has suggested that some of the same processes that are part of perspective-taking (according to an action theory based conceptualization) are also interpersonal problem-solving skills, and Shure (1982) has found that measures of perspective-taking and interpersonal problem-solving are often significantly intercorrelated.

Interpersonal problem-skills generally have been defined as a set of interrelated cognitive skills. Spivack, Shure, and their colleagues, the researchers who have done the most work on this topic, have identified five interpersonal problem-solving skills (Shure, 1982; Spivack, Platt, & Shure, 1976):

1.   Sensitivity of problems: "An awareness of the variety of possible problems that beset human interactions and a sensitivity to the existence of an interpersonal problem or at least the potential for such problems whenever people get together [Spivack et al., 1976, p. 5]."

2.   Alternative-solution thinking: The ability to generate a variety of different solutions (not to necessarily recognize the best solution).

3.   Means-ends thinking: The ability to articulate the step-by-step means that may be necessary in order to carry out the solution to any interpersonal problem (a skill that includes recognition of obstacles that could interfere with goal completion, and the realization that goal satisfaction may not occur immediately).

4.   Consequential thinking: The tendency to consider the consequences of one's social acts for others as well as oneself, and to generate alternative consequences to a social act before deciding what to do.

5.   Causal thinking: An understanding or appreciation of the fact that how one feels or acts may have been influenced by (and, in turn, may influence) how others feel and act.

Interpersonal problem-solving skills usually have been assessed with the interview techniques developed by Spivack, Shure, and their colleagues (Shure & Spivack, 1978; Spivack & Shure, 1974; Spivack et al., 1976). For example, to assess alternative-solution thinking, children are presented with hypothetical problem situations and then requested to think of different ways in which the story protagonist could solve the problem at hand. Alternatively, to assess means-end thinking, preadolescents or adults generally are presented with story themes and asked to fill in the middle of the story. Recently, Krasnor and Rubin (1981) have suggested that young children's social-problem skills should be assessed behaviorally rather than with verbal measures, and they have begun to develop measures for doing so (Krasnor & Rubin, 1983; see Butler & Meichenbaum, 1981, for a critical review of assessment instruments for interpersonal problem-solving skills).

Given the cognitive nature of interpersonal problem-solving skills, it is not surprising that there are developmental changes in these capacities. For example, Marsh (1982) examined four problem-solving abilities in kindergartners, second, fourth, and sixth graders. The older elementary-school children were able to define interpersonal problems more thoroughly, to generate more alternatives and consequences, and to select solutions that reflected more relevant perspectives. For problem definition, there was a significant increase in ability between grades 2 and 4; for all other abilities (generation of alternatives, consequential thinking, and selection of alternatives), there were significant increases between grades 4 and 6.

In general, interpersonal problem-solving skills have been positively related to adjustment. In a series of studies (see Spivack et al., 1976; Shure, 1982), well-adjusted children have been found to generate more solutions to problems than do inhibited or impulsive children. Alternative-solution thinking has also been related to low anxiety as well as low social withdrawal in 4–5-year-olds (Olson, Johnson, Parks, Barrett, & Belleau, 1983a). Moreover, inhibited children also appear to be deficient in consequential thinking (Shure, Newman, & Silver, 1973; reported in Shure, 1982). In adults and adolescents, low means-end thinking has been related to psychiatric and acting-out problems (e.g., Platt, Scura, & Hannon, 1973; Platt & Spivack, 1972; Platt, Spivack, Altman, Altman, & Peizer, 1974; cf. Butler & Meichenbaum, 1981). The degree of association between problem-solving skills and adjustment varies with the specific skill being examined, as well as with the age of the individual (Shure, 1982).

Problem-solving abilities have also been related to popularity and a variety of positive social behaviors in normal children. For example, the ability to generate alternative solutions has been positively related to positive peer interactions in 4–5-year-olds (Olson et al., 1983b). Similarly, a combination of interpersonal problem-solving skills (including problem definition, generation of alternatives, consequential thinking, and selection of alternative and means-end thinking have been related to teacher- or child-report of eighth graders' ability to make and maintain friendships, participation in group activities, and overall interpersonal skills (Marsh et al., 1981). Finally, means-end thinking (but not problem-solving skills) has also been related to low aggression for eighth-grade girls (but not boys; Marsh, Serafica, & Barenboim, 1981), whereas a combination of skills has been related to low levels of aggression for second-grade boys (but not girls; Gouze, Rayias, & Bieber-Schneider, 1983).

Although problem-solving skills have been associated with a variety of positive social behaviors, few researchers have examined the relation of interpersonal problem-solving skills to prosocial behavior. Nonetheless, according to the limited data, problem-solving skills do seem to be associated, at least to some degree, with prosocial action in childhood. In two different studies with fifth graders, Shure (1980) noted strong relations between prosocial tendencies (as rated by peers and/or teachers) and interpersonal problem-solving skills. Prosocial behavior was defined broadly as including popularity as well as concern for others. In the first study, both boys' and girls' prosocial tendencies were consistently correlated with means-end thinking. In the second study (which was an intervention study), the ability to formulate alternative solutions to problems was most highly related to the indices of prosocial behavior; moreover, for boys only, prosocial behavior was significantly correlated with means-end and consequential skills.

Other researchers have focused more specifically on prosocial behaviors such as helpfulness than did Shure. In a study with eighth graders, Marsh et al. (1981) found that means-end thinking and a measure of a combination of interpersonal problem-solving skills (problem definition, generation of alternatives, consequential thinking, and selection of alternatives) were associated with teachers' reports of girls' (but not boys') helpfulness. Means-end thinking was also negatively related to teacher report of girls' hurting other children, and positively related to girls' concern with the problems of others. For boys, self report of concern with the problems of others was positively related to the composite measure of problem-solving skills. In another study, teachers' ratings of 4–5-year-olds' social cooperativeness (including prosocial as well as compliant and cooperative behaviors) were negatively related to the number of aggressive solutions to hypothetical problem situations, but not to quantity or relevance of solutions (Olson et al., 1983b). Finally, training in interpersonal problem-solving skills as well as other social-cognitive skills has been associated with increases in preschoolers' prosocial behaviors (as rated by adults; Spivack & Shure, 1974).

Clearly, the evidence linking interpersonal problem-solving skills to prosocial behavior is scanty and inconclusive. Nonetheless, it seems logical that the ability to generate a variety of solutions to problems (prosocial as well as aggressive), and to think through the steps and consequences of actions when dealing with interpersonal situations, should enhance the likelihood of children choosing to perform prosocial rather than antisocial action. This idea is supported by Dodge and Newman's (1981) finding that aggressive boys, who tend to overattribute hostility to peers in unwarranted circumstances (Dodge, 1980), do so only when they respond quickly. Apparently, when aggressive boys analyze situations in more detail, they are less likely to make the type of attributions that have been associated with aggressive responses. Of course, as is true for the ability to role take, interpersonal problem-solving ability does not ensure positive or altruistic responding; people can use these skills for self-oriented, manipulative purposes. Nonetheless, in individuals with limited capacities to think through their behaviors and their consequences (e.g., children), the ability to do so relatively effectively should increase the probability that they will engage in other-oriented, rather than self-oriented, behaviors. Research in which interpersonal problem-solving skills are being used as one of a variety of procedures to enhance prosocial responding is now underway (e.g., Solomon et al., 1981).

CONCLUSION

There are a variety of socio-cognitive abilities involving inferences and related skills that seem to influence the likelihood of one individual assisting another. However, the role of these capacities (or the tendency to use these capacities) in prosocial behavior is not simple or constant; the use of these skills is probably related to prosocial behavior in some situations and not others, and apparently can serve to enhance the probability of some (e.g., altruistic) but not all types of prosocial behaviors. Moreover, these social-cognitive skills can be involved in diverse and/or multiple phases of prosocial action, including: (1) the detection of another's need (perspective-taking and interpersonal problem-solving skills); (2) evaluation of the merit of the need (attributions about controllability and source of dependency); (3) generation of a potential helper's affective (empathic or otherwise) motivation to assist (perspective-taking and attributions about the locus and controllability of the other's dependency); and (4) successfully formulating and executing appropriate helping behaviors (interpersonal problem-solving skills). Thus, although our understanding of the specific links between altruism and the social-cognitive processes discussed in this chapter is limited, it is clear that these and related processes are important factors in the capacity and tendency to behave in an altruistic manner.

7 Altruistic Values and Moral Judgment

Nancy Eisenberg, Randy Lennon, Jeannette F. Pasternack

The self-attributional research reviewed in Chapter 5 frequently has been interpreted as providing information about individuals' conscious, cognitive motives
for altruism and other types of prosocial behaviors (e.g., Bar-Tal, 1982; Eisenberg, 1982). However, researchers have studied cognitions related to altruism
by means of a variety of other approaches; most notably, they have delineated
cognitions concerning helping that occur prior to (rather than subsequent to)
prosocial behaviors or are associated with high levels of altruism across settings.
This research will now be considered in some detail.

NORMS AND INTERNALIZED VALUES

Central to many conceptualizations of altruism are notions such as internalized
norms and personal values (e.g., Bar-Tal, 1982; Eisenberg, 1982; Krebs, 1982;
Staub, 1978; Schwartz & Howard, 1981, 1982). Although not all psychologists
use these terms in an identical manner, most view norms as values that people
internalize sometime during the process of socialization and development—
values that are at least in part cognitive constructions. These values frequently
are those held by the larger society; however, they can be personally constructed
by the individual. Norms and values may differ across individuals, and also vary
in their relative importance to various persons.

Some norms associated with prosocial behavior are likely to lead to altruistic
behavior; others are not. For example, the norm of reciprocity, which refers to
the principle of the reciprocation or exchange of benefits (Gouldner, 1960), is
likely to be associated with nonaltruistic prosocial behavior. People who adher

to this norm assist another because the other either has previously benefited them or may reciprocate in the future. In contrast, the norm of social responsibility, which prescribes the giving of aid to needy or dependent others (Goranson & Berkowitz, 1966), is likely to engender true altruism. When this norm is internalized, we "act on behalf of others, not for material gain or social approval [Goranson & Berkowitz, 1966, p. 228]."

A fundamental issue is, of course, why we sometimes act in accordance with internalized values or norms. Various explanations have been proposed, but most are basically similar. Theorists typically have suggested that people develop general (Staub, 1978) or situation-specific (Schwartz & Howard, 1981, 1982) expectations that they will engage in behaviors consistent with personal values and beliefs (e.g., personal norms, Staub, 1978), and that adherence to these expectations is motivated by self-reactions such as positive or negative self-evaluation. Karylowski (1982b) and Reykowski (1982a) have labeled altruistic motivation that stems from the involvement of one's self-esteem with relevant norms as "endocentric," and they have contrasted this type of motive with "exocentric altruism" in which attention is directed toward the other person rather than the self (Karylowski, 1982b).

Although it is clear that mere exposure to or awareness of norms related to altruism is often insufficient in itself to motivate altruism (cf. Berkowitz, 1972; Bryan & Walbek, 1970; Krebs, 1970), there is evidence that personal norms (a person's expectations that he or she will engage in certain behaviors; Staub, 1978) constructed from internalized values are related to a wide variety of helping behaviors (e.g., Schwartz, 1973, 1978; Schwartz & Fleishman, 1978; cf. Schwartz & Howard, 1981, 1982). For example, Staub (1974) found that adults with a prosocial orientation (including the tendency to ascribe responsibility to oneself, low endorsement of Machiavellian values, high levels of moral judgment, and low ambition) exhibited more helping of a person in an emergency than did adults with less commitment to prosocial values. Similarly, Schwartz and other researchers have found that personal norms constructed from internalized values are significantly related to the performance of a variety of prosocial acts, including willingness to volunteer to donate bone marrow (Schwartz, 1973) or blood (Pomazal & Jaccard, 1976; Zuckerman & Reis, 1978), tutor blind children (Schwartz, 1978), or help elderly welfare recipients (Schwartz & Fleishman, 1982). The strength of the relation between personal norms or values and altruism may be mediated by a variety of factors including both the individual's tendencies to role take or spontaneously note the needs of others (Schwartz, 1968a; Malinowska, 1973; cited in Reykowski, 1982a) and to accept versus deny responsibility to conform with normative obligations (a defensive behavior, Schwartz, 1968b, 1973; Schwartz & Fleishman, 1983; Schwartz & Howard, 1980). Moreover, individuals seem to be more likely to act in accordance with altruistic personal norms or values if they recognize their own competence to assist (Schwartz & Ben David, 1976).

Some investigators have suggested that processes other than self-evaluation mediate the effectiveness of certain values associated with prosocial or altruistic behavior. Lerner (1975, 1981; Lerner & Meindl, 1981) has proposed that during childhood people develop the notion of a just world, one in which people get what they deserve. According to this view, the belief in a just world provides individuals with a greater sense of control over their own fates; if people admit that others are subjected to undeserved, unjust suffering or deprivation, they must acknowledge that they are themselves vulnerable to similar fates. Thus, to maintain one's belief in a just world, people often attempt to restore justice by assisting others who have experienced undeserved suffering.

Lerner's (1975, 1981; Lerner & Meindl, 1981) concept of justice is generally viewed as an internalized value or motive. This motive is egoistic in that it is based upon the desire to dispel doubts concerning the controllability of one's own fate. Consequently, the justice motive frequently should be associated with nonaltruistic helping. However, through the process of socialization and development, commitment to justice can become an important value and motive independent of its egoistic origins (Kohlberg, 1969, 1976). For example, through the exercise of role-taking and empathic skills, people may develop a sense of justice that is independent of their own needs and insecurities and becomes a moral orientation or value that guides their actions towards others (Karniol & Miller, 1981). Performance of behaviors consistent with this value is probably regulated, at least in part, by self-evaluative processes. Consequently, prosocial behaviors based upon internalized justice values are usually viewed as altruistic.

It is likely that other norms that are hedonistic in origin may, for some people, become internalized moral values. For example, Walster, Walster, and Berscheid (1978) have suggested that the norm of equity frequently motivates nonaltruistic helping. People who feel that they have an unequitable advantage in a relationship may assist a disadvantaged other in order to avoid social censure for being exploitive or to gain social approval for being concerned. Alternatively, people in inequitable relationships may assist to relieve the distress associated with an inequitable state. This nonmoral norm of equity may, however, be internalized as a moral principle during socialization. In other words, the norm of equity may become a value functionally autonomous of its hedonistic basis, one that can be used to construct personal norms and values and is of importance to the individual's self-evaluation (Schwartz & Howard, 1982). As such, the norm of equity may motivate altruistic helping.

To summarize, many investigators believe that cognitions underlying moral norms and values frequently motivate altruistic behavior. The process by which norm or value-related cognitions are associated with behavior is not entirely cognitive, however; emotions related to self-evaluation (e.g., guilt, self-praise) mediate the process. In our view, as well as that of others (e.g., Hoffman, 1984a; Staub, 1978), value or norm-based altruistic behavior is one of the two major types of altruism: the other is empathically motivated prosocial behavior (see Chapter 3). Although both types of altruism are based upon cognitive as well as affective processes, cognitive processes would seem to be more central to altruism based upon principles or values, whereas affect typically is viewed as the more salient contributor to empathically motivated altruism.

HIERARCHIES OF NORMS, VALUES, PREFERENCES, AND DESIRES

Most individuals undoubtedly have internalized a number of different values and adher to a variety of norms, some essentially moral and some not. Moreover, each individual has a variety of personal needs and preferences. These values, norms, needs, and preferences are the bases of what Staub (1978) has labeled as personal goals, that is, preferences "for certain outcomes or end states or an aversion to certain outcomes [p. 46]." Some personal goals are idiosyncratic, some more commonly held. For example, among a particular individual's personal goals could be desires for social approval, material gain, and success on academic tasks. Personal goals are, in part, cognitive in that a set of cognitions is likely to be associated with personal goals (Staub, 1978). For example, a person for whom helping others is a personal goal might evaluate others and their welfare positively, and view others' distresses as undesirable. According to Staub, altruistic values and norms, as well as the tendency to react empathically, should increase the desirability of altruistic personal goals such as improving another's welfare or acting in a helpful manner (which can be a goal in itself).

In any given situation, several personal goals may be activated. Thus, various personal goals, some derived from internalized values or norms, can come into conflict. For example, in a situation involving potential altruism, an individual's valuing of others' welfare may conflict with personal goals such as the desire for material gain. In other cases, especially when a prosocial behavior entails little cost to the benefactor, there may be little or no conflict among personal goals.

Given that people hold a variety of values and personal goals, an important issue is the way in which individuals resolve conflicts among values and/or goals. This issue is addressed, in part, by the large body of research on moral judgment. In this research, investigators have examined how people resolve moral conflicts between various values or personal goals on a cognitive (reasoning) level. It is to this literature that we now turn.

KOHLBERG'S APPROACH TO MORAL JUDGMENT

Lawrence Kohlberg's theorizing and research clearly has been central to the work on moral judgment. Kohlberg and his colleagues have focused on the qualitative form of children's and adults' moral reasoning, and on developmental change in that reasoning (Kohlberg, 1969, 1971, 1976, 1978, 1981; Colby & Kohlberg, 1984; Colby, Kohlberg, Gibbs, & Lieberman, 1983). In Colby and Kohlberg's words:

> Kohlberg has attempted to describe general organizational or structural features of moral judgment that can be shown to develop in a regular sequence of stages. The concept of structure implies that a consistent logic or form of reasoning can be abstracted from the content of an individual's responses to variety of situations. It implies that moral development may be defined in terms of the qualitative reorganization of the individual's pattern of thought rather than in the learning of new content. Each new reorganization integrates within a broader perspective the insights that were achieved at lower stages. The developing child becomes better able to understand and integrate diverse points of view on a moral-conflict situation and to take more of the relevant situational factors into account. In this sense, each stage presupposes the understanding gained at previous stages. As a result, each stage provides a more adequate way of making and justifying moral judgments. The order in which the stages develop is said to be the same in each individual not because the stages are innate but because of the underlying logic of the sequence [pp. 41–42].

Kohlberg (e.g., 1963, 1969) originally proposed a sequence of six developmental stages. However, over the past 25 years, these stages and the scoring system used to code level of moral judgment frequently have been revised. The goal of these revisions has been to better differentiate content (the concrete issues being considered) from structure (the more formal and abstract features of moral judgment that presumably are the basis for differentiating among stages). In his most recent work, Kohlberg (1978) eliminated the scoring of his highest stage (stage 6) which he now considers an elaboration of stage 5. Moreover, one of his colleagues who helped develop the recent coding system has suggested that Kohlberg's stage 5 is really an existential phase (a detached "meta" perspective) rather than a true moral stage (Gibbs, 1977, 1979; Gibbs & Widaman, 1982).

As they now stand, Kohlberg's stages are described by Colby and Kohlberg (1984) as stages of sociomoral perspective taking:

> The basic developmental concept underlying the revised stage sequence is level of sociomoral perspective, the characteristic point of view from which the individual formulates moral judgments. In regard to level of sociomoral perspective, we interpret the perspective-taking underlying the moral stages as intrinsically moral in nature rather than as a logical or social-cognitive structure applied to the moral domain . . . These levels provide a general organization of moral judgment and serve to inform and unite other more specific moral concepts, such as the nature of the morally right or good, moral reciprocity, rules, rights, obligation or duty, fairness, and welfare consequences, and moral values such as obedience to authority, preservation of human life, and maintenance of contracts and affectional relations [p. 43].

TABLE 7.1
The Six Moral Stages

| | Content of Stage | | |
Level and Stage	What is Right	Reasons for Doing Right	Social Perspective of Stage
LEVEL I—PRECONVENTIONAL Stage 1—Heteronomous Morality	To avoid breaking rules backed by punishment, obedience for its own sake, and avoiding physical damage to persons and property.	Avoidance of punishment, and the superior power of authorities.	*Egocentric point of view.* Doesn't consider the interests of others or recognize that they differ from the actor's; doesn't relate two points of view. Actions are considered physically rather than in terms of psychological interests of others. Confusion of authority's perspective with one's own.
Stage 2—Individualism, Instrumental Purpose, and Exchange	Following rules only when it is to someone's immediate interest; acting to meet one's own interests and needs and letting others do the same. Right is also what's fair, what's an equal exchange, a deal, an agreement.	To serve one's own needs or interests in a world where you have to recognize that other people have their interests, too.	*Concrete individualistic perspective.* Aware that everybody has his/her own interest to pursue and these conflict, so that right is relative (in the concrete individualistic sense).
LEVEL II—CONVENTIONAL Stage 3—Mutual Interpersonal Expectations, Relationships, and Interpersonal Conformity	Living up to what is expected by people close to you or what people generally expect of people in your role as son, brother, friend, etc. "Being good" is important and means having good motives, showing concern about others. It also means keeping mutual relationships, such as trust, loyalty, respect and gratitude.	The need to be a good person in your own eyes and those of others. Your caring for others. Belief in the Golden Rule. Desire to maintain rules and authority which support stereotypical good behavior.	*Perspective of the individual in relationships with other individuals.* Aware of shared feelings, agreements, and expectations which take primacy over individual interests. Relates points of view through the concrete Golden Rule, putting yourself in the other guy's shoes. Does not yet consider generalized system perspective.

Stage		Social Perspective of Stage
Stage 4—Social System and Conscience	Fulfilling the actual duties to which you have agreed. Laws are to be upheld except in extreme cases where they conflict with other fixed social duties. Right is also contributing to society, the group, or institution.	To keep the institution going as a whole, to avoid the breakdown in the system "if everyone did it," or the imperative of conscience to meet one's defined obligations (Easily confused with Stage 3 belief in rules and authority.)	*Differentiates societal point of view from interpersonal agreement or motives.* Takes the point of view of the system that defines roles and rules. Considers individual relations in terms of place in the system.
LEVEL III—POST-CONVENTIONAL, or PRINCIPLED Stage 5—Social Contract or Utility and Individual Rights	Being aware that people hold a variety of values and opinions, that most values and rules are relative to your group. These relative rules should usually be upheld, however, in the interest of impartiality and because they are the social contract. Some nonrelative values and rights like *life* and *liberty*, however, must be upheld in any society and regardless of majority opinion.	A sense of obligation to law because of one's social contract to make and abide by laws for the welfare of all and for the protection of all people's rights. A feeling of contractual commitment, freely entered upon, to family, friendship, trust, and work obligations. Concern that laws and duties be based on rational calculation of overall utility, "the greatest good for the greatest number."	*Prior-to-society perspective.* Perspective of a rational individual aware of values and rights prior to social attachments and contracts. Integrates perspectives by formal mechanisms of agreement, contract, objective impartiality, and due process. Considers moral and legal points of view; recognizes that they sometimes conflict and finds it difficult to integrate them.
Stage 6—Universal Ethical Principles	Following self-chosen ethical principles. Particular laws or social agreements are usually valid because they rest on such principles. When laws violate these principles, one acts in accordance with the principle. Principles are universal principles of justice: the equality of human rights and respect for the dignity of human beings as individual persons.	The belief as a rational person in the validity of universal moral principles, and a sense of personal commitment to them.	*Perspective of a moral point of view* from which social arrangements derive. Perspective is that of any rational individual recognizing the nature of morality or the fact that persons are ends in themselves and must be treated as such.

Reprinted with permission from Kohlberg (1976).

A relatively recent version of Kohlberg's stages is presented in Table 7.1. Kohlberg views his stages as being focused on justice; that is, morality is defined in terms of one's reasoning regarding justice. In Kohlberg's view, principles of justice are primary to an impartial, universal system of morality. The criterion of reversibility is viewed as the "ultimate criterion of justice [Kohlberg, Levine, & Hewer, 1983, p. 95]"; in other words, the truly just solution is one that is considered acceptable or fair from the point of view of all interested parties. However, although Kohlberg focuses on justice, he recently acknowledged the possibility that there are other broader ways to conceptualize morality (Kohlberg et al., 1983).

Despite Kohlberg's claim that his stages differ from one another primarily in terms of structure and not in content of reasoning, it is clear from Table 7.1 that his recent stages are still defined, in part, by content. At each stage, specific values or personal goals predominate. For example, at Stage 2 concrete instrumental goals and considerations are salient, whereas concern with others' expectations is central to a stage 3 orientation. Indeed, the contents of each stage (or level) seem to reflect a generalized value orientation (Berndt, 1981; Nisan, 1984a; Staub, 1978). Moreover, as was noted by Rest (1979), only certain issues (content) are coded at each specific stage.

Discussion of Kohlberg's schema of moral judgment and its derivatives (e.g., Gibbs & Widaman, 1982; Rest, 1979) can (and has) filled volumes (cf. Colby et al., 1983; Gibbs & Widaman, 1982; Kohlberg, 1981, 1983; Kohlberg et al., 1983; Rest, 1979; Weinreich-Haste & Locke, 1983). It is not our goal to summarize or evaluate in detail the research and extensive debate and theorizing concerning Kohlberg's work. Rather, we seek to extract from the research and thinking concerning Kohlbergian and other models of moral judgment that information most relevant to an understanding of people's thinking about and performance of altruistic behavior. Consequently, henceforth we will focus on the literature specifically relevant to prosocial responding.

MORAL JUDGMENTS CONCERNING ALTRUISTIC AND PROSOCIAL ACTIONS

Dilemmas Pitting Prosocial Values Against Other Values

In most of the research based on Kohlberg's stages of moral judgment, reasoning related to altruistic values is not salient. This is due to the nature of Kohlberg's moral dilemmas. In nearly all of the standard moral scenarios (dilemmas) used by Kohlberg and his colleagues to elicit moral reasoning, there is an explicit conflict between two different moral values or norms. Consider the following famous dilemma:

In Europe, a woman was near death from a special kind of cancer. There was only one drug that the doctors thought might save her. It was a form of radium that a druggist in the same town had recently discovered. The drug was expensive to make, but the druggist was charging ten times what the drug cost him to make. He paid $200 for the radium and charged $2,000 for a small dose of the drug. The sick woman's husband, Heinz, went to everyone he knew to borrow the money, but he could only get together about $1,000 which is half of what it cost. He told the druggist that his wife was dying, and asked him to sell it cheaper or let him pay later. But the druggist said, "No, I discovered the drug and I'm going to make money from it." So Heinz got desperate and broke into the man's store to steal the drug for his wife. Should the husband have done this? Why?

In this dilemma, values such as those concerning stealing, punishment, and disobeying laws are in direct conflict with values related to helping, duties implicit in relationships, and/or the value of life. In fact, when people choose to reason about the option of helping Heinz's wife, the issue of altruism per se is the focus of the reasoning much less frequently than other issues such as affiliative relationships, the value of life, moral law, and conscience (cf. Colby, Gibbs, Kohlberg, Speicher-Dubin, & Candee, 1979). This is, in part, because of the strong focus in the dilemma on the value of life (due to the life-or-death nature of the dilemma); people who say Heinz should help frequently orient primarily to this issue rather than to altruistic considerations.

In other dilemmas, issues related to others' welfare and altruism are even less salient. This is true despite the fact that Kohlberg has described four moral orientations that he believes are reflected in responses to his dilemmas, two of which (utilitarian maximizing of the welfare of each person and perfectionistic seeking of harmony or integrity of the self and social group) often can be viewed as primarily prosocial in nature (Colby et al., in press). For example, in another commonly used Kohlberg dilemma, a boy is promised by his father that he can go to camp if he earns the money to pay tuition. After the boy earns the money, the father asks for the money to go on a fishing trip. The person responding to this dilemma is asked whether or not the boy should refuse to give his father the money, and why. In this dilemma, issues such as authority, affiliative relationships, property, and contract (promises) are central. This dilemma is fairly typical of Kohlberg's other dilemmas in that issues related to prohibitions (laws, rules, authorities' dictates, formal obligations, and punishment) are salient, whereas altruistic and prosocial considerations, where relevant, are less central. Consequently, it is difficult to determine whether Kohlberg's stages are generalizable to moral reasoning about issues in which altruistic norms and values are more salient.

There is some research available in which authorities' dictates and rules have been pitted against the alternative of assisting another in a context in which the issue of helping (or altruism) per se is central to the moral dilemma. Blasi (in press), in a study of children's reasoning and attitudes regarding obedience, presented first, sixth, and tenth/eleventh graders with hypothetical dilemmas in

which there was a conflict between performance of prosocial behavior and either
(1) the commands or rules of an authority or (2) a city law (grades 6 and 10/11
only). Blasi's dilemmas were similar to those of Kohlberg's in that prohibition-
related issues were central; however, Blasi's moral conflicts were also less extreme
than Kohlberg's dilemmas (they involved relatively life-like conflicts rather than
situations with extreme consequences such as life-or-death outcomes). Consequently, altruistic issues were more salient than in the Kohlberg's dilemmas;
individuals who justified the decision to assist tended to focus more on the
prosocial behavior itself than on the issues of killing or the value of life.

Blasi's (in press) dilemmas concerning authorities' rules differed for each
grade. The conflict inherent in the dilemma presented to first graders was between
helping a fallen child in the yard and obeying a maternal command to stay in
the house; for sixth graders, between bringing food to a boy being punished at
camp and obeying the orders of the camp director; and for the tenth/eleventh
graders, between telling a hospital patient's family the patient's true condition
and disobeying a hospital rule that prohibits doing so. In the dilemma in which
helping and the law were pitted against one another, a city official could help a
businessman to avoid bankruptcy but would have to violate a city law in doing
so. Children were asked what the story protagonist should do and why, as well
as a variety of other questions concerning obligations, disobedience, and personal
accountability.

Although it is difficult to generalize from children's responses to only one
(first graders) or two (sixth and tenth/eleventh graders) dilemmas, especially
when the dilemmas vary somewhat across age, Blasi's (in press) results are
suggestive. Blasi noted rather dramatic age differences in reasoning. First graders
were much more sensitive to another's needs than to an authority's rules, although
they did not feel a strict obligation to assist. In justifying their decisions, first
graders tended to refer to "objective" considerations that were signs of the other's
need (e.g., the needs of the child, the danger of the child getting hurt, the child's
crying, or the anxiety of the child's mother) or to the circumstances (e.g., the
fact that nobody else was around to help or the baby was too little to know what
to do). Egocentric concerns (e.g., possible gain for the helper) were also relatively
frequent. Thus, first graders' concerns were concrete, referring to specific needs
or circumstances, and were rarely framed within more general concerns such as
doing one's duty. Moreover, younger children did not appear to view their
concerns as demanded by personal beliefs or interpersonal norms, or as being
relevant to broad humanistic values. Blasi noted that even vague expressions
such as "it's nice to help," which suggest a system of social expectations, were
infrequent.

In contrast to first graders, sixth graders were much less likely to reject
authorities and laws in favor of altruistic or prosocial behavior. In their justifications, sixth graders seldom verbalized egocentric reasons; they tended to cite
general principles of social interaction, laws and authority, or morality and duty.

More specifically, sixth graders mentioned issues such as loyalty and friendship, the intrinsic value of obedience to rules, laws, and authorities ("The director knows better; he is in charge") or considerations of duty and "wrong" or "right" (e.g., "It would be wrong to disobey").

The adolescents' reasoning did not differ greatly from that of sixth graders. However, some of these oldest children did exhibit types of reasoning not used by younger children. For example, 27% of the high-school students justified their decisions primarily with references to people's rights or contracts (mutual agreements), the perspective of other individuals, or societal and universal values. Moreover, the emphasis on the subjectivity of moral evaluations (e.g., "she should do it, because she feels inside that it's good" or "she has a good reason for breaking the law") increased dramatically from sixth grade to high school. Finally, in making moral judgments, high-school students, but not younger children, sometimes referred to subjective characteristics of the actor (the individual's personality, background, and interests) or the potential benefactor's overall moral philosophy and the meaning of one's personal philosophy, commitments, or integrity to the expression of self.

In summary, in Blasi's (in press) study children's reasoning concerning conflicts between prosocial behavior and obedience to rules or laws changed with age. Young children's reasoning was clearly more concrete and egocentric than that of older children, although young children seemed very aware of, and influenced by, the needs of others and the circumstances creating need. Older elementary-school children tended to emphasize issues related to social interaction, the moral value of authority, objective criteria of morality, and duty. High-school children generally expressed reasons similar to those used by sixth graders; however, some older students also emphasized more abstract principles (e.g., individual rights), the perspective of society, subjective evaluations or morality, and personal values, philosophies, and integrity. In brief, consistent with Kohlberg's scheme of moral judgment, children's reasons became more abstract, complex in structure, and internalized with age.

In a study of Israeli children aged 5–12, Levin and Bekerman-Greenberg (1980) also examined moral reasoning concerning situations in which the option of prosocial behavior was salient but was pitted against an authority's dictates. In specific, children were asked if and why they would share pretzels with a peer when sharing was prohibited by their mother. Justifications were scored into six levels of reasoning to reflect developmental maturity: (1) lack of generosity due to moral egocentrism; (2) generosity due to immediate, automatic reciprocity; (3) generosity due to a "good boy/good girl" morality (desire to behave "good" in accordance with social norms); (4) conditioned generosity (sharing has social meaning and depends on the relation between people); (5) generosity due to empathy; and (6) functional generosity due to the value of positive justice (sharing is conceived as a derivative of the general moral value of positive justice, a value than enhances social relations among people).

Levin and Bekerman-Greenberg (1980) found that older children tended to use higher level justifications than did younger children. However, because age trends were examined as part of a larger analysis including reasoning about other situations, it is unclear whether or not the age-related changes were significant for reasoning in any given dilemma. Nonetheless, Levin and Bekerman-Greenberg's data are consistent with those of Blasi (in press) in that children's justifications became less egoistic and based more on relationships between people with age.

Kohlberg's "Responsibility" Dilemmas

Altruistic considerations are not central in Kohlberg's standard moral dilemmas. Moreover, even when prosocial issues have been embedded in Kohlberg's dilemmas, two duties, values, or norms are presented as being in direct conflict (e.g., norms against killing versus stealing). However, in real life, altruistic concerns are not always, or even usually, in direct conflict with other nonaltruistic norms or values; they merely conflict with nonmoral, self-oriented personal goals.

In a recent paper, Kohlberg and his colleagues (Higgins, Powers, & Kohlberg, 1984) considered, for the first time, dilemmas in which the issue of caring was salient, and was in conflict with self-interest or responsibility to the self. More specifically, they discussed moral reasoning concerning the following dilemma:

The college Harry applied to had scheduled an interview with him for the coming Saturday at 9:00 am. As the college was 40 miles away from Harry's town and Harry had no way of getting there, his guidance counselor agreed to drive him. The Friday before the interview the guidance counselor told Harry that his car had broken down and was in the repair shop until Monday. He said he felt badly but there was no way he could drive him to his interview. He still wanted to help him out, so he went to Harry's homeroom and asked the students if there was anyone who could drive Harry to the college. No one volunteered to drive him. A lot of students in the class think Harry shows off and talks too much, and they do not like him. The homeroom teacher says he has to take his children to the dentist at that time. Some students say they cannot use the family car, others work, some do not have their licenses. One student, Billy, knows he can use his family car but wonders whether he should do something for Harry when the few students in class who know him best say they are busy or just cannot do it. Besides, he would have to get up really early on a Saturday morning, the only morning during the week he can sleep late.

1. Should Billy volunteer to drive Harry to college? Why or why not? [p. 82].

Higgins et al. (1984) found that students' reasoning about such a dilemma was not necessarily similar to reasoning in response to the standard Kohlberg dilemmas. They coded the students' responses to the caring dilemma primarily

TABLE 7.2
Stages of Responsibility Judgments[a]

Stage 1. Responsibility and obligation are seen as being the same. The person feels compelled to fulfill the commands of superiors or authority figures or the rules given by them.

Stage 2. Responsibility is differentiated from obligation from this stage onward. The person is responsible only to and for him/herself and his or her welfare, property, and goals.

Stage 2/3. There is a recognition that everyone is responsible to and for themselves, their welfare, property, and goals. Persons who are irresponsible or careless lose some of the right to have themselves, their welfare, and so on, respected. For example, being careless mitigates the right to have one's property respected as well as justifying a lessened concern for the person's welfare.

Stage 3. Responsibility for the self is to do the "good" thing, to live up to generally known and accepted standards of a "good person." Responsibility to others is limited to those with whom one has a personal relationship and is defined as meeting their needs or promoting their welfare.

Stage 3/4. Responsibility is seen more as a process for maintaining and enhancing feelings of closeness and affection in personal relationships. Being irresponsible is defined as "hurting the other's feelings" within a relationship and is considered a valid basis for a lessened concern of the other's welfare.

Stage 4. Responsibility is seen as a mutually binding set of feelings and agreements among people in relationships, groups, or communities. Being responsible for the self means one must act out of dependability, trustworthiness, and loyalty regardless of fluctuating feelings among people. Irresponsibility on the part of those people within the same group does not mitigate concern for their welfare or rights by other group members.

[a]Adapted from Higgins et al. (1984).

on the dimension of responsibility (to self or other; see Table 7.2), and found that high-school students frequently expressed lower level moral judgment when discussing the caring dilemma than when discussing standard dilemmas. From their examples, it appears that responsibility to self, often expressed in terms that appear rather hedonistic, frequently lowered an individual's reasoning about caring dilemmas. Quite likely, if Higgins et al.'s subjects had been younger, evidence of egoistic considerations would have been even clearer.

Higgins et al. (1984) also found that high-school students' moral reasoning about the caring dilemma was influenced by the social norms in their school. In alternative schools in which a sense of community was emphasized, students were relatively likely to refer to norms related to helping. Thus, alternative high schools' students' responsibility-related moral reasoning was somewhat higher than that of regular high-school students, although students from different schools did not differ on reasoning concerning the standard Kohlberg dilemmas.

Based on Higgins' and her colleagues' work (Higgins et al., 1984), one can conclude that responsibility for others, responsibility for the self, self-concern, norms related to helping, and the nature of helping in relationships are central issues in adolescents' moral reasoning about dilemmas in which the conflict is between helping another and one's own wishes or needs. Moreover, it appears that the level of this type of reasoning is influenced by the adolescent's social environment. However, because of the limited number of dilemmas and the small age range of the subjects, Higgins et al.'s finding must be considered as preliminary.

"Ethic of Caring"

Carol Gilligan (1977, 1979, 1982) has suggested that one reason that prosocial values such as caring have been assigned a relatively minor role in Kohlberg's schema of moral judgment is that Kohlberg's schema was based on the moral judgments of males. In her view, due to the differential socialization of males and females, males and females typically develop two different approaches to morality: an ethic of justice and rights and an ethic of caring and responsibility. The masculine approach, the ethic of justice and rights, is viewed as an expression of autonomy and the "individuated self"; the emphasis in morality is on how to exercise one's own rights without interfering with the rights of others. In contrast, the ethic of care and responsibility (the feminine approach) is viewed as developing from the individual's feelings of interconnectedness with others. The focus of this mode of morality is on how to lead a moral life that includes obligations to the self, the family, and people in general. This approach is guided by the goal of minimizing the harm done overall, and results in a focus on helping others, relationships, and the specific details of concrete situations in which moral dilemmas are embedded.

Gilligan (1982) has outlined a sequence of development for the ethic of caring. At the first level, the focus is on caring for the self, and relationships are viewed in self-serving terms. This period is followed by a transitional phase in which such concerns are criticized as selfish. This criticism "signals a new understanding of the connection between self and others which is articulated by the concept of responsibility [p. 74]." At the second level, good is equated with caring for others, and the self's own concerns are often subjugated. Indeed, concern with one's own needs tends to be viewed as selfish. The third level is viewed as developing out of the disequilibrium created by the problems in unequal, self-sacrifical relationships. Its focus is on the dynamics of relationships, and the interconnectedness of self and other. One is responsible for relationships, the quality of which depends on meeting the needs of both self and other. In Gilligan's words: "Care becomes the self-chosen principle of a judgment that remains psychological in its concern with relationships and response but becomes universal in its condemnation of exploitation and hurt [p. 74]."

Gilligan's (1971, 1979, 1982) theory has received considerable attention. It is not surprising, therefore, that some investigators have disagreed with Gilligan's assertions (e.g., Brabeck, 1983; Broughton, 1983; Code, 1983; Colby & Damon, 1983; Kohlberg et al., 1983; Nails, 1983; O'Loughlin, 1983). For example, Higgins et al. (1984), Nunner-Winkler (1984), and Colby and Damon (1983) believe that Gilligan's morality of caring can be assimilated into Kohlberg's scheme of moral judgment. In Nunner-Winkler's (1984) view, Gilligan's two ethical approaches are not differences in ethical position, but in emphasis on one versus the other of two categories of moral duties. These two types of duties are perfect duties (i.e., duties of omission such as do not kill, steal, etc.) and imperfect duties (i.e., duties of commission that do not prescribe specific acts but only formulate a maxim to guide action, e.g., practice charity). Higgins et al.'s (1984) response to Gilligan was simply to assimilate Gilligan's ethic of caring into Kohlberg's scheme by constructing stages of responsibility within his system.

Most relevant for our purposes is a critical analysis of the contribution of Gilligan's (1977, 1979, 1982) work to an understanding of altruism. A first consideration is the data base upon which many of Gilligan's conclusions are based. Most of her sample were part of Gilligan and Belenky's (1980) research on women's moral reasoning about the issue of abortion. Additional data were obtained from interviews in which women were asked questions such as "Why be moral?" and "How would you describe yourself to yourself?" Although Gilligan has claimed to assess moral reasoning related to caring, it is important to note that the issue of abortion does not necessarily have to be interpreted as a prosocial dilemma, that is, as a conflict between one's own needs and desires and those of another. In some circumstances, the individual needs of all individuals (the pregnant woman, fetus, and other significant individuals) can be met by a single course of action. For example, if the pregnant woman truly desires her unborn child even though she has some ambivilence, her needs and those of the fetus are consistent. Similarly, one could argue that bringing an unwanted child into the world is not acting in a manner consistent with the child's needs; in such a situation one could view the fetus' needs as consistent with those of the woman desiring an abortion. More important, however, is the fact that many people do not consider abortion a moral issue (because a young fetus is not viewed as a living human being); consequently, the issue of abortion may be viewed as a personal decision or a decision based on social conventional concerns, not a moral decision (cf. Turiel, 1983; Turiel & Smetana, 1984). Indeed, as was noted by Nunner-Winkler (1984), many of Gilligan's interviewees focused on morally neutral issues such as a choice between life-styles when discussing the abortion decision. This was true even for some women who were viewed by Gilligan as expressing the highest level of the ethic of caring. What was termed by Gilligan as a woman's attending to her responsibility to herself could often be interpreted as the woman's considering the issue of "What kind of life do I want to lead?"

Despite the fact that the issue of abortion may not be viewed as a moral dilemma by many persons, Gilligan and Belenky's (1980) work is of some relevance to an understanding of altruism. For those interviewees who considered abortion a moral issue, the consideration of another's welfare (be it the fetus', father's, or someone else's) was frequently a central concern. Thus, it can be concluded that altruistic concerns are frequently important in women's moral judgments, at least in some situations. Indeed, Gilligan apparently found that women expressed much more concern for others than is typically found in moral-judgment interviews involving Kohlberg's standard interview (although this finding has been questioned by other writers, e.g., Broughton, 1983; Nails, 1983).

Gilligan (1977, 1979, 1982) claimed that the difference between Kohlberg's findings and her own is due primarily to differences in samples (males versus females). However, it is quite possible that the difference in emphasis was due to a variety of other factors including differences in: (1) the content of Kohlberg's and Gilligan's moral dilemmas (see, however, Lyons, 1983, and Gibbs, Arnold, & Burkhart, 1984); (2) the respondent's point of view (third person in the Kohlberg interview; first person in Gilligan's); and (3) the reality of the situation (real-life or hypothetical). Moreover, Gilligan's subjects frequently were responding to the concrete issue of "What will *you* do?" (deonitic or practical reasoning; cf. Higgins et al., 1984), not to the prescriptive questions (e.g., "What should *he* do?") typical in Kohlberg's procedure. Researchers have found that reasoning about practical, everyday situations (Leming, 1976), first-person reasoning (Eisenberg-Berg & Neal, 1981; Weiss, 1982), and reasoning about real-life situations (Blotner & Bearison, 1980; Damon, 1977) is somewhat lower than deonitic, third-person, and hypothetical moral reasoning; thus, one would expect some difference between Kohlberg's and Gilligan's findings based merely on the structure of the interviews. Nonetheless, it is likely that the differing content of Kohlberg's and Gilligan's dilemmas is an important cause of the differences in their findings. We will return to this issue of prosocial versus justice or prohibition-related content shortly.

Positive Justice (Distributive Justice)

In the research derived from Kohlberg's scheme of moral judgment, the issue of positive or distributive justice—that is, how one makes decisions related to the distribution of commodities or privileges—has seldom been examined. However, because dilemmas concerning positive justice often involve potential prosocial or altruistic actions, some of the research on moral reasoning about positive justice is of relevance to the topic of altruistic cognitions.

To our knowledge, the earliest empirical investigations concerning moral reasoning about positive aspects of morality were conducted by Jean Piaget (1965). In his book *The Moral Judgment of the Child*, Piaget published a series of studies, most of which concerned children's cognitions about prohibition-related aspects of morality (e.g., rules, wrongdoing, and punishment). However, one section of his book is concerned with distributive (as well as retributive) justice.

To assess children's moral judgments about distributive and retributive justice, Piaget presented children with stories and questions related to the stories. In only one of these stories did the questions directly concern the possibility of prosocial behavior (helping another at some cost). Piaget's story was as follows:

A mother is on the lake in a little boat with her children. At four o'clock she gives them each a roll. One of the boys starts playing the fool at the end of the boat. He leans right over the boat and lets his roll fall in. What should be done to him? Should he have nothing to eat, or should they each have given him a little piece of theirs? [p. 269].

This story was designed to pit the issue of retributive justice against that of distributive justice. Piaget interviewed children aged 6–12 regarding the story and found that only 43% of the 6–8-year-old children believed that the boy who dropped his roll should be given more to eat (should be treated equally as the consequence of sharing rather than punished). In contrast, 75% of the 9–12-year-olds favored equality over punishment. These data were consistent with Piaget's (1965) overall findings; in general, he noted that children increasingly favored equality over retributive justice (even if the creation of conditions of equality did not involve prosocial behavior) with age.

Between 1932 and the 1970s, research on the topic of children's moral reasoning regarding the positive aspects of distributive justice was virtually nonexistent. However, in the mid- to late 1970s, investigators' interest in this type of moral judgment was sparked by the research of William Damon (1975, 1977, 1980, 1981; also see Enright, Enright, & Lapsley, 1981; Enright, Enright, Mannheim, & Harris, 1980; Enright, Franklin, & Mannheim, 1980; Kurdek, 1980; Larson & Kurdek, 1979; Levin & Bekerman-Greenberg, 1980). Damon's work, although pertaining to positive justice (distributive justice), is only tangentially concerned with reasoning regarding altruism (or even prosocial behavior in general). Consider the following dilemma that Damon (1977) used to elicit children's moral judgment:

Here are four little children just about your age [pictures are shown]. Well, actually, George here is a couple of years younger than the other three. Let's pretend that they were at school one day when their teacher, Miss Townsend, asked them to go outside with a couple of men. The men told the four kids that they really liked bracelets made by little children, and they asked the kids if they would make some bracelets for them. The kids spent about 15 or 20 minutes making lots of bracelets for the men. Michele, here, made a whole lot of bracelets, more than anyone else, and hers were the prettiest ones too. John and Ellen made some nice bracelets too; and, as you can see, John is the biggest boy there. George, the younger kid, didn't do so well. He only made half of a bracelet, and it was not very pretty.

Well, one of the men thanked them all for making bracelets, and put before them 10 candy bars, which he said was their reward for making the bracelets. But he said that the kids would have to decide what the best way was to split up the candy bars between themselves. Let's pretend that these are the 10 candy bars [represent with poker chips]. How do you think the kids should split them up between themselves?
1. Should Michele get some extra for making the most and the prettiest? Is that fair? Why?

2. Should John get some extra for being the biggest boy? Is that fair? Why? What about Ellen?
3. Should George, the younger kid, get less than the other kids because he didn't do so well? Is that fair? Why?
4. Should the boys get more than the girls? Or should the girls get more than the boys? Why?
5. What's the best way to divide the candy bars? Why is that a good way?
6. What if you were . . . [the kid who made the most, the biggest boy, girl; ask about each question in turn]? Would you think that this was the best way to split them up? Why? [pp. 64–65]

Additional elaborations and probes can also be included in the interview, including a few related to altruism (e.g., "Why do you share with people? How many of your things should you share? [p. 68])".

Damon's (1977) dilemmas primarily concern the concept of justice, for example, issues of fairness, equity, and equality. Altruism is less central because other valid criteria for the division of goods (e.g., differences in age and performance) are embedded in the dilemma; moreover, in the dilemmas, no one person really "owns" the objects to be distributed. Indeed, altruistic concerns are central to only one of Damon's six levels (and sublevels) of positive justice reasoning used to code the judgments of children aged 4–8. In specific, at Damon's lowest level (Level 0-A), positive justice choices derive from the child's wish that an act occur. The child simply asserts choices rather than attempting to justify them (e.g., "I should get it because I want it"). At Level 0-B, choices still reflect the child's desires but are now justified on the basis of external, observable realities such as size, sex, or other physical characteristics of persons (e.g., "We should get the most because we're the biggest"). Such justifications are used in a fluctuating manner, and are self-serving in the end. At Level 1-A, positive justice choices are based on the notion of strict equality (everyone should get the same). The child's justifications are consistent with this principle but are unilateral and inflexible. At Level 1-B, the child's positive justice choices are based upon the notion of reciprocity in actions; in other words, the child believes that people should be paid back in kind for doing good or bad things. Notions of merit and equity are evident; those who work hardest or contribute the most should get more. At Level 2-A, cognitions conducive to altruism finally emerge. At this level, the child develops a moral relativity based on the understanding that different persons can have different but equally valid claims, and that the claims of persons with special needs (e.g., who are poor) are weighted most heavily. However, the child also attempts quantitative compromises between competing claims (e.g., he should get the most, but she should also get some).[1]

---

[1]It is important to note, however, that Blotner and Bearison (1984) found virtually no 2-A reasoning in their sample of children in grades K to 5. Thus, altruistic concerns seldom were foremost among the children's considerations.

Finally, at the highest level (Level 2-B), children coordinate the considerations of equality and reciprocity so that they take into account the claims of various persons and the demands of the specific situation. Children's choices reflect their recognition that all persons should be given their due (Damon, 1977).

Damon's (1977) stages of moral judgment have, in general, been found to be positively related to age in the elementary-school years (e.g., Blotner & Bearison, 1984; Damon, 1977, 1980; Enright et al., 1980, 1981; Kurdek, 1980; Larson & Kurdek, 1979; Levin & Bekerman-Greenberg, 1980). Thus, based on Damon's stages, one would expect older elementary-school children to be more likely than younger children to consider another's need (and less likely to consider only their own needs) when making decisions concerning positive justice. However, older elementary-school children are also more likely than younger children to consider other formal criteria such as merit when dividing goods. Thus, in the types of situations considered by Damon, one would expect increased concern with altruistic considerations with age, but perhaps only a small increase in truly altruistic behavior. This is because other valid criteria or values for distribution besides one's own or others' needs and wants are salient in Damon's dilemmas. Nonetheless, there are some preliminary data consistent with the conclusion that higher level reasoning on Damon's assessment procedure is positively related to prosocial behavior (Blotner & Bearison, 1984).

In summary, Damon's (1977) positive-justice dilemmas, like Kohlberg's dilemmas, allow for the possibility of altruistic concerns. However, they do not reflect the types of situations in which issues related to altruism are the central focus, and altruism is likely to be the normatively desirable response. In Damon's dilemmas, the issues of deservedness and fairness are foremost; the issue of others' needs is brought into the dilemma only by indicating that one particular story character is needy (e.g., poor). Moreover, the commodity to be divided is not the sole property of any one person, so decisions regarding distribution will often be based upon cognitions regarding the expectations and desires of other persons with claims on the commodity (e.g., the person who did the most work would probably expect at least a fair share of payment, if not more). Thus, although Damon's work has contributed much to our understanding of children's conceptions of fairness, its usefulness in understanding cognitions about helping is relatively limited.

Prosocial Moral Reasoning

Both Higgins et al.'s (1984) and Gilligan's (1977, 1979, 1982) data provide some evidence that caring and altruistic considerations are frequently verbalized by adolescents and adults when reasoning about dilemmas in which another's welfare is salient. Moreover, both Higgins et al. and Gilligan view an egoistic, self-focused orientation as the initial, developmentally immature level of moral reasoning about caring dilemmas. Neither Kohlberg nor Gilligan, however, has examined younger children's moral reasoning about caring dilemmas, or developmental change in judgment prior to mid-adolescence. The primary goal of our own research program on moral reasoning has been to examine these issues.

At the time this research was begun, Kohlberg seemed to be asserting that his stages of moral judgment applied to moral reasoning about all types of moral conflicts. However, at that time, the only moral dilemmas studied by Kohlberg were those few in his set of standard dilemmas. As was discussed previously, altruism, if a relevant choice at all in these dilemmas, is generally embedded in a context in which assisting another constitutes a violation of a prohibition.

From Kohlberg's perspective, the crucial difference between his standard dilemmas and those of Gilligan (1977, 1982) and ourselves is in the focus on responsibility and caring. We would agree with this analysis. However, Kohlberg also has asserted that the difference in dilemmas is primarily in relation to reasoning about special relationships, for example, in regard to family, friends, and members of our social group (Kohlberg et al., 1983, pp. 20–21) and responsibility in relationships. Although it is true that the issue of caring is accentuated in personal relationships and that people, especially children, often apply principles related to caring more readily to those with a connection to the self (Eisenberg, 1983a), relationships are *not* central to reasoning elicited by our dilemmas. Indeed, our prosocial dilemmas were constructed in a manner that de-emphasizes personal relationships; the story protagonist in our dilemmas never has a close relationship with the potential recipient of aid. The fact that we find a relatively small amount of reasoning in which subjects refer to relationships attests to our success in minimizing the emphasis on relationships in our dilemmas (Eisenberg et al., 1983; Eisenberg-Berg, 1979a; Eisenberg-Berg & Roth, 1980). Thus, we feel that the primary difference between reasoning elicited by Kohlberg's and our own dilemmas is not with regard to reasoning about caring within relationships; the difference is in the emphasis on the enhancement of the welfare of others versus issues of justice (e.g., fairness). Nevertheless, it is clear that some individuals will respond to prosocial dilemmas on the basis of justice considerations; for example, they may interpret not assisting another as inflicting unwarranted harm or as perpetuating an injustice.

Given Kohlberg's emphasis on justice and perfect duties rather than caring, we were uncertain whether or not his scheme of moral reasoning was applicable to moral reasoning about prosocial behavior. Thus, in the mid-1970s, we began a program of research focusing on what we have called prosocial moral judgment, that is, moral reasoning about dilemmas in which one person's needs, wants, or desires conflict with those of another in a context in which the role of laws, rules, punishment, authorities and their dictates, formal obligations, and other formal criteria is irrelevant or minimized. Our goal was to delineate age-related changes in this type of judgment in childhood in the hope of gaining a better understanding of the conscious cognitions associated with prosocial behavior.

In pursuit of this goal, we and our colleagues have conducted a series of studies on prosocial moral judgment: some longitudinal, others crosssectional or involving only one group (Eisenberg, Boehnke, Schuhler, & Silbereisen, 1985; Eisenberg, Lennon, & Roth, 1983; Eisenberg, Pasternack, Cameron, & Tryon, 1984; Eisenberg, Pasternack, & Lennon, 1984; Eisenberg-Berg, 1979a, b; Eisenberg-Berg & Hand, 1979; Eisenberg-Berg & Neal, 1981; Eisenberg-Berg & Roth, 1980). The typical procedure in this research has been to present children or adolescents with four prosocial dilemmas, and to elicit their reasoning regarding these dilemmas (in private, individual interviews). In each dilemma, the needs or wants of one individual are in direct conflict with those of another individual or group in a context in which the roles of prohibitions, punishments, authorities, and other formal criteria/obligations are irrelevant or minimized. An example of such a dilemma used with younger children (preschool and elementary-school age) is as follows:

One day a girl (boy) named Mary (Eric) was going to a friend's birthday party. On her (his) way she (he) saw a girl (boy) who had fallen down and hurt her (his) leg. The girl asked Mary to go to her house and get her parents so the parents could come and take her to the doctor. But if Mary did run and get the child's parents, she would be late for the birthday party and miss the ice cream, cake, and all the games. What should Mary do? Why?

Research Findings: Crosssectional Data.   In an initial crosssectional study involving 125 second, fourth, sixth, ninth, eleventh, and twelfth graders, we examined developmental changes in children's reasoning about prosocial dilemmas (Eisenberg-Berg, 1979b; Mussen & Eisenberg-Berg, 1977). The children's reasoning was coded into a variety of categories, many of which resemble aspects of Kohlberg's stages (examples of some of the categories are presented in Table 7.3).

Justifications used to support the decision to assist were coded separately from those used to justify the decision not to assist. Summary scores for each category of justification used across the four dilemmas ranged from 1 (no use of a category) to 4 (a category of major concern; see Table 7.4). Interrater reliability for scoring of individual categories (computed for 37 protocols) was .70 for all but three categories (*considerations for helping:* stereotype of majority behavior, $\rho = .48$; *considerations against helping;* hedonistic gain, $\rho = .66$, direct reciprocity, $\rho = .69$). Test/retest reliability was computed over a 2-week period for 22 high-school students (for all categories with a mean of 1.1 or higher for either elementary- or high-school students) and was above .60 for all categories (combined across reasons for helping and not helping) except direct reciprocity (.52), pragmatic (.46), humanness (.52), sympathetic orientation (.46), role-taking (.44), positive affect related to consequences (.41), negative affect related to consequences

TABLE 7.3
Prosocial Moral-reasoning Categories[a]

1. *Obsessive and/or magical view of authority and/or punishments:* Avoidance of punishment and unquestioning deference to power are valued in their own right. The physical consequences of action determine its goodness regardless of human values and needs. Example: "If he didn't help, someone would find out and punish him."

2. *Hedonistic reasoning.*
   (a) *Pragmatic, hedonistic gain to the self:* Orientation to gain for oneself (besides gain resulting from direct reciprocity). Example: "She wouldn't help because she'd want to go to the party."
   (b) *Direct reciprocity:* Orientation to personal gain due to direct reciprocity (or lack of it) from the recipient of an act. Example: "She'd help because they'd give her food the next time she needed it."
   (c) *Affectional relationship:* Individuals' identifications with another, their liking for the other, and the other's relation to one's own needs are important considerations in the individual's moral reasoning. Example: "She'd share because she'd probably have friends in the town."

3. *Nonhedonistic pragmatism:* Orientation to practical concerns that are not directly related to either selfish considerations or the other's need. Example: "I'd help because I'm strong."

4. *Concern for others' needs (needs-oriented reasoning).*
   (a) *Concern for others' physical and material needs:* Orientation to the physical and material needs of the other person. Examples: "He needs blood," or "She's hurt."
   (b) *Concern for others' psychological needs:* Orientation to the psychological needs and affective states of the other person. Example: "They'd be happy if they had food."

5. *Reference to and concern with humanness:* Orientation to the fact that the other is human, living, a person. Example: He's help because "they're human," or "they are people, too."

6. *Stereotyped reasoning.*
   (a) *Stereotypes of a good or bad person:* Orientation to stereotyped images of a good or bad person. Example: A child would help because "it's nice."
   (b) *Stereotyped images of majority behavior:* Orientation to "natural" behavior and what most people would do. Example: "It's only natural to help."
   (c) *Stereotyped images of others and their roles:* Orientation to stereotyped image of others and what others do. Example: "I'd help because farmers are nice people."

7. *Approval and interpersonal orientation:* Orientation to others' approval and acceptance in deciding what is the correct behavior. Example: "They'd like her if she helped."

8. *Overt empathic orientations.*
   (a) *Sympathetic orientation:* Expression of sympathetic concern and caring for others. Examples: "He would feel sorry for them," "She'd be concerned."
   (b) *Role taking:* The individual takes the perspective of the other and explicitly uses this perspective in personal reasoning. Examples: "I'my trying to put myself in her shoes," or "She'd know how it feels."

9. *Internalized affect.*
   (a) *Simple internalized positive affect and positive affect related to consequences:* The individual simply states that he or she would "feel good" as a result of a particular course of action without giving a reason, or says that the consequences of his or her act for the other person would inspire good feelings. The affect must be used in a context that appears internalized. Example: "She'd help because seeing the villiagers fed would make her feel good."
   (b) *Internalized positive affect from self-respect and living up to one's values:* Orientation to feeling good as the result of living up to internalized values. Example: "I'd feel good knowing that I had lived up to my principles."
   (c) *Internalized negative affect over consequences of behavior:* Concern with feeling bad or

TABLE 7.3 (*continued*)

guilty due to the consequences of an act. Example: "She would feel guilty because the girl was hurt."

(d) *Internalized negative affect due to loss of self-respect and/or not living up to one's values*: Orientation to feeling bad as the result of not living up to internalized values. Example: "He'd think badly of himself if he didn't do the right thing."

10. *Other abstract and/or internalized types of reasoning.*

(a) *Internalized law, norm, and value orientation*: Orientation to an internalized responsibility, duty, or need to uphold the laws and accepted norms or values. Examples: "She has a duty to help needy others," or "He'd feel he had a responsibility to assist because of his values."

(b) *Concern with the rights of others*: Orientation to protecting individual rights and preventing injustices that violate another's rights. Example: "I'd help because her right to walk down the street was being violated."

(c) *Generalized reciprocity*: Orientation to indirect reciprocity in a society (i.e., exchange that is not one-to-one but eventually benefits all). Example: "If everyone helps one another, we'd all be better off."

(d) *Concern with the condition of society*: Orientation to improving the society or community as a whole. Example: "If everyone helps, society would be a lot better."

"Less frequently used categories such as those related to equality of individuals and social contract are omitted (See Eisenberg [1977] and Eisenberg-Berg [1979a]). Adapted from Eisenberg-Berg, 1979a.

(.42), and condition of society (.27). (As will be discussed later, test/retest for overall moral orientation was much higher.) Alpha coefficients computed for each category of reasoning with a mean above 1.1 (on a 1–4 scale) for either elementary- or high-school students ranged from .19 to .85 (see Table 7.4). Although the alphas for the internalized affect categories were, in general, relatively low, the alpha for all types of internalized affect (all four categories combined) was .64. Given that (1) the four dilemmas differed considerably in content; (2) the children could verbalize any of many types of reasoning; and (3) there were only four dilemmas (i.e., four items per category), it is surprising that as many of the alpha coefficients were as high as they were.

To examine the interrelations of the various moral consideration categories, correlations and a factor analysis were computed for the categories used to justify prosocial action. Only the consideration categories used to explain why someone should assist were subjected to the factor analysis because all but four subjects used primarily hedonistic reasoning when resolving the dilemmas in favor of not assisting the needy other. As can be seen in Table 7.5, the first factor in the factor analysis seemed to be organized on a more-mature versus less-mature axis. Factor 2 contained the moral considerations related to internalized values and norms and self-respect for one's behavior in regard to these values or norms. The category "stereotype of majority behavior" was positively associated with the internalized categories; however, this association was due to the responses

TABLE 7.4
Moral Consideration Categories: Means and Alpha Coefficients

Category	2nd	4th	6th	9th	11th	12th	Alpha[a]
			Means by Grade Level				
			Positive consideration[b]				
Hedonistic gain	1.37	2.04	1.30	1.32	1.32	1.48	.65
Direct reciprocity	1.86	1.89	1.64	1.79	1.41	1.52	.49
Affectional relationship	1.35	1.05	1.11	1.12	1.14	1.08	.49
Pragmatic	1.19	1.25	1.18	1.29	1.18	1.17	.20
Concern for others' physical needs	3.12	2.80	3.18	3.56	3.21	3.16	.50
Concern for others' psychological needs	1.54	1.66	1.48	2.20	1.91	1.68	.59
Reference to humanness	1.07	1.46	1.48	1.92	1.42	1.76	.73
Stereotype of good/bad person	3.15	1.99	1.72	1.48	1.37	1.28	.76
Stereotype of majority behavior	1.00	1.05	1.00	1.16	1.27	1.12	.42
Approval/interpersonal orientation	2.46	2.10	1.96	2.28	1.82	1.76	.68
Sympathetic orientation	1.00	1.25	1.61	1.44	1.87	1.58	.57
Role-taking	1.19	1.60	1.88	2.40	2.50	2.36	.64
Simple internalized positive affect and positive affect related to consequences	1.07	1.10	1.29	1.34	1.69	1.44	.19
Internalized positive affect from self-respect/living up to values	1.00	1.00	1.06	1.36	1.41	1.56	.43
Internalized negative affect over consequences of behavior	1.07	1.05	1.34	2.04	2.13	1.88	.51
Internalized negative affect due to loss of self-respect/not living up to values	1.00	1.00	1.00	1.08	1.32	1.52	.69
Internalized law, norm, and value orientation	1.00	1.00	1.06	1.48	2.28	2.28	.85
Concern with rights of others	1.00	1.00	1.00	1.04	1.05	1.24	.53
Generalized reciprocity	1.35	1.00	1.32	1.20	1.64	1.36	.47
Concern with condition of society	1.00	1.05	1.25	1.20	1.32	1.40	.60
			Negative considerations[c]				
Hedonistic gain to self	3.82	3.90	3.90	4.00	3.95	3.70	
Direct reciprocity	1.96	1.16	1.00	1.16	1.00	1.19	
Affectional relationship	1.54	2.84	2.80	2.84	2.45	2.79	
Hedonism with socially acceptable rationalization	1.00	1.28	1.20	1.47	1.67	1.45	
Approval/interpersonal orientation	1.00	1.42	1.00	1.00	1.00	1.07	

[a]Alpha coefficients were computed after combining scores for a single category across reasons for and against helping.

[b]These means were computed including only those individuals who decided for helping in at least one dilemma.

[c]These means were computed including only those individuals who decided against helping in at least one dilemma.

Adapted from Eisenberg-Berg (1979a). Copyright 1979 by the American Psychological Association. Adapted with permission of the publisher.

TABLE 7.5
Positive Moral Consideration Categories: Factors[a]

Category	Factor 1[b]	Factor 2[c]	Factor 3[d]
Direct reciprocity	− .38		
Concern with others' physical and material needs		.31	.49
Concern with others' psychological needs			.50
Reference to and concern with humanness	.33		.57
Stereotype of good/bad person	− .53		
Stereotype of majority behavior		− .44	
Approval/interpersonal orientation	− .42		
Sympathetic orientation			.39
Role-taking	.38		.40
Simple internalized positive affect and positive affect over consequences			.52
Internalized positive affect from self-respect and living up to one's values	.46	− .56	
Internalized negative affect over consequences of behavior	.41		.67
Internalized negative affect due to loss of self-respect and not living up to one's values	.43	− .40	
Internalized law, norm, and value orientation	.79	− .42	.29
Concern with rights of others	.40		
Generalized reciprocity	.38		
Concern with the condition of society	.29		.33

[a]Adapted from Eisenberg-Berg, 1979a.
[b]Factor 1 = high/low axis.
[c]Factor 2 = highly internalized.
[d]Factor 3 = emphathic.
Copyright 1979 by the American Psychological Association. Adapted with permission of the publisher.

of only a few individuals because this category was used very infrequently. Factor 3 was clearly an empathic factor involving role-taking and concern for others (and the consequences of one's behavior on others).

Although the hedonistic categories did not load heavily on any of the factors, two of the three hedonistic categories (direct reciprocity and pragmatic, hedonistic gain to the self) were significantly intercorrelated. The third hedonistic category, affectional relationship, was verbalized relatively infrequently. Moreover, when reasoning about the decision *not* to assist was considered, the various self-oriented, hedonistic categories were interrelated.

One especially interesting finding concerned needs-oriented reasoning (reasoning in which individuals simply oriented to and labeled others' needs when these needs conflicted with those of the story protagonist). This type of reasoning frequently has been labeled as Stage 2 in Kohlberg's system (or stage 1/2, 2, or 2/3 in Gibbs & Widaman's [1982] modification of Kohlberg's system, depending on the wording of the reasoning). We found that needs-oriented reasoning not only grouped with more sophisticated empathic reasoning categories in the factor analysis, but also was positively correlated with a number of these categories. In contrast, needs-oriented reasoning was unrelated or negatively correlated with the hedonistic, self-oriented categories of reasoning (Eisenberg-Berg, 1979a). These findings reinforced our belief that needs-oriented reasoning is a primitive mode of empathic reasoning, and is not analogous in developmental maturity to the egoistic or pragmatic categories of reasoning in Kohlberg's stage 2. Our more recent findings that (1) needs-oriented reasoning correlated with an index of empathy (Bryant, 1982) in 7–8-year-olds (Eisenberg, Pasternack, & Lennon, 1984); (2) needs-oriented reasoning is related to prosocial behavior (Eisenberg, Pasternack, & Lennon, 1984; Eisenberg, Boehnke, Schuhler, & Silbereisen, 1985; Eisenberg-Berg & Hand, 1979); and (3) needs-oriented and hedonistic reasoning generally are negatively related (e.g., Eisenberg, Boehnke, Schuhler, & Silbereisen, 1985; Eisenberg-Berg & Hand, 1979) are also consistent with the view that needs-oriented reasoning is a qualitatively different type of reasoning than the hedonistic and pragmatic types of reasoning grouped with it in Kohlberg's system.

As part of our own original crosssectional research (Eisenberg-Berg, 1979a), we also conducted multivariate and univariate linear trend analyses on the categories of considerations used to justify the decision to assist another. The results of the univariate analysis are presented in Table 7.6 (the multivariate F was significant at $p < .001$). The commonly used stereotypic category (stereotypes of good/bad persons and behaviors) and the approval/interpersonal orientation category decreased in usage with age as the children entered high school. In contrast, most of the more sophisticated self-reflective empathic and internalized affect and value categories were used more frequently with age. This is not surprising given the moral as well as cognitive sophistication of the latter categories; moreover, these findings are consistent with those of Kohlberg (1971, 1976).

In the linear trend analyses, the needs-oriented and hedonistic categories (when used to justify the decision to assist) did not decrease significantly in usage with age. However, according to additional chi-square analyses, these types of considerations dominated the reasoning of only the youngest children (see Eisenberg, 1977, for details). Clearly, the hedonistic categories were used more frequently by younger than older children when decisions both to assist and *not* to assist were considered.

Research Findings: Longitudinal Data.   In our early crosssectional research, it became clear that both hedonistic considerations and needs-oriented considerations (especially those related to physical and material rather than psychological needs) dominate the reasoning of preschool as well as young school-aged

TABLE 7.6
Positive Moral Consideration Categories:
Univariate Linear Trend Analyses

Moral Consideration Categories	$F(df = 1, 114)$	Direction of trends[a]
Direct reciprocity	3.61[b]	−
Reference to and concern with humanness	10.77[c]	+
Stereotype of good/bad person	39.70[c]	−
Stereotype of majority behavior	4.66[c]	+
Approval and interpersonal orientation	3.91[c]	−
Sympathetic orientation	11.04[c]	+
Role-taking	23.09[c]	+
Simple positive affect and positive affect related to consequences	11.72[c]	+
Internalized positive affect from self-respect and living up to one's values	19.59[c]	+
Internalized negative affect over consequences of behavior	37.34[c]	+
Internalized negative affect due to loss of self-respect and/or not living up to one's values	14.63[c]	+
Internalized law, norm, and value orientation	67.32[c]	+
Concern with the rights of others	7.41[d]	+
Generalized reciprocity	12.60[c]	+
Concern with the condition of society	6.97[d]	+

[a] "+" indicates that the category increases in frequency with age. "−" indicates a decrease with age.
[b] $= p < .10$
[c] $= p < .05$
[d] $= p < .01$
[e] $= p < .001$
Adapted from Eisenberg-Berg, 1979a.

children (e.g. Eisenberg-Berg, 1979a; Eisenberg-Berg & Hand, 1979; Eisenberg-Berg & Neal, 1981). However, in our crosssectional research, it was unclear whether one type of consideration was more mature developmentally.

As the result of an ongoing longitudinal study, it has been possible to chart age-related changes in moral reasoning from the preschool to elementary-school years. For example, in an initial 1 1/2 year longitudinal followup of 34 pre-schoolers (initially 4–5 years of age), Eisenberg-Berg and Roth (1980) found that use of hedonistic reasoning decreased significantly with age, whereas use of needs-oriented (physical and psychological combined) and approval-oriented/interpersonal considerations increased with age. Thus, it became clear that needs-oriented reasoning is empirically (as well as philosophically) a more developmentally mature type of moral consideration.

In additional followups of the same sample, we further examined the development of prosocial moral judgment in the elementary-school years. In the second longitudinal followup, 33 of the 34 children involved in the 1 1/2 year followup (Cohort 1) were reinterviewed 1 1/2 years later at age 7–8 (3 years after the initial interview). Moreover, a second longitudinal cohort (Cohort 2) of 16 5–6-year-olds was reinterviewed after a 1-year interval. A third group of 30 children (Cohort 3) of approximately the same age and background as the 7–8-year-old cohort was also interviewed for the first time; their moral judgment was compared with that of the primary cohort as a check for the effects of repeated testing (Eisenberg et al., 1983).

For coding the data, all interviews from the various cohorts and interview sessions (over the years) were mixed together and coded. This was done to ensure equivalent coding across all groups and interview sessions. For each of the moral consideration categories for each dilemma, the child was assigned a score indicating the frequency with which he or she used the category when discussing both the pros and cons of helping the needy other in the story (1 = no use of a category; 2 = vague, questionable use; 3 = clear use; 4 = a major type of reasoning used). The scores for each category were then summed across the four dilemmas, yielding summary scores ranging from 4 to 16 for each category of reasoning.

To examine for age changes in moral judgment in the longitudinal samples, multivariate and univariate analyses of variance with one between subjects factor (sex) and one within subjects factor (time of testing) were computed. For the 7–8 year olds (C_1), there were significant age-related changes for two categories of reasoning. Hedonistic reasoning, which had decreased in use from age 4–5 to 5 1/2–6 1/2, showed another significant decrement in use from age 5 1/2–6 1/2 to 7–8. Needs-oriented reasoning, which increased in use from age 4–5 to 5 1/2–6 1/2, was used significantly more by the children at 7–8 years of age than 1 1/2 years earlier. The same pattern of findings was obtained for the smaller cohort (C_2) tested after a 1-year interval; use of hedonistic reasoning decreased in frequency whereas the use of needs-oriented reasoning increased. Moreover, repeated testing did not seem to influence the children's moral reasoning; the 7–8-year-olds interviewed for the third time (C_1) differed from those interviewed for the first time (C_3) in scores for only two of the less frequently used categories of reasoning.

In 1982, 2 years after the second followup, children in the two longitudinal cohorts were reinterviewed (Eisenberg, Pasternack, & Lennon, 1984). The children in the primary cohort were 9–10 years of age, and the children in the smaller cohort were 7–8 years of age. The procedures for interviewing, scoring, and analysis were similar to those used previously. For the 9–10 year olds, there were significant decrements in hedonistic reasoning from ages 4–5 and 5 1/2–6 1/2 to age 9–10, but not from age 7–8 to 9–10 (although there was a nonsignificant decrease in use of hedonistic reasoning over this time period; see Table 7.7). Use of needs-oriented reasoning leveled off at age 9–10 and was used slightly less (nonsignificantly) than at age 7–8. However, the use of a number of other categories of reasoning increased over the 5-year period: pragmatic reasoning (from ages 4–5 and 7–8 to age 9–10), approval/interpersonal reasoning (from

TABLE 7.7
Moral Reasoning Categories: Means for Cohort 1[a]

Reasoning Categories	Time 1	Time 2	Time 3	Time 4
Authority/punishment	4.19	4.00	4.09	4.12
Hedonistic	12.12	8.66	6.31	5.88
Direct reciprocity	4.00	4.09	4.09	4.31
Affectional relationship	4.03	4.38	4.00	4.25
Pragmatism	4.12	4.47	4.28	5.03
Needs-oriented	8.53	11.59	13.62	13.12
Concern with humanness	4.00	4.25	4.12	4.25
Stereotypes of good/bad persons	4.50	4.31	4.68	5.12
Stereotypes of majority behavior	4.00	4.00	4.00	4.00
Stereotypes of others' roles	4.00	4.00	4.03	4.00
Approval/interpersonal	4.00	4.06	4.22	4.44
Sympathetic	4.00	4.03	4.00	4.19
Role-taking	4.00	4.00	4.06	4.59
Positive affect/simple or related to consequences	4.00	4.00	4.09	4.56
Positive affect regarding self-respect, etc.	4.00	4.00	4.09	4.03
Negative affect/simple or related to consequences	4.00	4.00	4.00	4.16
Negative affect regarding self-respect, etc.	4.00	4.00	4.00	4.06
Internalized law, norm, or value orientation	4.00	4.00	4.03	4.00
Generalized reciprocity	4.00	4.00	4.00	4.00
Condition of society	4.00	4.00	4.06	4.00
Concern with rights of others	4.00	4.00	4.00	4.03
Contractual orientation	4.00	4.00	4.00	4.00
Equality of humans	4.00	4.00	4.00	4.00

[a]Possible range = 4–16.

age 4–5 to 9–10), stereotypic reasoning (stereotypes of "good" and "bad" persons, from age 5 1/2–6 1/2 to age 9–10), and affectional relationship reasoning (from age 7–8 to 9–10). Moreover, two relatively sophisticated categories of reasoning (role taking and positive affect related to consequences) were used significantly more than at younger ages.

The results for the younger, smaller cohort were similar to those for the primary cohort at age 7–8. There was a decrement in the use of hedonistic reasoning over the 3-year period, and increments in needs-oriented and stereotypic reasoning. Moreover, a cohort of 9–10-year-olds (C_1) interviewed for the first time in 1982 did not differ in reasoning from the primary cohort; thus, there was no evidence of an effect of repeated testing.

Based on both the crosssectional and longitudinal research, we have delineated an age-related sequence of development of prosocial moral judgment. We view these levels as involving, to some degree, successively more advanced cognitive structures of sociomoral reasoning. However, we do not make Kohlberg's assumptions regarding universality, invariance of sequence, hierarchical sequencing, and homogeneity of the individual's reasoning (see Chapter 9 for more discussion of these issues).

The levels of prosocial reasoning are presented in Table 7.8. The lowest level has been found to be dominant in only the reasoning of preschool and elementary-school children; Levels 4b and 5 predominate in the reasoning of only a minority of high-school students. However, individuals do not reason exclusively at one level, or even at a given level and the adjacent levels. Even adolescents at Levels 4a, 4b, or 5 occasionally verbalize Level 1 reasoning when justifying the decision not to assist (Eisenberg-Berg, 1979a). Level of reasoning is relatively

TABLE 7.8
Levels of Prosocial Reasoning[a]

Level 1.   Hedonistic, self-focused orientation: The individual is concerned with self-oriented consequences rather than moral considerations. Reasons for assisting or not assisting another include consideration of direct gain to the self, future reciprocity, and concern for others because one needs and/or likes the other (due to the affectional tie.) (Predominant mode primarily for preschoolers and younger elementary-school children).

Level 2.   Needs-oriented orientation: The individual expresses concern for the physical, material, and psychological needs of others even though the other's needs conflict with one's own needs. This concern is expressed in the simplest terms, without clear evidence of self-reflective role taking, verbal expressions of sympathy, or reference to internalized affect such as guilt. (Predominate mode for many preschoolers and many elementary-school children).

Level 3.   Approval and interpersonal orientation and/or stereotyped orientation: Stereotyped images of good and bad persons and behaviors and/or considerations of other's approval and acceptance are used in justifying prosocial or nonhelping behaviors. (Predominant mode for some elementary- and high-school students.)

Level 4a: Self-reflective empathic orientation: The individual's judgments include evidence of self-reflective sympathetic responding or role taking, concern with the other's humanness, and/or guilt or positive affect related to the consequences of one's actions (predominant mode for a few older elementary-school children and many high-school students).

Level 4b: Transitional level: The individual's justifications for helping or not helping involve internalized values, norms, duties, or responsibilities, concern for the condition of the larger society, or refer to the necessity of protecting the rights and dignity of other persons; these ideas, however, are not clearly and strongly stated. (Predominant mode for a minority of people high-school age or older).

Level 5.   Strongly internalized stage: Justifications for helping or not helping are based on internalized values, norms, or responsibilities, the desire to maintain individual and societal contractual obligations or improve the condition of society, the belief in the dignity, rights, and equality of all individuals. Positive or negative affect related to the maintenance of self-respect for living up to one's own values and accepted norms also characterizes this stage. (Predominant mode for only a small minority of high-school students and no elementary-school children).

[a]Adapted from Eisenberg et al., 1983.

stable; test/retest reliability for high-school students' stage scores has been found to be 86% (exact agreement) over a 2-week period (reanalyzed data for 22 subjects from Eisenberg, 1977).

In summary, in both crosssectional and longitudinal research, we have found age-related changes in children's prosocial moral reasoning. A decrease in hedonistic reasoning occurs during the elementary school years, whereas needs-oriented reasoning increases until approximately age 7–8 (Eisenberg et al., 1983; Eisenberg, Pasternack, & Lennon, 1984). Moreover, stereotypic and approval-oriented concerns increase in use in the elementary-school years (Eisenberg, Pasternack, & Lennon, 1984), and then decrease in use into the high-school years (Eisenberg, 1977; Eisenberg-Berg, 1979a). The more sophisticated self-reflective, empathic categories (e.g., Level 4) are used occasionally in elementary school, and increase in frequency into the high-school years. Reasoning involving internalized values, principles, or responsibilities and affect associated with adherence to internalized values is very infrequent in elementary school (Eisenberg, Pasternack, & Lennon, 1984; Eisenberg-Berg, 1979a), and is salient in the reasoning of only a small minority of high-school students. For example, of 72 high-school students in one study (Eisenberg, 1977), only 17 were predominantly at Level 4b, whereas 12 were at Level 5. Thus, change in level of reasoning as well as type of reasoning (i.e., use of moral reasoning categories) has been found to be highly related to age.

The Relation Between Prosocial and Kohlbergian Moral Judgment

The nature of the empirical changes in reasoning described in our studies is consistent, on the whole, with prior research concerning moral judgment (e.g., Kohlberg, 1976; Rest, 1979). A self-focused or egoistic orientation has generally been viewed by psychologists as being morally immature. In contrast, an orientation to the approval and expectations of others and the adherence to global conceptions of societal norms and values has often been viewed as constituting an intermediate level of morality, one in which the individual is in the process of, or has achieved a moderate level of, internalization. A self-reflective orientation to others' welfare has also been viewed by Kohlberg (1969, 1971, 1976) and others (e.g., Gilligan, 1977) as a sign of at least a moderate level of moral development. Finally, concern with abstract ethical principles, the social system, imperatives of conscience, and meeting one's obligations has been viewed by Kohlberg (1976) and others (Gibbs & Widaman, 1982; Rest, 1979) as representing a relatively high level of development.

This is not to say that there are no differences between moral reasoning concerning prosocial and Kohlbergian moral dilemmas. Authority and punishment-oriented considerations, so evident in young children's reasoning in response to Kohlberg dilemmas, are virtually nonexistent in even preschoolers' prosocial moral judgment (Eisenberg, Pasternack, Cameron, & Tryon, 1984; Eisenberg-Berg & Hand, 1979; Eisenberg-Berg & Neal, 1981). Whether this difference is one of content or structure (i.e., do children use different types of Kohlberg's stage 1 reasoning in their prosocial judgments or do they fail to exhibit Kohlberg's stage 1) is not entirely clear, because the Kohlberg coding manual is not designed to code prosocial reasoning. Whatever the case may be, it is likely that children verbalize so few authority or punishment-oriented concerns because children, at least in this culture, are seldom punished for failing to assist another when they themselves have not caused the harm (Zahn-Waxler et al., 1979). Indeed, elementary-school children (but not kindergartners) seem to feel that acts such as stealing are governed by rules, but helping (and, to some degree, sharing) is not (Smetana, Bridgeman, & Turiel, 1983).

The degree and nature of the relation between prosocial and Kohlbergian moral reasoning is not clear. In our own studies, we generally have found a low to moderately high positive relation between the two aspects of moral judgment (Eisenberg, 1977; Eisenberg et al., 1983; Eisenberg, Pasternack, & Lennon, 1984; Eisenberg-Berg, 1976). However, whereas Higgs (1975) also noted a moderate association (.55 for a free-response index; .36 to .50 for objective responses) between first-year college students' reasoning on prosocial and Kohlberg stories, Kurdek (1981) found that high-school and college students' prosocial and Kohlberg moral judgment (as measured with Rest's [1979] objective instrument) were not significantly related.

Given the substantial modifications in Kohlberg's scoring system over the past 10 years, it is difficult to compare studies involving Kohlberg's dilemmas that they were conducted at different times. Indeed, because of the dramatic revisions in Kohlberg's schema in just the past few years, it is possible that the magnitude of the association between reasoning in response to prosocial dilemmas and reasoning concerning the standard Kohlberg dilemmas has changed from a few years ago. To our knowledge, the most recent comparison of the two aspects of moral judgment is that in our 5-year longitudinal followup. The Kohlberg data, when scored with the 1979 Kohlberg scoring manual (Colby et al., 1979), correlated .27 ($p < .03$) with level of prosocial reasoning for a sample of 9–10 year olds.

Data concerning the relative maturity of an individual's prosocial versus Kohlbergian reasoning, like those on the degree of correlation between the two types of reasoning, are inconsistent. We have found that children's prosocial reasoning tends to be somewhat more advanced than their Kohlbergian moral reasoning (Eisenberg, 1977). Similarly, Kurdek (1981) found that high-school and college students' prosocial moral judgment was more advanced than their reasoning concerning Kohlberg dilemmas. In contrast to these findings, Higgins et al. (1984) noted that high-school students' moral reasoning on prosocial dilemmas was either equally or less advanced than their reasoning on the standard Kohlberg dilemmas. Higgs (1975) obtained a similar pattern of findings for college students' free responses to prosocial and Kohlberg dilemmas; however, the pattern did not seem to hold when objective responses (subjects chose among predetermined reasons) were considered. Both Higgins et al. and Higgs used adaptations of Kohlberg's scoring system; thus, it is possible that their findings were influenced by the tendency for Kohlberg to score sympathetic, empathic reasoning as fairly immature unless embedded in a relatively abstract framework (cf. Gilligan, 1977, 1982). Another possible explanation for the inconsistencies in the data concerns age of the respondents; prosocial reasoning may be more advanced than Kohlbergian reasoning in childhood, whereas the reverse may be true in adulthood.

It is important to keep in mind that reasoning in response to the prosocial and Kohlberg dilemmas is scored with different systems. Kohlberg's most recent scoring system is more structurally based than is Eisenberg's (although the role of content in Kohlberg's scoring system is also obvious). More specifically, complexity of inferred perspective-taking is more central to scoring with Kohlberg's than Eisenberg's system. Thus, it is possible that individuals' responses to prosocial and Kohlberg dilemmas are more similar than the existing research would indicate; some of the difference in reasoning regarding prosocial and Kohlberg dilemmas could be due to discrepancies in scoring system. Indeed, there is some evidence to suggest that this is the case, especially for younger children's reasoning. Eisenberg et al. (1983) scored 7–8-year-olds' reasoning on two Kohlberg dilemmas with both Kohlberg's scoring system and their own system for scoring prosocial moral judgment.[2] Whereas the correlation between reasoning on prosocial and Kohlberg dilemmas was only .24 when the Kohlberg dilemmas were scored with Kohlberg's system, the association was .49 when reasoning on both types of dilemmas was coded with the prosocial scoring system. However, this pattern of findings did not hold at age 9–10. The latter finding may have occurred because the system for coding prosocial dilemmas does not contain a number of differentiations useful for scoring older children's judgments about prohibition-oriented moral dilemmas.

Other Research Regarding Developmental Change in Prosocial Moral Judgment

Although several researchers have examined prosocial moral reasoning in adolescence or adulthood (Eisenberg-Berg, 1979a; Higgins et al., 1984; Higgs, 1975; Kurdek, 1981), only a few besides Eisenberg have investigated developmental changes in prosocial moral judgment in childhood. Moreover, due to differences

---

[2]The correlations between the two scoring systems when both were used to score responses to Kohlberg dilemmas were .73 when the children were age 7–8 and .46 when the children were 9–10.

in methods and coding systems, the results of this research are difficult to compare with that of Eisenberg.

Reykowski (1977) reported the results of a study conducted by Zwolinski with 4–9-year-old Polish children. The children were told three stories; in two stories the children had to resolve a conflict between competing needs (e.g., there were three children at the river but only space for one in a canoe). Zwolinski found that the children's solutions for the hypothetical dilemmas became less self-interested with age. Moreover, other-oriented solutions increased in frequency until approximately age 5, then decreased with age. "Just" solutions, in which the child tried to reconcile the interests of all individuals, increased consistently with age. This pattern of findings is reminiscent of that discussed by Gilligan (Gilligan and Belenky, 1980) with regard to women's decisions concerning abortion.

In a study with Israeli children aged 5–12, Levin and Bekerman-Greenberg (1980) asked children to indicate if and why they would share pretzels with three kinds of potential recipients: (1) a peer who previously had refused to share crayons with the child; (2) a "bad" child who often disturbs lessons; and (3) a poor and needy child. Moreover, the children were asked whether a child should share in general with peers, and why. The children's justifications were coded into six levels of reasoning ranging from moral egocentrism to functional generosity due to the value of positive justice (these levels are presented in more detail on page 125). Justifications for sharing increased in level with age. Level of reasoning about these helping situations was positively correlated with both reasoning about Damon's (1977) positive-justice dilemma and reasoning about sharing when prohibited by an authority, even when the effect of age was partialled out of the correlations.

In another study with Israeli children, Bar-Tal, Raviv, and Shavit (1981) interviewed 4–5- and 7–8-year-olds about hypothetical helping, sharing, and comforting situations. Based on the one example of a dilemma in the Bar-Tal et al. article, it appears that the potential prosocial behavior in these dilemmas was not very costly. Children were asked whether the story protagonist would assist another and why. Subsequently, subjects chose from among four predetermined answers, each representing a different motive for assisting, the one they believed was the best reason for assisting.

Bar-Tal et al. (1981) coded the children's responses into the following eight categories believed to reflect six developmental stages of motives for helping (Bar-Tal, 1981): (1) external initiation with a tangible reward; (2) external initiation with no reward; (3) self-initiation with a tangible reward; (4) self-initiation with a social reward (normative stage); (5) self-initiation with an expectation of unspecified future reciprocity from the child in need; (6) self-initiation with generalized reciprocity; (7) self-initiation with a self (internal) reward; and (8) self-initiation with no reward. Older children both expressed and chose higher level justifications than did younger children. The majority of older children said that help is given because the recipient of help will someday reciprocate the assistance. In contrast, the majority of younger children said that help is given when an external reward is promised. Justifications for helping, sharing, and comforting were significantly interrelated, and were associated with children's responses to questions concerning why the children themselves and other children help in general.

The children in the Bar-Tal et al. (1981) study apparently exhibited more reward-oriented (hedonistic) and reciprocity-related reasons for assisting than has been found in our own research. This difference could be due to the nature of the moral dilemmas used by Bar-Tal et al. and Eisenberg (Eisenberg et al., 1983; Eisenberg-Berg, 1979a), as well as to the nature of the questions directed to the children. Bar-Tal et al. used dilemmas in which helping was apparently not extremely important for the recipient; for example, in one dilemma, the story protagonist merely was present when another child fell down, was injured, and cried. In this situation, the benefit to the fallen child of comforting was not large. In contrast, in our prosocial dilemmas, the potential recipient of aid has an obvious, salient need that can be addressed by the story protagonist. It is likely that children think about or express hedonistic concerns more frequently when another's need is relatively minor. Moreover, although we generally have obtained fewer reward-oriented reasons for assisting than did Bar-Tal et al., we have found that children express much hedonistic, self-oriented reasoning when they decide *not* to assist. Finally, in the Bar-Tal et al. study, children were asked what the story protagonist "would" do, whereas in our own research children have been asked what "should" be done. Older children tend to use lower level reasoning when reasoning about what *would* be done than about what *should* be done (Leming, 1976); thus, the wording of Bar-Tal et al.'s questions may have affected the responses of their older children. However, it is not clear that younger children differentiate between what would and should be done in their moral reasoning.

Summary: Development of Prosocial Moral Judgment

It should be clear from the review of the work of Higgins et al., Gilligan, Eisenberg, and others that researchers conceptualize and score prosocial moral reasoning in a variety of ways. The dilemmas investigators have used to study moral reasoning about helping or caring range from those utilizing real-life situations (which may or may not be perceived as dilemmas involving others' needs, Gilligan, 1977, 1982), to those involving very simple, low-cost, low-benefit hypothetical helping acts (e.g., Bar-Tal et al., 1981; Levin & Bekerman-Greenberg, 1980), to those involving a clear conflict between a hypothetical other's own needs and those of a potential recipient (e.g., Eisenberg et al., 1983; Eisenberg-Berg, 1979a; Higgs, 1975; Higgins et al., 1984). Moreover, some researchers have questioned subjects concerning what *should* be done, but others have asked for reasons to justify what *would* be done. With regard to scoring of responses, Kohlberg and his colleagues have tended to emphasize the issues of responsibility and relationships; Gilligan has discussed both caring and responsibility in relationships; and others (e.g., Bar-Tal et al., 1981) have focused on the dimension of type of initiation and reward (external or internal) for assisting. Whereas Higgins et al., Gilligan, Higgs, and Eisenberg have coded reasons supporting decisions not to assist as well as those to assist, Bar-Tal et al. (1981) and Levin and Bekerman-Greenberg (1980) did not (all children in Bar-Tal et al.'s study said that the story protagonist would help). Finally, the age of respondents used in the various investigations has varied considerably from preschool and elementary-school children (Bar-Tal et al., 1981; Eisenberg et al., 1983; Eisenberg, Pasternack, & Lennon, 1984; Eisenberg-Berg, 1979a, Eisenberg-Berg & Neal, 1981; Eisenberg-Berg & Roth, 1980; Levin & Bekerman-Greenberg, 1980) to adolescents and adults (Gilligan, 1977, 1982; Higgs, 1975; Higgins et al., 1984; Kurdek, 1981).

Despite all the differences in design and scoring, some general conclusions can be drawn from the body of literature on prosocial moral judgment. Young children frequently express egoistic or hedonistic concerns in their moral reasoning. They also express primitive empathic concerns; however, these empathic concerns become stronger and more self-reflective with age. In middle childhood, the quality of relationships, social approval, and issue of adherence to social norms also become considerations in many children's justifications. In adolescence and adulthood, issues related to internalized values, responsibilities and duties, and the welfare of the larger group may become important to the individual; however, self-reflective empathic concerns often retain their importance. Thus, although the exact nature and sequence of transition from one mode of reasoning to another has not yet been adequately delineated, it is clear that age-related changes in prosocial moral judgment do occur.

PERSONAL CORRELATES OF MODE AND LEVEL OF PROSOCIAL MORAL JUDGMENT

Although the emphasis of this book is not on the socialization and personality correlates of altruistic behavior, it is useful to an understanding of altruism to briefly review the personal correlates of level of prosocial moral judgment.[3] Moreover, data concerning the personal characteristics that are associated with level or mode of prosocial moral reasoning are relevant to a model of moral judgment that will be presented in Chapter 9. In this model, mode or level of

---

[3]For research concerning the relation of parental socializations practices to prosocial moral judgment, see Eisenberg et al. (1983) and Eisenberg, Pasternack, and Lennon (1984).

moral reasoning used with regard to a particular situation is viewed as influenced by personal factors.

Empathy/Sympathy

Theorists and researchers frequently have posited a causal relation between empathy and altruism. Moreover, sympathetic considerations are salient in many individuals' prosocial moral reasoning. Thus, it is not surprising that degree of sympathetic and empathic responding has been associated with level or mode of prosocial moral reasoning. In specific, in young children (7–8-year-olds), scores on Bryant's (1982) self-report measure of empathy (which assesses a combination of both vicarious affective responsiveness and sympathic concern) have been postively associated with needs-oriented (primitive empathic) reasoning (Eisenberg, Pasternack, & Lennon, 1984). For 9–10-year-olds, scores on the Bryant empathy measures were positively correlated with both sympathetic moral reasoning, and overall level of reasoning, and were negatively related to hedonistic reasoning. Empathic children apparently expressed relatively high levels of the types of empathic judgments that were sophisticated for their age group (self-reflective empathic reasoning for older children, needs-oriented reasoning for younger children).

Empathic responding has also been associated with adolescents' (Eisenberg-Berg & Mussen, 1978) level of prosocial moral judgment. Moreover, Hogan's (1969) self-report measure of social sensitivity (which is a measure of role taking and social sensitivity) has also been positively related to high-school and college-aged females', but not males', prosocial moral reasoning (Kurdek, 1981). In brief, the limited available research is consistent with the conclusion that level of prosocial moral reasoning is positively associated with self report of empathic, sympathetic responsiveness and social sensitivity (especially for females). Whether or not this relation would hold for measures of empathy/sympathy that are nonverbal rather than self report has not been examined.

Role Taking

The ability to cognitively assume the perspective of another is viewed by some theorists as a component of empathy (e.g., Feshback, 1978), as well as a possible mediator or determinant of altruism (Krebs & Russell, 1981) and level of moral judgment (e.g., Kohlberg, 1969). However, in research with children, a measure of cognitive role taking (Flavell et al.'s [1968], 7-picture task) was not significantly related to 5 1/2–6 1/2- (Eisenberg-Berg & Roth, 1980) or 7–8-year-olds' (Eisenberg et al., 1983 study, unpublished data) mode (type) or level of prosocial moral judgment. In contrast, Kurdek (1981) found a positive relation between high-school and college-aged females', but not males', prosocial moral judgment and a composite score of cognitive and affective role taking (assessed with several tasks). Thus, the association between role taking and prosocial moral judgment does not appear to be strong or consistent. However, given the broad range of role-taking capacities and corresponding assessment instruments used in research, it is possible that the association between role taking and prosocial moral judgment varies as a function of aspect and level of role taking considered.

Political Orientation

Liberal and/or humanitarian political attitudes frequently concern the welfare of others, especially the needy members of society. Consequently, it is logical to expect some relation between prosocial moral judgment and political attitudes. However, in only two studies has the association between level of prosocial moral judgment and political orientation been explored. Eisenberg-Berg (1976) found a positive association between level of prosocial moral judgment (assessed with an objective measure similar to that of Rest, 1979) and seventh to twelfth graders' liberal and humanitarian political attitudes. Level of prosocial moral judgment was a better predictor of liberal attitudes (but not humanitarian attitudes) than were age and religious affiliation. Similarly, in a study involving ninth, eleventh, and twelfth graders, level of prosocial moral reasoning was positively related to political liberalism, but only for females, when the effects of age were controlled (Eisenberg-Berg, 1979b).

The findings concerning the positive relation between prosocial moral judgment and political attitudes are, in general, consistent with the research on Kohlbergian moral reasoning and altruism. Maturity of moral judgment has been positively associated with individuals' conceptions of laws and the dynamics of legal compliance (e.g., Tapp & Kohlberg, 1971; Torney, 1971), political activism (Haan, Smith, & Block, 1968), and political ideology and attitudes (Candee, 1975; Fishkin, Keniston, & McKinnon, 1973; Fontana & Noel, 1974; Haan et al., 1968; Rest, 1979). In general, conventional levels of reasoning have been related to more conservative political attitudes, and high levels of moral reasoning have been associated with liberal political attitudes.

Scholastic Aptitude

A basic assumption of cognitive-developmental theory is that a certain level of cognitive development is necessary for the emergence of corresponding levels of moral judgment (e.g., Kohlberg, 1969, 1971). In general, the research has supported this assertion; cognitive development, as assessed by IQ (e.g., Arbuthnot, 1973; Harris, Mussen, & Rutherford, 1976; Kohlberg, 1969; Kuhn, Langer, Kohlberg, & Haan, 1977) or performance on Piagetian logical tasks (e.g., Cauble, 1976; Kuhn et al., 1977; Tomlinsen-Keasey, & Keasey, 1974; Walker, 1980; Walker & Richards, 1979) has been empirically associated with level of moral judgment on Kohlberg-type dilemmas. However, although Kohlberg (1969) has claimed that a given level of logical level is necessary (although not sufficient) for each stage of moral judgment, data concerning the cognitive prerequisites of stage of Kohlbergian moral judgment are inconsistent (e.g., Haan, Weiss, & Johnson, 1982; Kuhn et al., 1977; Krebs & Gillmore, 1982; Walker, 1980). Nonetheless, it is obvious that cognitive development is at least involved in moral judgment; mature levels of moral judgment clearly reflect more sophisticated cognitive conceptualizations than do lower levels.

Research concerning the relation between prosocial moral judgment and cognitive development is sparse. Eisenberg (1977; Eisenberg-Berg, 1979b) examined the association between scholastic aptitude (scores on standardized tests of academic achievement) and level of prosocial moral judgment. Scholastic aptitude scores should be expected to reflect intelligence if the child is motivated to achieve. Eisenberg found a moderately high association between the two for middle-class high-school boys, but not for high-school girls or elementary-school children. This pattern of findings may have occurred because social norms tend to reinforce adolescent males', but not females', academic achievement (Douvan & Adelson, 1966; Maccoby, 1966); thus, males, especially those approaching adulthood, may be more motivated to achieve than are adolescent females or younger children. As a consequence, their test scores may be a more accurate measure of intelligence than are the scores of females or younger children.

To examine the relation between prosocial moral judgment and cognitive development, logical development on Piagetian tasks should be assessed. To our knowledge, such research has not been conducted. Nonetheless, the findings reported here provide some initial support for the view that cognitive development is related to level of prosocial moral judgment.

Social Desirability

When one assesses an aspect of moral development via verbal report, there is always the concern that individuals with a strong need to appear in a socially desirable light will report not what they believe, but what they think others view as correct or moral. Although data concerning this issue are limited, it appears that self-presentational issues are not a major contaminant of elementary-school children's prosocial moral judgment. Eisenberg, Pasternack, & Lennon (1984) found that 9–10-year-olds' scores on Crandall's (Crandall, Crandall, & Katkowsky, 1965) social desirability scale for children were unrelated to nearly all categories of prosocial moral reasoning, as well as to a composite score of reasoning. Scores on this scale (and on a subscale composed of the 5 items concerning prosocial behavior) were positively related to only one type of reasoning, approval/interpersonally oriented reasoning. Moreover, the 5-item prosocial subscale (but not the entire scale) was negatively related to sympathetic concerns and positively related to the number of stories in which the children said the story protagonist would assist. These findings are consistent with those of Karniol (1984) in indicating that children generally are unable or uninterested in faking high level moral responses.

THE RELATION OF MORAL JUDGMENT TO
PROSOCIAL BEHAVIOR

The study of moral judgment would be of limited interest to most theorists and researchers if moral judgment bore no relation to moral behavior. Indeed, it was in the interest of obtaining a better understanding of moral behavior that many researchers began to investigate moral judgment.

The nature of the relation between moral behavior and moral judgment is undoubtedly complex. This is for several reasons. First, any single behavior may be due to a variety of motives, some moral and some nonmoral. For example, an individual may assist a needy other to obtain a reward or recognition, to incur a debt, to improve his/her relationship with the needy other, to live up to internalized values, or as a consequence of an emotional empathic response. In the latter two cases, the resultant behavior would be considered altruistic; in the former three, it would not. In fact, it appears that some prosocial behaviors frequently serve a nonmoral function; for example, young children may often help in an attempt to initiate social interaction or avoid interpersonal conflict (e.g., Eisenberg, Pasternack, Cameron, & Tryon, 1984; Eisenberg-Berg & Hand, 1979). Thus, it is not surprising that some prosocial behaviors are infrequently related to moral judgment.

An additional point to consider is that many prosocial behaviors are undoubtedly performed rather automatically, with little or no prior cognitive processing (Langer et al., 1978; Piliavin et al., 1981). People apparently have cognitive scripts (structures of knowledge consisting of a coherent sequence of actions and events expected in a given situation) stored in their memory that they frequently use to guide their behavior; when such a script is used, people may behave with relatively little cognitive processing. Behavior of this sort can be viewed as habitual. Moreover, in severe crisis situations, people frequently help in an almost reflexive manner. In both of the aforementioned situations, one would expect relatively little association between moral judgment and moral behavior (unless one's social script was originally constructed as the result of careful consideration of moral issues).

Despite the issues just discussed and the obvious fact that our methods for assessing both moral judgment and altruism are far from perfect, researchers have found some association between moral judgment and various forms of prosocial behaviors. Both mature levels of Kohlbergian moral reasoning (e.g., Harris et al., 1976; Kohlberg, 1969; Kohlberg & Candee, 1984; McNamee, 1978; Staub, 1974; cf. Blasi, 1980; Underwood & Moore, 1982) and distributive-justice reasoning (Blotner & Bearison, 1984; Emler & Rushton, 1974) have been related to frequency or amount of prosocial behavior. Level of Kohlbergian moral reasoning appears to be positively associated with the tendency to assign responsibility to the self to assist (McNamee, 1978). Moreover, as might be expected, level of moral reasoning about prosocial situations has been associated with prosocial behavior, perhaps more closely than have been other types of moral reasoning.

The research concerning the association between prosocial moral judgment and prosocial behavior is presented in Table 7.9. As can be seen in this table, there is some relation between behavior and reasoning, although not in all situations. In studies of preschoolers' naturally occurring prosocial behaviors, moral reasoning—particularly modes of reasoning that most clearly reflect empathic or egoistic considerations—has been more closely related to spontaneous sharing behaviors than to helping behaviors (which, in these studies, have no material cost) or behaviors performed in response to a peer's request (Eisenberg, Cameron, & Tryon, 1984; Eisenberg, Pasternack, Cameron, & Tryon, 1984; Eisenberg-Berg & Hand, 1979). In laboratory studies involving elementary-school or high-school students, prosocial moral reasoning has been more highly correlated with prosocial behaviors involving a cost (e.g., donating or volunteering an hour or time after school) than those that are low in cost (e.g., helping pick up paper clips; Eisenberg, Pasternack, & Lennon, 1984; Eisenberg, Boehnke, Schuhler, & Silbereisen, 1985; Eisenberg-Berg, 1979b). Moreover, the relation between reasoning and behavior appears to be strongest when the situation about which the individual reasons is similar to that in which behavior is assessed (Levin & Bekerman-Greenberg, 1980).

The pattern of relations presented in Table 7.9 is consistent with the view that the relation between prosocial moral reasoning and prosocial behavior is mediated, in part, by costliness of the prosocial act. This is quite logical; if a given behavior is low in cost to the actor, it frequently may be performed without much cognitive reflection, moral or otherwise. Furthermore, if the benefit to the other is small, moral concerns related to the other's welfare are unlikely to arise. Of course, if the price of helping is too high, there also may be little relation between moral reasoning and behavior because of limited variation in helping behavior (few individuals may help).

In a recent study, Eisenberg and Shell (1985) examined the degree of association between preschoolers' and third graders' prosocial moral reasoning and behavior as a function of cost of the helping act. Moral reasoning was assessed with Eisenberg's dilemmas (Eisenberg-Berg & Hand, 1979), and children were given the opportunity to donate to poor children on two separate occasions. On one occasion, the cost of donating was relatively low; preschoolers could share any of 10 identical, relatively unattractive stickers whereas third graders' could share some of ten pennies. On the other occasion, the cost of assisting was higher; the preschoolers were given the opportunity to donate some of ten attractive, nonidentical stickers, whereas the older children could donate some of ten

TABLE 7.9

Studies of the Relationship between Prosocial Behavior and Reasoning

Study	Subjects	Measure of Prosocial Behavior	Measure of Reasoning	Relationship	Direction and Comments
Eisenberg, Boehnke, Schuhler, & Silbereisen, 1985	M & F grades 2, 4	Helping pick up spilled paper clips and donating candies to orphans	Several categories in Table 7.3	Between categories of reasoning and helping	+—Donating (negatively related to hedonistic, positively to needs-oriented) / 0—Helping
Eisenberg, Pasternack, Cameron, & Tryon, 1984	M & F preschoolers	Spontaneous or "asked for" (compliant) naturally occurring prosocial behaviors	Several categories in Table 7.3	Between frequency of prosocial behaviors and amount of various modes of reasoning	+—for spontaneous sharing (− with hedonistic) / 0—for other prosocial behaviors
Eisenberg, Pasternack, Lennon, 1984	M & F 9–10 year olds	Helping pick up paper clips and toys and donating nickels to charity	Several categories in Table 7.3 / Composite measure of reasoning	Between various categories of reasoning and both a composite measure of helping and donating	+—for donating (negatively related to hedonistic reasoning) / +—for helping (negatively related to affectional relationship reasoning) / 0—for donating / 0—for helping
Eisenberg & Shell, 1985	M & F preschoolers & grade 3	Donating high- or low-cost items to peers	Several categories of reasoning in Table 7.3	Between various categories of reasoning and amount donated	+—for high-cost donating and several categories of reasoning / 0—between low cost donating and reasoning

Study	Subjects	Behavior	Reasoning measure	Relationship	Results
Eisenberg, 1979b	M & F grades 9, 11, 12	Donating an hour to help the experimenter with a dull task	Eisenberg's prosocial moral reasoning stages	Between volunteering and level of reasoning	+—for boys, 0—for girls
Eisenberg-Berg, & Hand, 1979	M & F preschoolers	Spontaneous or "asked for" (compliant) naturally occurring prosocial behaviors	Categories of reasoning derived from those in Table 7.3	Between frequency of prosocial behaviors and amount of various modes of reasoning	+—for spontaneous sharing (+ with needs-oriented reasoning; – with hedonistic) 0—for other prosocial behaviors
Levin & Bekerman-Greenberg, 1980	Israeli M & F grades K, 2, 4, 6	Sharing pretzels won in a lottery with a peer	Reasoning about a hypothetical situation similar to the sharing assessment, a somewhat similar situation, or a very different situation dealing with distributive justice; level of reasoning (from high to low); positive justice, empathy, conditional generosity, good boy-girl morality; immediate reciprocity, egocentrism	Between level of reasoning and number of pretzels shared	+—for all types of stories; + with similar situation when the effects of grade were controlled; 0—for somewhat different situation when age controlled; – with distributive justice when age controlled
Wright, 1942b	M & F ages 8, 11	Sharing attractive and unattractive toys with peers	Reasons about hypothetical situation involving distribution of toys (few details given)	Reasons for sharing and actual sharing	+—ideology and behavior related (few details given)

nickels. As hypothesized, the relation between moral reasoning and donating in the high-cost condition was significant (donating was negatively related to donating and/or positively related to needs-oriented reasoning, depending on the age of the child); however, donating of low-cost items was unrelated to moral reasoning. These findings are consistent with the notion that the relation between moral judgment and behavior is stronger in situations in which the cost of assisting is high enough to invoke moral conflict. Moreover, the association probably would have been even stronger in the high-cost condition if one could have determined the significance of the stickers or money to the children, and taken this factor into account.[4]

In summary, it appears that there is a moderate positive association between individuals' moral reasoning and their prosocial behavior in some circumstances. Although cause and effect are not entirely clear, the values represented in individuals' moral reasoning apparently influence behavior in a given context either directly (by affecting decision-making in the situation) or, perhaps, indirectly (by serving to establish certain habitual patterns of behavior that are likely to occur in a variety of settings). Thus, it would appear that the question to be addressed in future investigations is not "Is there an association between moral reasoning and altruistic behavior?", but "In what circumstances is there an association between moral judgment and altruistic behavior?"

CONCLUSION

The existing research is consistent with the view that internalized moral values and personal goals are related to individuals' prosocial behaviors. Moreover, because these values and goals often are reflected in individuals' moral judgments, it is not surprising that researchers have found some association between moral reasoning (especially reasoning about prosocial actions) and moral behaviors.

The values that individuals express in their reasoning about prosocial moral dilemmas typically change dramatically with age. In general, the change that is observed is from a concrete, egoistic orientation in early childhood to a more empathic and value-based orientation in adolescence. Thus, despite considerable individual differences in children's moral reasoning, such reasoning tends to become more altruistic with age.

It is interesting to note the similarities between the self-attributions children make at various ages and their prosocial moral reasoning at the same age. In

---

[4]High- and low-cost helping were also assessed; however, even high-cost helping apparently was perceived as low in cost by the older children (it correlated with low-cost donating in the first study). Low-cost helping was not correlated with moral judgment; high-cost helping was positively related to developmentally mature moral reasoning for preschoolers (for whom there was a positive association between high-cost helping and high-cost donating) in Study 1, and for third graders in Study 2.

general, children's self-attributions develop in a manner consistent with changes in their moral reasoning (see Chapter 5); their attributions become less concrete and egoistic and more empathic and altruistic with age. Thus, the bodies of research on moral judgment and self-attributions are consistent in indicating that children's reasons for performing prosocial acts change systematically with development.

Although a few researchers (e.g., Bar-Tal et al., 1981; Levin & Bekerman-Greenberg, 1980; Reykowski, 1977) have studied the prosocial moral reasoning of children in cultures other than the United States, it is difficult to directly compare their data with those collected in America. This is due to gross differences in the moral dilemmas and scoring systems used for coding the children's responses. Thus, it is useful to consider the research in which similar dilemmas and coding systems were used in different cultures. This is the focus of Chapter 8.

8 Prosocial Moral Judgment: Cross-cultural Research

Nancy Eisenberg, Anne Tietjen, Rainer K. Silbereisen, Petra Schuhler, Rachel Hertz-Lazarowitz, Ina Fuchs, Klaus Boehnke[1]

Altruism and other prosocial behaviors are social behaviors, set in a given social context, and nearly always involve other persons. Consequently, the psychological significance of a prosocial act is a function, in part, of individuals' cognitions related to the norms, values, and customs of their culture and the emotional reactions they have learned to attach to various behaviors, values, and goals. Indeed, in some social settings or cultures, a given prosocial act may be viewed by a benefactor, recipient, and observers as altruistic and helpful, whereas in other settings or cultures, the same act may be perceived to be degrading to the recipient (cf. Fisher, Nadler, & Whitcher-Alagnor, 1983; Gergen, Ellsworth, Maslach, & Seipel, 1975; Gergen & Gergen, 1983; Gergen, Morse, & Kristeller, 1973). Thus, given the role of social learning in the interpretation of actions, it is important to consider cultural and subcultural influences when studying reasoning about altruistic action (cf. Nisan, 1984a).

Some similarities in the development of moral judgment are to be expected across cultures (cf. Kohlberg, 1969). This is due simply to the fact that the capacities for abstract thought and complex perspective taking seem to be necessary for (or at least facilitive of) higher level reasoning (see Chapter 7). However, it is also clear that individual differences in the level of moral judgment are a consequence, in part, of variations in socialization history (e.g., Eisenberg, Lennon, & Roth, 1983; Holstein, 1969; Leahy, 1981; Parikh, 1980). The socialization of children varies dramatically across cultures (e.g., Whiting & Whiting, 1975); these differences in socialization should be reflected in children's moral judgment.

---

[1] Order of authors other than the first author is counter-alphabetical.

It is likely that cross-cultural and cross-national differences in moral reasoning are due to at least two factors. First, differences may emerge because of the values, norms, and attitudes brought to the decision-making task. These values, norms, and attitudes are most likely taught either directly or indirectly (e.g., through modeling), and should influence the relative importance of different goals and modes of reasoning. Second, variation across cultures in socialization practices and in the range of children's experiences probably influences, to some degree, level of socio-cognitive skills (such as perspective-taking; Kohlberg, 1969) available to the child when engaging in moral decision-making. Children who are encouraged to be autonomous, to become actively involved in decision-making, and are not overprotected tend to exhibit higher level moral reasoning (e.g., Eisenberg, 1977; Eisenberg et al., 1983; Holstein, 1969; Leahy, 1981; Parikh, 1980), presumably because of increased opportunities to take the role of others and exercise their role-taking and reasoning capacities. Thus, socialization experiences within or across cultures would be expected to affect the child's capabilities for processing sociomoral information, and therefore should be reflected in level of moral judgment. Of course, it is likely that level of prosocial reasoning differs most markedly across cultures that are very different in social structure; indeed, Kohlberg (1969) and others (Nisan & Kohlberg, 1982; Turiel, Edwards, & Kohlberg, 1978; White, Bushnell, & Regnemer, 1978) have noted the greatest differences between the Kohlbergian reasoning of individuals from Western, industrial versus nonindustrial, traditional cultures.

Kohlberg (1969, 1971) has claimed that although mean level of moral judgment varies across cultures, the sequence of development does not. Whether or not this is true has been a topic of debate (Kurtines & Grief, 1974; Simpson, 1974). In this chapter, we will examine this and related issues with regard to prosocial moral judgment. Only research in which moral judgment was assessed in a manner similar to that of Eisenberg (Eisenberg et al., 1983) will be discussed. This is because, to our knowledge, no other procedure for measuring moral reasoning about prosocial behavior has been used in more than one society. Thus, to render cross-cultural comparisons interpretable, we must confine our review to this relatively limited body of research.

GERMAN DATA

In a first attempt to systematically study prosocial moral judgment in another culture, Eisenberg, Boehnke, Schuhler, and Silbereisen (1985) compared the prosocial moral reasoning of American and West German children. Although the German and American cultures are similar in many aspects, there are differences in the two cultures that might lead to differences in the development of moral reasoning.

As mentioned previously, researchers have found that levels of both Kohl-bergian (e.g., Leahy, 1981; Parikh, 1980) and prosocial (e.g., Eisenberg et al., 1983) reasoning are positively related to nonrestrictive childrearing practices and, to some degree, maternal warmth. Thus, cross-national differences in child-rearing practices are likely to be associated with cross-national variations in moral judgment. According to children's reports, German parents appear to provide more love and support than do American parents (Devereux, Bronfen-brenner, & Suci, 1962). Given the association between maternal warmth and prosocial moral judgment in the early but not mid-elementary-school years (Eisenberg et al., 1983), one might predict that young German children's pro-social moral reasoning would be more advanced than that of their American counterparts. However, the fact that American mothers apparently allow their 6- and 14-year-old children more autonomy than do German mothers (Wesley & Karr, 1968) is consistent with the hypothesis that American children may be more advanced in their reasoning in the later school years.

The research on sociopolitical thinking suggests that the prosocial moral judgment of Americans and Germans may, indeed, differ in some respects. For example, although Adelson (1971) found that German children were more likely than American or English children to trust authorities, view authorities as wise and benevolent, and to advocate strong leadership, in more recent research American adolescents scored higher than German adolescents on authoritarianism (Lederer, 1982). Thus, it would not be surprising if German and American children differed in their use of some types of moral reasoning, especially for dilemmas in which concern for authorities' approval and deference to the existing social order were likely to be salient issues.

Eisenberg et al.'s (1985) goal was to examine differences in both level and developmental sequence of German and American children's prosocial moral reasoning. Thus, they conducted a cross-national, cross-sectional study. The participants in this study were 92 Germans and 99 Americans in preschool, second, or fourth grade. The children were nearly all Caucasian, and from working and middle-class families. The mean ages of the children were very similar across the samples of children.

Prosocial moral judgment was assessed with the same four moral dilemmas used in the American research with elementary-school children (Eisenberg et al., 1983; Eisenberg, Pasternack, & Lennon, 1984; Eisenberg-Berg & Hand, 1979). The stories were very slightly modified for use with the German children, for example, the word "courtyard" was used instead of "yard." German children were interviewed by German experimenters (all of whom also spoke English); American children were interviewed by Americans. However, the procedures were nearly identical in both countries. The interviews with German children were translated into English by German psychologists fluent in English. Interview protocols for both the American and German were coded by the same person (an American); interrater reliability was scored by German psychologists for the

German sample and by Americans for the American sample. Interrater reliabilities were adequate.

In the analyses, we first examined age changes in German children's prosocial moral judgment. Fourth graders used less hedonistic reasoning than both preschoolers and second graders; moreover, second graders verbalized less hedonistic reasoning than did preschoolers. Direct reciprocity reasoning was more common among fourth graders than preschoolers; the differences between adjacent age groups were not significant. Second graders verbalized significantly more needs-oriented reasoning than did preschoolers; the decrease in needs-oriented reasoning from second to fourth grade was not significant. Approval/interpersonal reasoning and reference to humanness were used significantly more by fourth graders than preschoolers; moreover, for reference to humanness, the increase was also significant from second to fourth grade (see Table 8.1).

To determine whether the pattern of developmental change for German children was similar to that for American children, multivariate and univariate analyses of variance were computed to examine for any interactions of country with sex or age; none even approached marginal significance. Thus, the developmental patterns were similar for German and American children. However, German children verbalized significantly more direct reciprocity reasoning than did American children, whereas Americans used considerably more stereotypic reasoning than did Germans.

Interestingly, the relations between the second and fourth grade German children's prosocial behavior (donating, helping pick up paper clips) and reasoning were similar to those found for American children (Eisenberg et al., 1984). Number of candies donated was significantly, positively related to needs-oriented reasoning (and to the moral-judgment composite), and negatively related to hedonistic reasoning. Low-cost helping was unrelated to reasoning. Thus, as has been found for American children (see Chapter 7), German children's reasoning was related to high-cost prosocial behaviors, but not low-cost prosocial behaviors.

In summary, the results of the present study were quite consistent with findings concerning prosocial development in American children. The age-related developmental changes in the German children's prosocial moral judgment were very similar to those noted in prior cross-sectional and longitudinal research with American children (Eisenberg et al., 1983, 1984; Eisenberg-Berg, 1979). Indeed, when the German and American children's reasoning was directly compared, there were no differences in the pattern of age-related change. These findings are consistent with the view that prosocial moral judgment develops similarly in different Western cultures, probably due to both the role of cognition in development and some basic similarities in the socialization of children in Western cultures.

Cross-cultural differences in use of specific prosocial reasoning categories (regardless of age) were also few. German children did verbalize somewhat more

TABLE 8.1

Moral Reasoning Categories: Means for German and American Children

Reasoning Categories	German Children Grade			American Children Grade		
	Preschool	2	4	Preschool	2	4
Hedonistic	8.17	6.66	5.21	10.13	6.63	5.69
Direct reciprocity	4.00	4.34	4.76	4.00	4.17	4.28
Affectional relationship	4.07	4.24	4.15	4.00	4.23	4.36
Pragmatism	4.63	5.14	5.48	4.37	4.90	5.33
Needs-oriented	10.73	12.90	12.27	9.67	12.87	13.18
Concern with humanness	4.00	4.38	4.91	4.03	4.90	4.64
Stereotypes of good/bad persons	4.33	4.38	4.39	4.70	5.13	5.67
Approval/interpersonal orientation	4.00	4.03	4.21	4.00	4.00	4.26
Sympathetic	4.00	4.10	4.18	4.00	4.13	4.49
Role-taking	4.00	4.03	4.09	4.00	4.10	4.41
Positive affect/simple or related to consequences	4.00	4.03	4.00	4.00	4.00	4.31

Note: The possible range for scores was 4.00 to 16.00. Only categories with means of 4.25 or higher for at least one age group in one country are shown. Reprinted from Eisenberg, Boehnke, Schuhler, & Silbereisen, 1985, with permission of the publisher.

reasoning concerning direct reciprocity, whereas American children made more references to stereotypic conceptions of good and bad persons or behaviors. Perhaps the relative importance of norms relating to direct reciprocity versus norms related to helping varies across the two countries. However, it is important to note that neither direct reciprocity nor stereotyped reasoning were frequently verbalized, especially by the preschoolers or second graders. Nonetheless, there were minor differences in German and American children's use of different modes of prosocial reasoning, even if there were no differences in the sequence of their development.

ISRAELI DATA

Another country in which prosocial moral judgment has been studied is Israel. Israel is a particularly interesting country in which to examine moral reasoning because of the existence of the kibbutz. The kibbutz is a society within the larger society, a communal society in which many child-care responsibilities as well as material goods are shared by the group. The kibbutz is noted for its ideological orientation, albeit the specific ideologies of various kibbutzim differ considerably.

Although the social structure, ideologies, and methods of child rearing in the kibbutz have received considered attention in the psychological literature (e.g., Beit-Hallahimi & Rabin, 1977; Rabin, 1965; Spiro, 1965), there is relatively little empirical research directly comparing prosocial behaviors or reasoning in Israeli kibbutz versus city children. However, researchers have found that: (1) kibbutz children tend to score higher on scales of social responsibility than do city children (Nadler, Romek, & Shapiro-Friedman, 1976); (2) kibbutz children and adults are more prosocial than are city dwellers (Avgar, Brofenbrenner, & Henderson, 1977; Nadler et al., 1976; Yinon, Sharon, Azgad, & Barshir, 1981); and (3) kibbutz children score higher than city children on Kohlberg's measure of moral judgment (Bar-Yam, Kohlberg, & Naame, 1980; Firstenberg-Havazelet; cited in Bar-Tal et al., 1981). Moreover, there appears to be more emphasis on socialist, egalitarian ideologies in the kibbutz than in urban Israeli settings (Garber-Talman, 1972; Spiro, 1965), one that is reflected in children's distribution of rewards (Nisan, 1984b). However, contrary to what most researchers would predict, in the one study of prosocial moral reasoning that we have located, kibbutz and city children did not differ in level of reasoning (Bar-Tal et al., 1981).

In the Bar-Tal et al. (1981) study, 4–5- and 7–8-year-old children reasoned about hypothetical situations in which the cost of helping was low, and the individual to be assisted was not in great need. Indeed, the cost of assisting was so low that all children, even the 4–5-year-olds, said they would help. Moreover, only mean level of reasoning, not mode of reasoning (e.g., self-oriented, empathic), was examined. Differences between kibbutz and city children might have been evident if the children had reasoned about situations involving more of a moral dilemma (e.g., one in which there was more cost to the actor).

The prosocial moral reasoning of Israeli children (kibbutz or city) in comparison to that of American children is also of interest. Israel is a country in which people from many countries have immigrated in the past few decades. Thus, it is a rather diverse society, and is influenced by both Eastern and Western European (as well as Arabic) cultures. For this reason alone, it is interesting to explore the differences in the reasoning of American and Israeli children. Moreover, because a considerable amount of research on attributions about prosocial actors (e.g., Bar-Tal, 1982; Bar-Tal et. al, 1980; Guttman et al., 1979; Hertz-Lazarowitz, 1983; Raviv et al., 1980) and moral reasoning about prosocial behaviors (Bar-Tal et al., 1981; Levin & Bekerman-Greenberg, 1980) has been conducted in Israel, information concerning similarities and dissimilarities in American and Israeli children's reasoning would be useful for interpreting patterns of findings in the existing literature.

In a recent study, Fuchs, Hertz-Lazarowitz, Eisenberg, & Sharabany, (1984; Fuchs, Eisenberg, Hertz-Lazarowitz, & Sharabany, in press) compared the moral reasoning of American and Israeli (kibbutz and city) children in third grade. Fifty-five American, 29 kibbutz children, and 36 Israeli city children of comparable age responded to the same four prosocial moral reasoning dilemmas used by Eisenberg in her longitudinal research. Children were interviewed by adults from their own cultures, and the stories were coded in the original languages. Interrater reliability was obtained not only between Israeli coders and between American coders, but also between the primary Israeli coder and the primary coder for the American data. Satisfactory reliability was obtained for all commonly used categories except pragmatic reasoning, which was therefore excluded from analyses. Two sets of analyses were computed, one in which the American data and that of the combined Israeli sample were compared, and one in which all three groups (American, Israeli city, and Israeli kibbutz) were compared.

In the first set of multivariate and univariate analyses of variance, the dependent variables were all categories of reasoning that were used with any real frequency (hedonistic, direct reciprocity, affectional relationship, physical needs-oriented, psychological needs-oriented, humanism, stereotypes of good/bad persons or stereotypes of norms, role-taking, internalized law and norm orientation). To reduce the possibility of small differences in coding leading to significant findings, only types of reasoning which occurred relatively frequently for at least one gender in one country were included in analyses. Significant cross-national differences were found for all types of reasoning *except* stereotypic reasoning and psychological needs-oriented reasoning (the effect for hedonistic reasoning was marginally significant at $p < .053$). American children verbalized much more physical needs-oriented reasoning. In contrast, Israeli children used more hedonistic, direct reciprocity, affectional relationship, humanism, role-taking, and internalized law/norm orientation reasoning (see Table 8.2).

TABLE 8.2
Moral Judgment Categories Used by American and Israeli Children:
Means

Moral Reasoning Category[a]	American Children (N = 55)	Israeli City Children (N = 36)	Israeli Kibbutz Children (N = 29)
Hedonistic	4.94	6.36	4.86
Direct reciprocity	4.13	4.47	4.97
Affectional relationship	4.06	4.50	4.72
Needs-oriented (physical needs)	14.11	7.81	7.07
Needs-oriented (psychological need)	4.53	4.67	5.07
Concern with humanness	4.22	4.56	5.52
Stereotypes of good/bad persons or norms	5.87	6.19	6.28
Stereotypes of majority behavior	4.06	4.53	4.14
Approval/interpersonal	4.27	4.39	4.28
Role-taking	4.07	5.50	4.59
Law and norm orientation	4.00	4.14	4.55

[a]Only the categories used with any real frequency are listed. Pragmatic reasoning is not listed due to its low interrater reliability. Reprinted from Fuchs, Eisenberg, Hertz Lazarowitz, & Sharabany (in press). Kibbutz, Israeli city, and American children's moral reasoning about prosocial moral conflicts. *Merrill-Palmer Quarterly.* By permission of Wayne State University.

In a similar analysis, the responses of the children from all three groups were compared. Univariate analyses for the effect of group (American, kibbutz, Israeli city) were significant for the same categories of reasoning as in the previous analysis (including hedonism). According to post-hoc tests comparing the three groups, there were significant differences among the groups in physical needs-oriented, concern with humanness, role-taking, and internalized law/norm orientation reasoning. American children verbalized significantly more physical needs-oriented reasoning than did either kibbutz or Israeli city children. In contrast, kibbutz children used more concern with humanness and internalized law/ norm orientation reasoning than did either American or Israeli city children, and Israeli city children verbalized more role-taking reasoning than did either of the other two groups (see Table 8.2). In none of the analyses was there an effect for sex of the children; nor were there interactions of sex with country or group.

To summarize, the American children were especially likely to base their decisions on the relatively immature type of reasoning in which individuals simply orient to the others' needs. In contrast, kibbutz children were more likely than other children to justify their decisions by refering to the notion that the needy other was a "person" (with the implication, direct or implied, that people are special); moreover, they were most likely to verbalize reasoning that appealed to internalized norms, rules, or values. Both of these types of reasoning preferred by the kibbutz children are relatively mature developmentally and seem to reflect the ideological emphasis of the kibbutz.

The Israeli city children expressed more of only one type of reasoning than did kibbutz and American children; they were more likely to explicitly put themselves or the story protagonist in the shoes of the needy other. The reason for this finding is not entirely clear. In Israeli schools, there is often considerable emphasis on prosocial values. Perhaps in the Israeli city, the emphasis is on the welfare of the other in a dyad, whereas the welfare of the group (rather than specific others) is of central concern to kibbutz socializers. This possibility is consistent with Sharabany's (1974) finding of more intimacy in city Israeli children's than kibbutz children's friendships.

Role taking in moral situations is viewed as being enhanced by socializers' demands for autonomy (cf. Kohlberg, 1969), however, researchers have found that Israeli urban children tend to report receiving fewer achievement demands and independence demands, and less autonomy than do kibbutz children (Avgar et al., 1977; Devereaux, Shouval, Bronfenbrenner, Rodgers, Kav-Venaki, Kiely, & Karson, 1974). Consequently, it is unlikely that the high level of role-taking reasoning among urban Israeli children was due to socializers' emphasis on autonomy. However, because the use of higher level moral reasoning has been associated with parental emphasis on autonomy (e.g., Eisenberg, 1977; Eisenberg et al., 1983; Leahy, 1981), kibbutz children's use of some more sophisticated modes of reasoning could be due, in part, to the press for autonomy and independence in the kibbutz.

Overall, it appears that the Israeli children used several of the more advanced modes of prosocial moral reasoning more than did the American children, but also expressed somewhat more of several types of developmentally immature types of reasoning (hedonistic, affectional relationship, direct reciprocity). However, two of the immature types of reasoning that were used frequently by the Israeli children (direct reciprocity, affectional relationship) were used considerably (although not significantly) more by kibbutz children, and are consistent with the emphasis on relationships and exchange among group members that is characteristic of a communal society (c.f. Furby, 1978). Moreover, the fact that Israeli city children expressed somewhat more hedonistic reasoning (the difference between Israelis' and Americans' use of this category was primarily due to the high rate of hedonistic reasoning among Israeli city children) is probably due to the emphasis on consumerism in Israeli cities, combined with the fact that many commodities are scarce or expensive. In the kibbutz, a communal philosophy is salient, and the emphasis on personal ownership of material goods is downplayed.

The city Israeli and kibbutz children differed little in their reasoning, although in many cases, the mean scores for the city Israeli children were intermediate to those for American and kibbutz children. The largest differences seemed to be across cultures, with Israeli children verbalizing a broader range of reasons, both high and low level. It should be noted, however, that the patterns of reasoning were not that different for American and Israeli children; both used physical needs-oriented reasoning more than any other type of reasoning, and hedonistic and stereotypic reasoning were also common modes of reasoning for both groups (see Table 8.2). Authority and punishment concerns, as well as most highly internalized modes of reasoning, were seldom used by the children. Unfortunately, because data were collected for only one age group, it was impossible to determine whether patterns of developmental change are similar across cultures.

JAPANESE DATA

Both Germany and Israel are basically western cultures, similar to the United States in many fundamental features. Thus, it is not surprising that reasoning about prosocial moral dilemmas was somewhat similar among children in the United States, Israeli, and Germany. However, one might expect children's moral reasoning in nonwestern cultures to be less similar to that of American children, due to differences in both socialization influences and the salience of various norms or values.

Data from nonwestern cultures concerning prosocial moral reasoning would be particularly useful for examining the role of culture in the development of moral judgment. Few such data are available. However, in a study with 159 Japanese fifth graders, Sakagami and Namiki (1982) examined the factor structure of Japanese children's prosocial moral judgment. The children were presented with four prosocial dilemmas, two of those used by Eisenberg and two similar dilemmas. The children indicated their reasoning by choosing reasons representing the categories used by Eisenberg (Table 7.3) from a predetermined list and indicating the importance of each reasoning. The subjects' ratings for the various reasons were summed across stories, and the resultant scores were subjected to a factor analyses.

Three factors emerged from this analysis. In the first factor, several highly internalized moral categories (internalized law, norm, and value orientation, concern with rights of others, and generalized reciprocity) loaded heavily, as did the categories concerned with humanness and stereotyped images of majority behavior. Authority/punishment reasoning, hedonistic reasoning, and direct reciprocity, all developmentally immature modes of reasoning, were the primary contributors to the second factor. Approval/interpersonal orientation reasoning loaded next highest on this factor. In the third factor, affective and empathic categories loaded heavily. In specific, all four categories concerning internalized affect (simple internalized positive affect and positive affect related to consequences, internalized positive affect from self-respect and living up to one's values, internalized negative affect over consequences of behavior, internalized negative affect due to loss of self-respect and/or not living up to one's values) as well as reasoning about the physical needs of others (concern for others' physical and material needs) loaded highly. Thus, although the factor structure is not identical with that found by Eisenberg-Berg (1979a), it is consistent with the general findings of Eisenberg. Types of reasoning that have been found to be developmentally immature grouped together; developmentally mature categories clustered together; several categories concerning internal affective reactions such as guilt and pride grouped together. Given that Sakagami and Namiki's (1982) methods of obtaining data and their sample (with regard to age) differed considerably from those used in the factor analyses with American children, one would not expect the structure of the factors to be identical.

PAPUA NEW GUINEA (MAISIN) DATA

The most informative data concerning prosocial moral reasoning in a nonwestern culture are those collected by Anne Tietjen from people in two Maisin coastal villages, Uiaku and Ganjiga, Papua New Guinea. A complete report of the study is given in Tietjen (1985).

The Maisin villagers are hardworking subsistence gardeners who also gather wild foods, fish, and hunt. The little cash income they have comes primarily from relatives in the towns, and from the sale of bark cloth made by the women. Although their villages first came into contact with Europeans around 1890 and most men in the village have spent some time working or attending school in an urban center, the village presently is relatively isolated and underdeveloped, even in relation to many other villages in Papua New Guinea.

In the Maisin villages, many traditional beliefs and customs have survived and coexist with the teachings of the Anglican church and the influences of the modified western-style government. The traditional social organization is strong; the people are tightly bound by kinship obligations. Moreover, the Maisin are collectivistic rather than individualistic in orientation (see Barker, 1983, 1984; Tietjen, 1984, 1985; Tietjen & Walker, in press, for more details).

It should be noted that the Maisin are one of many cultural groups in New Guinea; they number approximately 1,500 individuals in six coastal villages. Although the great majority of Papua New Guineans live in rural villages similar to the Maisin, there are major cultural differences among the more than 300 different language groups in the country. Thus, it would not be appropriate to generalize from the Maisin to other cultural groups in Papua New Guinea.

To assess prosocial moral judgment of the Maisin, Tietjen (1985) interviewed individuals using a slightly modified version of Eisenberg's stories. The stories were adapted so that the situations described would be recognizable to the village residents. Sixty-nine children (virtually all of the children in the school that serves three Maisin villages) were interviewed in 1982; 34 of these children were reinterviewed in 1983. In addition, 8 adolescents and 24 parents responded to stories. All children in grades 1–3 were interviewed in their native language.

Children in grades 5 and 6 were interviewed in English, the language in which the school is taught. All but three adolescents were interviewed in English, although a translator was present to help if needed. The adults were parents of the school children; they were interviewed at their homes, most in Maisin. All stories had been previously translated into Maisin and translated back into English to check the accuracy of translation before they were used. To insure that Tietjen was coding data in the same manner as the American data have been coded, she and Eisenberg both scored 30 protocols. Interrater reliability between the two was relatively high.

Maisin children, as well as adolescents and adults, used more physical needs-oriented reasoning than any other type of reasoning. Next most frequently used was hedonistic reasoning. The pattern of findings for the younger Maisin children was similar to that of American children of comparable age in that physical needs-oriented and hedonistic reasoning were the most common modes of judgment, with the former being more prevalent than the latter. However, the reasoning of the older children and adults differed relatively little from that of the children, especially when compared to the findings for American children and adults. The most salient developmental changes were significant moderate increases in affectional relationship, sympathetic and psychological needs-oriented reasoning (especially the latter) with age. Hedonistic reasoning peaked in third grade (perhaps because of the initial effects of exposure to Western values) and dropped off somewhat thereafter. Authority and punishment reasoning was low at all ages, as was the use of higher-level reasoning categories.

In brief, although the moral reasoning of the Maisin clearly fit the coding scheme of Eisenberg (there ware no "new" types of reasoning noted by the coders), there are both similarities and some clear differences between the reasoning of the Maisin and that of American respondents in other research. Early elementary school American and Maisin children appear to be quite similar in reasoning (except American children may use somewhat more stereotypic reasoning). The patterns of development from early elementary school into adulthood are quite different, however. Although Maisin adolescents and adults verbalized somewhat less hedonistic reasoning than younger children—a finding consistent with the American data—the Maisin adolescents and adults exhibited very little of the more sophisticated modes of reasoning. This latter finding is consistent with the fact that people from nonwestern, rural, and nonindustrial societies exhibit relatively little higher-level Kohlbergian reasoning (e.g., Nisan & Kohlberg, 1982; Turiel et al., 1978; White et al., 1978). One possible explanation for the difference in moral reasoning of persons from industrial and traditional societies is that moral reasoning patterns correspond to characteristics of social structure (Edwards, 1982).

In a small, face-to-face, traditional society such as that of the Maisin, it is not surprising that needs-oriented reasoning is the primary mode of moral judgment. Tietjen (1985) argues that reasoning of this type (if considered empathic and other-oriented) is appropriate for societies such as the Maisins', because in such societies, individuals must cooperate with one another to survive. Good interpersonal relationships are necessary and of great importance to the Maisin villagers. They believe that the best way to maintain good relations with others is to help them, always when they are asked for help, and even when there is no request for assistance. Children are taught early to help and to be aware of others' needs (Tietjen, 1984). Given the nature of the society and the need for people to get along and attend to one another's needs, it is not surprising that the types of reasoning used by the Maisin reflect attention to others' needs (physical needs-oriented, psychological needs-oriented, and sympathetic reasoning), as well as concern with that which is possible for them to give to others (hedonistic and perhaps pragmatic concerns).

CONCLUSION

Although the cross-cultural data on prosocial moral judgment are limited, several conclusions can be drawn from this research. First, the similarity across cultures in terms of the modes of reasoning that develop first is striking. Needs-oriented and hedonistic reasoning clearly dominate the reasoning of preschool and early elementary children in all cultures studied. Moreover, certain types of reasoning—authority and punishment and the more sophisticated internalized and self-reflective categories of reasoning—are seldom verbalized by elementary school aged children.

Despite the similarities across cultures, differences in the moral reasoning of individuals from diverse cultures are also evident. The moral judgments of children seem to reflect, to some degree, the values and concerns of the culture. Once children are capable of understanding a certain type of reasoning, differential use of that reasoning seems to be linked to the importance of the concerns embedded in the reasoning for persons in the society. Nonetheless, children, regardless of culture, seldom verbalize types of reasoning that are very advanced for their age (e.g., are abstract and/or involve high levels of perspective taking) despite the relevance of the specific type of reasoning for those in the culture. Thus, cultural differences seem to affect choice of reasoning within that domain of moral reasoning accessible to the individual as a consequent of his or her level of socio-cognitive development.

9 A Model of Prosocial Moral Reasoning

In previous chapters, research concerning the development of children's and adolescents' prosocial moral reasoning was presented. While reviewing this research, we occasionally alluded to a conceptual model, or assumptions that might be expected to be part of a model. However, an explicit model of the development of prosocial moral judgment was never outlined in any detail. At this point, I will take what may seem to be a step backwards and will present such a "model," albeit not fully developed. This model is described subsequent to the review of the literature because an understanding of both the categories of reasoning used by children and developmental change in prosocial reasoning is necessary for the discussion that will follow.

As was mentioned previously, the most detailed and influential model of moral judgment is that of Kohlberg and his colleagues (e.g., Colby, Kohlberg, & Kauffman, in press; Kohlberg, 1969, 1976). Kohlberg has outlined a number of specific assertions regarding the nature of the development of moral judgment, and the characteristics of developmental stages. Because of the familiarity of Kohlberg's model to all researchers and theorists in the area of moral development and the role it has played in this domain of study, our thinking will be compared with that of Kohlberg, Colby, and their colleagues. As will become clear, there are both important similarities and differences between Kohlberg's and our assumptions.

To conduct the proposed comparison, it is necessary to briefly outline both Kohlberg's theory and his coding system. The latter is important because the manner in which moral reasoning is measured has a direct effect on the degree to which some theoretical assertions are supported. Moreover, differences in the

173

ways in which Kohlberg and we have assessed moral reasoning have resulted in somewhat disparate views concerning the development of moral reasoning.

KOHLBERG'S CONCEPTUAL MODEL

Assertions

In Kohlberg and his colleagues' view, moral judgments are interpreted as the individual's perceptions of moral reality. Thus, individuals' thinking about moral questions and their interpretation of moral issues are perceived as important determinants of moral conduct (Colby et al., in press).

An important distinction in Kohlberg's theory is between content of moral judgment (specific moral beliefs or opinions) and structure of reasoning (the general organizing principles or patterns of thought). Kohlberg has focused primarily on structure because it is the structure, not the content, that is believed to exhibit developmental regularity and generalizability within and across individuals. Moreover, the meaning of an individual's moral beliefs is viewed as dependent on an understanding of the individual's general moral view or conceptual framework (Colby et al., in press). According to this model, people construct meaning as a result of the process of dealing with various situations; however, the individual's meaning structure is limited by his or her current developmental level of structure, as well as the individual's prior history.

Kohlberg has differentiated between what he labels as hard structural and soft structural stage models. As discussed in Chapter 2, the criteria for hard stages (borrowed from Piaget) are as follows:

1. Stages imply a distinction of qualitative difference in structures (modes of thinking) that still serve the same basic function (for example, intelligence) at various points in development.

2. These different structures form an invariant sequence, order, or succession in individual development. While cultural factors may speed up, slow down, or stop development, they do not change its sequence.

3. Each of these different and sequential modes of thought forms a "structural whole." A given stage response on a task does not just represent a specific response determined by knowledge and familiarity with that task or tasks similar to it; rather, it represents an underlying thought-organization. The implication is that various aspects of stage structures should appear as a consistent cluster of responses in development.

4. Stages are hierarchical integrations. As noted, stages form an order of increasingly differentiated and integrated structures for fulfilling a common function. Accordingly, higher stages displace (or, rather, integrate) the structures found at lower stages [Colby et al., in press. MS. pp. 12–13].

Soft stages are described as adhering to the first two criteria enumerated above, but not the latter two criteria. Kohlberg's stages are an example of hard-structural stages; Loevinger's (Loevinger & Wessler, 1970) stages of ego development are considered an example of soft stages.

Several aspects of these criteria require further elaboration. The criterion of "structured wholeness" implies that much of the individual's moral reasoning is at a single level. Indeed, Kohlberg and his colleagues (Colby et al., 1983) assert that most of an individual's moral reasoning at a given point in time is at one stage and the adjacent stages. Thus, at least at first glance, it would appear that Kohlberg is asserting that people do not use and/or have access to reasoning two or more stages below or above their dominant stage. However, due to the way in which Kohlberg has operationalized moral judgment, this is not what is being asserted.

Colby et al. (in press) differentiated among comprehension of judgments made by others; preference for, or evaluation of, statements made by others (as studied by Rest, 1979); and spontaneous production of moral judgments in response to questions about what is right and wrong and why. It is also possible to differentiate between competence and performance with regard to spontaneous production. To some degree, Kohlberg and his colleagues have examined competence, not performance, in the domain of moral reasoning. In other words, the coding system is designed to emphasize the most advanced or highest-level reasoning that an individual uses with any consistency, not the range of reasoning verbalized by individuals in their moral reasoning. Indeed, Kohlberg's coding system includes several techniques that systematically exclude, to some degree, reasoning that varies greatly from that of individual's dominant stage, especially lower-level reasoning. First, stages of reasoning that comprise less than 25% of the individual's reasoning are discarded when computing the person's global moral judgment score (Colby et al., 1983). This is not the case for the weighted composite scores used in much of the research (the MMS scores), however, types of reasoning used less than 10% of the time are discarded when computing composite scores. Second, if a lower-level idea is expressed in a manner that is not viewed as being prescriptive (i.e., is not used as a moral justification), it is not coded. This procedure has resulted in the systematic deletion of some lower-level reasoning that other persons might choose to code. Consider Colby et al.'s (1983) sample of reasoning for an individual responding to questions about Kohlberg's euthanasia dilemma:

SHOULD THE DOCTOR DO WHAT SHE ASKS AND GIVE HER THE DRUG?

No, I don't think so. I think it's asking too much of a doctor for one thing, that she should ask this even though she is in great pain. A doctor isn't suppose to do this. WHY? I believe it's in their code that you shouldn't give a drug to any person to help them die sooner or to put them to death right away. *If he were found out to have given her this drug, he'd probably be kicked out of his profession and he might not be able to get into something else.* [case 41–B, p. 88].

For this sample of reasoning, the lower level Stage 2 reasoning (the last sentence) would not be scored. In Colby et al.'s (1983) opinion:

> The risk of undesirable consequences is not used as the central argument against mercy killing as the critical indicators specify. The requirement that the risk of losing his job be used as a central justification reflects the fact that at higher stages a pragmatic concern such as this maintains some validity (the stages are "hierarchically integrated") but is no longer seen as a sufficient justification from the moral point of view. In fact, longitudinal case 41 (time B) was scored globally at stage 3 [p. 89].

A third procedure in the Kohlberg scoring system that tends to lessen the heterogeneity in individuals' scores is that reasoning at lower levels is eliminated if the same basic idea or concern is also expressed in a more mature version. The rationale for this scoring rule is that the lower-level reason is viewed as being conceptually consistent with the higher level reasoning, only expressed incompletely or inadequately (Colby, personal communication, 1984). Although this may often be the case, it is debatable whether or not this assumption always is valid.

In brief, as a consequence of scoring rules, an individual's reasoning generally is rendered more homogeneous, as well as rated at a higher level, than would be the case if all the individual's reasoning were coded. This does not mean, however, that all heterogenity is eliminated; an individual can still be scored as quite heterogeneous in reasoning with the Kohlberg system. However, the fact that heterogenity is reduced is very important when comparing the results of research on prosocial and Kohlbergian moral judgment.

Scoring

In comparing prosocial and Kohlbergian moral judgment, it is useful to have a basic understanding of both coding systems. Such information is necessary to understand exactly what is being labeled as moral judgment. In Kohlberg's latest scoring system (Standard Issue Scoring; Colby et al., in press), there are three levels or units on which individuals' responses to dilemmas are coded: the issue, norm, and element. These three coding units will now be reviewed.

In each Kohlbergian dilemma, there is a conflict between two moral issues and their associated courses of action. For example, in the Heinz dilemma, there is a conflict between life (the choice to steal a drug to save the wife's life; see dilemma on p. 175) and law (the decision not to save the wife's life). The first step in scoring responses to Kohlberg dilemmas is simply to determine which issue (i.e., course of action) was being considered by the individual for a given "chunk" of reasoning (part of the individual's reasoning may be in support of one issue whereas the remainder is in support of the other). The choice of issue is seen as representing a choice of one value over another (e.g., the valuing of life over law).

The next step in scoring is to determine which of nine norms is being referred to in a given chunk of reasoning. The norm is the moral value or object of concern that the individual refers to in justifying a choice of action in a dilemma (i.e., life, preservation, quality/quantity, property, truth, affiliation, authority, law, contract, conscience, punishment). Identifying the norm constitutes a first step in determining why the individual believes a chosen course of action is appropriate. Thus, if a person starts to justify a personal action-choice by refering to property-related issues, the norm would be property. Put simply, the norm refers to the content or object of concern that is referred to in the justification of a moral choice. An individual may use one or several norms when discussing a moral dilemma.

Certain norms are much more likely to be used than others in relation to a given dilemma; the individual's choice of norms is determined, to a large degree, by the content of a specific dilemma as well as by the interviewer's questions (e.g., if the interviewer asks a question related to the value of life, the respondent is likely to refer to the life norm in responding). Nonetheless, the individual's own values are viewed as influencing which of various relevant norms are emphasized in his or her reasoning.

A complete moral judgment is viewed as going beyond specifying a value or object of concern (a norm). The ultimate reason or principle for a given norm being of interest is of importance. These ultimate reasons or principles are designated as "elements" in Kohlberg's coding system. Elements, but not issues or norms, are strongly related to stage of reasoning.

A simple example is helpful in clarifying the difference between a norm and an element. Consider the following justification for saying that Heinz should save his wife's life by stealing the drug (the life issue in the Heinz dilemma): "Heinz should steal the drug because his wife will die without it." The basic object of concern being discussed is life or death; thus, the "life" norm is being evoked. The real *justification* for stealing, however, is focused on the issue of good or bad consequences for the wife. Thus, the element coded in this example would be "good individual consequences/bad individual consequences."

Elements are actually of two types, modal and value (see Table 9.1). In a fully elaborated moral judgment, both a modal and value element (as well as an issue and norm) can be coded. However, especially for lower-stage reasoning, it is often the case that only a modal element can be scored. The modal elements are, in a sense, key moral words such as "should," "must," "approves," or "has

TABLE 9.1
Kohlberg's Moral Elements[a]

Modal Elements
Upholding normative order:
1. Obeying/consulting persons or deity. Should obey, obtain consent (should consult, persuade).
2. Blaming/approving. Should be blamed for, disapproved (should be approved).
3. Retributing/exonerating. Should retribute against (should exonerate).
4. Having a right/having no right.
5. Having a duty/having no duty.

Value Elements
Egoistic consequences
6. Good reputation/bad reputation.
7. Seeking reward/avoiding punishment.
Utiltarian consequences:
8. Good individual consequences/bad individual consequences.
9. Good group consequences/bad group consequences
Ideal or harmony-serving consequences:
10. Upholding character.
11. Upholding self-respect.
12. Serving social ideal or harmony.
13. Serving human dignity and autonomy.
Fairness:
14. Balancing perspectives or role-taking.
15. Reciprocity or positive desert.
16. Maintaining equity and procedural fairness.
17. Maintaining social contract or freely agreeing.

[a]Adapted from Colby et al. (in press).

a right." They express the mood or modality of the moral judgment, for example, if the moral reasoning is an expression of duty, of rights, or of blame (Colby et al., in press).

Modal elements do not provide reasons or values in themselves; for example, they do not indicate why duties or rights are valued or why such duties or rights exist. However, in some cases (especially with individuals reasoning at lower levels), additional justification is not provided (e.g., the individual says something like "it's her right, that's why you should do it."). In cases such as this, the modal element is coded. However, if further justification is provided, a value element is coded.

The value elements are used to provide final justifications that go beyond that of the norm or modal element. Value elements are viewed as representing the ultimate ends, values, or reasons held by the individual. These ends, values, or reasons include concern with egoistic consequences, utilitarian consequences, ideal or harmony-serving consequences, or fairness (see Table 9.1 for details). People reasoning at lower stages sometimes use value elements but sometimes do not.

In summary, in contrast to the norms, elements are the reasons, motivations, or concerns behind action. Thus, some people may have a fundamental concern for maintaining a good reputation; others are concerned with human dignity. Norms define the kind of moral action (e.g., law breaking, life saving), whereas ethical reasons for those actions are provided by the elements. In other words, norms tell us what the individual values (e.g., life, property); elements tell us why it is valued (Colby et al., in press).

There are numerous reasons for the complexity of the Kohlberg scoring system. One is that Kohlberg's dilemmas are concerned with a variety of moral issues; for example, in two of the interview forms, the three dilemmas concern conflicts about morality/conscience (whether or not to be lenient toward someone who has broken the law), punishment (whether to punish someone who has broken the law), and authority versus contract (obeying one's parents versus abiding by or holding someone to an agreement). Thus, individuals are likely to cite a wide range of objects of concern (norms) as well as justifications (elements), and the scoring system must be sufficiently differentiated to accomodate this variation.

A second reason for the complexity of the scoring system (i.e., the use of issues, norms, and elements) is to provide a means of classifying moral reasoning into small units for ease of coding. The new scoring manual contains numerous examples of reasoning for each combination of an issue, norm, and element that is appropriate to a given stage level (not all possible combinations are scored at each stage). By classifying subjects' responses into small units that can be matched to the examples, scoring errors decrease whereas interrater reliability increases. Thus, issues and norms are useful devices for classifying reasoning into units for coding into stages.

The preceeding summary of the Kohlberg coding system obviously is too incomplete and insufficiently detailed to equip the reader to use Kohlberg's scoring system. The reader is referred to the new scoring manual (Colby et al., in press) for more detail regarding the scoring system.

PROSOCIAL MORAL REASONING

Scoring

The procedures and categories for scoring prosocial moral reasoning were presented in Chapter 7. Rather than re-introduce these, at this time the similarities and differences in the scoring of prosocial and Kohlberg moral dilemmas will be considered.

The scoring system that has been used to code prosocial moral judgment is less complex than that used to code Kohlberg's dilemmas. This is due, in part, to the greater homogeneity of content across the prosocial dilemmas, resulting

in a much smaller range of typical responses (e.g., reasoning related to authorities, formal obligations, and social contract are less relevant to prosocial than
Kohlberg's dilemmas and therefore are seldom discussed). The relative simplicity
of the prosocial moral reasoning coding system also is due to the fact that most
of the research on this type of moral judgment has been conducted with preschool
or elementary-school children. The responses of children are much simpler and
less diverse than those of older persons (Eisenberg-Berg, 1979a); thus, it is not
surprising that a scoring system used primarily to code the reasoning of adolescents and adults (Kohlberg's system) is much more complex than one used to
code the responses of children. In fact, the range of categories used to score the
prosocial reasoning of young children (e.g., in Eisenberg et al., 1983; Eisenberg-
Berg & Hand, 1979; Eisenberg-Berg & Roth, 1980) is much narrower than the
range of categories in the total scoring system (Eisenberg, 1977; Eisenberg-Berg,
1979a).

At a very basic level, different aspects of moral reasoning are scored with
the prosocial and Kohlberg's scoring systems. Individuals' competence (capacity),
rather than performance (entire range of reasoning), is emphasized, to some
degree, with the Kohlbergian moral-judgment score. In contrast, with the prosocial scoring system, all of the individual's reasoning usually is scored regardless
of whether it occurs less than 25% of the time (a criterion for computing the
global scores in the Kohlberg system) and regardless of whether higher-level
reasoning concerning the same general idea (i.e., in Kohlberg's system, the same
issue, norm, and element) is used. This simple difference in scoring criteria
undoubtedly has an effect on the diversity and homogeneity of a single individual's reasoning.

With regard to the units of coding used by Kohlberg (issues, norms, modal
elements, and value elements), the prosocial moral reasoning categories are most
similar to Kohlberg's modal and value elements. Although the names given to
the prosocial categories are often quite similar to those for Kohlberg's norms,
the intent behind the prosocial categories is to code the concern or motive behind
the reasoning. For example, at first glance, it might seem that the prosocial
reasoning category "affectional relationship" is similar to Kohlberg's norm of
"affiliation." However, reasoning related to objects of affiliation is frequently
coded into a variety of prosocial categories including "hedonistic reasoning"
(e.g., if the child wants to make a friend merely to have someone to play with),
"approval/interpersonal orientation" (e.g., a course of action is chosen to enhance
a relationship or to gain another's approval), and "affectional relationship" (a
course of action is chosen becuase one likes, or is a friend of, the potential
recipient). Thus, not all references to relationships and objects of relationship
(the focus of Kohlberg's norm of affiliation) are coded in the prosocial category
"affectional relationship." Similarly, not all references to authorities would be
coded in the prosocial category "authority/punishment orientation"; for example,
references to authorities could be scored as "hedonistic" (e.g., "It wouldn't be

worth getting in a fight because my mother would not let me play outdoors anymore") or "concern with society" (e.g., "It is important that people obey authorities because if everyone adhers to authorities' dictates, everyone in society would be better off").

Indeed, some of the prosocial moral-judgment categories can be considered as analogous to specific value elements. For example, the element "good reputation/bad reputation" is similar to the prosocial category "approval/interpersonal orientation;" "seeking reward/avoiding punishment" is similar to "hedonistic reasoning;" "good group consequences/bad group consequences" to "concern with condition of society;" "concern with human dignity and autonomy" to "concern with human dignity;" and "maintaining social contract or freely agreeing" to "social-contract orientation." Similarly, "upholding character" and "upholding self-respect" are similar to the prosocial categories concerning positive or negative affect related to living up to one's values and self-image and/ or the law and norm orientation category (depending on the specifics of the response).

In the prosocial moral-judgment coding system, modal and value elements are not clearly differentiated. Moreover, the prosocial moral reasoning scoring system is not explictedly based on levels of sociomoral perspective taking. Nonetheless, the similarity between Kohlberg's value elements and the prosocial categories is striking, and reflects basic similarities in the conceptualization of moral judgment.

Much of the difference in what is indexed by Kohlberg's and our prosocial scoring system is attributable to variations in procedures used to produce summary indices of moral judgment. In Kohlberg's system, the individual's use of elements for specific objects of concern (i.e., norms) is used to compute a single summary score. In computing this score, information related to infrequently used modes of reasoning and some lower-level reasoning is omitted, resulting in a single composite score that reflects competence more than performance. In contrast, prosocial moral-reasoning scores have been derived in three different ways. First, in many studies, the prosocial categories themselves, not a summary score based on some amalgamation of the prosocial category scores, have been the unit of analysis. In these instances, the entire range of the individual's responses is considered (Eisenberg, Boehnke, Schuhler, & Silbereisen, 1985; Eisenberg, Pasternack, Cameron, & Tryon, 1984; Eisenberg-Berg & Hand, 1979). In several more recent studies, a composite score that is designed to reflect the proportion of each type of reasoning used has been computed (e.g., Eisenberg et al., 1984; Eisenberg, Lennon, & Roth, 1983). Although this composite is a single score, the range of the individual's reasoning is represented in the composite. Finally, in some research the individual's reasoning has been classified into one of various levels (Eisenberg, 1983a; Eisenberg-Berg, 1979b; see Table 7.8 for these levels). In doing so, the highest level of reasoning that was used with some frequency was the basis for the classification process. Thus, this index of prosocial moral reasoning can be viewed as reflecting competence more than performance, although the individual's reasoning was not assigned to the highest level verbalized if that type of reasoning was used very infrequently. It is likely that this index of prosocial moral reasoning is most similar to that of Kohlberg. However, it has seldom been used in the research.

Conceptual Assumptions

Due, in part, to the fact that Kohlberg and those examining prosocial moral reasoning have coded somewhat different aspects of moral judgment, we do not make all the same assumptions about prosocial moral judgment that Kohlberg has made with regard to Kohlbergian moral judgment. For example, because all of the individual's prosocial moral reasoning is scored (judgments at different levels are not collapsed), we do not find that stages are "structured wholes." Indeed, a single individual often exhibits reasoning at a variety of levels.

We also do not claim that our levels of prosocial reasoning are invariant in sequence. We are still attempting (via longitudinal and cross-cultural research) to further verify the sequence of development. At this point in time, it is not altogether clear which categories are at equivalent levels; some of those we have combined into a single level may not be entirely equivalent in developmental maturity. For example, direct reciprocity and hedonistic reasoning are combined into a single level although the former seems to develop somewhat later than the latter (e.g., Eisenberg et al., 1985; Eisenberg et al., 1983).

Even if we were more confident that our levels of reasoning were entirely accurate, it would be quite possible that we would discover that the levels were not invariant in sequence. For example, level 3 (see Table 7.8), including stereotypic and approval/interpersonal oriented reasoning, seems to emerge at an earlier age than level 4 (self-reflective empathic reasoning) in both our cross-sectional and cross-cultural research. Not all of our longitudinal subjects, however, have exhibited level 3 reasoning prior to level 4 reasoning. Moreover, in crosssectional research, children too young to have "passed through" level 3 often exhibit some level 4 reasoning. Although levels 3 and 4 could, depending on the exact wording, be coded at an equivalent level with Kohlberg's scoring system, we have found that components of level 3 and level 4 reasoning (i.e., the categories included at each level) are unrelated or negatively related, and follow different developmental courses. Thus, based on our data, it would seem that these two levels of reasoning are neither developmentally equivalent nor invariant in sequence. It should be noted, however, the even if our levels of reasoning are not invariant in sequence, this would not mean that Kohlberg's stages based on level of sociomoral perspective-taking are not.

Just as it is too soon to determine whether the levels of prosocial moral reasoning are invariant in sequence, it also is too early to make definitive statements regarding the universality of the levels. Clearly, if the levels prove not to be invariant, they could not be universal. Thus, although the data presented in Chapter 8 are consistent with the view that the ordering of levels (not the use of a particular mode of reasoning at a specific age) is somewhat similar across cultures, this issue has not been adequately examined.

Another of Kohlberg's assertions concerns the issue of hierarchical integration. In Kohlberg's view, later stages not only replace but transform earlier stages. Each new stage is viewed as representing an integration or transformation of the previous stage. Other theorists have disagreed with Kohlberg's assertion regarding hierarchical integration. Rest (1979) rejected Kohlberg's model and proposed an additive or "layer-cake" model in which higher level stages are added to the individual's repertoire (generally as the individual ages) with no loss of access to lower-stage reasoning. In other words, the individual still uses lower-stage reasoning even when he or she is capable of higher-stage reasoning. This model of development is inconsistent with Kohlberg's assumption that stages of reasoning are structured wholes.

Our data are consistent with Rest's (1979), not Kohlberg's, model of development. We have found that even adolescents capable of using relatively high-level moral reasoning sometimes simultaneously use a variety of lower-level modes of reasoning (Eisenberg-Berg, 1979a). This difference between our findings and those of Kohlberg could be due to differences in procedures for scoring of individuals' lower-level reasoning. Nonetheless, when the entire range of an individual's prosocial moral reasoning is considered, it is clear that the model of hierarchical integration does not accurately describe the nature of prosocial moral judgment.

The last of Kohlberg's assertions with regard to moral stages is that each stage is qualitatively different from other stages of moral reasoning. Given the dramatic change in the structure of children's reasoning with age, it is our belief there might be qualitative changes in children's moral reasoning as they develop more sophisticated levels of social-cognitive skills. However, we are uncertain whether our levels of prosocial moral reasoning accurately depict qualitatively different stages of reasoning. For example, it is possible that some types of reasoning included in level 4 are not qualitatively different than some categories of reasoning included in level 5; rather, some level 4 and 5 modes of reasoning may represent differences in value orientations (e.g., other-oriented versus rule-oriented values). Additional research is necessary to determine whether there are qualitative changes in prosocial moral judgment, and if so, which modes of reasoning are characteristic of each qualitative stage.

A Model of Prosocial Development

Although prosocial moral judgment levels are not asserted to embody all of the criteria of "hard" developmental stages (qualitative change, structural wholeness, invariant sequence, and hierarchical integration), there are important conceptual similarities between Kohlberg's model of moral judgment and our own model of the development of prosocial moral judgment. The most important of these is the underlying assumption that development is limited, in part, by the individual's level of socio-cognitive development, that is, the complexity of the individual's cognition with regard to social phenomena. In Kohlberg's and his colleagues' view, a certain level of logical and socio-cognitive skills is necessary but not sufficient for a given level of moral reasoning (Colby et al., in press). For example, 9-year-olds could not be expected to exhibit Kohlberg's stage 4 reasoning because their ability to conceptualize notions as abstract as "society," the societal point of view, and the role of the individual in society is limited. The implication of this perspective is that there is a ceiling set on individuals' levels of moral judgment by their levels of cognitive sophistication, which, in turn, are in part developmentally determined. In other words, individuals who are at a low or moderate level with regard to logical and socio-cognitive functioning—often due to their young age and corresponding incomplete development—cannot be expected to understand or use higher-level modes of moral judgment (see Chapter 7 for more discussion of the relations of moral judgment to cognitive and perspective-taking skills)

The assumption that there is a ceiling set on the individual's level of moral reasoning due to the individual's level of logical and/or socio-cognitive development seems applicable to the domain of prosocial moral judgment. Young children clearly are incapable of expressing higher-level modes of reasoning; level 4 or 5 reasoning is quite rare even among children in elementary school (e.g., Eisenberg-Berg, 1979a; Eisenberg-Berg & Hand, 1979; Eisenberg-Berg & Roth, 1980). Thus, logical and socio-cognitive capabilities—capabilities associated with chronological age—appear to limit the range of potential levels of moral reasoning available to the individual for use (see Figure 9.1).

Within the range of prosocial reasoning accessible to a given individual, a variety of levels may be verbalized. For example, a child who is capable of level 3 reasoning often also uses level 1 and 2 reasoning (although the child might be expected to use greater amounts of reasoning that is closer in level to personal level of competence than reasoning further from personal level of competence; cf. Davidson, King, Kitchener, & Parker, 1980). Consequently, an interesting question concerns the factors that influence individuals' choices of reasoning within their range of competence.

Colby et al. (in press) believe that there is a developmental press for people to use the highest level of reasoning that they are capable of using. In our view, there is such a press, but it is mild. We believe that the individual's choice of moral reasoning is also influenced by personal values and goals (which, in turn, are based in part on the individual's socialization history). For example, individuals who are concerned about social appearances and others' approval should tend to use approval/interpersonally oriented reasoning, whereas empathic persons with other-oriented value systems should tend to use whichever mode of

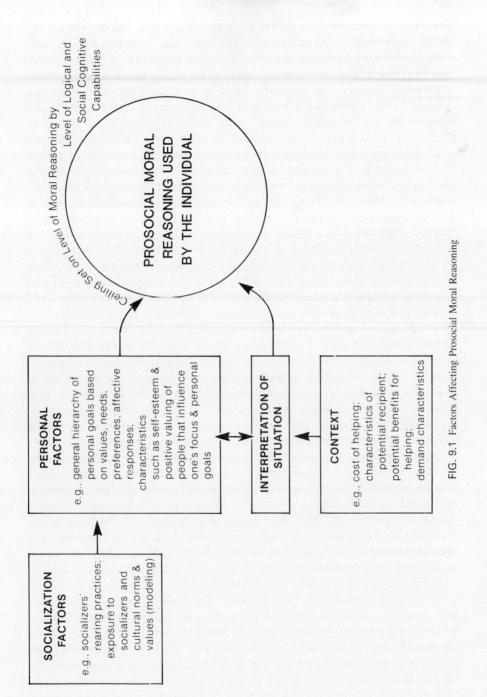

FIG. 9.1 Factors Affecting Prosocial Moral Reasoning

empathic moral reasoning is appropriate for their age (e.g., needs-oriented reasoning for younger children; sympathetic or role-taking reasoning for older children). In contrast, those concerned with material outcomes for the self should tend to prefer hedonistic reasoning, whereas the desire to behave in a manner condoned by society would be expected to be associated with stereotypic reasoning. In other words, the type of reasoning preferred by a given individual is expected to be a function of aspects of the person frequently labeled as components of "personality." These include the individual's value-orientation and other individual characteristics such as degree of positive valuing of people, level of self-esteem, and degree of self-concern, all of which color the individual's needs, preferences, and values (cf. Berkowitz, 1972; Jarymowicz, 1977; Reykowski, 1982a, b; Staub, 1984). Although the individual's level of competence with regard to moral reasoning is limited by developmental factors, performance within one's sphere of competence is believed to be a function, in part, of individual differences on a variety of personal variables.

Although the data are limited, there is some evidence to support this view. Among fourth graders, we have found that individuals concerned with presenting a socially desirable image tend to use relatively high levels of approval-oriented reasoning (Eisenberg, Pasternack, & Lennon, 1984). Similarly, American children who scored high on Bryant's (1982) empathy scale were found to use relatively high amounts of empathic modes of reasoning (needs-oriented reasoning for second graders; sympathetic reasoning for fourth graders; Eisenberg et al., 1984). A similar relation between needs-oriented reasoning (psychological needs) and empathy scores has been noted among the Maisin in New Guinea (Tietjen, personal communication).

All individuals have a number of personal goals based upon personal values, needs and preferences (cf. Staub, 1978, 1984). As was noted by Staub (1978), in a given situation, several of these personal factors may be relevant to moral decision-making. Moreover, in many situations, various personal goals activated in a given context may conflict with one another. For example, in a situation in which one can publically assist another at a cost to the self, the desire for social approval and/or empathically-based concern may conflict with the desire to preserve one's own resources. In such circumstances, the relative importance of the various relevant goals in the individual's hierarchy of personal goals should be reflected in the choice of moral justifications, as well as in the relative salience of various modes of reasoning (when more than one mode is used).

Despite our focus on the role of personal characteristics (e.g., values, goals), it is clear that the context is also an important influence on individuals' choices of moral reasoning from those modes available to them. For example, young children (Eisenberg-Berg & Neal, 1981) and adults (Sobesky, 1983) tend to use more lower-level reasoning as the cost of assisting another increases. Moreover, there is undoubtedly an interaction beween the factors of context and personal characteristics; which personal goals are most salient in a specific situation will be a function, in part, of components of both the context and the person. For example, the degree to which the goal of obtaining others' approval is activated is a function of somewhat different contextual cues (e.g., different degrees of public visability or the presence of different observers) for different persons, depending upon pre-existing personality characteristics. Of course, it is also true that the individual's interpretation of a situation—including which aspects of the situation are apprehended, perceived as salient, and/or distorted—is a function, in part, of personal characteristics. Indeed, it is unlikely that context alone ever is the sole influence on choice of moral reasoning; even in extreme situations in which contextual influences are overwhelming (e.g., if the cost of acting in a manner consistent with higher level reasoning were death), there would probably be individual differences in the level of moral judgment expressed with regard to a specific moral conflict (e.g., consider the behavior and reasoning of Socrates prior to his death).

This perspective on prosocial moral reasoning is presented in Figure 9.1. The lists of personal, contextual, and socializations factors in the figure are not exhaustive; nor would we limit the factors influencing moral reasoning exhibited by the individual to those in the figure. Nonetheless, it is our view that such a heuristic model is useful when considering the factors that contribute to the individual's level of prosocial moral reasoning concerning moral conflicts in specific contexts.

CONCLUSION

Our view of the processes influencing the individual's use of moral reasoning differs somewhat from that of Kohlberg. This is due to differences in theoretical orientation, in the types of moral dilemmas studied, and (perhaps of most importance) in the scoring systems. Personal characteristics, and the socialization influences affecting these characteristics, are much more prominent in our model than in Kohlberg's. Similarly, contextual factors, and their interaction with personal factors, are viewed as more important in our model. However, the precise manner in which personal and contextual variables influence mode of level judgment (when performance rather than competence is the focus) has been insufficiently studied; future research concerning this issue could do much to clarify our understanding of moral judgment.

10 The Role of Altruistic Affect and Cognitions in Behavior

In 1964, Kitty Genovese was murdered in Queens, New York within the sight or sound of 38 persons. Although the stabbing took place over a considerable length of time, none of the witnesses called the police until after the woman was dead. Surely some of the witnesses, upon hearing Kitty's screams, felt empathy or sympathy for her. Others must have known that they would suffer pangs of guilt for not assisting. Similarly, cognitions regarding values or norms of helping must have crept into the thoughts of some witnesses. Yet none helped.

The Kitty Genovese incident is a dramatic example illustrating the commonly known fact that people do not always assist others even when they think they should help or feel emotions consistent with benevolent behavior. This notion is true for adults as well as children, although children may be less likely than adults to assist in some circumstances (cf. Moore & Eisenberg, 1984; Radke-Yarrow et al., 1983). An important question, then, concerns the links between altruistic behavior and altruistic emotions and cognitions, and the nature of other factors that mediate or moderate these interrelations.

The issues of when, how, and why prosocial behavior are enacted are complex. Many theorists and researchers have proposed models of prosocial action (e.g., Latane & Darley, 1970; Piliavin et al., 1981; Schwartz & Howard, 1981, 1984; Staub, 1978); indeed, entire books have been written on the topic. The processes included in extant models have differed across theorists and researchers, depending upon the type of prosocial behavior (e.g., helping in emergencies versus nonemergency situations) and the age of the actors of interest (child versus adult). The processes related to prosocial action—from the first step of attending to another's need to the action itself and its consequences—are so complex and varied that no one model has, or probably can, delineate the entire phenomenon.

In this final chapter, a model of prosocial action will be outlined, one designed to delineate the role of altruistic emotions and cognitions in altruistic and prosocial action. In this model, we will include a variety of factors that influence prosocial action besides altruistic affects and cognitions; however, many of these will not be discussed in detail. We present this model for heuristic purposes, with the hope of stimulating further thinking and research. Certainly we have captured neither the complexity of prosocial action in all circumstances nor the breath of research findings and theoretical conceptualizations available in the literature. For example, biological factors are not included in the model, although they may affect role taking and empathic capacities (see Chapter 2).

Our model concerns prosocial action that is directed toward alleviating another's need. This fact in itself limits the generalizability of the model. Clearly, some acts of assistance are directed toward individuals who have no discernable physical or psychological need (Eisenberg, Pasternack, Cameron, & Tryon, 1984). Assistance of this sort seems to be based on the benefactor's style of social interaction (Eisenberg, Cameron, Tryon, & Dodez, 1981; Eisenberg et al., 1984) or the benefactor's own desires (e.g., the desire to initiate social interaction; Eisenberg-Berg & Hand, 1979). In cases such as these, when the other's needs or wants are not discernable via either perceptual processing (e.g., visual cues) or sophisticated cognitive perspective-taking (e.g., envisioning of needs in the other's ongoing life circumstances), associated prosocial behavior is relatively unlikely to be altruistically motivated. Consequently, given that the primary focus in this book is on altruism, prosocial acts that are not based on the perception of another's needs or desires will not be considered.

A simplified overview of the model is presented in Figure 10.1. This model is subdivided and presented in greater detail in Figures 10.2, 10.3 and 10.4. The remainder of this chapter will be organized around this model.

ATTENTION TO ANOTHER'S NEED: A FIRST STEP

Before a person can assist another who is in need, he or she must process and consciously recognize the other's need or desires. This point frequently has been discussed by Schwartz and his colleagues (e.g., Schwartz & Howard, 1981, 1982, 1984), and is the first step in their value-based, decision-making model of altruism.

Attention to another's need is influenced by both personal factors and the individual's interpretation of the given situation. Moreover, characteristics of individuals that affect both their interpretation of the situation and the likelihood of their noting another's need appear to be influenced by socialization history. The ways in which these factors interact and influence attention to another's need are illustrated in Figure 10.2, and will now be discussed in some detail.

190

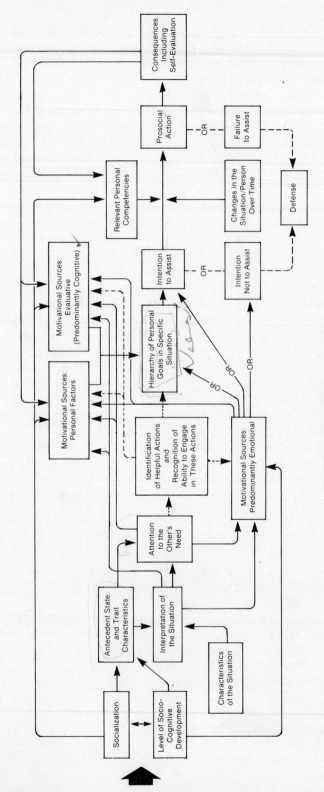

FIG. 10.1 A Model of Prosocial Behavior

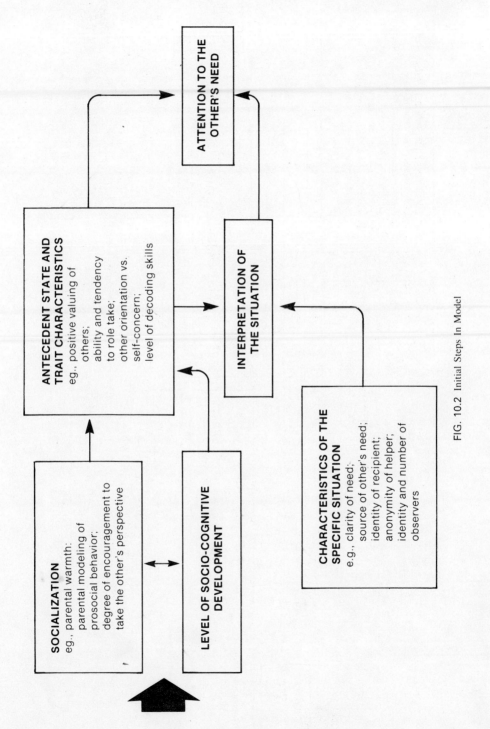

FIG. 10.2 Initial Steps In Model

ATTENTION TO THE OTHER'S NEED

ANTECEDENT STATE AND TRAIT CHARACTERISTICS
eg., positive valuing of others;
ability and tendency to role take;
other orientation vs. self-concern;
level of decoding skills

INTERPRETATION OF THE SITUATION

SOCIALIZATION
eg., parental warmth;
parental modeling of prosocial behavior;
degree of encouragement to take the other's perspective

LEVEL OF SOCIO-COGNITIVE DEVELOPMENT

CHARACTERISTICS OF THE SPECIFIC SITUATION
e.g., clarity of need;
source of other's need;
identity of recipient;
anonymity of helper;
identity and number of observers

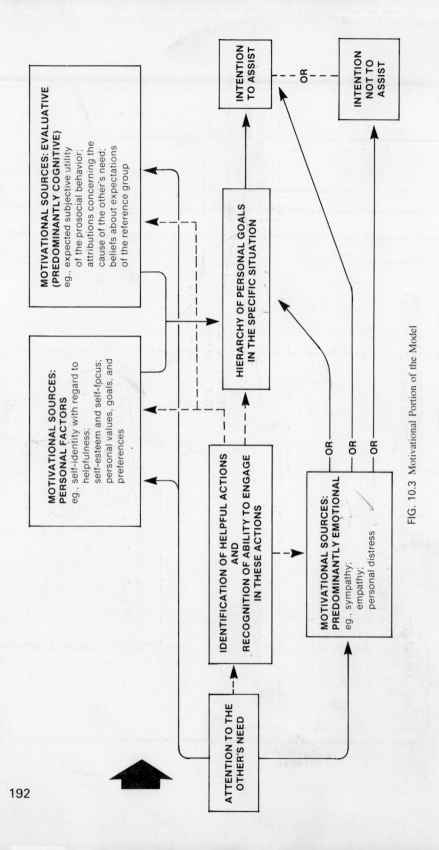

FIG. 10.3 Motivational Portion of the Model

192

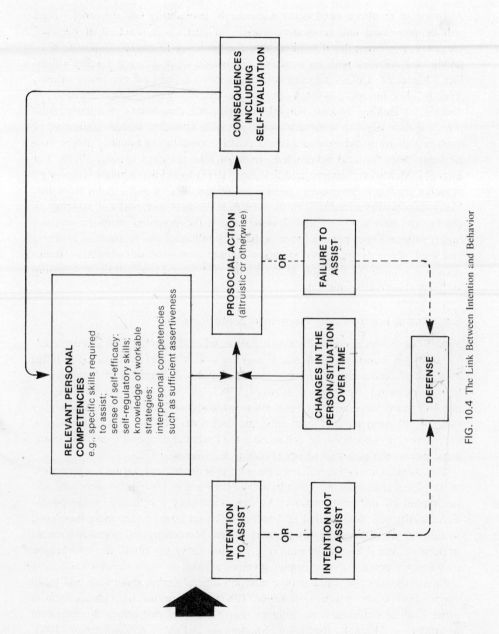

FIG. 10.4 The Link Between Intention and Behavior

CONSEQUENCES INCLUDING SELF-EVALUATION

RELEVANT PERSONAL COMPETENCIES
e.g., specific skills required to assist; sense of self-efficacy; self-regulatory skills; knowledge of workable strategies; interpersonal competencies such as sufficient assertiveness

PROSOCIAL ACTION (altruistic or otherwise)

FAILURE TO ASSIST

CHANGES IN THE PERSON/SITUATION OVER TIME

DEFENSE

INTENTION TO ASSIST

OR

INTENTION NOT TO ASSIST

OR

Personal Factors

Attention to another's need is not a given; the probability that the other's need will be processed and recognized varies, in part, as a function of personal variables. For example, it is likely that the tendency to engage in perspective-taking is associated with an increased likelihood of perceiving another's need (see Chapter 6). Unless the cues denoting another's need are extremely salient, some level of inference is often necessary to discern that another is unhappy, in distress, or lacking in some tangible or intangible commodity. Similarly, self-preoccupation may, in some situations, preclude attending to cues indicative of another's distress, whereas a general positive orientation towards others may facilitate detection and acknowledgement of relevant cues (Staub, 1978). For example, McMillen, Sanders, and Solomon (1977) found that adults who received negative feedback designed to induce temporary loss of self-esteem were less likely than positive-feedback or no-feedback subjects to report not noticing an emergency, and also exhibited less helping if the potential recipient was not highly salient. Other personal factors that may influence one's attention to others and their needs in any given situation include degree of self-directed (nonnegative) attention (Stephenson & Wicklund, 1983) and one's skill at decoding verbal and nonverbal messages.

Situational Factors and Their Interpretations

Situational factors undoubtedly also influence whether another's need is detected. For example, clarity and salience of another's need would be expected to influence initial processing of another's need and the designation of that need as being serious (cf. Schwartz & Howard, 1982). In fact, explicitly detailing the needs of individuals requiring bone-marrow transplants has been related to higher rates of volunteering to donate an organ (Schwartz, 1970). Similarly, helping in emergencies appears to be enhanced if the potential recipient is in close visual proximity to the potential helper (Piliavin & Piliavin, 1972).

Situational factors that influence awareness of another's need are not processed in an identical manner by all individuals; they are differentially perceived and interpreted by different persons. As was previously mentioned, some people undoubtedly are more skilled at detecting relevant cues, or are more motivated to seek out information regarding others' states. Moreover, individual differences in personal variables and in state (e.g., mood) serve to "filter" the information in the environment. For example, level of arousal (a state variable) seems to influence the ways in which people interpret others' verbal statements and facial expressions (Clark, Milberg, & Erber, 1983); furthermore, individuals seem to differ in their willingness to decipher nonverbal cues that others do not intent to emit (e.g., Blanck, Rosenthal, Snodgrass, DePaulo, & Zuckerman, 1981; Zuckerman, Blanck, DePaulo, & Rosenthal, 1980). In brief, personal variables not only directly influence whether one attends to a need, but also affect the way in which potential environmental cues, possibly indicative of need, are interpreted.

Socialization History

Many of the personal characteristics that influence attention to and interpretation of cues concerning others' needs can be related to socialization history. For example, level of perspective-taking skills seems to be enhanced by maternal warmth and support, low maternal use of physical punishment, a tendency for mothers to avoid dominating or overcontrolling the child, and maternal emphasis on "person-centered rationales" (rationales that refer to people in a personal fashion rather than to roles or positional attributes; Light, 1979). Exposure to experiences (Iannotti, 1978) and disciplinary practices (e.g., other-oriented reasoning, Hoffman, 1970b) that focus the child's attention on others and their thoughts and feelings also seem to promote the ability or tendency to role take. Similarly, warm, supportive parenting is likely to produce positive affect toward and trust of other persons (e.g., Ainsworth, Blehar, Waters, & Wall, 1978; Pastor, 1981; Waters, Wippmann, & Sroufe, 1979), characteristics that one would expect to lead to a general positive orientation towards others and, consequently, to a tendency to attend to others and their needs (Staub, 1978).

Many personal characteristics involved in interpreting cues concerning another's need change dramatically as a function of socio-cognitive development. For example, level of perspective-taking capabilities improves dramatically with age (see Chapter 6). Furthermore, young children seem to be less able than older children to interpret subtle cues indicative of another's need. Pearl (1979) found that 4-year-olds were less likely than 8-year-olds to recognize that actors in a videotape had a problem when cues related to the distress itself and the cause of the distress were subtle. Moreover, young children were less likely to infer sadness on the part of the child with the problem, especially when the problem was due to lack of skill rather than lack of physical ability.

Identification of Helpful Actions and Recognition of One's Ability to Assist

Schwartz and Howard (1982, 1984) included three steps in the attention stage of their model: (1) awareness of a person in need; (2) identification of potentially helpful actions; and (3) recognition of one's own ability to engage in these actions. In their model, these three steps preceed both the activation of value and motivational components that feed into the decision-making process and the evaluation of the costs and benefits of the helping act.

Obviously, it is true that steps (1), (2), and (3) often may proceed the activation of feelings related to motivation to assist or evaluation of costs and benefits. Furthermore, in many situations people may never develop feelings of obligation to assist if they have not identified ways of assisting and have not recognized that they have the capacity to assist. However, it is logical to assume that steps (2) and (3) are not always a prerequisite to the generation of the motivation to assist and the processing of costs and benefits. For example, in emergencies people may feel that they should help before they have thought through whether or not they have the ability to assist or have identified potential means of assisting. In other situations, people may make the decision to try to assist, and then seek information with regard to the means of assisting and the possibility of their actually doing so. Indeed, the values that are activated in the decision-making process may influence identification of potential means of helping (e.g., different values might lead to different views about whether one should assist indigent people by feeding them, providing job training, or attempting to enact laws related to their needs). In brief, it is likely that identifying a means for assisting and recognizing one's own ability to engage in these actions can occur at various places in the process leading to prosocial behavior; some of the possibilities are illustrated in Figures 10.1 and 10.3.

MOTIVATIONAL FACTORS

Once potential helpers or benefactors have attended to another's need (and perhaps have identified actions that might relieve this need and have recognized their own ability to assist), they must decide whether they plan to assist. There are at least two ways in which this process can proceed (see Figure 10.1). In some instances, primarily emergencies, the process underlying the decision to assist is primarily affective; in other situations, the process is one in which cognitive processing as well as specific characteristics of the individual play a larger role.

In yet other situations, an individual may assist semi-automatically, that is, may respond without much conscious cognitive processing or emotionally responding. Such behavior can be viewed as habitual or based on well-learned cognitive scripts (e.g., Langer, Blank, & Chanowitz, 1978). In situations such as these, the roles of contemporaneous cognitive, personal, and affective motivational sources are probably minimal. However, because people are unlikely to assist if the various costs of a habitual prosocial act are high, it can be assumed that people generally do evaluate aspects of the helping context, if only in a minimal or global manner. For this reason, there is no separate path in Figure 10.1 for habitual or scripted prosocial behaviors.

Motivational Source: Primarily Affective

Empathy, Sympathy, and Personal Distress.   Consider the situation in which a toddler falls into a wading pool and is likely to drown. Most people would immediately assist; thus, the role of cognitive processing and personality variables in the process of deciding to help must be minimal. Few people would engage in an extensive analysis of costs and benefits, in part because the potential costs are not very high. However, even if the costs were somewhat higher (e.g., if the toddler had waded into a turbulent ocean), many people would probably still attempt to assist. In such crises, it appears that the motive to assist is primarily affective—either sympathy for the other in distress or the desire to relieve one's own feelings of personal distress (e.g., anxiety, fear) that are engendered by viewing the other's distress.

Whether one experiences sympathy or personal distress when confronted with another in distress is probably a function, in part, of one's needs, values, and preferences as reflected in one's hierarchy of personal goals (e.g., the importance of others and their welfare in one's hierarchy). These values, preferences, and needs are shaped, to some degree, by socializers. For example, warm, supportive parenting, parental expression of emotion, and parental empathy have been related to the development of empathic tendencies (Barnett et al., 1980; Eisenberg-Berg & Mussen, 1978; cf. Barnett, 1982). Moreover, whether arousal is experienced as personal distress, sympathy, or some other emotion seems to be a function of the observer's interpretation of the cause of the arousal (based on situational cues). For example, when someone is aroused upon seeing another person staggering, attributions related to the cause of the other's staggering (e.g., whether it is due to drunkenness or a heart attack) will probably affect whether observers interpret their arousal as distress or sympathy (cf. Paliavin et al., 1981, for more discussion of related issues and a more detailed model of emergency helping).

If the observer whose initial reaction is primarily affective experiences a high degree of personal distress, he or she will search for the best way to reduce that distress (cf. Batson, 1984). If assisting will reduce the personal distress (especially if the cost of assisting is not too high), the observer may decide to help the needy other. However, if there is an easier, less costly way of reducing one's distress, for example, escape from the situation, the observer is likely to choose that route for handling the arousal. If the individual does choose to escape, he or she is likely to defend against negative self-evaluative reactions by devaluing the victim or redefining the situation (e.g., through denying the other's need, denying that an effective means of assisting was available, denying that one has the ability or competence to assist, and/or denying that one has a responsibility to conform with obligations stemming from normative or personal standards in that particular set of circumstances; cf. Schwartz & Howard, 1981, 1982, 1984 for more details).

Developmental factors may also influence whether an observer responds to another's distress with personal distress, sympathy, or some other reaction. Very young children (10–14 months of age) do not seem to differentiate the other's distress from their reaction to viewing the other (e.g., Radke-Yarrow & Zahn-Waxler, 1984). If infants view another in distress, they are likely to exhibit signs of agitation or distress themselves and may also seek out the mother. Thus, young children apparently react to the vicarious sharing of emotion in a manner that suggests they often are experiencing personal distress. In contrast, slightly older children sometimes attempt to assist another, even when escape from the circumstances is easy; thus, it would appear that by the middle of the second year, many children are capable of experiencing sympathy as well as personal distress.

Whether the ratio of predominantly sympathetic to predominantly personal distress reactions increases with age after the first 2–3 years is difficult to ascertain. The increased assisting with age noted in some situations during childhood (cf. Moore & Eisenberg, 1984; Radke-Yarrow et al., 1983) could be due to any number of factors, including greater understanding with age that helping can be a means of reducing one's own personal distress or raising one's own mood (Cialdini & Kenrick, 1976). Nonetheless, age-related increments in role-taking skills and the internalization of other-oriented values and norms may be associated with an increasing tendency during the school years for children to experience vicarious arousal as predominantly sympathy rather than personal distress.

Motivation: Evaluative (Predominantly Cognitive) Factors

Observers do not decide whether they intend to assist a needy other primarily on the basis of their affective responses to the specific circumstances. In many situations, the other's need is not so compelling that a strong affective response is forthcoming; moreover, in most situations the decision to assist or not to assist need not be made instantaneously because help need not be immediate to be useful. In brief, most situations in which an individual is faced with a decision regarding a prosocial act are not crises, emergencies, or circumstances in which the other's need is gripping and extremely compelling.

Analysis of Subjective Utility: Costs versus Benefits. When the decision whether to assist is not made impulsively, numerous other factors may influence one's decision, some of which are primarily cognitive in nature. One such factor is the expected utility of the act in question. Both the perceived outcomes of assisting or not assisting, and the individual's beliefs concerning the probability of these outcomes seem to influence the decision-making process (cf. Lynch & Cohen, 1978). Extreme or negative consequences may get disproportionate weight in making decisions regarding helping (Lynch & Cohen, 1978); nonetheless, positive consequences such as lifting one's own mood may also influence one's decision whether or not to help (cf. Cialdini et al., 1982).

It is clear that as the probable costs for assisting increase, people both are less likely to say that one should or would assist (Eisenberg-Berg & Neal, 1981; Lynch & Cohen, 1978; Sobesky, 1983), and are less likely to actually engage in prosocial behavior (e.g., Eisenberg & Shell, 1985; Midlarsky & Midlarsky,

1973; Wagner & Wheeler, 1969). Indeed, if the cost of assisting is high, helping seemingly can be inhibited for most persons, even for those who generally are empathic and predisposed to assist (Batson et al., 1983). Costs for helping may include feelings of aversion that are likely to arise when helping (e.g., if the victim is drunk or bloody; cf. Piliavin, Rodin & Piliavin, 1969; Piliavin, Piliavin, & Rodin, 1975), material losses (Wagner & Wheeler, 1969), possible physical harm (Midlarsky & Midlarsky, 1973; Shotland & Straw, 1976), or loss of social approval and potential social sanctions (e.g., Staub, 1970, 1971). These potential costs must be considered in light of potential gains such as social approval or recognition for helping (e.g., McGovern, Ditzian, & Taylor, 1975; Paulhus, Shaffer, & Downing, 1977) and the avoidance of emotional costs (e.g., empathic arousal or personal distress) for not helping (see Batson, 1984 and Piliavin et al., 1981, for a more detailed discussion of these issues). However, because one often cannot know for certain the exact costs and rewards for a given behavior prior to enacting the behavior, it is the individual's *estimate* of the subjective utility of an act, not the actual utility, that influences the decision-making process.

As discussed by Kurtines and Schneider (1983), there are at least three models to explain the manner in which estimates of expected utility and situational cues jointly influence subsequent prosocial behavior. Situational cues may influence perceptions of the utility of prosocial action, which in turn affect prosocial behavior. In contrast, subjective expected utilities may affect the way in which the individual processes information available in the environment which then influences the probability of prosocial action. Finally, both situational factors and subjective utilities may have a direct causal effect on prosocial behavior.

Kurtines and Schneider (1983) examined the plausibility of the three afore-mentioned models by studying two sharing behaviors of elementary-school children. Amount of information provided to the children about the potential recipient of sharing (situational information) was varied and children's perceptions regarding the expected utility of assisting were assessed with interview data. Kurtines and Schneider obtained support for two of the three models; one index of sharing was best explained by the causal model in which person and situation variables were independent causal influences, whereas the other index of sharing was best accounted for by the model in which the effects of the situational variable (information) on behavior were mediated by the expected utility of the potential prosocial behavior.

In summary, individuals' expectations regarding the utility of a given prosocial act (often based on situational information) seem to influence whether or not they intend to, and actually do, assist. However, as will be discussed shortly, the subjective utility of an act generally is but one of several factors considered by the individual when weighing and ranking various behavioral options.

Attributions Concerning the Cause of the Other's Need.   As was discussed in some detail in Chapter 6, attributions that potential helpers make with regard to the cause or origin of another's need are related to the likelihood that the potential helper will intend to or will actually assist. These attributions, which are primarily cognitive in nature, elicit emotional responses such as sympathy or disgust (Weiner, 1980; Zillman & Cantor, 1977). Such attributions are, of course, highly influenced by information embedded in the situation concerning the other's need (whether or not the other is needy due to factors within his or her control). However, information in the situation, including that related to the cause of another's need, may be distorted or redefined if a potential benefactor experiences conflict when deciding whether to assist. Such distortion can serve as a defense against negative evaluations if a potential helper chooses not to assist (cf. Schwartz & Howard, 1981, 1982, 1984).

Motivation: Personality Factors

In many situations, the motivation to assist once an individual is aware of another's need is likely to be based on more than just the individual's cognitive evaluation of the situation and his or her immediate affective response to the needy other. Characteristics of the self can influence individuals' abiding goals and values, and also motives and concerns in specific contexts. For example, the ways in which we think about ourselves (e.g., our level of self-esteem and self-perceptions with regard to moral character) will affect which personal goals are highlighted in specific circumstances (which, in turn, affects whether one decides to assist).

Personality characteristics that can influence decision-making in helping contexts do not, of course, materialize out of thin air. They have a socialization history, and also may vary as a function of the individual's level of socio-cognitive development. For example, as will be discussed shortly, self-perceptions regarding one's own helpfulness seem to vary in childhood, in part, as a function of understanding of consistency of personality over time. Examples of the role of socialization and developmental factors in personal factors that affect prosocial behavior will be included in the following discussion.

Self-identity with Regard to the "Trait" of Helpfulness or Kindness. One factor that seems to influence the decision to assist is the individual's self-perception with regard to his or her own kindness, helpfulness, or generosity. People who view themselves as altruistic, that is, as the type of person who assists another for internal reasons, are somewhat more likely to assist others than are people who do not view themselves as altruistic.

In specific, social psychologists have found that adults who are induced to comply with an initial small request are more receptive to a subsequent larger request (the "foot-in-the-door effect"; Freedman & Fraser, 1966; cf. Beaman, Cole, Preston, Klentz, & Steblay, 1983; DeJong, 1979). One proposed explanation for this phenomenon is that compliance with the initial request induces an altruistic self-image, and that people strive to act in ways consistent with their self-image (DeJong, 1979). Consistent with the adult research, researchers have found that children who have been induced to act in a prosocial manner and then are provided with prosocial attributions (i.e., are told that they have behaved as they did because they are generous or kind) are more helpful or generous on subsequent opportunities than are children who have not been provided with any attributions (Grusec & Redler, 1980), or have been provided with externally-oriented attributions (i.e., the children are told that they were helpful simply to comply with adults' expectations; Grusec, Kuczynski, Rushton, & Simutis, 1978; cf. Chapter 5). As for the findings with adults, these data have been interpreted as indicating that children attempt to act in ways consistent with their own (and perhaps others') conceptions of their character (cf. Eisenberg & Cialdini, 1984).

Although there is little direct evidence that the desire to maintain a consistent image mediates the findings concerning the provision of attributions to children, there is indirect evidence. Grusec and Redler (1980) found that provision of prosocial attributions by adults to children was associated with 8- and 10-year-olds' subsequent prosocial behavior, but not with that of 5-year-olds. This is interesting because children do not consistently conceptualize people in terms of stable psychological dispositions prior to 7–8 years of age (e.g., Dix & Grusec, 1983; Rholes & Ruble, 1984). Moreover, children do not seem to base self-attributions upon prior behavior until age 7 or older (e.g., Nicholls, 1979; Ruble, Parsons, & Ross, 1976). Thus, consistent with Grusec and Redler's findings, one would not expect the provision of generous attributions to enhance prosocial responding prior to age 8 because young children should not view themselves in terms of stable dispositions, and consequently, should not be concerned with maintaining a stable self-image (or public image).

In brief, for people approximately aged 8 and older, self-perceptions regarding one's own altruistic tendencies seem to be associated with the inclination to assist others. Altruistic self-perceptions apparently can be induced by the provision of altruistic attributions (at least for children), and by subtly inducing the individual to assist others (cf. Grusec, 1982; Moore & Eisenberg, 1984; Staub, 1979). Thus, socialization practices can be viewed as affecting the nature of self-perceptions concerning altruism which, in turn, has a causal influence on the inclination to perform prosocial actions.

Self-esteem and Self-focus.   Other personal factors that appear to influence one's intention to assist a needy other are level of self-esteem and degree of self-focus. However, the relations of these factors to prosocial intentions and behaviors are complex.

Various theorists and researchers have posited a relation between self-worth and the prosocial proclivities (e.g., Reykowski, 1984; Staub, 1978, 1979). In Reykowski's view, when a cognitive structure (e.g., dealing with the self, other people, social organizations, sociocentric standards, socially defined tasks, or representations of beliefs and ideological standards) is in a state of tension, the content of the structure is more likely to be the source of evaluation. Thus, concern regarding oneself tends to activate self-oriented standards. In other words, if someone is experiencing conflict or concern with regard to personal self-worth, that individual will tend to evaluate events in terms of their effects on the self.

Reykowski's (1984) view has received some empirical support. In a study with 16- to 18-year-old Polish boys, Jarymowicz (1977) divided her subjects into three groups: (1) those low in self-acceptance; (2) those with medium to high self-acceptance whose self-evaluations were inconsistent with how they would like to see themselves; and (3) those without self-worth problems (i.e., those with high self-acceptance and consistent self-evaluations). Some of the boys in each group were administered a treatment designed to raise self-esteem. The treatment enhanced willingness to volunteer to assist others, but only for the group low in volunteering (group 2). On a measure of social sensitivity (receptivity to external signals that indicate the states of other people and recognition of these states), there were no differences across the three experimental groups. However, in the control groups (those without treatment), subjects with no self-worth problems scored highest in social sensitivity, followed by those with inconsistent self-evaluations, and then those low in self-acceptance.

In summary, Jarymowicz (1977) found that high, consistent self-esteem was associated with greater social sensitivity; both high self-esteem and low self-esteem (but not inconsistent self-esteem) were associated with volunteering to assist. Jarymowicz suggested that low self-evaluation was related to high willingness to help because of fear of rejection (cf. Nowakowska, 1977). According to both Jarymowicz (1977) and Reykowski (1984), the treatment designed to enhance self-esteem influenced willingness to assist because egocentric, self-oriented cognitions are reduced when tension concerning self-worth is lessened, resulting in increased sensitivity to others and their needs. However, the measure of willingness to assist was willingness to sign a declaration to help immediately after reading a statement in which the needs of others were explicitly stated. Thus, the increase in willingness to assist was not due to failure to attend to another's need, but due to enhanced or differential processing of information related to the other's need.

Staub (1979) suggested that there may be a curvilinear relation between self-esteem and prosocial behavior, with those moderate in self-esteem being most prosocial. In his view, people with very high self-esteem may be so self-satisfied that they are unquestioning with regard to their relationships with others, and therefore are somewhat insensitive to others. In support of this view, he cited the work of Reykowski and Jarymowicz (1976, cited in Staub, 1979, p. 237) in which a medium level of self-esteem was associated with relatively high levels of sensitivity to perceiving the problems and needs of another. It is not clear, however, if those with medium-level self-esteem are more motivated to assist, or are only more likely to detect another's need.

In my view, the research on the relation between self-worth and prosocial behavior is consistent with the notion that people with different levels of self-esteem may tend to assist for different reasons. People with medium and low self-esteem may be more likely than those with higher self-esteem to use prosocial behavior as a means of avoiding rejection or obtaining social approval. This pattern should hold, however, only in situations in which there is the potential for rejection if one does not assist, or the potential for approval if one does assist. In contrast, if rejection is likely to be associated with a given prosocial behavior, persons with high self-esteem, who would be expected to have less need for social approval, may be more likely to assist than other persons. Of course, issues related to social acceptance or rejection are probably not salient for all people with medium and low self-esteem; I am merely suggesting that there is some association between level of self-worth and relative concern with social evaluation.

Temporary shifts in self-esteem and self-focus can also affect the motivation to engage in prosocial behavior. For example, temporary decrements in self-esteem due to experimental manipulations have been associated with increased helping in adults (e.g., McMillen, 1971). Moreover, focusing of attention on the self prior to exposure to an opportunity to assist has been found to enhance subsequent helping, apparently because increasing one's self-focus enhances self-attribution for a situation or event, that is, increases felt responsibility for others (Duval, Duval, & Neely, 1979). However, self-focus may enhance helping only when the other's needs are salient; otherwise, self-focus may obstruct awareness of others' needs (Rogers, Miller, Mayer, & Duval, 1982). Thus, self-focus seems to affect both attention to the other's need and motivation to assist the other, depending upon a variety of factors such as salience of the other's need and the valence of affect associated with focusing on the self (cf. Cialdini et al., 1982).

Values, Needs, and Preferences. In most decision-making situations, some of the individual's personal values, needs, and preferences will be considered in the course of deciding upon a course of action. This is certainly true in many situations in which individuals must choose whether to assist another. The values relevant to the specific situation may be moral (e.g., may concern internalized values) or nonmoral (e.g., concern the important of achievement). Because moral values seem to develop and solidify with age, it is likely that their influence on decision-making (especially in comparison to that of personal needs and preferences) increases during childhood into adulthood. The relevant needs and preferences can be quite varied, from the need for approval, to the desire for hedonic pleasure, to the desire to maintain a consistent self-image. Moral values that are especially relevant to altruism were discussed in Chapter 7. We will turn now to the issue of how relevant preferences, needs, and values are weighed, along with other factors, in the decision-making process.

HIERARCHIES OF PERSONAL GOALS

Staub's (1978, 1979, 1984) concept of personal goals was discussed in some detail in Chapters 7 and 9. In Staub's terms, personal goals are motivational preferences for certain end-states and aversions to others. Moreover, conscious thoughts, beliefs, or values are believed to contribute to the aversive or positive aspects of a goal.

Personal goals can be moral or nonmoral. In some cases they are based on personal needs and desires; in other cases, they are based on moral values. Indeed, in Staub's (1978, 1979, 1984) view, value orientations are basically synonymous with moral personal goals.

For all people, certain needs, desires, or goals are more important than others; however, the ordering of importance of goals undoubtedly varies across individuals. For example, obtaining social approval may be an important goal for some people and not others. Moreover, in many situations, various personal goals are relevant and may even conflict with one another. Different situations highlight different personal goals, and to varying degrees. Thus, in one situation desire for approval and the need to achieve may be relevant goals, whereas in other situations they are of little or no relevance (e.g., Erkut, Jaquette, & Staub, 1981).

When various personal goals conflict and one or more of these goals is of a moral nature, this conflict can be considered a moral dilemma. For example, a prosocial value orientation based on either internalized values related to duty or a positive orientation to and concern for others (Staub, 1984) could conflict with the nonmoral goal of desire for material goods or the need for social approval. The resolution of such a moral dilemma (at least at a hypothetical level) is what has been assessed in the research on prosocial moral judgment.

In real-life situations, the hierarchy of personal goals is a function of not only the individual's a priori personal goals and the circumstances themselves, but also the individual's cognitive evaluation of features of the given situation (e.g., attributions regarding the source of the other's need and subjective expected utilities) and the degree and type of affect (e.g., sympathy or personal distress) elicited in the specific context. For example, if the situation elicits a high level of sympathy, an altruistic personal goal may be especially salient.

The values, goals, and needs that underlie personal goals and their relative importance clearly change with development (see Chapter 7). These developmental shifts are reflected in age-related changes in one's typical hierarchy of personal goals (one's general hierarchy rather than one's hierarchy in a specific situation) and, consequently, in level of moral judgment. Given that both other-oriented values based upon self-reflective role taking or sympathetic responsiveness and internalized principles concerning the morality or prescriptiveness of altruism are much more common with age, one would expect moral personal goals to rank higher in the hierarchies of older children and adults than those of younger children.

As was discussed in Chapters 6, 7, and 8, the relative importance of an individual's various values, goals, and needs as reflected in moral judgment are influenced by socio-cognitive development (e.g., level of perspective-taking) and socialization (including familial and cultural) history. Thus, hierarchies of personal goals seem to reflect aspects of the individual that are rooted in prior experience and current level of socio-cognitive functioning, as well as the individual's interpretation of, and affective reaction to, a specific situation.

INTENTION TO ASSIST

Based upon the individual's hierarchy of personal goals in a specific situation (and self-evaluative emotions that may be associated with some personal goals), the individual will attempt to decide whether to assist. If the decision-making process is inconclusive, the individual is likely to defend against feelings of obligation toward the needy other by denying responsibility for the other, minimizing the other's need, or some other defensive technique (Schwartz & Howard, 1981, 1982). In such a situation, the decision-making process may recycle (see Janis & Mann, 1977 and Piliavin et al., 1981 for further discussions of the resolution of decisional conflict); for example, the initial situation may be reinterpreted. Moreover, in our view, defensive reactions can occur not only when decisional conflict is present, but also if an actor decides not to assist. Especially if the individuals hold prosocial values or have altruistic self-images, they may defend their inaction in order to avoid negative self-evaluation and related aversive affective reactions.

THE INTENTION-BEHAVIOR LINK

Just because an individual holds beliefs consistent with prosocial action or decides to assist another does not necessarily mean that he or she will actually do so. For a long time, psychologists have noted that there is not necessarily a close relation between attitudes and actual behavior (cf. Ajzen & Fishbein, 1977). However, the association appears to be higher if intentions rather than general attitudes are assessed (Ajzen & Fishbein, 1977); if there is a high correspondence between the attitude and behavior (Ajzen, 1982; Ajzen & Fishbein, 1977); if actors expect the utility of the behavior to be high and positive in valence (e.g.,

Pomazal & Jaccard, 1976; Saltzer, 1981); and if individuals explicitly define their attitudes as relevant and appropriate guides to action (Snyder, 1982).

Fishbein and Ajzen (1975) presented a model for the prediction of behavior which is useful for our purposes. In this model, intentions lead to behavior, and intentions are a function of: (1) the subjective probability that performing a given behavior will lead to a given consequence, multiplied by the value that the expected consequence has for the individual; added to (2) beliefs about the expectations of reference group members, multiplied by the individual's motivation to comply with the expectations of the reference group. Thus, as in our model, intentions to assist are a function of subjective expected utilities, the relative weighting (often reflected in moral reasoning) of these nonmoral, pragmatic, or hedonistic consequences, and the desire to conform with perceived social normative expectations. In other words, the Fishbein-Ajzen model can be interpreted as implying that behavioral intentions are a function of both the subjective expected utility of an action and the relative weighting of nonmoral and social-referential personal goals.

There has been considerable empirical support for the Fishbein-Ajzen model. With reference to prosocial behavior, social psychologists have found that the intention to assist is positively related to actually assisting (e.g., Pomazal & Jaccard, 1976; Zuckerman & Reis, 1978). Moreover, there is some evidence that people who feel helping to be valued by significant others will be more likely to intend to assist (Zuckerman & Reis, 1978; but not Pomazal & Jaccard, 1976), and that the subjective expected utility of a prosocial behavior is related to intention to assist (see pp. 198–199).

In an early version of the Fishbein-Ajzen model, moral values were one of the components used to predict intentions and behavior. However, the moral component was dropped from the model, because Fishbein and Ajzen found that it often served as little more than an alternative measure of behavioral intention (Ajzen & Fishbein, 1970). However, a number of researchers have suggested that moral norms should be a part of the model (e.g., Berndt, 1981; Schwartz & Tessler, 1972). In fact, researchers have found that moral norms or values held by the individual do affect intentions (feelings of moral obligation) in moral situations (e.g., Gorsuch & Ortberg, 1983; Pomazal & Jaccard, 1976; Rholes & Bailey, 1983; Zuckerman & Reis, 1978); however, they do not directly influence behavior once their effects on intentions are considered (Zuckerman & Reis, 1978). Thus, it appears that felt motivation to act in accordance with personal moral norms and values influences altruism and other moral behaviors primarily via their effect on intentions.

The idea of felt moral obligation is captured both in Schwartz and Howard's (1982) and Staub's (1978) notion of "personal norms." For example, Schwartz and Howard define personal norms as "situation-specific behavioral expectations generated from one's own internalized values, backed by self-administered sanctions and rewards [p. 329]." However, neither Schwartz and Howard nor Staub have been concerned with determining the degree to which personal norms directly influence intentions versus actual behavior. Because the relevant research concerning personal norms and moral values was discussed in some detail in Chapter 7, this work will not be reviewed again. However, it is important to note that this research generally is consistent with the idea that motivation to comply with internalized moral values has an effect on the performance of prosocial behavior.

The Role of Competence

Even the best-intentioned and most moral persons may not follow through on their intention to assist another. One reason for the lack of consistency in some situations between behavior and values or intentions is that the individual may be unable to assist, or feel incompetent to assist. For example, Pomazal and Jaccard (1976) found that some people positively disposed toward donating blood could not do so because they did not meet the necessary requirements. Along somewhat different lines, Peterson (1983a, b) found that competence training which provided knowledge or skills relevant to assisting in a specific situation enhanced subsequent helping. Moreover, the fact that adults are less likely to assist in an emergency if another, more competent person is present (Latane & Nida, 1981) suggests that relative level of competence may affect whether or not individuals assist.

Another type of competence that appears to influence prosocial responding in some settings is the ability to effectively handle social interactions. Some individuals who desire or intend to assist another may not do so because they are too socially inhibited to initiate planned actions. Support for this notion is available in the developmental literature; children who have the social skills to handle difficult social situations seem to be relatively likely to donate time and energy to others (Larrieu, 1984a). Moreover, researchers have found that children who are relatively social (engage in more peer interactions; Eisenberg, Cameron, Tryon, & Dodez, 1981; Eisenberg, Pasternack, Cameron, Tryon, 1984) and assertive (Barrett & Yarrow, 1977; Larrieu, 1984b) are more likely than other children to spontaneously initiate prosocial behaviors. These same children, however, seem to be better able than the less socially assertive children to refuse to assist when requested by peers to assist (i.e., they are less compliant; Eisenberg et al., 1981; Larrieu, 1984b). In brief, although socially skilled and assertive individuals may not always choose to assist a needy other and may not have other capabilities that facilitate prosocial responding (e.g., inferential skills; Barrett & Yarrow, 1977), a certain degree of social assertiveness may sometimes be necessary to carry out prosocial intentions.

Other Relevant Personal Capabilities

To enact an intended action requires more than the initial intention and the capacity to perform the intended behavior. It requires knowledge of effective helping strategies (Barnett, Darcie, Holland, & Kobasigawa, 1982), sufficient self-regulation (e.g., delay of gratification) to adhere to a chosen course rather than succumbing to attractive alternatives, and the ability to maintain one's attention (i.e., to avoid distractions; Grim, Kohlberg, & White, 1968; cf. Kanfer, 1979). Moreover, carrying out an intended behavior, especially one costly to the self, sometimes may require an abiding sense of responsibility or obligation. Relevant self-regulatory processes undoubtedly increase with age (cf. Kopp, 1982); moreover, judgments of moral responsibility and obligation appear to be associated with higher-stage moral reasoning (Kohlberg & Candee, 1984), which of course is positively related to age. Thus, older children and adults should be considerably more likely than younger children to have the personal capabilities necessary to enact intended prosocial behaviors, although even adults undoubtedly may lack the self-control or felt responsibility to carry through on their initial intentions.

Changes In Personal Characteristics And The Situation

If there is a lapse of time between the point at which an individual decides to assist another and the opportunity to do so, numerous other factors can preclude execution of the prosocial act. For example, situational factors may change in a manner that affects one's estimate of the subjective utility of the act (e.g., the costs of helping or the opportunity for social approval may change). Moreover, the salience of various values, norms and personal needs, desires, or affective reactions may shift if the situation is altered. For example, if cues related to the other's state of need (e.g., facial expressions) are not as salient as previously had been the case, an individual who had intended to help based upon sympathetic responding may be less inclined to assist. Furthermore, there may be actual changes in the other's need state or behavior (e.g., their attempts at self-help) over time, changes that lessen the potential benefactor's desire or commitment to assist.

In summary, a variety of factors can intervene between the decision to assist and performance of the actual prosocial act, even if the potential helper is competent to assist. This reality accounts, in part, for the slippage between prosocial intentions and behavior.

THE CONSEQUENCES OF PROSOCIAL BEHAVIOR

The performance of prosocial behavior in itself can influence the probability of enacting subsequent altruistic or prosocial behaviors. Indeed, researchers have found that engaging in prosocial behaviors is associated with enhanced probability of prosocial responding in the future (e.g., Beaman et al., 1983; DeJong, 1979; Staub, 1979). Consequently, a feedback loop by which performance of altruism affects the individual's characteristics is included in our model.

The consequences of engaging in prosocial behaviors for the individual's functioning are of several types. First, as was discussed previously, participation in prosocial behavior may alter the individual's self-perceptions with regard to their own helpfulness. Especially if people feel that their prosocial behavior was performed for internal, altruistic reasons, enactment of the behavior should reinforce or bolster one's image as an altruistic person (cf. Eisenberg & Cialdini, 1984; Grusec, 1982; Grusec et al., 1978). In contrast, failure to perform an altruistic act may engender a selfish self-image. Moreover, even if the prosocial behavior was externally imposed, over time people may forget that the motive was external and may begin to view themselves as prosocial individuals (Perry & Perry, 1983).

The mere performance of a prosocial behavior may also serve to shape moral values which may then affect future prosocial responding. People appear to have a need to maintain consistency between their behaviors and beliefs (as in cognitive dissonance theory, cf. Festinger, 1957; Wicklund & Brehm, 1976); thus, people may realign their values and moral-reasoning processes pertaining to altruism to be consistent with prior behavior. Moreover, if Piaget (1965) was correct in assuming that moral thought in childhood often drives from action, the development of conscious, altruistic moral values may be based, at least in part, on the experience of behaving in a prosocial manner (cf. Locke, 1983).

Another reason that performance of prosocial behaviors may enhance future prosocial proclivities is that prosocial actors are sometimes reinforced for the performance of prosocial activities. Rewards can be material, social, or internal, for example, feelings of competence or empathic/sympathetic rewards. Thus, performance of prosocial actions could affect both actors' evaluations of the utility of future prosocial actions and their level of self-esteem (both of which could influence future prosocial responding).

When people assist others, they also may be provided with opportunities to role take and learn about others' feeling and perspectives. This experience could lead to greater receptivity to others' expressions of need in future situations and enhanced role-taking capabilities. Moreover, people (especially children) who engage in prosocial activities may learn more or different prosocial behaviors that can be repeated in future situations, that is, they may increase their competence with regard to prosocial functioning.

In brief, performance of a prosocial act can have repercussions that affect future prosocial responding. Thus, a model of prosocial or altruistic action should include sequelae of performance or nonperformance of prosocial behavior.

ALTRUISM: ITS PLACE IN THE MODEL

The model presented in Figures 10.1 to 10.4 is a model of prosocial behavior, not solely altruistic behavior. In this model, prosocial behaviors can be motivated by nonaltruistic motivations, such as reducing one's own externally generated personal distress or the desire for social or material rewards. Thus, given that it is altruism, not other kinds of prosocial responding, that is of primary interest, it may be useful to specifically note the role of altruistic emotions and cognitions in the model.

According to the definition of altruism guiding our model, a behavior is altruistic if motivated by: (1) sympathy; (2) self-evaluative emotions (or anticipation of these emotions) associated with specific internalized moral values and norms or one's responsibility to act in accordance with these values or norms; (3) cognitions concerning the values, norms, responsibilities, and duties unaccompanied by discernable self-evaluative emotions; or (4) cognitions and accompanying affect (e.g., feelings of discomfort due to inconsistencies in one's self-image) related to self-evaluation vis a vis one's moral self-image (Blasi, 1983). One could argue that some of these motivations (especially 2 and 4) are not altruistic because they involve regulation of one's own negative affect; however, such motives are consistent with most definitions of altruism because there is no expectation of external reward for any of these motivations, and any negative affect is internally generated.

The motives listed above are included in the model of prosocial behavior presented in Figure 10.1. Internalized values and norms are listed in the figure; moreover, these values are reflected in the individual's hierarchy of personal goals. Self-evaluation emotions are viewed as associated with these values and personal goals; if a personal goal is moral, behavior consistent with the goal often will elicit positive self-evaluation, whereas inconsistent behavior may produce self-condemnation or guilt.

In contrast, sympathy is viewed as a primarily (although not solely) emotional response that can motivate relatively reflexive altruism, or can contribute, along with other factors, to the prosocial decision-making process. Moreover, self-attributions concerning the consistency of one's behavior with one's self-image are presented in the model and are relevant to an understanding of altruism if altruistic or egoistic traits are part of the individual's self-image.

Because altruism is differentiated from other prosocial behaviors on the basis of motive, it is primarily with regard to motivational inputs (represented in Figure 10.3) that the model differs somewhat for altruistic and nonaltruistic acts of assistance. Of course, the socialization antecedents of personal characteristics that are associated with altruistic versus nonaltruistic prosocial motivations and behavior differ somewhat, and higher levels of socio-cognitive development are likely to be more closely associated with altruistic than nonaltruistic motives and behavior. Moreover, whether a prosocial act is altruistic will likely affect the nature of the actor's self-evaluative reaction subsequent to performance of an act of assistance. In brief, altruism is one of various modes of prosocial responding depicted in the model; moreover, different possible antecedents, consequences, and motivational sources for altruistic behavior are encompassed by the model.

CONCLUSION

Altruistic behavior, like most social behaviors, is complex and multiply determined. Moreover, its significance to the actor can vary, and is difficult to ascertain. In this book, the cognitive and emotional bases for altruism were examined, as were developmental changes in individuals' conceptions regarding the nature of altruism and other prosocial acts. Moreover, models for conceptualizing the manner in which cognitive and affective factors interact with other factors in influencing prosocial development (reasoning and behavior) were presented.

As is often the case when dealing with a complex social behavior, the research and models presented throughout this book raise more questions than they answer. Some of the thorniest questions concern the ways in which cognition and emotion interact, and the causal nature of such interactions. For example, it is unclear whether the cognitive components of moral personal goals are firmly established prior to the development of the tendency to self-reinforce for actions consistent with a given moral value (or self-punish for behavior inconsistent with the value), or if children first learn from socializers to self-reinforce behaviors consistent with a value and only later internalize the relevant value. Similarly, the degree to which cognitive processing (e.g., related to the source of the other's need or the subjective expected utility of a potential prosocial behavior) precedes versus follows sympathetic or empathic responding and reflexive helping in a crisis needs clarification.

Another question of considerable importance concerns the degree to which altruistic moral judgment is limited by developmental factors. To what extent is the individual's level of moral judgment (and, consequently, motives for assisting) a direct function of level of socio-cognitive capabilities versus situational factors and nonmoral values and needs? To what degree do individuals feel a press to reason at the highest level they are capable of hold (as hypothesized by cognitive developmentalists)? What factors affect the directionality of the relation between moral judgment and behavior?

Throughout this book, we hope we have suggested not only questions and issues that need to be examined, and directions in which to move. For example, with regard to the altruistic emotions, it is clear that our thinking must be more differentiated than has generally been the case. Sympathy, empathy, and feelings of personal distress must be differentiated conceptually and empirically; moreover, we need to move from asking *if* there is a relation between empathy and altruism to asking *when*, on a conceptual basis, can a relation between sympathy (or empathy or personal distress) and altruism (or other types of prosocial behaviors) be expected. A similar approach is needed when defining socio-cognitive skills (such as role taking) and examining their role in altruism. Furthermore, we must take seriously the notion of social scripts and the automatic quality of behavior in some situations, as well as the internal conflicts that can arise from the activating of several, often conflicting, values, norms, needs, and preferences in a single situation.

Obviously, there is much to be done. In all likelihood, we will never fully understand the interplay of factors that affect the probability of altruistic behavior, and the role that development plays in the process. Nonetheless, the quest to understand the positive side of human nature is not only an exciting one, but one that could enhance the quality of life for all.

References

Abelson, R. P. (1981). Psychological status of the script concept. *American Psychologist, 36,* 715–729.

Abramovitch, R., & Freedman, J. (1981). Actor-observer differences in children's attributions. *Merrill-Palmer Quarterly, 27,* 53–59.

Adelson, J. (1971). The political imagination of the young adolescent. *Daedalus, 100,* 1013–1050.

Aderman, D., & Berkowitz, L. (1970). Observational set, empathy, and helping. *Journal of Personality and Social Psychology, 14,* 141–148.

Ainsworth, M. D., Blehar, M. C., Waters, E., & Wall, S. (1978). *Patterns of attachment: A psychological study of strange situations.* Hillsdale, NJ: Lawrence Erlbaum Associates.

Ajzen, I. (1982). On behavior in accordance with one's attitudes. In M. P. Zanna, E. T. Higgins, & C. P. Herman (Eds.), *Consistency in social behavior: The Ontario Symposium.* Hillsdale, NJ: Lawrence Erlbaum Associates.

Ajzen, I., & Fishbein, M. (1970). The prediction of behavior from attitudinal and normative variables. *Journal of Experimental Social Psychology, 6,* 466–487.

Ajzen, I., & Fishbein, M. (1973). Attitudinal and normative variables as predictors of specific behaviors. *Journal of Personality and Social Psychology, 27,* 41–57.

Ajzen, I., & Fishbein, M. (1977). Attitude-behavior relations: A theoretical analysis and review of empirical research. *Psychological Bulletin, 84,* 888–918.

Apsler, R. (1975). Effects of embarrassment on behavior towards others. *Journal of Personality and Social Psychology, 32,* 145–153.

Arbuthnot, J. (1973). Relationships between maturity of moral judgment and measures of cognitive abilities. *Psychological Reports, 33,* 945–946.

Archer, R. L. (1984). The farmer and the cowman should be friends: An attempt at reconciliation with Batson, Coke, and Pych. *Journal of Personality and Social Psychology, 46,* 709–711.

Archer, R. L., Diaz-Loving, R., Gollwitzer, P. M., Davis, M. H., & Foushee, H. C. (1981). The role of dispositional empathy and social evaluation in the empathic mediation of helping. *Journal of Personality and Social Psychology, 40,* 786–796.

Arkin, R. M., Gleason, J. M., & Johnsten, S. (1976). Effects of perceived choice, expected outcome, and observed outcome, of an actor on the causal attributions of actors. *Journal of Experimental Social Psychology, 12,* 151–158.

213

Aronfreed, J. (1968). *Conduct and conscience: The socialization of internalized control over behavior.* New York: Academic Press.

Aronfreed, J. (1970). The socialization of altruistic and sympathetic behavior: Some theoretical and experimental analyses. In J. Macaulay & L. Berkowitz (Eds), *Altruism and helping behavior.* New York: Academic Press.

Aronfreed, J., Cutick, R. A., & Fagen, S. A. (1963). Cognitive structure, punishment, and nurturance in the experimental induction of self-criticism. *Child Development, 34,* 281–294.

Averill, J. R. (1980). The emotions. In E. Staub (Ed.), *Personality: Basic aspects and current research.* Englewood Cliffs, NJ: Prentice-Hall.

Avgar, A., Bronfenbrenner, U., & Henderson, C. R., Jr. (1977). Socialization practices of parents, teachers, and peers in Israel: Kibbutz, moshav, and city. *Child Development, 48,* 1219–1227.

Bailey, C. (1980). Morality, reason and feeling. *Journal of Moral Education, 9,* 114–121.

Baldwin, A. L., Baldwin, C. P., Castillo-Vales, V., & Seegmiller, B. (1971). Cross-cultural similarities in the development of the concept of kindness. In W. W. Lambert & K. Weisbrod (Eds.), *Comparative perspectives in social psychology.* Boston, MA: Little, Brown.

Baldwin, A., Baldwin, C., Hilton, I., & Lambert, N. (1969). The measurement of social expectations and their development in children. *Monographs of the Society of Research in Child Development, 34,* (4, Serial No. 128).

Baldwin, C. P., & Baldwin, A. L. (1970). Children's judgments of kindness. *Child Development, 41,* 29–47.

Bandura, A. (1973). *Aggression: A social learning analysis.* Englewood Cliffs, NJ: Prentice-Hall.

Bandura, A. (1977). *Social learning theory.* Englewood Cliffs, NJ: Prentice-Hall.

Bandura, A. (1978). The self system in reciprocal determinism. *American Psychologist, 33,* 344–358.

Barenboim, C. (1981). The development of person perception in childhood and adolescence: From behavioral comparisons to psychological constructs. *Child Development, 52,* 129–144.

Barker, J. (1983). *Western medicine and the continuity of belief: The Maisin of Collingwood Bay, Papua New Guinea.* Unpublished manuscript, University of British Columbia.

Barker, J. (1984). *Missionaries and mourning: Continuity and change in the death ceremonies of a Melanesian people.* Unpublished manuscript, University of British Columbia.

Barnes, R. D., Ickes, W., & Kidd, R. F. (1979). Effects of the perceived intentionality and stability of another's dependency on helping behavior. *Personality and Social Psychology Bulletin, 5,* 367–372.

Barnett, K., Darcie, G., Holland, C. J., & Kobasigawa, A. (1982). Children's cognitions about effective helping. *Developmental Psychology, 18,* 267–277.

Barnett, M. A. (1975). Effects of competition and relative deservedness of the other's fate on children's generosity. *Developmental Psychology, 11,* 665–666.

Barnett, M. A. (1982). Empathy and prosocial behavior in children. In T. M. Field, A. Huston, H. C. Quay, L. Troll, & G. E. Finley (Eds.). *Review of human development.* New York: Wiley.

Barnett, M. A. (1984). The role of perspective taking and empathy in the child's prosocial behavior. In H. E. Sypher & J. L. Applegate (Eds.), *Social cognition and communication.* Beverly Hills, CA: Sage.

Barnett, M. A., Howard, J. A., King, L. M., & Dino, G. A. (1980). Antecedents of empathy: Retrospective accounts of early socialization. *Personality and Social Psychology Bulletin, 6,* 361–365.

Barnett, M. A., Howard, J. A., King, L. M., & Dino, G. A. (1981). Helping behavior and the transfer of empathy. *Journal of Social Psychology, 115,* 125–132.

Barnett, M. A., Howard, J. A., Melton, E. M., & Dino, G. A. (1982). Effect of inducing sadness about self or other on helping behavior in high and low empathic children. *Child Development, 53,* 920–923.

Barrett, D. E., & Yarrow, M. R. (1977). Prosocial behavior, social inferential ability, and assertiveness in young children. *Child Development, 48,* 475–481.

Bar-Tal, D. (1982). Sequential development of helping behavior: A cognitive-learning approach. *Developmental Review, 2,* 101–124.

Bar-Tal, D., Korenfeld, D., & Raviv, A. (in press). The relationships between the development of helping behavior and the development of social perspective and moral judgment. *Genetic Psychology Monographs.*

Bar-Tal, D., Nadler, A., & Blechman, N. (1980). The relationship between Israeli children's helping behavior and their perception on parents' socialization practices. *Journal of Social Psychology, 111,* 159–167.

Bar-Tal, D., & Nissim, R. (1984). Helping behavior and moral judgment among adolescents. *British Journal of Developmental Psychology, 2,* 329–336.

Bar-Tal, D., & Raviv, A. (1982). A cognitive-learning model of helping behavior development: Possible implications and applications. In N. Eisenberg (Ed.), *The development of prosocial behavior.* New York: Academic Press.

Bar-Tal, D., Raviv, A., & Leiser, T. (1980). The development of altruistic behavior: Empirical evidence. *Developmental Psychology, 16,* 516–524.

Bar-Tal, D., Raviv, A., & Shavit, N. (1981). Motives for helping behavior: Kibbutz and city children in kindergarten and school. *Developmental Psychology, 17,* 766–772.

Bar-Yam, M., Kohlberg, L., & Naame, A. (1980). Moral reasoning of students in different cultural, social, and educational settings. *American Journal of Education, 88,* 345–362.

Batson, C. D. (1984). *A theory of altruistic motivation.* Unpublished manuscript, University of Kansas.

Batson, C. D., & Coke, J. S. (1981). Empathy: A source of altruistic motivation for helping? In J. P. Rushton & R. M. Sorrentino (Eds.), *Altruism and helping behavior: Social, personality, and developmental perspectives.* Hillsdale, NJ: Lawrence Erlbaum Associates.

Batson, C. D., Coke, J. S., & Pych, V. (1983). Limits on the two-stage model of empathic mediation of helping: A reply to Archer, Diaz-Loving, Gollwitzer, Davis, and Foushee. *Journal of Personality and Social Psychology, 45,* 895–898.

Batson, C. D., Duncan, B. D., Ackerman, P., Buckley, T., & Birch, K. (1981). Is empathic emotion a source of altruistic motivation? *Journal of Personality and Social Psychology, 40,* 290–302.

Batson, C. D., O'Quin, K., Fultz, J., Vanderplus, M., & Isen, A. M. (1983). Influence of self-reported distress and empathy on egoistic versus altruistic motivation to help. *Journal of Personality and Social Psychology, 45,* 706–718.

Battistich, V., Watson, M., & Solomon, D. (1983, August). *Children's cognitions about helping relationships.* Paper presented at the annual meeting of the American Psychological Association, Anaheim, CA.

Baumgardt, C., Kueting, H. J., & Silbereisen, R. K. (1981, September). *Social competence as an objective of road safety education in primary schools.* Paper presented at the International Conference on Road Safety, Cardiff, Wales.

Beaman, A. L., Cole, C., Preston, M., Klentz, B., & Steblay, N. M. (1983). Fifteen years of foot-in-the-door research. *Personality and Social Psychology Bulletin, 9,* 181–196.

Beit-Hallahimi, B., & Rabin, A. I. (1977). The kibbutz as a social experiment and child-rearing laboratory. *American Psychologist, 32,* 532–541.

Bem, D. J. (1972). Self perception theory. In L. Berkowitz (Ed.), *Advances in experimental social psychology* (Vol. 6). New York: Academic Press.

Benson, N. C., Hartmann, D. P., & Gelfand, D. M. (1981, April). *Intentions and children's moral judgments.* Paper presented at the biennial meeting of the Society for Research in Child Development, Boston, MA.

Berkowitz, L. (1969). Resistance to improper dependency relationships. *Journal of Experimental Social Psychology, 5,* 283–294.

Berkowitz, L. (1972). Social norms, feelings, and other factors affecting helping and altruism. In L. Berkowitz (Ed.), *Advances in experimental social psychology* (Vol. 6). New York: Academic Press.

Berkowitz, L., & Lutterman, K. G. (1968). The traditional socially responsible person. *The Public Opinion Quarterly, 32,* 169–185.

Berlyne, D. E. (1960). *Conflict, arousal and curiosity.* New York: McGraw-Hill.

Berndt, T. J. (1977). The effects of reciprocity norms on moral judgment and causal attribution. *Child Development, 48,* 1322–1330.

Berndt, T. J. '(1981). Relations between social cognition, nonsocial cognition, and social behavior: The case of friendship. In J. H. Flavell & L. Ross (Eds.), *Social cognitive development: Frontiers and possible futures.* Cambridge, UK: Cambridge University Press.

Berndt, T. J., & Berndt, E. G. (1975). Children's use of motive and intentionality in person perception and moral judgments. *Child Development, 46,* 904–912.

Best, D. L., Williams, J. E., Cloud, J. M., Davis, S. W., Robertson, L. S., Edwards, J. R., Giles, H., & Fowles, J. (1977). Development of sex-trait stereotypes among young children in the United States, England, and Ireland. *Child Development, 48,* 1375–1384.

Bickman, L., & Kamzan, L. (1973). The effect of race and need on helping behavior. *Journal of Social Psychology, 89,* 73–77.

Blanck, P. D., Rosenthal, R., Snodgrass, S. E., De Paulo, B. M., & Zuckerman, M. (1981). Sex differences in eavesdropping on nonverbal cues: Developmental changes. *Journal of Personality and Social Psychology, 1981, 41,* 391–396.

Blasi, A. (1980). Bridging moral cognition and moral action: A critical review of the literature. *Psychological Bulletin, 88,* 1–45.

Blasi, A. (1983). Moral cognition and moral action: A theoretical perspective. *Developmental Review, 3,* 178–210.

Blasi, A. (in press). Autonomy in obedience: The development of distancing in socialized action. In W. Edelstein (Ed.), *Contemporary approaches to social cognition.* Frankfort: Suhrkamp.

Block, J. H. (1973). Conceptions of sex role: Some cross-cultural and longitudinal perspectives. *American Psychologist, 28,* 512–526.

Block, J. H. (1981). Gender differences in the nature of premises developed about the world. In E. K. Shapiro & E. Weber (Eds.), *Cognitive and affective growth: Developmental interaction.* Hillsdale, NJ: Lawrence Erlbaum Associates.

Blotner, R., & Bearison, D. J. (1984). Developmental consistencies in children's sociomoral knowledge: Justice reasoning and altruistic behavior. *Merrill–Palmer Quarterly, 30,* 349–367.

Blum, L. A. (1980). *Friendship, altruism and morality.* London: Routledge & Kegan Paul.

Borke, H. (1971). Interpersonal perception of young children: Egocentrism or empathy. *Developmental Psychology, 5,* 262–269.

Borke, H. (1973). The development of empathy in Chinese and American children between three and six years of age. *Developmental Psychology, 9,* 102–108.

Boski, P. (1983). Egotism and evaluation in self and other attributions for achievement related outcomes. *European Journal of Social Psychology, 13,* 287–304.

Braband, J., & Lerner, M. J. (1975). "A little time and effort" . . . Who deserves what from whom. *Personality and Social Psychology Bulletin, 1,* 177–179.

Brabeck, M. (1983). Moral judgment: Theory and research in differences between males and females. *Developmental Review, 3,* 274–291.

Bradley, G. W. (1978). Self-serving biases in the attribution process: A re-examination of the fact or fiction question. *Journal of Personality, 36,* 56–71.

Brandstadter, J. (1981, September). *Entwicklungs-beratung unter dem aspecktder Lebensspanne: Thesen zur programmatik und methodologie.* Paper presented at Entwicklungspsychologie, Augusburg.

Brandstadter, J. (1983, April). *Action development and development through action.* Paper presented at the biennial meeting of the Society for Research in Child Development, Detroit, MI.

Brandt, R. B. (1959). *Ethical theory.* Englewood Cliffs, NJ: Prentice-Hall.

Breger, L. (1973). *From instinct to identity.* Englewood Cliffs, NJ: Prentice-Hall.

Brehm, S. S., Powell, L. K., & Coke, J. S. (1984). The effects of empathic instructions upon donating behavior: Sex differences in young children. *Sex Roles, 10,* 405–416.

Breznitz, S., & Kugelmass, S. (1968). The moral judgment of positive acts. *Journal of Social Psychology,* *76,* 253–258.

Brody, L. R. (1983, August). *Children's emotional attributions to themselves and others: A measure* *of children's defensiveness.* Paper presented at the annual convention of the American Psychological Association, Anaheim, CA.

Broughton, J. M. (1983). Woman's rationality and men's virtues: A critique of gender dualism in Gilligan's theory of moral development. *Social Research, 50,* 597–642.

Bryan, J. H., & Walbek, N. H. (1970). Preaching and practicing generosity: Children's actions and reactions. *Child Development, 41,* 329–353.

Bryant, B. (1982). An index of empathy for children and adolescents. *Child Development, 53,* 413–425.

Buck, R. (1977). Nonverbal communication of affect in preschool children: Relationships with personality and skin conductance. *Journal of Personality and Social Psychology, 35,* 225–236.

Buck, R., Miller, R. E., & Caul, W. F. (1974). Sex, personality, and physiological variables in the communication of affect via facial expression. *Journal of Personality and Social Psychology, 30,* 587–596.

Buck, R. W., Savin, V. J., Miller, R. E., & Caul, W. F. (1972). Communication of affect through facial expression in humans. *Journal of Personality and Social Psychology, 23,* 362–371.

Buckley, N., Siegel, L., & Ness, S. (1979). Egocentrism, empathy, and altruistic behavior in young children. *Developmental Psychology, 15,* 329–330.

Burleson, B. R. (1982). The development of comforting strategies in childhood and adolescence. *Child* *Development, 53,* 1578–1588.

Burleson, B. R. (1984). Comforting communication. In H. E. Sypher & S. L. Applegate (Eds.), *Communication by children and adults: Social cognitive and strategic processes.* Beverly Hills, CA: Sage.

Burleson, B. R., & Fennelly, D. A. (1981). The effects of persuasive appeal form and cognitive complexity on children's sharing. *Child Study Journal, 11,* 75–90.

Butler, L., & Meichenbaum, D. (1981). The assessment of interpersonal problem-solving skills. In P. Kendall & S. Hollon (Eds.), *Assessment strategies for cognitive-behavioral assessment.* New York: Academic Press.

Butzin, C. (1979, March). *Children's moral judgments of ulterior motives.* Paper presented at the biennial meeting of the Society for Research in Child Development, San Francisco, CA.

Campbell, D. T. (1975). On the conflicts between biological and social evolution and between psychology and moral tradition. *American Psychologist, 30,* 1103–1126.

Candee, D. (1975). The moral psychology of Watergate. *Journal of Social Issues, 31,* 183–192.

Carlsmith, J. M., & Gross, A. (1969). Some effects of guilt on compliance. *Journal of Personality* *and Social Psychology, 11,* 240–244.

Cauble, M. A. (1976). Formal operations, ego identity, and principled morality: Are they related? *Developmental Psychology, 12,* 363–364.

Chandler, M. J., & Greenspan, S. (1972). Ersatz egocentrism: A reply to H. Borke. *Developmental* *Psychology, 7,* 104–106.

Chapman, M., & Skinner, E. A. (1985). Action in development—development in action. In M. Frese & J. Sabini (Eds.), *Goal-directed behavior: The concept of action in psychology.* Hillsdale, NJ: Lawrence Erlbaum Associates.

Cialdini, R. B., Baumann, D. J., & Kenrick, D. T. (1981). Insights from sadness: A three-step model of the development of altruism as hedonism. *Developmental Review, 1,* 207–223.

Cialdini, R. B., Darby, B. L., & Vincent, J. E. (1973). Transgression and altruism: A case for hedonism. *Journal of Experimental Social Psychology, 9,* 502–516.

Cialdini, R. B., & Kenrick, D. T. (1976). Altruism as hedonism: A social development perspective on the relationship of negative mood state and helping. *Journal of Personality and Social Psychology,* *34,* 907–914.

Cialdini, R. B., Kenrick, D. T., & Baumann, D. J. (1982). Effects of mood on prosocial behavior in children and adults. In N. Eisenberg (Ed.), *The development of prosocial behavior*. New York: Academic Press.

Clark, M. S., Milberg, S., & Erber, R. (1983). Effects of arousal on judgments of others' emotions. *Journal of Personality and Social Psychology, 46,* 551–560.

Code, L. B. (1983). Responsibility and the epistemic community: Woman's place. *Social Research, 50,* 537–555.

Cohen, E. A., Gelfand, D. M., & Hartmann, D. P. (1981). Causal reasoning as a function of behavioral consequences. *Child Development, 52,* 514–522.

Coke, J. S. (1980). Empathic mediation of helping: Egoistic or altruistic? (Doctoral dissertation, University of Kansas, 1979). *Dissertation Abstracts International, 41,* 405B. (University Microfilms No. 8014371).

Coke, J. S., Batson, C. D., & McDavis, K. (1978). Empathic mediation of helping: A two-step model. *Journal of Personality and Social Psychology, 36,* 752–766.

Colby, A., Gibbs, J., Kohlberg, L., Speicher-Dubin, B., & Candee, D. (1979). *Standard for scoring manual*. Cambridge, MA: Harvard University, Center for Moral Education.

Colby, A., & Damon, W. (1983). Listening to a different voice: A review of Gilligan's *In a Different Voice. Merrill-Palmer Quarterly, 29,* 473–481.

Colby, A., & Kohlberg, L. (1984). Invariant sequence and internal consistency in moral judgment stages. In W. M. Kurtines & J. L. Gewirtz (Eds.), *Morality, moral behavior and moral development*. New York: Wiley.

Colby, A., Kohlberg, L., Gibbs, J., & Lieberman, M. (1983). A longitudinal study of moral judgment. *Monographs of the Society for Research in Child Development*, 48 (Serial No. 200), 1–124.

Colby, A., Kohlberg, L., & Kauffman, K. (in press). Theoretical introduction to the measurement of moral judgment. In A. Colby & L. Kohlberg (Eds.), *The measurement of moral judgment* (Vol. 1). New York: Cambridge University Press.

Costanzo, P. R., Coie, J. D., Grumet, J. F., & Farnell, D. (1973). A re-examination of the effects of intent and consequence on children's moral judgments. *Child Development, 44,* 154–161.

Constanzo, P. R., Grumet, J. F., & Brehm, S. S. (1974). The effects of choice and source of constraint on children's attributions of preference. *Journal of Experimental Social Psychology, 10,* 352–364.

Cowan, P. A. (1982). The relationship between emotional and cognitive development. *New Directions for Child Development, 16,* 49–81.

Crandall, V. C., Crandall, V. J., & Katkowsky, W. (1965). A child's social desirability questionnaire. *Journal of Consulting Psychology, 29,* 27–36.

Crittenden, B. (1979). The limitations of morality as justice in Kohlberg's theory. In D. B. Cochrane, C. N. Hamm, & A. C. Kazepides (Eds.), *The domain of moral education*. New York: Paulist Press.

Cunningham, J. D., Starr, P. A., & Kanouse, D. E. (1979). Self as actor, active observer, and passive observer: Implications for causal attribution. *Journal of Personality and Social Psychology, 37,* 1146–1152.

Cunningham, M. R., Steinberg, J., & Grev, R. (1980). Wanting to and having to help: Separate motivations for positive mood and guilt-induced helping. *Journal of Personality and Social Psychology, 38,* 181–192.

Damon, W. (1971). *A developmental analysis of the positive justice concept from childhood through adolescence*. Unpublished masters thesis, University of California, Berkeley.

Damon, W. (1975). Early conceptions of positive justice as related to the development of logical operations. *Child Development, 46,* 301–312.

Damon, W. (1977). *The social world of the child*. San Francisco, CA: Jossey-Bass.

Damon, W. (1980). Patterns of change in children's social reasoning: A two-year longitudinal study. *Child Development, 51,* 1010–1017.

Damon, W. (1981). The development of justice and self-interest during childhood. In M. J. Lerner & S. C. Lerner (Eds.), *The justice motive in social behavior*. New York: Plenum Press.

Darlington, R. B., & Macker, C. E. (1966). Displacement of guilt produced altruistic behavior. *Journal of Personality and Social Psychology, 4,* 442–443.

Darwin, C. (1965). *The expression of emotions in man and animals.* Chicago, IL: University of Chicago Press, (Originally published, 1872).

Davidson, M. L., King, P. M., Kitchener, K. S., & Parker, C. A. (1980). The stage sequence concept in cognitive and social development. *Developmental Psychology, 16,* 121–131.

Davis, M. H. (1983a). Empathic concern and the muscular dystrophy telephon: Empathy as a multidimensional construct. *Personality and Social Psychology Bulletin, 9,* 223–229.

Davis, M. H. (1983b). Measuring individual differences in empathy: Evidence for a multidimensional approach. *Journal of Personality and Social Psychology, 44,* 113–126.

Deci, E. L. (1975). *Intrinsic motivation.* New York: Plenum Press.

DeJong, W. (1979). An examination of self-perception mediation of the foot-in-the-door effect. *Journal of Personality and Social Psychology, 37,* 2221–2239.

Deutsch, F., & Madle, R. A. (1975). Empathy: Historic and current conceptualizations, measurement, and a cognitive theoretical perspective. *Human Development, 18,* 267–287.

Devereux, E. C., Bronfenbrenner, U., & Suci, G. J. (1962). Patterns of parent behavior in the United States of America and in the Federal Republic of Germany: A cross-national comparison. *International Sociological Science Journal, 14,* 488–506.

Devereux, E. C., Shouval, R., Bronfenbrenner, U., Rodgers, R. R., Kav-Venaki, S., Kiely, E., & Karson, E. (1974). Socialization practices of parents, teachers, and peers in Israel: The kibbutz versus the city. *Child Development, 45,* 269–281.

Dienstbier, R. A. (1978). Attribution, socialization, and moral decision making. In J. H. Harvey, W. Ickes, & R. F. Kidd (Eds.), *New directions in attribution research* (Vol. 2). Hillsdale, NJ: Lawrence Erlbaum Associates.

DiVitto, B., & McArthur, L. Z. (1978). Developmental differences in the use of distinctiveness, consensus, and consistency information in making causal judgments. *Developmental Psychology, 14,* 474–482.

Dix, T., & Grusec, J. E. (1983). Parental influence techniques: An attributional analysis. *Child Development, 54,* 645–652.

Dix, T., & Herzberger, S. (1983). The role of logic and salience in the development of causal attribution. *Child Development, 54,* 960–967.

Dlugokinski, E., & Firestone, I. J. (1973). Congruence among four methods of measuring other-centeredness. *Child Development, 44,* 304–308.

Dlugokinski, E. L., & Firestone, I. J. (1974). Other-centeredness and susceptibility to charitable appeals: Effects of perceived discipline. *Developmental Psychology, 10,* 21–28.

Dodge, K. A. (1980). Social cognition and children's aggressive behavior. *Child Development, 51,* 162–170.

Dodge, K. A., & Newman, J. P. (1981). Biased decision-making processes in aggressive boys. *Journal of Abnormal Psychology, 90,* 375–379.

Douvan, E. A., & Adelson, J. (1966). *The adolescent experience.* New York: Wiley.

Dreman, S. B. (1976). Sharing behavior in Israeli school children: Cognitive and social learning factors. *Child Development, 47,* 186–194.

Dreman, S. B., & Greenbaum, C. W. (1973). Altruism or reciprocity: Sharing behavior in Israeli kindergarten children. *Child Development, 44,* 61–68.

Dressel, S., & Midlarsky, E. (1978). The effects of model's exhortations, demands, and practices on children's donation behavior. *Journal of Genetic Psychology, 132,* 211–223.

Duffy, E. (1972). Activation. In N. S. Greenfield & R. A. Sternback (Eds.), *Handbook of psychophysiology.* New York: Holt.

Duval, S., Duval, V. H., & Neely, R. (1979). Self-focus, felt responsibility, and helping behavior. *Journal of Personality and Social Psychology, 37,* 1769–1778.

Dymond, R. F. (1949). A scale for the measurement of empathic ability. *Journal of Consulting Psychology, 13,* 27–33.

Earle, W. B., Diaz-Loving, R., & Archer, R. L. (1982, August). *Antecedents of helping: Assessing the role of empathy and values.* Paper presented at the annual meeting of the American Psychological Association, Washington,DC.

Eckensberger, L. H. (1979). A metamethodological evaluation of psychological theories from a cross-cultural perspective. In L. H. Eckensberger, W. J. Lonner, & Y. H. Poortinga (Eds.), *Cross-cultural contributions to psychology.* Lisse: Swets & Zeitlinger.

Eckensberger, L. H., & Reinshagen, H. (1980). Kohlberg's Stufentheorie der Entwicklung des Moralischen Urteils: Ein Versuch ihrer Reinterpretation im Bezugrahmen handlungstheoretischer Konzepte. In L. H. Eckensberger & R. K. Silbereisen (Eds.), *Entwicklung sozialer Kognitionen: Modelle, Theorien, Methoden, Anwendung.* Stuggart: Klett.

Eckensberger, L. H., & Silbereisen, R. K. (1980a). Einleitung: Handlungstheoretische fur die Entwicklungspsychologie Sozialer Kognitionen. In L. H. Eckensberger & R. K. Silbereisen (Eds.), *Entwicklung Sozialer Kognitionen: Modelle, Theorien, Methoden, Anwendung.* Stuttgart: Klett.

Eckensberger, L. H., & Silbereisen, R. K. (1980b). *Entwicklung Sozialer Kognitionen: Modelle, Theorien, Methoden, Anwendung.* Stuttgart: Klett.

Edwards, C. P. (1982). Moral development in comparative cultural perspective. In D. Wagner & W. Stevenson (Eds.), *Cultural perspectives on child development.* San Francisco, CA: Freeman.

Eisen, S. V. (1979). Actor-observer differences in information inference and causal attribution. *Journal of Personality and Social Psychology, 37,* 261–272.

Eisenberg, N. (1977). The development of prosocial moral judgment and its correlations (Doctoral dissertation, University of California, Berkeley, 1976). *Dissertation Abstracts International, 37,* 4753B. (University Microfilms No. 77–444, 184).

Eisenberg, N. (1982). The development of reasoning regarding prosocial behavior. In N. Eisenberg (Ed.), *The development of prosocial behavior.* New York: Academic Press.

Eisenberg, N. (1983a). Children's differentiations among potential recipients of aid. *Child Development, 3,* 594–602.

Eisenberg, N. (1983b). Developmental aspects to recipients' reactions to aid. In J. D. Fisher, A. Nadler, & B. M. DePaulo (Eds.), *New directions in helping.* New York: Academic Press.

Eisenberg, N. (1983c). The relation between empathy and altruism: Conceptual and methodological issues. *Academic Bulletin, 5,* 195–208.

Eisenberg, N., Boehnke, K., Schuhler, P., & Silbereisen, R. K. (1985). The development of prosocial behavior and cognitions in German children. *Journal of Cross-Cultural Psychology, 16,* 69–82.

Eisenberg, N., Cameron, E., & Tryon, K. (1984). Prosocial behavior in the preschool years: Methodological and conceptual issues. In E. Staub, D. Bar-Tal, J. Karylowski, & J. Reykowski (Eds.), *The development and maintenance of prosocial behavior: International perspectives on positive morality.* New York: Plenum Press.

Eisenberg, N., Cameron, E., Tryon, K., & Dodez, R. (1981). Socialization of prosocial behavior in the preschool classroom. *Developmental Psychology, 17,* 773–782.

Eisenberg, N., & Cialdini, R. B. (1984). The role of consistency pressures in behavior: A developmental perspective. *Academic Psychology Bulletin, 6,* 115–126.

Eisenberg, N., & Lennon, R. (1983). Sex differences in empathy and related capacities. *Psychological Bulletin, 94,* 100–131.

Eisenberg, N., Lennon, R., & Roth, K. (1983). Prosocial development: A longitudinal study. *Developmental Psychology, 19,* 846–855.

Eisenberg, N., Lundy, T., Shell, R., & Roth, K. (1985). Children's justifications for their adult- and peer-directed compliant (prosocial and nonprosocial) behaviors. *Developmental Psychology, 21,* 325–331.

Eisenberg, N., Pasternack, J. F., Cameron, E., & Tryon, K. (1984). The relations of quantity and mode of prosocial behavior to moral cognitions and social style. *Child Development, 55,* 1479–1485.

Eisenberg, N., Pasternack, J. F., & Lennon, R. (1984, March). *Prosocial development in middle childhood.* Paper presented at the biennial meeting of the Southwest Society for Research on Human Development, Denver, CO.

Eisenberg, N., Pasternack, J. F., & Lundy, T. (1984). *Children's justifications for their adult-directed and adult-requested compliant prosocial behaviors.* Unpublished manuscript, Arizona State University.

Eisenberg, N., Pasternack, J. F., & Lundy, T. (1985). *Preschoolers' self-attributions for adult-instigated prosocial behaviors.* Unpublished manuscript, Arizona State University.

Eisenberg, N., & Shell, R. (1985, April). *The relation of prosocial moral judgment and behavior in children.* Paper presented at the biennial meeting of the Society for Research in Child Development, Toronto, Canada.

Eisenberg-Berg, N. (1976). The relation of political attitudes to constraint-oriented and prosocial moral reasoning. *Developmental Psychology, 12,* 552–553.

Eisenberg-Berg, N. (1979a). Development of children's prosocial moral judgment. *Developmental Psychology, 15,* 128–137.

Eisenberg-Berg, N. (1979b). The relationship of prosocial moral reasoning to altruism, political liberalism, and intelligence. *Developmental Psychology, 15,* 87–89.

Eisenberg-Berg, N., & Geisheker, E. (1979). Content of preachings and power of the model/preacher: The effect on children's generosity. *Developmental Psychology, 15,* 168–175.

Eisenberg-Berg, N., & Hand, M. (1979). The relationship of preschoolers' reasoning about prosocial moral conflicts to prosocial behavior. *Child Development, 50,* 356–363.

Eisenberg-Berg, N., & Lennon, R. (1980). Altruism and the assessment of empathy in the preschool years. *Child Development, 51,* 552–557.

Eisenberg-Berg, N., & Mussen, P. (1978). Empathy and moral development in adolescence. *Developmental Psychology, 14,* 185–186.

Eisenberg-Berg, N., & Neal, C. (1979). Children's moral reasoning about their spontaneous prosocial behavior. *Developmental Psychology, 15,* 228–229.

Eisenberg-Berg, N., & Neal, C. (1981). The effects of person of the protagonist and costs of helping on children's moral judgment. *Personality and Social Psychology Bulletin, 7,* 17–23.

Eisenberg-Berg, N., & Roth, K. (1980). The development of children's prosocial moral judgment: A longitudinal follow-up. *Developmental Psychology, 16,* 375–376.

Elder, J. L. D. (1983, April). *Role-taking and prosocial behavior revisited: The effects of aggregation.* Paper presented at the biennial meeting of the Society for Research in Child Development, Detroit, MI.

Emler, N. P., & Rushton, J. P. (1974). Cognitive-developmental factors in children's generosity. *British Journal of Social and Clinical Psychology, 13,* 277–281.

Enright, R. D., Enright, W. F., & Lapsley, D. K. (1981). Distributive justice development and social class: A replication. *Developmental Psychology, 17,* 826–832.

Enright, R. D., Enright, W. F., Mannheim, L. A., & Harris, B. E. (1980). Distributive justice and social class. *Developmental Psychology, 16,* 555–563.

Enright, R. D., Franklin, C. C., & Mannheim, L. A. (1980). Children's distributive justice: A standardized and objective scale. *Developmental Psychology, 16,* 193–202.

Enzle, M. E., & Schopflocker, D. (1978). Instigation of attribution processes by attribution questions. *Personality and Social Psychology Bulletin, 4,* 595–599.

Epstein, S. (1979). The stability of behavior: 1. On predicting most of the people most of the time. *Journal of Personality and Social Psychology, 37,* 1097–1126.

Erkut, S., Jaquette, D., & Staub, E. (1981). Moral judgment-situation interaction as a bases for predicting prosocial behavior. *Journal of Personality, 49,* 1–49.

Eysenck, H. J. (1960). The development of moral values in children: The contribution of learning theory. *British Journal of Educational Psychology, 30,* 11–21.

Fay, B. (1971). The relationships of cognitive moral judgment, generosity, and empathic behavior in six and eight year old children (Doctoral dissertation, University of California, Los Angeles, 1970). *Dissertation Abstracts International*, 31, 3951A (University Microfilms No. 71-4868, 122).

Feinberg, H. K. (1978). Anatomy of a helping situation: Some personality and situational determinants of helping in a conflict situation involving another's psychological distress. *Dissertation Abstracts International*, 257-258B (University Microfilms No. 78-10713).

Feldman, N. S., Klosson, E. C., Parsons, J. E., Rholes, W. S., & Ruble, D. N. (1976). Order of informational presentation and children's moral judgments. *Child Development, 47,* 556-559.

Fellner, C. H., & Marshall, J. R. (1981). Kidney donors revisited. In J. P. Rushton & R. M. Sorrentino (Eds.), *Altruism and helping behavior: Social, personality, and developmental perspectives.* Hillsdale, NJ: Lawrence Erlbaum Associates.

Fenichel, O. (1945). *The psychoanalytic theory of neurosis.* New York: Norton.

Feshbach, N. D. (1975). The relationship of child-rearing factors to children's aggression, empathy, and related positive and negative behaviors. In J. deWit & W. W. Hartup (Eds.), *Determinants and origins of aggressive behavior.* The Hague, Netherlands: Mouton.

Feshbach, N. D. (1978). Studies of empathic behavior in children. In B. A. Maher (Ed.), *Progress in experimental personality research* Vol. 8. New York: Academic Press.

Feshbach, N. D. (1982). Sex differences in empathy and social behavior in children. In N. Eisenberg (Ed.), *The development of prosocial behavior.* New York: Academic Press.

Feshbach, N. D., & Roe, K. (1968). Empathy in six and seven year olds. *Child Development, 39,* 133-145.

Festinger, L. (1957). *A theory of cognitive dissonance.* Stanford, CA: Stanford University Press.

Fiedler, K. (1982). Causal schemata: Review and criticism of research on a popular construct. *Journal of Personality and Social Psychology, 42,* 1001-1013.

Filter, T. A., & Gross, A. E. (1975). Effects of public and private deviancy on compliance with a request. *Journal of Experimental Social Psychology, 11,* 553-559.

Fincham, F., & Jaspars, J. (1979). Attribution of responsibility to the self and other in children and adults. *Journal of Personality and Social Psychology, 37,* 1589-1602.

Fishbein, M., & Ajzen, I. (1975). *Beliefs, attitudes, intentions, and behavior: An introduction to theory and research.* Reading, MA: Addison-Wesley.

Fisher, J. D., Nadler, A., & Whitcher-Alagnor, J. (1983). Four conceptions of reactions to aid. In J. D. Fisher, A. Nadler, & B. M. DePaulo (Eds.), *New directions in helping. Vol. 1. Recipient reactions to aid.* New York: Academic Press.

Fishkin, J., Keniston, K., & McKinnon, C. (1973). Moral reasoning and political ideology. *Journal of Personality and Social Psychology, 27,* 109-119.

Flavell, J. H., Botkin, P., Fry, C., Wright, J., & Jarvis, P. (1968). *The development of role-taking and communication skills in children.* New York: Wiley.

Flugel, J. C. (1961). *Man, morals, and society.* London: Duckworth.

Fontana, A. F., & Noel, B. (1973). Moral reasoning in the university. *Journal of Personality and Social Psychology, 27,* 419-429.

Ford, M. E. (1979). The construct validity of egocentrism. *Psychological Bulletin, 86,* 1169-1188.

Fouts, G. T. (1972). Charity in children: The influence of "charity" stimuli and an audience. *Journal of Experimental Child Psychology, 13,* 303-309.

Freedman, J. L. (1970). Transgression, compliance and guilt. In J. R. Macaulay & L. Berkowitz (Eds.), *Altruism and helping behavior.* New York: Academic Press.

Freedman, J. L., & Fraser, S. C. (1966). Compliance without pressure: The foot-in-the-door technique. *Journal of Personality and Social Psychology, 4,* 195-202.

Freedman, J. L., Wallington, S. A., & Bless, E. (1967). Compliance without pressure: The effect of guilt. *Journal of Personality and Social Psychology, 7,* 117-124.

Freud, A. (1937). *The ego and mechanisms of defense.* London: Hogarth.

Freud, S. (1925). *Collected papers.* London: Hogarth.

Freud, S. (1926). *Inhibitions, symptoms and anxiety.* London: Hogarth.

Freud, S. (1930). *Civilization and its discontents.* London: Hogarth.

Freud, S. (1955). Group psychology and the analysis of the ego. *The complete Psychological Works of Sigmund Freud.* (Vol. XVIII). London: Hogarth.

Freud, S. (1959). The passing of the Oedipus complex. *Collected papers,* Vol. II. New York: Basic Books (originally published in 1924).

Freud, S. (1968). *New introductory lectures on psychoanalysis.* London: Hogarth (originally published 1933).

Fuchs, I., Eisenberg, N., Hertz-Lazarowitz, R., & Sharabany, R. (in press). *Kibbutz, Israeli city, and American children's moral reasoning about prosocial moral conflicts. Merrill–Palmer Quarterly.*

Fuchs, I., Hertz-Lazarowitz, R., Eisenberg, N., & Sharabany, R. (1984, August). *Prosocial reasoning and prosocial behavior of kibbutz and city children in Israel.* Paper presented at the annual meeting of the American Psychological Association, Toronto, Canada.

Fultz, J. N. (1982). *Influence of potential for self-reward on egoistically and altruistically motivated helping.* Unpublished masters thesis, University of Kansas.

Furby, L. (1978). Sharing: Decisions and moral judgment about letting others use one's possessions. *Psychological Reports, 43,* 595–609.

Gaertner, S. L., & Dovidio, J. F. (1977). The sublety of white racism, arousal, and helping behavior. *Journal of Personality and Social Psychology, 35,* 691–707.

Gaertner, S. L., Dovidio, J. F., & Johnson, G. (1979). *Race of victim, nonresponsive bystanders, and helping behavior.* Paper presented at the annual meeting of the American Psychological Association, New York.

Garber-Talman, Y. (1972). *Family and community in the kibbutz.* Cambridge, MA: Harvard University Press.

Gelfand, D. M., & Hartmann, D. P. (1982). Response consequences and attributions: Two contributors to prosocial behavior. In N. Eisenberg (Ed.), *The development of prosocial behavior.* New York: Academic Press.

Gergen, K. J., Ellsworth, P., Maslach, C., & Seipel, M. (1975). Obligation, donor resources, and reactions to aid in three nations. *Journal of Personality and Social Psychology, 3,* 390–400.

Gergen, K. J., & Gergen, M. M. (1983). The social construction of helping relationships. In J. D. Fisher, A. Nadler, & B. M. DePaulo (Eds.), *New directions in helping. Vol. 1. Recipient reactions to aid.* New York: Academic Press.

Gergen, K. J., Morse, J. J., & Kristeller, J. L. (1973). The manner of giving: Cross-national continuities in reactions to aid. *Psychologia, 16,* 121–131.

Gibbs, J. C. (1977). Kohlberg's stages of moral judgment: A constructive critique. *Harvard Educational Review, 47,* 43–61.

Gibbs, J. C. (1979). Kohlberg's moral stage theory: A Piagetian revision. *Human Development, 22,* 89–112.

Gibbs, J. C., Arnold, K. D., & Burkhart, J. E. (1984). Sex differences in the expression of moral judgment. *Child Development, 55,* 1040–1043.

Gibbs, J. C., & Widaman, K. F. (1982). *Social intelligence measuring the development of sociomoral reflection.* Englewood Cliffs, NJ: Prentice-Hall.

Giblin, P. T. (1981). Affective development in children: An equilibrium model. *Genetic Psychology Monographs, 103,* 3–30.

Giblin, P. T., Bezaire, M. M., & Agronow, S. J. (1982). Affective investments of preschool children: Positive responsivity. *Journal of Genetic Psychology, 141,* 183–195.

Gilligan, C. (1977). In a different voice: Women's conceptions of self and of morality. *Harvard Educational Review, 47,* 481–517.

Gilligan, C. (1979). Women's place in man's life cycle. *Harvard Educational Review, 49,* 431–446.

Gilligan, C. (1982). *In a different voice: Psychological theory and women's development.* Cambridge, MA: Harvard University Press.

Gilligan, C., & Belenky, M. F. (1980). A naturalistic study of abortion decisions. *New Directions for Child Development, 7*, 69–90.

Glover, E. (1968). *The birth of the ego*. London: Allen & Unwin.

Goffman, E. (1963). *Behavior in public places*. New York: The Free Press.

Goffman, E. (1969). *The presentation of self in everyday life*. London: Penguin Books.

Goranson, R. E., & Berkowitz, L. (1966). Reciprocity and responsibility reactions to prior help. *Journal of Personality and Social Psychology, 3*, 227–232.

Gorsuch, R. L., & Ortberg, J. (1983). Moral obligations and attitudes: Their relation to behavioral intentions. *Journal of Personality and Social Psychology, 44*, 1025–1028.

Gouldner, A. W. (1960). The norm of reciprocity: A preliminary statement. *American Sociological Review, 25*, 161–178.

Gouze, K., Rayias, M., & Bieber-Schneider, R. (1983, August). *Cognitive correlates of aggression in second grade children*. Paper presented at the annual convention of the American Psychological Association, Anaheim, CA.

Graziano, W. G., Brody, G. H., & Bernstein, S. (1980). Effects of information about future interaction and peer's motivation on peer reward allocations. *Developmental Psychology, 16*, 475–482.

Green, S. K. (1975). Causal attribution and its relationship to role-taking and helping behavior in children. (Doctoral Dissertation, Loyola University, 1975). *Dissertation Abstracts International, 36*, 1966B (University Microfilms No. 75–9848).

Greenglass, E. R. (1969). Effects of prior help and hindrance on willingness to help another: Reciprocity or social responsibility. *Journal of Personality and Social Psychology, 11*, 224–231.

Grim, P., Kohlberg, L., & White, S. (1968). Some relationships between conscience and attentional processes. *Journal of Personality and Social Psychology, 8*, 239–253.

Grodman, S. M. (1979). The role of personality and situational variables in responding to and helping an individual in distress. *Dissertation Abstracts International, 40*, 1421B. (University Microfilms No. 79–20850).

Grueneich, R. (1982). Issues in the developmental study of how children use intention and consequence information to make moral evaluations. *Child Development, 53*, 29–43.

Grusec, J. E. (1982). The socialization of altruism. In N. Eisenberg (Ed.), *The development of prosocial behavior*. New York: Academic Press.

Grusec, J. E., Kuczynski, L., Rushton, J. P., & Simutis, Z. M. (1978). Modeling, direct instruction, and attributions: Effects on altruism. *Developmental Psychology, 14*, 51–57.

Grusec, J. E., & Redler, E. (1980). Attribution, reinforcement, and altruism: A developmental analysis. *Developmental Psychology, 16*, 525–534.

Guttman, J., Bar-Tal, D., & Leiser, T. (1979). *The effect of various reward situations on children's helping behavior*. Unpublished manuscript, Tel-Aviv University.

Haan, N. (1978). Two moralities in action contexts: Relationships to thought, ego regulation, and development. *Journal of Personality and Social Psychology, 36*, 286–305.

Haan, N., Smith, M., & Block, J. (1968). Moral reasoning of young adults: Political-social behavior, family background, and personality correlates. *Journal of Personality and Social Psychology, 10*, 183–201.

Haan, N., Weiss, R., & Johnson, V. (1982). The role of logic in moral reasoning and development. *Developmental Psychology, 18*, 245–256.

Hacker, W. (1978). *Allgemeine Arberstund Ingenieurpsychologie*. Bern: Huber Verlag.

Hall, C. S., & Lindzey, G. (1954). Psychoanalytic theory and its applications in the social sciences. In G. Lindzey (Ed.), *Handbook of social psychology*. Cambridge, MA: Addison-Wesley.

Hamilton, W. D. (1964). The genetical evolution of social behaviour. *Journal of Theoretical Biology, 7*, 1–52.

Hamilton, W. D. (1971). Selection of selfish and altruistic behavior in some extreme models. In J. F. Eisenberg & W. S. Dillon (Eds.), *Man and beast: Comparative social behavior*. Washington, DC: Smithsonian Institution Press.

Hamilton, W. D. (1972). Altruism and related phenomena, mainly in social insects. *Annual Review of Ecology and Systematics, 3,* 193–232.

Harris, M. B., & Huang, L. C. (1973). Helping and the attribution process. *Journal of Social Psychology, 90,* 291–297.

Harris, P. (1983, April). *Children's theories of emotions.* Paper present at the biennial meeting of the Society for Research in Child Development, Detroit, MI.

Harris, S., Mussen, P., & Rutherford, E. (1976). Some cognitive, behavioral, and personality correlates of maturity of moral judgment. *Journal of Genetic Psychology, 128,* 123–135.

Harter, S. (1982). A cognitive-developmental approach to children's understanding of affect and trait labels. In F. C. Serafica (Ed.), *Social-cognitive development in context.* New York: Guilford Press.

Harvey, M. D., & Enzle, M. E. (1981). A cognitive model of social norms for understanding the transgression-helping effect. *Journal of Personality and Social Psychology, 41,* 866–875.

Heider, R. (1958). *The psychology of interpersonal relations.* New York: Wiley.

Heller, K. A., & Berndt, T. J. (1981). Developmental changes in the formation and organization of personality attributes. *Child Development, 52,* 683–691.

Hertz-Lazarowitz, R. (1983). Prosocial behavior in the classroom. *Academic Psychology Bulletin, 2,* 319–338.

Hesse, P., & Cicchetti, D. (1982). Perspectives on an integrated theory of emotional development. *New Directions for Child Development: Emotional Development, 16,* 3–48.

Higgins, A., Power, C., & Kohlberg, L. (1984). The relationship of moral atmosphere to judgments of responsibility. In W. M. Kurtines & J. L. Gewirtz (Eds.), *Morality, moral behavior, and moral development.* New York: Wiley.

Higgins, E. T. (1981). Role taking and social judgment: Alternative perspectives and processes. In J. H. Flavell & L. Ross (Eds.), *Social cognitive development.* New York: Cambridge University Press.

Higgins, E. T., Feldman, N. S., & Ruble, D. N. (1980). Accuracy and differentiation in social prediction: A developmental perspective. *Journal of Personality, 48,* 520–540.

Higgins, E. T., & Parsons, J. E. (1983). Social cognition and the social life of the child: Stages as subcultures. In E. T. Higgins, D. N., Ruble, & W. W. Hartup (Eds.), *Social cognition and social development: A sociocultural perspective.* New York: Cambridge University Press.

Higgs, A. C. (1975). An investigation of the similarities between altruistic and moral judgments. (Doctoral dissertation, University of Maryland, Baltimore, 1974). *Dissertation Abstracts International, 35,* 4269B (University Microfilms No. 75–7336).

Hobbs, T. (1973). Philosophical rudiments concerning government and society. In R. D. Milo (Ed.), *Egoism and altruism.* Belmont, CA: Wadsworth Publishing Co. (Original work published in 1642).

Hoffman, M. L. (1970a). Conscience, personality, and socialization techniques. *Human Development, 13,* 90–126.

Hoffman, M. L. (1970b). Moral development. In P. H. Mussen (Ed.), *Carmichael's manual of child development.* New York: Wiley.

Hoffman, M. L. (1975). Developmental synthesis of affect and cognition and its implications for altruistic motivation. *Developmental Psychology, 11,* 607–622.

Hoffman, M. L. (1976). Empathy, role-taking, guilt, and development of altruistic motives. In T. Lickona (Ed.), *Moral development and behavior: Theory, research and social issues.* New York: Holt.

Hoffman, M. L. (1977). Moral internalization: Current theory and research. In L. Berkowitz (Ed.), *Advances in experimental social psychology* (Vol. 10). New York: Academic Press.

Hoffman, M. L. (1981). Is altruism part of human nature? *Journal of Personality and Social Psychology, 40,* 121–137.

Hoffman, M. L. (1982a). Development of prosocial motivation: Empathy and guilt. In N. Eisenberg (Ed.), *The development of prosocial behavior.* New York: Academic Press.

Hoffman, M. L. (1982b). The measurement of empathy. In C. E. Izard (Ed.), *Measuring emotions in infants and children*. Cambridge, UK: Cambridge University Press.

Hoffman, M. L. (1984a). Empathy, its limitations, and its role in a comprehensive moral theory. In W. M. Kurtines & J. L. Gewirtz (Eds.), *Morality, moral behavior, and moral development*. New York: Wiley.

Hoffman, M. L. (1984b). Interaction of affect and cognition on empathy. In C. E. Izard, J. Kagan, & R. B. Zajonc (Eds.), *Emotions, cognition, and behavior*. Cambridge, UK: Cambridge University Press.

Hogan, R. (1969). Development of an empathy scale. *Journal of Consulting and Clinical Psychology, 33,* 307–316.

Holmes, S. J. (1945). The reproductive beginnings of altruism. *Psychological Review, 52,* 109–112.

Holstein, C. B. (1969). *The relation of children's moral judgment level to that of their parents and to communication patterns in the family*. Paper presented at the biennial meeting of the Society for Research in Child Development, Santa Monica, CA.

Holte, C. S., Jamruszka, V., Gustafson, J., Beaman, A. L., & Camp, G. C. (1984). Influence of children's positive self-perceptions on donating behavior in naturalistic settings. *Journal of School Psychology, 22,* 145–153.

Horowitz, I. A. (1968). Effect of choice and locus of independence on helping behavior. *Journal of Personality and Social Psychology, 8,* 373–376.

Hudson, L. M., Forman, E. A., & Brion-Meisels, S. (1982). Role taking as a predictor of prosocial behavior in cross-age tutors. *Child Development, 53,* 1320–1329.

Hume, D. (1966). *Enquiries concerning the human understanding and concerning the principles of morals* (2nd Ed.). Oxford: Clarendon Press. (Originally published in 1777).

Iannotti, R. J. (1975, April). *The many faces of empathy: An analysis of the definition and evaluation of empathy in children*. Paper presented at the biennial meeting of the Society for Research in Child Development, Denver, CO.

Iannotti, R. J. (1977, March). *A longitudinal investigation of role-taking, altruism, and empathy*. Paper presented at the biennial meeting of the Society for Research in Child Development, New Orleans, LA.

Iannotti, R. J. (1978). Effect of role-taking experiences on role taking, empathy, altruism, and aggression. *Developmental Psychology, 14,* 119–124.

Iannotti, R. J. (1981), April). *Prosocial behavior, perspective taking, and empathy in preschool children: An evaluation of naturalistic and structured settings*. Paper presented at the biennial meeting of the Society for Research In Child Development, Boston, MA.

Iannotti, R. J. (1985). Naturalistic and structured assessments of prosocial behavior in preschool children: The influence of empathy and perspective taking. *Developmental Psychology, 21,* 46–55.

Ickes, W. J., & Kidd, R. F. (1976). An attributional analysis of helping behavior. In J. H. Harvey, W. J. Ickes, & R. F. Kidd (Eds.), *New directions in attribution research* (Vol. 1). Hillsdale, NJ: Lawrence Erlbaum Associates.

Ickes, W. J., Kidd, R. F., & Berkowitz, L. (1976). Attributional determinants of monetary help-giving. *Journal of Personality, 44,* 163–178.

Izard, C. E. (1977). *Human emotions*. New York: Plenum.

Izard, C. (1984). Emotion-cognition relationships and human development. In C. E., Izard, J. Kagan, & R. B. Zajonc (Eds.), *Emotions, cognition, and behavior*. Cambridge, UK: Cambridge University Press.

James, W. (1884). What is emotion? *Mind, 9,* 188–205.

James, W. (1890). *Principles of psychology*. New York: Henry Holt.

Janis, I. L., & Mann, L. (1977). *Decision making*. New York: The Free Press.

Jarymowicz, M. (1977). Modification of self-worth and increment of prosocial sensitivity. *Polish Psychological Bulletin, 8,* 45–53.

Jensen, A. M., & Moore, S. G. (1977). The effect of attribute statements on cooperativeness and competitiveness in school-age boys. *Child Development, 48,* 305–307.

Jensen, L. C., & Hughston, K. (1973). The relationship between type of sanction, story content, and children's judgments which are independent of sanction. *The Journal of Genetic Psychology, 122,* 49–54.

Jones, E. E., & Nisbett, R. E. (1971). *The actor and the observer: Divergent perceptions of the causes of behaviors.* Morristown, NJ: General Learning Press.

Kagan, J. (1978). On emotion and its development: A working paper. In M. Lewis & L. Rosenblum (Eds.), *The development of affect.* New York: Plenum Press.

Kalliopuska, M. (1980). Children's helping behaviour: Personality factors and parental influences related to helping behaviour. *Dissertationes Humanarum Litterarum, 24.* Helsinki.

Kanfer, F. H. (1979). Personal control, social control, and altruism: Can society survive the age of individualism? *American Psychologist, 34,* 231–239.

Kant, I. (1949). *Critique of practical reasoning* (L. W. Beck, Trans.). Chicago, IL: University of Chicago Press. (Originally published, 1788)

Kant, I. (1964). *The doctrine of virtue.* New York: Harper & Row. (Originally published, 1797)

Karniol, R. (1978). Children's use of intention cues in evaluating behavior. *Psychological Bulletin, 85,* 76–85.

Karniol, R. (1982). Settings, scripts, and self-schemata: A cognitive analysis of the development of prosocial behavior. In N. Eisenberg (Ed.), *The development of prosocial behavior.* New York: Academic Press.

Karniol, R. (1984). A response set analysis of developmental differences in children's moral judgments. *Journal of Research in Personality, 18,* 15–26.

Karniol, R., & Miller, D. T. (1981). Morality and the development of conceptions of justice. In M. J. Lerner & S. C. Lerner (Eds.), *The justice motive in social behavior.* New York: Plenum Press.

Karniol, R., & Ross, M. (1976). The development of causal attributions in social perception. *Journal of Personality and Social Psychology, 34,* 455–464.

Karniol, R., & Ross, M. (1979). Children's use of a causal attribution schema and the inference of manipulative intentions. *Child Development, 50,* 463–468.

Karylowski, J. (1982a). Doing good to feel good vs. doing good to make others feel good: Some child-rearing antecedents. *School Psychology International, 3,* 149–156.

Karylowski, J. (1982b). Two types of altruistic behavior: Doing good to feel good or to make the other feel good. In V. J. Derlega & J. Grzelak (Eds.), *Cooperation and helping behavior: Theories and research.* New York: Academic Press.

Kassin, S. M., & Lepper, M. R. (in press). Over-sufficient and insufficient justification effects: Cognitive and behavioral development. In J. Nicholls (Ed.), *The development of achievement motivation.* Greenwich, CT: JAI Press.

Keasey, C. B. (1977). Young children's attribution of intentionality to themselves and others. *Child Development, 48,* 261–264.

Keasey, C. B. (1978). Children's developing awareness and usage of intentionality and motives. In H. E. Howe, Jr. (Ed.), *Nebraska Symposium of Motivation.* Lincoln, NE: University of Nebraska Press.

Kelley, H. H. (1967). Attribution theory in social psychology. In D. Levine (Ed.), *Nebraska Symposium on Motivation* (Vol. 15). Lincoln, NE: University of Nebraska Press.

Kelley, H. H. (1972). *Causal schemata and the attribution process.* New York: General Learning Press.

Kenrick, D. T., Baumann, D. J., & Cialdini, R. B. (1979). A step in the socialization of altruism and hedonism: Effects of negative mood on children's generosity under public and private conditions. *Journal of Personality and Social Psychology, 37,* 747–755.

Kenrick, D. T., Reich, J. W., & Cialdini, R. B. (1976). Justification and compensation: Rosier skies for the devalued victim. *Journal of Personality and Social Psychology, 34,* 654–657.

Kidd, R. F., & Berkowitz, L. (1976). Dissonance, self-concept, and helpfulness. *Journal of Personality and Social Psychology, 33,* 613–622.

King, M. (1971). The development of some intention concepts in young children. *Child Development, 42,* 1145–1152.

Kohlberg, L. (1963). The development of children's orientation toward a moral order: I. Sequence in the development of moral thought. *Vita Humana, 6,* 11–33.

Kohlberg, L. (1969). Stage and sequence: The cognitive-developmental approach to socialization. In D. A. Goslin (Ed.), *Handbook of socialization theory and research.* New York: Rand McNally.

Kohlberg, L. (1971). From is to ought: How to commit the naturalistic fallacy and get away with it in the study of moral development. In T. Mischel (Ed.), *Cognitive development and genetic episomology.* New York: Academic Press.

Kohlberg, L. (1973). Stages and aging in moral development: Some speculations. *The Gerontologist,* Winter, 497–502.

Kohlberg, L. (1976). Moral stage and moralization: The cognitive-developmental approach. In T. Lickona (Ed.), *Moral development and behavior: Theory, research, and social issues.* New York: Holt.

Kohlberg, L. (1978). Revisions in the theory and practice of moral development. *New Directions for Child Development, 2,* 83–88.

Kohlberg, L. (1981). *The philosophy of moral development: Moral stages and the idea of justice.* San Francisco: Harper & Row.

Kohlberg, L., & Candee, D. (1984). The relationship of moral judgment to moral action. In W. M. Kurtines & J. L. Gewirtz (Eds.), *Morality, moral behavior and moral development.* New York: Wiley.

Kohlberg, L., Levine, C., & Hewer, A. (1983). *Contributions to human development, Vol. 10. Moral Stages; A current formulation and a response to critics.* Basel: Karger.

Konecni, V. J. (1972). Some effects of guilt on compliance: A field replication. *Journal of Personality and Social Psychology, 23,* 30–32.

Kopp, C. B. (1982). Antecedents of self-regulation: A developmental perspective. *Developmental Psychology, 18,* 199–214.

Krasnor, L. R., & Rubin, K. H. (1981). The assessment of social problem-solving skills in young children. In T. Merluzzi, C. Glass, & M. Genest (Eds.), *Cognitive assessment.* New York: Guilford Press.

Krasnor, L. R., & Rubin, K. H. (1983). Preschool social problem solving: Attempts and outcomes in naturalistic interaction. *Child Development, 54,* 1545–1558.

Krebs, D. (1970). Altruism: An examination of the concept and a review of the literature. *Psychological Bulletin, 73,* 258–302.

Krebs, D. (1975). Empathy and altruism. *Journal of Personality and Social Psychology, 32,* 1134–1146.

Krebs, D. (1982). Altruism - A rational approach. In N. Eisenberg (Ed.), *The development of prosocial behavior.* New York: Academic Press.

Krebs, D., & Gillmore, J. (1982). The relationship among the first stages of cognitive development, role-taking abilities, and moral development. *Child Development, 53,* 877–886.

Krebs, D., & Russell, C. (1981). Role-taking and altruism. In J. P. Rushton & R. M. Sorrentino (Eds.), *Altruism and helping behavior: Social, personality, and developmental perspectives.* Hillsdale, NJ: Lawrence Erlbaum Associates.

Krebs, D., & Sturrup, B. (1982). Role-taking ability and altruistic behaviour in elementary school children. *Journal of Moral Education, 11,* 94–100.

Kritt, D., & Baldwin, A. (1980, September). *Children's concepts of kindness: Consideration of the recipient's need.* Paper presented at the annual convention of the American Psychological Association, Montreal, Canada.

Kuhn, D., Langer, J., Kohlberg, L., & Haan, N. S. (1977). The development of formal operations in logical and moral judgments. *Genetic Psychology Monographs, 95,* 97–188.

Kun, A., Murray, J., & Sredl, K. (1980). Misuses of the multiple sufficient scheme as a model of naive attributions: A case of mistaken identity. *Developmental Psychology, 16,* 13–22.

Kurdek, L. A. (1977). Structural components and intellectual correlates of cognitive perspective taking in first- through fourth grade children. *Child Development, 48,* 1503–1511.

Kurdek, L. (1978). Perspective taking as the cognitive basis of children's moral development: A review of the literature. *Merrill-Palmer Quarterly, 24,* 3–27.

Kurdek, L. A., (1980). Developmental relations among children's perspective taking, moral judgment, and parent-rated behavior. *Merrill-Palmer Quarterly, 26,* 103–121.

Kurdek, L. A. (1981). Young adults' moral reasoning about prohibitive and prosocial dilemmas. *Journal of Youth and Adolescence, 10,* 263–272.

Kurtines, W., & Grief, E. G. (1974). The development of moral thought: Review and evaluation of Kohlberg's approach. *Psychological Bulletin, 81,* 453–470.

Kurtines, W. M., & Schneider, P. J. (1983, August). *Sharing and giving as rule governed behavior: A psychological role-theoretical approach to pro- and anti-social behavior.* Paper presented at the annual meeting of the American Psychological Association, Aneheim, CA.

Lang, P. J. (1971). The application of psychophysiological methods to the study of psychotherapy and behavior modification. In A. E. Bergin & S. L. Garfield (Eds.), *Handbook of psychotherapy and behavior change: An empirical analysis.* New York: Wiley.

Langer, E. J., Blank, A., & Chanowitz, B. (1978). The mindlessness of ostensibly thoughtful action. *Journal of Personality and Social Psychology, 36,* 635–642.

Lantermann, E. D. (1980). *Intesaktionen: Person, Situation and Handlung.* Munden: Urban & Schwarzenberg.

Larson, S., & Kurdek, L. A. (1979). Intratask and intertask consistency of moral judgment indices in first-, third-, and fifth-grade children. *Developmental Psychology, 15,* 462–463.

Larrieu, J. A. (1984a, March). *Children's commitment to others, social efficacy, and prosocial behavior.* Paper presented at the biennial meeting of the Southwestern Society for Research in Human Development, Denver, CO.

Larrieu, J. A. (1984b, March). *Prosocial values, assertiveness, and sex: Predictors of children's naturalistic helping.* Paper presented at the biennial meeting of the Southwestern Society for the Research in Human Development, Denver, CO.

Latané, B., & Darley, J. (1970). *The unresponsive bystander: Why doesn't he help?* New York: Appleton.

Latané, B., & Nida, S. (1981). Ten years of research on group size and helping. *Psychological Bulletin, 89,* 308–324.

Laucken, V. (1973). *Naive Verhaltenshtheorie.* Stuttgart: Klett.

Lazarus, R. S. (1968). Emotions and adaptation: Conceptual and empirical relations. In W. J. Arnold (Ed.), *Nebraska Symposium on Motivation.* Lincoln, NE: University of Nebraska Press.

Lazarus, R. S., Averill, J. R., & Optin, E. M., Jr. (1970). Towards a cognitive theory of emotion. In M. B. Arnold (Ed.), *Feelings and emotions.* New York: Academic Press.

Leahy, R. L. (1979). Development of conceptions of prosocial behavior: Information affecting rewards given for altruism and kindness. *Developmental Psychology, 15,* 34–37.

Leahy, R. L. (1981). Parental practices and the development of moral judgment and self-image disparity during adolescence. *Developmental Psychology, 17,* 580–594.

Lederer, G. (1982). Trends in authoritarianism: A study of adolescents in West Germany and the United States since 1945. *Journal of Cross-Cultural Psychology, 13,* 299–314.

Leiman, B. (1978, August). *Affective empathy and subsequent altruism in kindergarteners and first graders.* Paper presented at the annual meeting of the American Psychological Association, Toronto, Canada.

LeMare, L., & Krebs, D. (1983). Perspective-taking and styles of (pro) social behavior in elementary school children. *Academic Psychology Bulletin, 2,* 289–298.

Leming, J. S. (1976). An exploratory inquiry into the multi-factor theory of moral behavior. *Journal of Moral Behavior, 5,* 179–188.

Lennon, R., Eisenberg, N., & Carroll, J., (1983a). The assessment of empathy in early childhood. *Journal of Applied Developmental Psychology, 4*, 295–302.

Lennon, R., Eisenberg, N., & Carroll, J. (1983b, April). *The relation between empathy and prosocial behavior in the preschool years.* Paper presented at the biennial meeting of the Society for Research in Child Development, Detroit, MI.

Lepper, M. R., Greene, D., & Nisbett, R. E. (1973). Undermining children's intrinsic interest with extrinsic rewards: A test of the "overjustification" hypothesis. *Journal of Personality and Social Psychology, 28*, 129–137.

Lerner, M. J. (1975). The justice motive in social behavior: Introduction. *Journal of Social Issues, 31*, 1–79.

Lerner, M. J. (1981). The justice motive in human relations: Some thoughts on what we know and need to know about justice. In M. J. Lerner & S. C. Lerner (Eds.), *The justice motive in social behavior.* New York: Plenum Press.

Lerner, M. J., & Matthews, G. (1967). Reactions to suffering of others under conditions of indirect responsibility. *Journal of Personality and Social Psychology, 5*, 319–325.

Lerner, M. J., & Meindl, J. R. (1981). Justice and altruism. In J. P. Rushton & R. M. Sorrentino (Eds.), *Altruism and helping behavior.* Hillsdale, NJ: Lawrence Erlbaum Associates.

Lerner, M. J., & Miller, D. T. (1978). Just world research and the attribution process: Looking back and ahead. *Psychological Bulletin, 85*, 1030–1051.

Lerner, M. J., & Simmons, C. H. (1966). The observer's reaction to the "innocent victim": Compassion or rejection? *Journal of Personality and Social Psychology, 4*, 203–210.

Levin, I., & Bekerman-Greenberg, R. (1980). Moral judgment and moral behavior in sharing: A developmental analysis. *Genetic Psychology Monographs, 101*, 215–230.

Lewis, M., & Michalson, L. (1983). *Children's emotions and moods: Theory and measurement.* New York: Plenum.

Lewis, M., Sullivan, M. W., & Michalson, L. (1984). The cognitive-emotional fugue. In C. E. Izard, J. Kagan, & R. B. Zajonc (Eds.), *Emotions, cognition, and behavior.* Cambridge: Cambridge University Press.

Liebhart, E. H. (1972). Empathy and emergency helping: The effects of personality, self-concern and accquaintance. *Journal of Experimental Social Psychology, 8*, 404–411.

Light, P. (1979). *The development of social sensitivity: A study of social aspects of role-taking in children.* Cambridge, UK: Cambridge University Press.

Locke, D. (1983). Theory and practice in thought and action. In H. Weinreich-Haste, & D. Locke (Eds.), *Morality in the making.* Chichester, England: Wiley.

Locke, D., & Pennington, D. (1982). Reasons and other causes: Their role in attribution processes. *Journal of Personality and Social Psychology, 42*, 212–223.

Loevinger, J., & Wessler, R. (1970). *Measuring ego development: Construction and use of a sentence completion test.* San Francisco, CA: Jossey-Bass.

Lorenz, K. (1966). *On aggression.* New York: Harcourt, Brace, & World.

Luria, Z., Goldwasser, M., & Goldwasser, A. (1963). Response to transgression in stories by Israeli children. *Child Development, 34*, 271–280.

Lynch, J. G., & Cohen, J. L. (1978). The use of subjective expected utility theory as an aid to understanding variables that influence helping behavior. *Journal of Personality and Social Psychology, 36*, 1138–1151.

Lyons, N. P. (1983). Two perspectives: On self, relationships and morality. *Harvard Educational Review, 53*, 125–145.

Lyons-Ruth, K. (1978). Moral and personal value judgments of preschool children. *Child Development, 49*, 1197–1207.

Maccoby, E. (1966). Differences in intellectual functioning. In E. E. Maccoby (Ed.), *The development of sex differences.* Stanford, CA: Stanford University Press.

MacLean, P. D. (1982, May). *Evolutionary brain roots of family, play, and the isolation call.* The

Adolph Meyer Lecture, 135th annual meeting of the American Psychological Association, Toronto, Canada.

Major, B. (1980). Information acquisition and attribution processes. *Journal of Personality and Social Psychology, 39, 6,* 1010–1023.

Mandler, G. (1975). *Mind and emotion.* New York: Wiley.

Mandler, G. (1980). The generation of emotion: A psychological theory. In R. Plutchik & H. Kellerman (Eds.), *Emotion: Theory, research and experience: Theories of emotion.* New York: Academic Press.

Mandler, G., Mandler, J. M., Kremen, I., & Skoliton, R. D. (1961). The response to threat: Relations among verbal and physiological indices. *Psychological Monographs, 75*(9, Whole No. 513), 1–19.

Marcus, R. F., Telleen, S., & Roke, E. J. (1979). Relation between cooperation and empathy in young children. *Developmental Psychology, 15,* 346–347.

Marks, E. L., Penner, L. A., & Stone, A. V. W. (1982). Helping as a function of empathic responses and sociopathy. *Journal of Research in Personality, 16,* 1–20.

Marsh, D. T. (1982). The development of interpersonal problem solving among elementary school children. *Journal of Genetic Psychology, 140,* 107–118.

Marsh, D. T., Serafica, F. C., & Barenboim, C. (1980). Effect of perspective-taking training on interpersonal problem solving. *Child Development, 51,* 140–145.

Marsh, D. T., Serafica, F. C., & Barenboim, C. (1981). Interrelationships among perspective taking, interpersonal problem solving, and interpersonal functioning. *Journal of Genetic Psychology, 138,* 37–48.

Matthews, K. A., Batson, C. D., Horn, J., & Rosenman, R. H. (1981). "Principles in his nature which interest him in the fortunes of others . . . ": The heritability of empathic concern for others. *Journal of Personality, 49,* 237–247.

McArthur, L. A. (1972). The how and what of why: Some determinants and consequences of causal attribution. *Journal of Personality and Social Psychology, 22,* 171–193.

McArthur, L. A. (1976). The lesser influence of consensus than distinctiveness information on causal attributions: A test of the person-thing hypothesis. *Journal of Personality and Social Psychology, 33,* 733–742.

McArthur, L. A., & Baron, R. M. (1983). Toward an ecological theory of social perception. *Psychological Review, 90,* 215–238.

McGovern, L. P., Ditzian, J. L., & Taylor, S. P. (1975). Sex and perceptions of dependency in a helping situation. *Bulletin of the Psychonomic Society, 5,* 336–338.

McMillen, D. L. (1971). Transgression, self-image, and compliant behavior. *Journal of Personality and Social Psychology, 20,* 176–179.

McMillen, D. L., & Austin, J. B. (1971). Effect of positive feedback on compliance following transgression. *Psychonomic Science, 24,* 59–60.

McMillen, D. L., Jackson, J. A., & Austin, J. B. (1974). Effects of positive and negative requests on ompliance following transgression. *Bulletin of the Psychonomic Society, 3,* 80–82.

McMillen, D. L., Sanders, D.Y., & Solomon, G. S. (1977). Self-esteem, attentiveness, and helping behavior. *Personality and Social Psychology Bulletin, 3,* 257–261.

McNamee, S. (1978). Moral behavior, moral development and motivation. *Journal of Moral Education, 7,* 27–31.

Mead, G. H. (1934). *Mind, self and society.* Chicago, IL: University of Chicago Press.

Mehrabian, A., & Epstein, N. A. (1972). A measure of emotional empathy. *Journal of Personality, 40,* 523–543.

Mercer, P. (1972). *Sympathy and ethics.* Oxford: Clarendon Press.

Meyer, J. P., & Mulherin, A. (1980). From attribution to helping: An analysis of the mediating effects of affect and expectancy. *Journal of Personality and Social Psychology, 39,* 201–210.

Midlarsky, E., & Bryan, J. H. (1972). Affect expressions and children's imitative altruism. *Journal of Experimental Research on Personality, 6,* 195–203.

Midlarsky, E., & Midlarsky, M. (1973). Some determinants of aiding under experimentally induced stress. *Journal of Personality, 41,* 305–327.

Miller, D. T. (1976). Ego involvement and attributions for success and failure. *Journal of Personality and Social Psychology, 34,* 901–906.

Miller, D. T. (1978). What constitutes a self-serving attributional bias? A reply to Bradley. *Journal of Personality and Social Psychology, 11,* 1221–1223.

Miller, D. T., & Ross, M. (1975). Self-serving biases in the attribution of causality: Fact or fiction? *Psychological Bulletin, 2,* 213–225.

Miller, D. T., & Smith, J. (1977). The effect of own deservingness and deservingness of others on children's helping behavior. *Child Development, 48,* 617–620.

Miller, G. A., Galanter, E., & Pribram, K. H. (1960). *Plans and The structure of behavior.* New York: Holt.

Miller, R. L., Brickman, P., & Bolen, D. (1975). Attribution versus persuasion as a means for modifying behavior. *Journal of Personality and Social Psychology, 31,* 430–441.

Miller, S. M. (1977, March). *Dependency, empathy, and altruism.* Paper presented at the biennial meeting of the Society for Research in Child Development, New Orleans, LA.

Milo, R. D. (1973). *Egoism and altruism.* Belmont, CA: Wadsworth.

Mischel, H. N. (1983, April). *From intention to action: The role of rule knowledge in the development of self-regulation.* Paper presented at the Society for Research in Child Development, Detroit, MI.

Mischel, W., & Mischel, H. N. (1976). A cognitive social-learning approach to morality and self-regulation. In T. Lickona (Ed.), *Moral development and behavior: Theory, research and social issues.* New York: Holt.

Monson, T. C., & Snyder, M. (1977). Actors, observers, and the attribution process: Toward a reconceptualization. *Journal of Experimental Social Psychology, 13,* 89–111.

Moore, B. S., & Eisenberg, N. (1984). The development of altruism. In G. Whitehurst (Ed.), *Annuals of Child Development.* Greenwich, CT: JAI Press.

Morency, N. L., & Krauss, R. M. (1982). Children's nonverbal encoding and decoding of affect. In R. S. Feldman (Ed.), *Development of nonverbal behavior in children.* New York: Spring-Verlag.

Morris, P. (1981). The cognitive psychology of self-reports. In C. Antaki (Ed.), *The psychology of ordinary explanations of social behaviour.* London: Academic Press.

Murdoch, I. (1971). *The sovereignty of good.* New York: Shocken.

Mussen, P., & Eisenberg-Berg, N. (1977). *Roots of caring, sharing, and helping: The development of prosocial behavior.* San Francisco, CA: Freeman.

Mussen, P., Rutherford, E., Harris, S., & Keasey, C. (1970). Honesty and altruism among pre-adolescents. *Developmental Psychology, 3,* 169–194.

Nadler, A., Romek, E., & Shapiro-Friedman, A. (1976). Giving in the kibbutz: Prosocial behavior of city and kibbutz children as affected by social responsibility and social pressure. *Journal of Cross-Cultural Psychology, 10,* 57–72.

Nagel, T. (1970). *The possibility of altruism.* Oxford: Clarendon Press.

Nails, D. (1983). Social-scientific sexism: Gilligan's mismeasure of man. *Social Research, 50,* 643–664.

Nelson, S. A. (1980). Factors influencing young children's use of motives and outcomes as moral criteria. *Child Development, 51,* 823–829.

Nicholls, J. G. (1979). The development of perception of own attainment and causal attributions for success and failure. *Journal of Educational Psychology, 71,* 94–99.

Nisan, M. (1984a). Content and structure in moral judgment: An integrative view. In W. M. Kurtines & J. L. Gewirtz (Eds.), *Morality, moral behavior, and moral development.* New York: Wiley.

Nisan, M. (1984b). Distributive justice and social norms. *Child Development, 55,* 1020–1029.

Nisan, M., & Kohlberg, L. (1982). Universality and variation in moral judgment: A longitudinal and cross-sectional study in Turkey. *Child Development, 53,* 865–876.

Nisbett, R. E., Caputo, C., Legant, P., & Marecek, J. (1973). Behavior as seen by the actor and as seen by the observer. *Journal of Personality and Social Psychology, 27,* 154–164.

Nisbett, R., & Ross, L. (1980). *Human inference: Strategies and shortcomings of social judgment.* Englewood Cliffs, NJ: Prentice-Hall.

Nisbett, R. E., & Wilson, T. D. (1977). Telling more than we can know: Verbal reports on mental processes. *Psychological Review, 84,* 231–259.

Notarius, C. I., & Levenson, R. W. (1979). Expressive tendencies and physiological response to stress. *Journal of Personality and Social Psychology, 37,* 1204–1210.

Nowakowska, M. (1977). Prosocial behavior: A decision model. *Polish Psychological Bulletin, 8,* 177–186.

Nummedal, S. G., & Bass, S. C. (1976). Effects of the salience of intention and consequence in children's moral judgments. *Developmental Psychology, 12,* 475–476.

Nunner-Winkler, G. (1984). Two moralities? A critical dimension of an ethic of care and responsibility versus an ethic of rights and justice. In W. M. Kurtines & J. L. Gewirtz (Eds.), *Morality, moral behavior, and moral development.* New York: Wiley.

O'Connor, M., & Cuevas, J. (1982). The relationship of children's prosocial behavior to social responsiblity, prosocial reasoning, and personality. *Journal of Genetic Psychology, 140,* 33–45.

O'Connor, M., Cuevas, J., & Dollinger, S. (1981). Understanding motivations behind prosocial acts: A developmental analysis. *Journal of Genetic Psychology, 139,* 267–276.

O'Loughlin, M. A. (1983). Responsibility and moral majority in the control of fertility—Or, a woman's place is in the wrong. *Social Research, 50,* 536–575.

Olejnik, A. B. (1975, April). *Developmental changes and interrelationships among role-taking, moral judgments, and children's sharing.* Paper presented at the biennial meeting of the Society for Research in Child Development, Denver, CO.

Olson, S. L., Johnson, J., Parks, K., Barrett, E., & Belleau, K. (1983a, April). *Behavior problems of preschool children: Dimensions and social and cognitive correlates.* Paper presented at the biennial meeting of the Society for Research in Child Development, Detroit, MI.

Olson, S. L., Johnson, J., Belleau, K., Parks, J., & Barrett, E. (1983b, April). *Social competence in preschool children: Interrelations with sociometric status, social problem-solving, and impulsivity.* Paper presented at the biennial meeting of the Society for Research in Child Development, Detroit, MI.

Ornum, W. V., Foley, J. M., Burns, P. R., DeWolfe, A. S., & Kennedy, E. C. (1981). Empathy, altruism, and self-interest in college students. *Adolescence, 64,* 799–808.

Pahel, K. (1979). Moral motivation. In D. B. Cochrane, C. M. Hamm, & A. C. Kazepides (Eds.), *The domain of moral education.* New York: Paulist Press.

Parikh, B. (1980). Development of moral judgment and its relation to family environment factors in Indian and American families. *Child Development, 51,* 1030–1039.

Pastor, D. L. (1981). The quality of mother-infant attachment and its relationship to toddlers' initial sociability with peers. *Developmental Psychology, 17,* 326–335.

Paulhus, D. L., Shaffer, D. R., & Downing, L. L. (1977). Effects of making blood donors motives salient upon donor retention: A field experiment. *Personality and Social Psychology Bulletin, 3,* 99–102.

Pearl, R. A. (1979, March). *Developmental and situational influences on children's understanding of prosocial behavior.* Paper presented at the biennial meeting of the Society for Research in Child Development, San Francisco, CA.

Peevers, B. H., & Secord, P. F. (1973). Developmental changes in attribution of descriptive concepts to persons. *Journal of Personality and Social Psychology, 27,* 120–128.

Peraino, J. M. (1977). *Role-taking training, affect arousal, empathy, and generosity.* Unpublished manuscript, University of California, Berkeley.

Peraino, J. M., & Sawin, D. B. (1981, April). *Empathic distress: Measurement and relation to prosocial behavior.* Paper presented at the biennial meeting of the Society for Research in Child Development, Boston, MA.

Perry, D. G., Bussey, K., & Freiberg, K. (1981). Impact of adults' appeals for sharing on the development of altruistic dispositions in children. *Journal of Experimental Child Psychology, 32*, 127–138.

Perry, D. G., & Perry, L. C. (1983). Social learning, causal attribution, and moral internalization. In J. Bisanz, G. L. Bisanz, & R. Kail (Eds.), *Learning in children: Progress in cognitive development research.* New York: Springer-Verlag.

Peters, R. S. (1979). Form and content in moral education. In D. B. Cochrane, C. M. Hamm, & A. C. Kazepides (Eds.), *The domain of moral education.* New York: Paulist Press.

Peterson, L. (1980). Developmental changes in verbal and behavioral sensitivity to cues of social norms of altruism. *Child Development, 51*, 830–838.

Peterson, L. (1983a). Influence of age, task competence, and responsibility focus on children's altruism. *Developmental Psychology, 19*, 141–148.

Peterson, L. (1983b). Role of donor competence, donor age, and peer presence on helping in an emergency. *Developmental Psychology, 19*, 873–880.

Peterson, L., & Gelfand, D. M. (1984). Causal attributions of helping as a function of age and incentives. *Child Development, 55*, 504–511.

Peterson, L., Hartmann, D. P., & Gelfand, D. M. (1977). Developmental changes in the effects of dependency and reciprocity cues on children's moral judgments and donation rates. *Child Development, 48*, 1331–1339.

Petrovich, O. (1982). Moral development among mildly mentally handicapped school children. *Journal of Moral Education, 11*, 233–246.

Piaget, J. (1965). *The moral judgment of the child.* New York: Free Press. (Originally published, 1932).

Piaget, J. (1970). Piaget's theory. In P. H. Mussen (Ed.), *Carmichael's manual of child psychology* (Vol. 1). New York: Wiley.

Piaget, J. (1981). *Intelligence and affectivity.* Palo Alto, CA: Annual Reviews.

Piliavin, J. A., Dovidio, J. F., Gaertner, S. L., & Clark, R. D., III. (1981). *Emergency intervention.* New York: Academic Press.

Piliavin, J. A., Dovidio, J. F., Gaertner, S. L., & Clark, R. D., III. (1982). Responsive bystanders: The process of intervention In V. J. Derlega & J. Grzelak (Eds.), *Cooperation and helping behavior: Theories and research.* New York: Academic Press.

Piliavin, J. A., & Piliavin, I. M. (1972). The effects of blood on reactions to a victim. *Journal of Personality and Social Psychology, 23*, 253–261.

Piliavin, I. M., Rodin, J., & Piliavin, J. A., (1969). Good samaritanism: An underground phenomenon? *Journal of Personality and Social Psychology, 13*, 289–299.

Piliavin, I. M., Piliavin, J. A., & Rodin, J. (1975). Costs, diffusion, and the stigmatized victim. *Journal of Personality and Social Psychology, 32*, 429–438.

Platt, J. J., Scura, W. C., & Hannon, J. R. (1973). Problem-solving thinking of youthful incarcerated heroine addicts. *Journal of Community Psychology, 1*, 248–281.

Platt, J. J., & Spivak, G. (1972). Problem-solving thinking of psychiatric patients. *Journal of Consulting and Clinical Psychology, 39*, 148–151.

Platt, J. J., Spivack, G., Altman, N., Altman,D., & Peizer, S. B. (1974). Adolescent problem-solving thinking. *Journal of Consulting and Clinical Psychology, 42*, 787–793.

Plutchik, R. (1977). Cognitions in the service of emotions: An evolutionary perspective. In D. K. Candland, J. P. Fell, E. Keen, A. I. Leshner, R. M. Tarpy, & P. Plutchik (Eds.), *Emotion.* Monterey, CA: Brooks/Cole.

Pomazal, R. J., & Jaccard, J. J. (1976). An informational approach to altruistic behavior. *Journal of Personality and Social Psychology, 33*, 317–326.

Rabin, A. I. (1965). *Growing up on the kibbutz.* New York: Springer.

Radke-Yarrow, M., & Zahn-Waxler, C. (1984). Roots, motives, and patterns in children's prosocial behavior. In E. Staub, D. Bar-Tal, J. Karylowski, & J. Reykowski (Eds.), *Development and maintenance of prosocial behavior: International perspectives on positive development.* New York: Plenum Press.

Radke-Yarrow, M., Zahn-Waxler, C., & Chapman, M. (1983). Prosocial dispositions and behavior. In P. Mussen (Ed.), *Manual of child psychology: Vol. 4. Socialization, personality and social development.* New York: Wiley.

Raviv, A., Bar-Tal, D., & Lewis-Levin, T. (1980). Motivations for donation behavior by boys of three different ages. *Child Development, 51,* 610–613.

Rawlings, E. I. (1968). Witnessing harm to others: A re-assessment of the role of guilt in altruistic behavior. *Journal of Personality and Social Psychology, 10,* 377–380.

Regan, J. W. (1971). Guilt, perceived injustice, and altruistic behavior. *Journal of Personality and Social Psychology, 18,* 124–132.

Reisenzein, R. (1983). The Schachter theory of emotion: Two decades later. *Psychological Bulletin, 94,* 239–264.

Rest, J. R. (1973). The hierarchical nature of stages of moral judgment. *Journal of Personality, 41,* 86–109.

Rest, J. R. (1979). *Development in judgment moral issues.* Minneapolis, MN: University of Minnesota Press.

Reykowski, J. (1977). Cognitive development and prosocial behavior. *Polish Psychological Bulletin, 8,* 35–43.

Reykowski, J. (1982a). Motivation of prosocial behavior. In V. J. Delaga & J. Grzelak (Eds.), *Cooperation and helping behavior: Theories and research.* New York: Academic Press.

Reykowski, J. (1982b). Social motivation. In M. R. Rosenzweig & L. W. Porter (Eds.), *Annual Review of Psychology* (Vol. 33). Palo Alto, CA: Annual Reviews.

Reykowski, J. (1984, August). *Evaluative systems: Rules of change.* Invited address presented at the annual meeting of the American Psychological Association, Toronto, Canada.

Rholes, W. S. (1982). The effects of personality trait attributions on modeling: A developmental study. *Child Study Journal, 3,* 187–203.

Rholes, W. S., & Bailey, S. (1983). The effects of level of moral reasoning on consistency between moral attitudes and related behaviors. *Social Cognition, 2,* 32–48.

Rholes, W. S., & Ruble, D. N. (1984). Children's understanding of dispositional characteristics of others. *Child Development, 55,* 550–560.

Ridley, M., & Dawkins, R. (1981). The natural selection of altruism. In J. P. Rushton & R. M. Sorrentino (Eds.), Altruism and helping behavior. Hillsdale, NJ: Lawrence Erlbaum Associates.

Roe, K. (1982, March). Personal communication.

Rogers, M., Miller, N., Mayer, F. S., & Duval, S. (1982). Personal responsibility and salience of the request for help: Determinants of the relation between negative affect and helping behavior. *Journal of Personality and Social Psychology, 43,* 956–970.

Rosenthal, T. L., & Zimmerman, B. J. (1978). *Social learning and cognition.* New York: Academic Press.

Ross, M., & Sicoly, F. (1979). Egocentric biases in availability and attribution. *Journal of Personality and Social Psychology, 37,* 322–336.

Ross, W. D. (1930). *The right and the good.* Oxford: Clarendon Press.

Rotenberg, K. J. (1982). Development of character constancy of self and other. *Child Development, 53,* 505–515.

Royce, J. R., & Diamond, S. R. (1980). A multifactor-system dynamics theory of emotion: Cognition-affective interaction. *Motivation and Emotion, 4,* 263–298.

Rubin, K. H., & Schneider, F. W. (1973). The relationship between moral judgment, egocentrism, and altruistic behavior. *Child Development, 44,* 661–665.

Ruble, D. N., Parsons, J. E., & Ross, J. (1976). Self-evaluation responses of children in an achievement setting. *Child Development, 47,* 990–997.

Rushton, J. P. (1980). *Altruism, socialization, and society.* Englewood Cliffs: Prentice-Hall.

Rushton, J. P. (1982). Social learning theory and the development of prosocial behavior. In N. Eisenberg (Ed.), *The development of prosocial behavior*. New York: Academic Press.

Rushton, J. P., Brainerd, C. J., & Pressley, M. (1983). Behavioral development and construct validity: The principle of aggregation. *Psychological Bulletin, 94,* 18–38.

Rushton, J. P., Russell, R. J. H., & Wells, P. A. (1984). Genetic similarity theory: Beyond kin selection. *Behavior Genetics, 14,* 179–193.

Rushton, J. P., & Wiener, J. (1975). Altruism and cognitive development in children. *British Journal of Social and Clinical Psychology, 14,* 341–349.

Rutherford, E., & Mussen, P. (1968). Generosity in nursery school boys. *Child Development, 39,* 755–765.

Saarni, C. (1979). Children's understanding of display rules for expressive behavior. *Developmental Psychology, 15,* 424–429.

Saarni, C. (1982). Social and affective functions of nonverbal behavior: Developmental concerns. In R. S. Feldman (Ed.), *Development of nonverbal behavior in children*. New York: Springer-Verlag.

Sakagami, M., & Namiki, H. (1982). Structure of prosocial moral judgment. *Studies in Sociology, Psychology, and Education, 22,* 51–57.

Saltzer, E. B. (1981). Cognitive mediators of the relationship between behavioral intentions and behavior. *Journal of Personality and Social Psychology, 41,* 260–271.

Saltzstein, H. D., & Weiner, A. S. (1982, August). *Moral intentionality: Children's representation of adult judgments and attribution processes*. Paper presented at the annual meeting of the American Psychological Association, Washington, DC.

Sawin, D. (1979, March). *Assessing empathy in children: A search for an elusive concept*. Paper presented at the biennial meeting of the Society for Research in Child Development, San Francisco, CA.

Sawin, D. B., Underwood, B., Weaver, J., & Mostyn, M. (1981). *Empathy and altruism*. Unpublished manuscript, University of Texas, Austin.

Schachter, S., & Singer, J. (1962). Cognitive, social and physiological determinants of emotional state. *Psychological Review, 69,* 378–399.

Schlenker, B. R., Hallam, J. R., & McCown, N. E. (1983). Motives and social evaluation: Actor-observer differences in the delineation of motives for a beneficial act. *Journal of Experimental Social Psychology, 19,* 254–273.

Schopenhauer, A. (1965). *On the basis of morality* (Translated by E. F. J. Payne). Indianapolis, IN: Bobbs-Merrill. (Originally published, 1841).

Schopler, J., & Matthews, M. W. (1965). The influence of perceived causal locus of partner's dependence on the use of interpersonal power. *Journal of Personality and Social Psychology, 4,* 609–612.

Schultz, T. R., & Butkowsky, I. (1977). Young children's use of the scheme for multiple sufficient causes in the attribution of real and hypothetical behavior. *Child Development, 48,* 464–469.

Schwartz, S. H. (1968a). Awareness of consequences and the influence of moral norms on interpersonal behavior. *Sociometry, 31,* 355–369.

Schwartz, S. H. (1968b). Words, deeds, and the perception of consequences and responsibility in action situations. *Journal of Personality and Social Psychology, 10,* 232–242.

Schwartz, S. H. (1970). Elicitation of moral obligation and self-sacrificing behavior: An experimental study of volunteering to be a bone marrow donor. *Journal of Personality and Social Psychology, 15,* 283–293.

Schwartz, S. H. (1973). Normative explanations of helping behavior: A critique, proposal, and empirical test. *Journal of Experimental Social Psychology, 9,* 349–364.

Schwartz, S. H. (1978). Temporal instability as a moderator of the attitude-behavior relationship. *Journal of Personality and Social Psychology, 36,* 715–724.

Schwartz, S. H., & Ben David, A. (1976). Responsibility and helping in an emergency: Effects of blame, ability and denial of responsibility. *Sociometry, 39,* 406–415.

Schwartz, S. H., & Clausen, G. T. (1970). Responsibility, norms, and helping in an emergency. *Journal of Personality and Social Psychology, 16,* 299–310.

Schwartz, S. H., & Fleishman, J. A. (1978). Personal norms and the mediation of legitimacy effects on helping. *Social Psychology, 41,* 306–315.

Schwartz, S. H., & Fleishman, J. A. (1982). Effects of negative personal norms on helping behavior. *Personality and Social Psychology Bulletin, 8,* 81–86.

Schwartz, S. H., & Fleishman, J. A. (1983). *Personal norms as a distinctive attitudinal variable.* Unpublished manuscript, Hebrew University, Jerusalem.

Schwartz, S. H., & Howard, J. A. (1980). Explanations for the moderating effect of responsibility denial on the personal norms-behavior relationship. *Social Psychology Quarterly, 43,* 441–446.

Schwartz, S. H., & Howard, J. A. (1981). In J. P. Rushton & R. M. Sorrentino (Eds.), *Altruism and helping behavior.* Hillsdale, NJ: Lawrence Erlbaum Associates.

Schwartz, S. H., & Howard, J. A. (1982). Helping and cooperation: A self-based motivational model. In V. J. Derlaga & J. Grzelak (Eds.), *Cooperation and helping behavior: Theories and research.* New York: Academic Press.

Schwartz, S. H., & Howard, J. A. (1984). Internalized values as motivators of altruism. In E. Staub, D. Bar-Tal, J. Karylowski, & J. Reykowski (Eds.), *The development and maintenance of prosocial behavior: International perspectives on positive development.* New York: Plenum Press.

Schwartz, S., & Tessler, R. (1972). A test of a model for reducing measured attitude-behavior discrepancies. *Journal of Personality and Social Psychology, 24,* 225–236.

Sears, R. R. (1957). Identification as a form of behavioral development. In D. B. Harris (Ed.), *The concept of development.* Minneapolis, MN: University of Minnesota Press.

Sears, R. R., Rau, L., & Alpert, R. (1965). *Identification and childrearing.* Stanford, CA: Stanford University Press.

Sedlak, A. J., & Kurtz, S. T. (1981). A review of children's use of causal inference principles. *Child Development, 52,* 759–784.

Seegmiller, B. R., & Suter, B. (1977). Relations between cognitive and behavioral measures of prosocial development in children. *The Journal of Genetic Psychology, 131,* 161–162.

Selman, R. (1971). The relation of role taking to the development of moral judgment in children. *Child Development, 42,* 79–91.

Selman, R. L. (1980). *The growth of interpersonal understanding: Developmental and clinical analyses.* New York: Academic Press.

Settlage, C. F. (1972). Cultural values and the superego in late adolescence. *Psychoanalytic Study of the Child, 27,* 57–73.

Shantz, C. U. (1975). The development of social cognition. In E. M. Hetherington (Ed.), *Review of child development research* (Vol. 5). Chicago, IL: University of Chicago Press.

Shantz, C. U. (1983). Social cognition. In P. H. Mussen (Ed.), *Handbook of child psychology:* Vol. 3.*Cognitive Development.* New York: Wiley.

Sharabany, R. (1974). Intimate friendship among kibbutz and city children and its measurement (Doctoral dissertation, Cornell University). *Dissertation Abstracts International, 35,* 1028–1029B. (University Microfilms No. 74–17682.)

Shatz, M. (1978). The relationship between cognitive processes and the development of communication skills. In H. E. Howe, Jr., & C. B. Keasey (Eds.), *Nebraska Symposium on Motivation, 1977: Social cognitive development.* Lincoln, NE: University of Nebraska Press.

Shennum, W. A., & Bugenthal, D. B. (1982). The development of control over affective expression in nonverbal behavior. In R. S. Feldman (Ed.), *Development of nonverbal behavior in children.* New York: Springer-Verlag.

Shotland, R. L., & Straw, M. K. (1976). Bystander response to an assault: When a man attacks a woman. *Journal of Personality and Social Psychology, 34,* 990–999.

Shotter, J. (1981). Telling and reporting: Prospective and retrospective uses of self-ascriptions. In C. Antaki (Ed.), *The psychology of ordinary explanations of social behavior.* London: Academic Press.

Shultz, T. R., & Butkowsky, I. (1977). Young children's use of the scheme for multiple sufficient causes in the attribution of real and hypothetical behavior. *Child Development, 48,* 464–469.

Shure, M. B. (1968). Fairness, generosity, and selfishness: The naive psychology of children and young adults. *Child Development, 30,* 857–886.

Shure, M. B. (1980). *Interpersonal problem solving in ten-year-olds.* Final grant report to the National Institute of Mental Health (Grant # R01 MH 27741).

Shure, M. B. (1982). Interpersonal problem solving: A cog in the wheel of social cognition. In F. C. Serafica (Ed.), *Social-cognitive development in context.* New York: The Guilford Press.

Shure, M. B., & Spivack, G. (1978). *Problem solving techniques in childrearing.* San Francisco, CA: Jossey-Bass.

Sicoly, F., & Ross, M. (1977). Facilitation of ego-based attributions by means of self-serving observer feedback. *Journal of Personality and Social Psychology, 35,* 734–741.

Sidgwick, H. (1962). *The methods of ethics.* Chicago, IL: University of Chicago Press. (Originally published, 1874).

Silbereisen, R. K. (1985). Action theory perspective in research on social cognition. In M. Frese & J. Sabini (Eds.), *Goal directed behavior: The concept of action in psychology.* Hillsdale, NJ: Lawrence Erlbaum Associates.

Silbereisen, R. K., Boehnke, K., & Reykowski, J. (1984, September). *Prosocial motives: A comparison of German and Polish adolescents.* Paper presented at the International Congress of Psychology, Acapulco, Mexico.

Simpson, E. L. (1974). Moral development research: A case of scientific bias. *Human Development, 17,* 81–106.

Sims, S. A. (1978). Sharing by children: Effects of behavioral example, induction, and resources. *The Journal of Psychology, 100,* 57–65.

Skinner, B. F. (1971). *Beyond freedom and dignity.* New York: Knopf.

Skinner, E. A., & Chapman, M. (1983, April). *Control beliefs in an action perspective.* Paper presented at the biennial meeting of the Society for Research in Child Development, Detroit, MI.

Smetana, J. G., Bridgeman, D. L., & Turiel, E. (1983). Differentiation of domains and prosocial behavior. In D. L. Bridgeman, *The nature of prosocial development.* New York: Academic Press.

Smith, C. L., Gelfand, D. M., Hartmann, D. P., & Partlow, M. P. (1979). Children's causal attributions regarding help giving. *Child Development, 50,* 203–210.

Smith, E. R. (1984). Attributions and other inferences: Processing information about the self versus others. *Journal of Experimental Social Psychology, 20,* 97–115.

Smith, E. R., & Miller, F. D. (1978). Limits on perception of cognitive processes: A reply to Nisbett and Wilson. *Psychological Review, 85,* 355–362.

Snodgrass, S. R. (1976). The development of trait inference. *Journal of Genetic Psychology, 128,* 163–172.

Snyder, M. (1982). When believing means doing: Creating links between attitudes and behavior. In M. P. Zanna, E. T. Higgins, & C. P. Herman (Eds.), *Consistency in social behavior: The Ontario Symposium.* Hillsdale, NJ: Lawrence Erlbaum Associates.

Snyder, M. L., Stephan, W. G., & Rosenfield, D. (1978). Attributional egotism. In J. H. Harvey, W. Ickes, & R. F. Kidd (Eds.), *New directions in attribution research* (Vol. 2). New York: Wiley.

Sobesky, W. E. (1983). The effects of situational factors on moral judgments. *Child Development, 54,* 575–584.

Solnit, A. J. (1972). Youth and the campus: The search for a social conscience. *Psychoanalytic Study of the Child, 27,* 98–105.

Soloman, D., Watson, M., Battistich, V., Solomon, J., & Schaps, E. (1981, August). *A program to promote interpersonal consideration and cooperation in children.* Paper presented at the annual convention of the American Psychological Association, Los Angeles, CA.

Spiro, M. E. (1965). *Kibbutz: Venture in utopia*. New York: Schocken.

Spivack, G., Platt, J. J., & Shure, M. B. (1976). *The problem solving approach to adjustment*. San Francisco, CA: Jossey-Bass.

Spivack, G., & Shure, M. B. (1974). *Social adjustment in young children: A cognitive approach to solving real problems*. San Francisco, CA: Jossey-Bass.

Sroufe, L. A., & Waters, E. (1977). Heart rate as a convergent measure in clinical and developmental research. *Merrill-Palmer Quarterly, 23*, 3–25.

Staub, E. (1970). A child in distress: The effects of focusing responsibility on children on their attempts to help. *Developmental Psychology, 2*, 152–153.

Staub, E. (1971). A child in distress: The influence of nurturance and modeling on children's attempts to help. *Developmental Psychology, 5*, 124–132.

Staub, E. (1974). Helping a distressed person: Social, personality, and stimulus determinants. In L. Berkowitz (Ed.), *Advances in experimental social psychology* (Vol. 7). New York: Academic Press.

Staub, E. (1978). *Positive social behavior and morality: Social and personal influences* (Vol. 1). New York: Academic Press.

Staub, E. (1979). *Positive social behavior and morality: Socialization and development* (Vol. 2). New York: Academic Press.

Staub, E. (1982, September). *Toward a theory of moral conduct: Goal orientations, moral judgment, and behavior*. Paper presented at the annual meeting of the American Psychological Association, Washington, DC.

Staub, E. (1984). Steps toward a comprehensive theory of moral conduct: Goal oreintation, social behavior, kindness and cruelty. In W. M. Kurtines & J. L. Gewirtz (Eds.), *Morality, moral development, and moral behavior: Basic issues in theory and research*. New York: Wiley.

Staub, E., & Feinberg, H. K. (1980, September). *Regularities in peer interaction, empathy, and sensitivity to others*. Paper presented at the Annual Meeting of the American Psychological Association, Montreal, Canada.

Stephan, W. G. (1975). Actor vs. observer: Attributions to behavior with positive or negative outcomes and empathy for the other role. *Journal of Experimental Social Psychology, 11*, 205–214.

Stephenson, B., & Wicklund, R. A. (1983). Self-directed attention and taking the other's perspective. *Journal of Experimental Social Psychology, 19*, 58–77.

Sterling, B., & Gaertner, S. L. (1984). The attribution of arousal and emergency helping: A bidirectional process. *Journal of Experimental Social Psychology, 20*, 286–596.

Stotland, E. (1969). Exploratory studies in empathy. In L. Berkowitz (Ed.), *Advances in experimental social psychology* (Vol. 4). New York: Academic Press.

Stotland, E., Mathews, K. E., Sherman, S. E., Hansson, R. O., & Richardson, B. E. (1978). *Empathy, fantasy, and helping*. Beverly Hills, CA: Sage.

Strayer, F. F., Wareing, S., & Rushton, J. P. (1979). Social constraints on naturally occurring preschool altruism. *Ethology and Sociobiology, 1*, 3–11.

Suls, J., Witenberg, S., & Gutkin, D. (1981). Evaluating reciprocal and nonreciprocal prosocial behavior: Developmental changes. *Personality and Social Psychology Bulletin, 7*, 25–31.

Surber, C. F. (1982). Separable effects of motives, consequences, and presentation order on children's moral judgments. *Developmental Psychology, 18*, 257–266.

Tapp, J. L., & Kohlberg, L. (1971). Developing senses of law and legal justice. *Journal of Social Issues, 27*, 65–92.

Tetlock, P. E., & Levi, A. (1982). Attribution bias: On the inclusiveness of the cognition-motivation debate. *Journal of Experimental Social Psychology, 18*, 68–88.

Thompson, R. A., & Frodi, A. M. (1984). The sociophysiology of infants and their caregivers. In W. M. Waid (Ed.), *Sociophysiology*. New York: Springer-Verlag.

Thompson, R. A., & Hoffman, M. L. (1980). Empathy and development of guilt in children. *Developmental Psychology, 16*, 155–156.

Tietjen, A. M. (1985). *Prosocial reasoning among children and adults in a Papua New Guinea society.* Manuscript submitted for publication.

Tietjen, A. M. (1984). Infant care and feeding and the beginnings of socialization among the Maisin of Papua New Guinea. *Ecology of Food and Nutrition, 15,* 39–48.

Tietjen, A. M. & Walker, L. J. (in press). Moral reasoning and leadership among men in a Papua New Guinea society. *Developmental Psychology.*

Toi, M., & Batson, C. D. (1982). More evidence that empathy is a source of altruistic motivation. *Journal of Personality and Social Psychology, 43,* 281–292.

Tomkins, S. S. (1963). *Affect, imagery, consciousness: The negative affects.* New York: Springer.

Tomkins, S. S. (1981). The quest for primary motives: Biography and autobiography of an idea. *Journal of Personality and Social Psychology, 41,* 306–329.

Tomlinson-Keasey, C., & Keasey, C. B. (1974). The mediating role of cognitive development in moral judgment. *Child Development, 45,* 291–298.

Toner, I. J., Moore, L. P., & Emmons, B. A. (1980). The effect of being labeled on subsequent self-control in children. *Child Development, 51,* 618–621.

Torney, J. V. (1971). Socialization of attitudes toward the legal system. *Journal of Social Issues, 27,* 137–154.

Trivers, R. L. (1971). The evolution of reciprocal altruism. *Quarterly Review of Biology, 46,* 35–57.

Turiel, E. (1983). *The development of social knowledge: Morality and convention.* Cambridge, UK: Cambridge University Press.

Turiel, E., Edwards, C. P., & Kohlberg, L. (1978). Moral development in Turkish children, adolescents, and young adults. *Journal of Cross-Cultural Psychology, 9,* 75–85.

Turiel, E., & Smetana, J. G. (1984). Social knowledge and action: The coordination of domains. In W. M. Kurtines & J. L. Gewirtz (Eds.), *Morality, moral behavior and development.* New York: Wiley.

Ugurel-Semin, R. (1952). Moral behavior and moral judgment of children. *Journal of Abnormal and Social Psychology, 47,* 463–474.

Underwood, B., & Moore, B. (1982). Perspective-taking and altruism. *Psychological Bulletin, 91,* 143–173.

van der Pligt, J. (1981). Actors' and observers' explanations: Divergent perspectives or divergent evaluations? In C. Antaki (Ed.), *The psychology of ordinary explanations of social behavior.* London: Academic Press.

von Cranach, M., & Harre, R. (1982). (Eds.), *The analysis of action: Recent theoretical and empirical advances.* Cambridge, UK: Cambridge University Press.

von Cranach, M., Kalbermatten, U., Indermuhle, K., & Gugler, B. (1982). *Goal-directed action.* London: Academic Press.

Volpert, W. (1974). *Handlungsstruk-turanalyse als Beitrag zur Qualifikationsforschung.* Koln: Pahl Rugenstein.

Wagner, C., & Wheeler, L. (1969). Model, need and cost effects in helping behavior. *Journal of Personality and Social Psychology, 12,* 111–116.

Walden, T. A. (1982). Mediation and production deficiencies in children's judgments of morality. *Journal of Experimental Child Psychology, 33,* 165–181.

Walker, L. J. (1980). Cognitive and perspective-taking prerequisites for moral development. *Child Development, 51,* 131–139.

Walker, L. J., & Richards, B. S. (1979). Stimulating transitions in moral reasoning as a function of cognitive development. *Developmental Psychology, 15,* 95–103.

Wallace, J., & Sadalla, E. (1966). Behavioral consequences of transgression: I. The effects of social recognition. *Journal of Experimental Research in Personality, 1,* 187–194.

Walster, E., Berscheid, E., & Walster, G. W. (1970). The exploited: Justice or justification? In J. R. Macauley & L. Berkowitz (Eds.), *Altruism and helping behavior.* New York: Academic Press.

Walster, E., Walster, G. W., & Berscheid, E. (1978). *Equity: Theory and research*. Boston, MA: Allyn and Bacon.

Waters, E., Wippmann, J., & Sroufe, L. A. (1979). Attachment, positive affect, and competence in the peer group: Two studies in construct validation. *Child Development, 50*, 821–829.

Watson, J. B. (1922). *Behaviorism*. New York: People's Institute.

Watson, J. B. (1928). *The ways of behaviorism*. New York: Harpers.

Weary, G. (1979). Self-serving attributional biases: Perceptual or response distortions? *Journal of Personality and Social Psychology, 37*, 1418–1420.

Weary, G. (1980). Examination of affect and egocentrism as mediators of bias in causal attributions. *Journal of Personality and Social Psychology, 38*, 348–357.

Weiner, B. (1980). A cognitive (attribution)-emotion-action model of motivated behavior: An analysis of judgments of help giving. *Journal of Personality and Social Psychology, 39*, 186–200.

Weiner, B. (1983). Some methodological pitfalls in attributional research. *Journal of Educational Psychology, 75*, 530–543.

Weinreich-Haste, H., & Locke, D. (Eds.) (1983). *Morality in the making: Thought, action, and social context*. Chichester, England: Wiley.

Weiss, R. J. (1982). Understanding moral thought: Effects on moral reasoning and decision making. *Developmental Psychology, 18*, 852–861.

Wesley, F., & Karr, C. (1968). Vergleich der ansichten und Erziehungshaltungen deutscher und amerikanishcher mutter. *Psychologische Rundschaw, 19*, 35–46.

Weyant, J. M. (1978). Effects of mood states, costs, and benefits of helping. *Journal of Personality and Social Psychology, 36*, 1169–1176.

White, C. B., Bushnell, N., & Regnemer, J. L. (1978). Moral development in Bahamian school children: A 3-year examination of Kohlberg's stages of moral development. *Developmental Psychology, 14*, 58–65.

White, P. (1980). Limitations on verbal reports of internal events: A refutation of Nisbett and White and of Bem. *Psychological Review, 87*, 105–112.

Whiting, B. B., & Whiting, J. W. M. (1975). *Children of six cultures: A psychocultural analysis*. Cambridge, MA: Harvard Unversity Press.

Whiting, J. W. M., & Child, L. L. (1953). *Child training and personality*. New Haven, CT: Yale University Press.

Wicklund, R. A., & Brehm, J. W. (1976). *Perspectives on cognitive dissonance*. Hillsdale, NJ: Lawrence Erlbaum Associates.

Williams, B. (1973). *Problems of the self*. Cambridge, UK: Cambridge University Press.

Williams, J. E., Bennett, S. M., & Best, D. L. (1975). Awareness and expression of sex stereotypes in young children. *Developmental Psychology, 11*, 635–642.

Wilson, B. J., & Cantor, B. (1985). Developmental differences in empathy with a television protagonist's fear. *Journal of Experimental Child Psychology, 39*, 284–299.

Wilson, E. O. (1975). *Sociobiology: The new synthesis*. Cambridge, MA: Harvard University Press.

Wilson, E. O. (1978). *On human nature*. Cambridge, MA: Harvard University Press.

Wispe, L. (1984). *The distinction between sympathy and empathy: To call forth a concept a word is needed*. Unpublished manuscript, University of Oklahoma.

Wispe, L., Kiecolt, J., & Long, R. E. (1977). Demand characteristics, moods, and helping. *Social Behavior and Personality, 5*, 249–255.

Wright, B. A. (1942a). Altruism in children and the perceived conduct of others. *Journal of Abnormal and Social Psychology, 37*, 218–233.

Wright, B. A. (1942b). The development of ideology of altruism and fairness in children. *Psychological Bulletin, 39*, 485.

Wynn-Edwards, V. C. (1962). *Animal dispersion in relation to social behavior*. New York: Harper.

Yinon, Y., Sharon, I., Azgad, Z., & Barshir, I. (1981). Helping behavior of urbanites, moshavniks, and kibbutzniks. *Journal of Social Psychology, 113*, 143–144.

Youniss, J. (1980). *Parents and peers in social development: A Sullivan-Piaget perspective*. Chicago, IL: University of Chicago Press.

Zahn-Waxler, C., Friedman, S. L., & Cummings, E. M. (1983). Children's emotions and behaviors in response to infants' cries. *Child Development, 54*, 1522–1528.

Zahn-Waxler, C., Iannotti, R., & Chapman, M. (1982). Peers and prosocial development. In K. H. Rubin & H. S. Ross (Eds.), *Peer relationships and social skills in childhood*. New York: Springer-Verlag.

Zahn-Waxler, C., & Radke-Yarrow, M. (1982). The development of altruism: Alternative research strategies. In N. Eisenberg (Ed.), *The development of prosocial behavior*. New York: Academic Press.

Zahn-Waxler, C., Radke-Yarrow, M., & Brady-Smith, J. (1977). Perspective-taking and prosocial behavior. *Developmental Psychology, 13*, 87–88.

Zahn, Waxler, C., Radke-Yarrow, M., & King, R. A. (1979). Childrearing and children's prosocial initiations toward victims of distress. *Child Development, 50*, 319–330.

Zahn-Waxler, C., Radke-Yarrow, M., & King, R. A. (1983). Early altruism and guilt. *Academic Psychology Bulletin, 5*, 247–260.

Zajonc, R. B. (1980). Feeling and thinking: Preferences need no inferences. *American Psychologist, 35*, 151–175.

Zajonc, R. B., & Markus, H. (1984). Affect and cognition: The hard interface. In C. E. Izard, J. Kagan, & R. B. Zajonc (Eds.), *Emotions, cognitions, and behavior*. Cambridge, UK: Cambridge University Press.

Zillman, D., & Cantor, J. R. (1977). Affective responses to the emotions of a protagonist. *Journal of Experimental Social Psychology, 13*, 155–165.

Zinser, O., & Lydiatt, E. W. (1976). Mode of recipient definition, affluence of the recipient, and sharing behavior in preschool children. *Journal of Genetic Psychology, 129*, 261–266.

Zinser, O., Perry, J. S., & Edgar, R. M. (1975). Affluence of the recipient, value of donations, and sharing behavior in preschool children. *Journal of Psychology, 89*, 301–305.

Zuckerman, M., Blanck, P. D., DePaulo, B. M., & Rosenthal, R. (1980). Developmental changes in decoding discrepant and nondiscrepant nonverbal cues. *Developmental Psychology, 16*, 220–228.

Zuckerman, M., Klorman, K., Larrance, D. T., & Spiegel, N. H. (1981). Facial, autonomic, and subjective components of emotion: The facial feedback hypothesis versus externalizer-internalizer distinction. *Journal of Personality and Social Psychology, 41*, 929–944.

Zuckerman, M., & Reis, H. T. (1978). Comparison of three models for predicting altruistic behavior. *Journal of Personality and Social Psychology, 36*, 498–510.

Author Index

Bennett, S. M., 39
Benson, N. C., 70, 71
Berkowitz, L., 36, 54, 107, 109, 116, 186
Berlyne, D. E., 3
Berndt, E. G., 65
Berndt, T. J., 59, 65, 70, 96, 122, 206
Bernstein, S., 76
Berscheid, D. E., 54, 117
Best, D. L., 39, 40
Bezaire, M. M., 40
Bickman, L., 107
Bieber–Schneider, R., 112
Birch, K., 34, 36, 37, 42, 43, 47
Blanck, P. D., 194
Blank, A., 97, 100, 104, 154, 196
Blasi, A., 123, 124, 125, 126, 154, 210
Blechman, N., 44
Blehar, M. C., 195
Bless, E., 53
Block, J., 152
Block, J. H., 39
Blotner, R., 130, 132, 133, 154
Blum, L. A., 1, 12, 13, 30, 41
Boehnke, K., 44, 90, 135, 140, 155, 156,
    161, 164, 181
Bolen, D., 96
Borke, H., 30, 39, 105
Boski, P., 79
Botkin, P., 105, 151
Braband, J., 108
Brabeck, M., 128
Bradley, G. W., 78, 79
Brady-Smith, J., 103, 105
Brandstadter, J., 26
Brandt, R. B., 7
Brainerd, C. J., 105
Breger, L., 16
Brehm, J. W., 209
Brehm, S. S., 36, 41, 48, 69
Breznitz, S., 64
Brickman, P., 96
Bridgeman, D., 146
Brion-Meisels, S., 103
Brody, G. H., 76
Brody, L. R., 38
Bronfenbrenner, U., 162, 168
Broughton, J. M., 128, 130
Bryan, J. H., 44, 107, 116
Bryant, B., 31, 151, 186
Buck, R., 40
Buckley, N., 103

Buckley, T., 34, 36, 37, 42, 43, 47, 48
Bugenthal, D. B., 40
Burkhart, J. E., 130
Burleson, B. R., 44, 106
Burns, P. R., 42
Bushnell, N., 161, 171
Bussey, K., 44
Butler, L., 111, 112
Butkowsky, I., 171
Butzin, C., 69, 70

C

Cameron, E., 44, 84, 88, 89, 91, 93, 97, 99,
    100, 135, 146, 154, 155, 156, 163, 181,
    186, 189, 207
Camp, G. C., 96
Campbell, D. T., 25
Candee, D., 123, 146, 152, 154, 208
Cantor, B., 36
Cantor, J. R., 200
Caputo, C., 78
Carlsmith, J. M., 54
Carroll, J., 36, 38, 40, 41, 43, 48
Castillo-Vales, V., 64, 65, 68, 70
Cauble, M. A., 152
Caul, W.F., 40
Chandler, M. J., 105
Chanowitz, B., 97, 100, 104, 154, 196
Chapman, M., 26, 31, 41, 103, 188, 198
Child, L. L., 55
Cialdini, R. B., 2, 54, 55, 96, 110, 198, 201,
    203, 209
Cicchetti, D., 23, 24
Clark, M. S., 194
Clark, R. D., III, 33, 34, 35, 36, 42, 46, 50,
    55, 104, 154, 188, 197, 199, 205
Clausen, G. T., 52
Cloud, J. M., 39
Code, L. B., 128
Cohen, E. A., 69, 70, 82
Cohen, J. L., 198
Coie, J. D., 66
Coke, J. S., 5, 13, 31, 34, 35, 36, 37, 38,
    41, 42, 43, 46, 47, 48, 49, 55, 199
Colby, A., 119, 122, 123, 128, 146, 173,
    174, 175, 176, 178, 179, 184
Cole, C., 200, 208
Costanzo, P. R., 66, 69, 70
Cowan, P.A., 3, 23, 24

Subject Index